REPRESENTING FEMININITY

REPRESENTING FEMININITY

*Middle-Class Subjectivity in
Victorian and Edwardian
Women's Autobiographies*

MARY JEAN CORBETT

New York   Oxford
OXFORD UNIVERSITY PRESS
1992

Oxford University Press

Oxford   New York   Toronto
Delhi   Bombay   Calcutta   Madras   Karachi
Petaling Jaya   Singapore   Hong Kong   Tokyo
Nairobi   Dar es Salaam   Cape Town
Melbourne   Auckland

and associated companies in
Berlin   Ibadan

Published by Oxford University Press, Inc.,
200 Madison Avenue, New York, New York 10016

Oxford is a registered trademark of Oxford University Press

Parts of Chapter 2 have appeared in Corbett, Mary Jean. "Feminine Authorship and Spiritual Authority in
Victorian Women Writers' Autobiographies." *Women's Studies* 18, no. 1 (1990): 13–29.

Library of Congress Cataloging-in-Publication Data
Corbett, Mary Jean, 1962–
Representing femininity : middle-class subjectivity in Victorian
and Edwardian women's autobiographies / Mary Jean Corbett.
p. cm.   Includes bibliographical references (p.   ) and index.
ISBN 0-19-506858-0
1. English prose literature—Women authors—History and criticism.
2. Women authors, English—19th century—Biography—History and criticism.
3. English prose literature—19th century—History and criticism.
4. Women—Great Britain—History—19th century—Historiography.
5. Women and literature—Great Britain—History—19th century.
6. Women—Great Britain—Biography—History and criticism.
7. Femininity (Psychology) in literature.   8. Middle classes in literature.
9. Autobiography—Women authors.   10. Subjectivity in literature.   I. Title.
PR788.W65C6   1992   828'.80809'9287—dc20   91-17499

1 3 5 7 9 8 6 4 2

Printed in the United States of America
on acid-free paper

Acknowledgments

I HAVE WRITTEN this book under enormously congenial conditions, created in large part by the generosity of institutions and individuals. The Green Library staff at Stanford University, and particularly Sonya Moss of the Inter-Library Loan division, met my scholarly demands with good humor and speed. The Stanford Humanities Center, staff of 1987–88 and fellows alike, provided material support of diverse kinds. A Whiting Foundation Fellowship in 1988–89, and a Summer Research Appointment from Miami University in 1990, helped me bring this work to completion.

No less vital were the intellectual support and personal encouragement my teachers have given me. Herbert Lindenberger provided more than his customary energy and attention. Barbara Gelpi prodded me onward with her careful eye for the project and the prose. To Rob Polhemus, I owe a less specifiable but no less substantial debt for his inability to be persuaded and his unstinting concern for my work and well-being. And Regenia Gagnier, gifted in all things, has been in turn all things to me: teacher, critic, scholar, friend. I like to think of this work as being hers as well.

My friends—who are also my teachers—have played equally important parts in the process. Over ten years ago, Patricia Skarda first taught me the value of loving what you do and doing what you love; I would never have gotten this far without her. From several thousand miles away, Lauren Goldberg, Rochelle Hanson, Lucy Jackson Norvell, Joe Perettine, Claire Poles, and Mary Rutkowski remained ideal readers and dear companions. In new surroundings, Art Casciato, Barry Chabot, Fran Dolan, Chris Knight, and Nedra Reynolds offered all kinds of comforts and gifts that I was only too delighted to accept. And I want to thank the people who have lived with me and with this, many of whom have read and so shaped portions of the manuscript, listened to me talk about it, or simply held my hand: Shay Brawn, Greg Coleman, Elizabeth Heckendorn Cook, Annie Finch, Miranda Joseph, Madeleine Kahn, John Kleiner, Jean Lee, Ira Livingston, and Kathy Veit. Alexandra Chasin and Kelly Mays—critics, kindred spirits, and card players extraordinaire—made everything possible and infinitely pleasurable. My thanks and love to all—you have been more than colleagues, more than friends, utterly indispensable.

And I am grateful, too, for the support and love of my family: my brothers and sisters—Bill, Judy, Dennis, and Susan—have helped me over and over again to pay the price of doing what I do. For my father and to my mother, each of whom—in very different ways and without ever meaning to—made me what I am, I give my love and my work.

Oxford, Ohio   M.J.C.
August, 1991

Contents

REPRESENTING FEMININITY

Introduction

ONE PURPOSE OF this book is to show that even Virginia Woolf was occasionally wrong. "I was thinking the other night," she wrote to her friend, Ethel Smyth, "that there's never been a woman's autobiography." Herself a prolific autobiographer, Smyth might have reminded Woolf that women *had* written autobiography even if what they had produced was, in Woolf's words, "nothing to compare with Rousseau."[1] It is not surprising that Woolf takes Rousseau as her standard, for most readers of modern autobiography have accepted his *Confessions* as the very type of self-representation or, limiting themselves to the English context, have looked to Mill or Newman as the generic prototype. And the introspective mode that Rousseau pioneered for the French and the Francophile tradition on the one hand, or the less obsessively intimate "life-and-work" document favored by the middle-class Victorian literary man on the other, may indeed seem to exhaust the range of autobiographical possibilities. Yet I mean to demonstrate that relying on these categories alone denies a place for women's experience as both historical actors and autobiographers. Although I obliquely address Woolf's question as to why there had been neither a female Rousseau nor a feminine tradition of autobiography to place alongside the work of the great nineteenth-century English women novelists, I am most concerned with exploring the ways in which some Victorian and Edwardian women *did* represent themselves in writing.

This book aims to contest the boundaries of genre, gender, and the autobiographical tradition by piecing together a partial history of middle-class women's subjectivities in the nineteenth and early twentieth centuries that will be both historically and culturally specific. Until very recently, the received generic understanding of autobiography has disempowered women by making women's lives and texts invisible; thus in bringing forward some portion of the vast quantity of middle-class women's autobiographical vritings from this period, I counter that received knowledge. *Representing Femininity* opens up the archives of women's history by including for analysis not only texts by women who wrote for a living, but also works by Victorian and Edwardian actresses

3

and suffragettes, and I situate those texts in a variety of contexts, with particular attention to the ways in which discourses of professional work shape wom-
en's self-representations. I maintain throughout that autobiography is first and
foremost a popular genre, read by common readers and written, more often
than not, by common writers; academic discourse has unjustifiably limited the
range of "readable" texts here, just as it once did in novel studies, by clinging
to an elitist distinction between high cultural and mass cultural forms. Thus in
taking a critical stance toward notions of professional authorship and in including several chapters on texts by women who were not "writers by profession,"
I redirect attention away from questions of literary form and aesthetic worthiness and toward an awareness of the ideological uses of autobiography as a
mode of constituting middle-class women's subjectivities. In meeting these aims,
I have consciously positioned this book at the intersection of my own professional, intellectual, and political concerns as a reader, writer, and teacher; thus
my feminism, my inquiry into autobiography, and my period interests—Romantic, Victorian, Edwardian—coalesce in ways that should make this book
useful to a variety of readers.

My work is very much concerned with the historical specificity of both autobiographies and subjectivities. I argue that concepts of the self and the forms
that self-representations take are historically and culturally variable; grounding
my analysis of a text or a group of texts within particular contexts, I hope to
avoid Woolf's error—measuring all works against an inflexible normalizing
standard of what autobiography should be. For one of the usual critical moves
among those who have focused on autobiography, as in literary studies more
generally, has been to adopt a universalizing standard, and so to occlude the
local conditions within which subjects and texts are produced. As Felicity A.
Nussbaum argues in her work on eighteenth-century autobiographical subjectivity, "the critical methodologies most commonly employed to read these texts
often wrench the subject from her or his cultural and historical moment."[2]
With Nussbaum, I insist instead that it is through cultural and historical analysis that we can begin to understand not only the constitution of autobiographical subjects, but also the specific uses of autobiography for writers and readers
and the particular forms that subjectivities take.

Just as they have downplayed the relevance of historical contexts to self-
representational texts, critics of autobiography have similarly neglected to consider the historical embeddedness of their own notions about self and have assumed that subjectivity is always and everywhere the same. Writing in 1960,
Roy Pascal holds up a moral standard for autobiographers. He claims that "bad"
autobiography "arises above all from a certain falling short in respect to the
whole personality. With the greatest number of autobiographies this is simply
an inadequacy in the persons writing, a lack of moral responsibility towards
their task, a lack of awareness and insight."[3] But judged by these criteria, even
the canonized work of Henry Adams—which displays a reticence about its author's personal life fairly typical for its period—falls short, suggesting to me
not "an inadequacy" in Adams, but in the criteria.

These same standards for evaluating autobiographies have also elided differences among the experiences of autobiographical subjects, differences constructed at least in part by gender, class, and race. Writing in 1972, James Olney prescribes a set of norms for autobiography: each work must demonstrate "an individual point of view, from which one sees things in order" and that point of view "must be (1) unitary; (2) specifically human; (3) personally unique."[4] Olney derives his tenets, as does Pascal, from liberal humanist fictions that support the primacy of "the individual point of view," the coherence of the "unitary" self, and the uniqueness of one's own personality. Not surprisingly, his effort to establish a common thread connecting all these "unique" representations of "individual" lives must conserve itself by excluding texts in which neither individuality nor uniqueness is as much of a concern as it is to those who occupy dominant subject positions.

That critics have based the normative theory of "proper" autobiography on readings of a few men's texts is itself a function of historical overdeterminations. That the texts that have been studied situate their authors as autonomous white male liberal subjects—a subject position by no means equally available or desirable to all those who have written autobiography—seriously undermines the claims to universality that their readers have made on their behalf. One of my working assumptions, by contrast, is that subjectivities themselves have histories: our contemporary notions of selfhood and our generic expectations for autobiography are not timeless and transcendent any more than the Victorians' were, but are rather produced by—and productive of—cultural and material practices.

Although the recent shift in thinking about the subject has dispelled the humanist fictions of Pascal and Olney, it has inserted a new norm for subjectivity that still continues to elide the specificity of diverse subject positions and subjectivities. Deconstruction and post-Freudian psychoanalysis have been instrumental in altering contemporary understandings of identity; the apparently autonomous, self-determining subject is no longer promoted as a model of the ideally integrated self, while the current conception of the subject understands it as radically decentered. In reading *The Prelude*, for instance, poststructuralists seek out the textual marks of Wordsworth's elaborate defense against his own instability as a speaking and writing subject, looking not for the signs of his insight but of his blindness. Reading the implications of Derridean and Lacanian theory back into nineteenth-century texts means recognizing that the subject of language is always a rhetorical construct and as such consistently undone by the inconsistencies of language itself: for example, Wordsworth's continual revision of *The Prelude*, as Paul Jay has shown, is in the last analysis a futile effort to fix linguistically a self that changes over time.[5] Like most other linguistically based formalist readings of autobiographical subjectivity, however, Jay's account lacks grounding in the material conditions that produce subjects and that they reproduce in language, which is itself a historically changing construct.

Although I share many of the assumptions that underlie the deconstructive critique of language and subjectivity, I have not pursued their implications in any systematic way; instead, I have tried to correct the tendency to seal off texts from their material determinants by bringing history, ideology, and gender to the fore in my analysis. My interests lie more in reconstructing than in deconstructing lives: the poststructuralist desire to celebrate what Paul de Man called the "de-facement" of the autobiographical subject proceeds from an imperative that makes very little sense to those of us—e.g., women, sexual and ethnic minorities—whose histories and subjectivities have always been effaced.[6] As Andreas Huyssen persuasively argues, to follow the poststructuralist lead of "[denying] the subject altogether" would be to "jettison the change of challenging the *ideology of the subject* (as male, white, and middle-class) by developing alternative and different notions of subjectivity," and so to make a political mistake of major proportions.[7] While the poststructuralist critique of the unified subject has thus changed the terms of the investigation into subjectivity and autobiography, those terms are still too narrowly focused, particularly as they fail to account for the social elements of the constitution of subjectivity, and especially the differences that gender, race, and class make to the process of acquiring language, identity, and power.

In the meantime, practitioners of a new feminist inquiry into autobiography have deliberately sought to establish the grounds for speaking of differences between men's and women's texts without making essentialist claims for "women's inherently different voice" (Nussbaum, p. xix): the most useful current work on women's autobiography, by and large available only in edited volumes, is deliberately multicultural and consciously critical of generic boundaries.[8] Some feminist critics have also forcefully inquired into why most male critics of autobiography have overlooked women's writing, and Sidonie Smith's work in particular reveals the androcentric assumptions that have shaped much scholarly work on the genre; she convincingly establishes that women's autobiographies have been undervalued because they do not fit generic terms derived solely from masculine experiences.[9] However, while feminist insights have provided important new ways of reading women's autobiographies, this new research seems unconsciously to replicate some shortcomings of the work it seeks to critique. For example, much scholarship on women's writings in this genre has taken the single-author approach, with essays devoted to individual autobiographies.[10] One indirect result of this tactic has been to reinforce the notion that texts worth reading are few and far between, even as certain texts have been brought to the forefront. This way of proceeding also inadvertently suggests that each work stands alone and bears no affinities to works produced within similar ideological and cultural contexts. I counter the tendency to make certain texts "representative" by looking at a broad range of works. My practice in the chapters that follow combines the particularity of close reading with an effort to draw out the affinities between and among texts by juxtaposition, for it has seemed to me appropriate to argue for some similarities among texts by women from similar class backgrounds and/or of the same profession in order to undercut the notion that autobiography is a unique production of a unique self. By examining a cross section of texts instead of just one or two, I have also been able to generalize about middle-class women's self-representational strategies even as I have tried to attend to differences among women. By putting autobiographical works back into those contexts, and by putting them into relation to one another, I hope to break the hold over critical practice that other kinds of thinking have come to possess.

More problematically, because liberal feminists have not adequately contested the ideological definition of "true" autobiography as the narrative unfolding of a significant public life, recorded by a subject whose achievements warrant preservation for posterity, certain modes of thought characteristic of earlier criticism have been uncritically reproduced. As Cora Kaplan puts it, "humanist feminist criticism does not object to the idea of an immanent, transcendent subject but only to the exclusion of women from those definitions which it takes as an historically accurate account of subjectivity rather than as an historically constructed ideology."[11] Along these lines, Harriet Martineau has usually been designated as the "representative" woman autobiographer of the nineteenth century. While her work and life differ greatly from those of most of her female contemporaries, Martineau's life and her writing of it approximate the masculinist standard of significance, and so have been taken up by feminist critics who have not interrogated the values and the subjectivity that standard implies.[12] Yet the impulse guiding feminist critique surely depends on inquiring into the ways in which masculinist categories have unjustifiably limited the range of what "counts" in generic and cultural terms; to contest the meaning and value of autobiography, as I do here, is one way to continue the work of recovering what Woolf called "the lives of the obscure." In reading texts that have gone largely unread by academics, I undermine prevalent notions of what qualifies as autobiography, for adhering to masculinist generic standards would only ensure that texts by women writers of "lesser" status, with a particular relation to androcentric norms of individual selfhood, would continue to be overlooked.[13] And in deliberately choosing to read and write about works by women much less conventionally unconventional than Martineau, I seek to establish new paradigms for analyzing women's stories.

Part of my overall thesis for the book, then, is that women's historical experiences make their autobiographical works different from those produced by men; since men and women have been differently situated in relation to the public sphere of work and the public form of autobiography, male and female self-representations are unlikely to conform to a single model. Rather than judge the texts I have read by norms derived from an almost wholly masculine tradition, I have reconstructed the autobiographical discourses of middle-class Victorian and Edwardian women through close analysis of the texts they created and the various contexts in which they wrote. This work argues that women's lives must be culturally and historically contextualized within specific ideological sites if they are to be visible at all.

If *Representing Femininity* challenges traditional notions of "authorship," "genius," and the "individual," then it also seeks to establish the grounds on which the women it discusses constitute their subjectivities. My primary concerns, as demonstrated earlier, are neither aesthetic nor generic; I am not interested in establishing a literary tradition of women's autobiography or a new feminist canon of women's self-representations. Rather, my task is specifying and examining the interplay of ideologies and experiences that is ever-present in written expressions of particular lives.

For someone self-consciously poststructuralist to speak of "experience" as I do may seem anomalous, for the word has fallen into disrepute among those feminists who wish to distance themselves from earlier feminist work of the 1970s, which claimed (naively, some think) "the authority of experience" as the crucial ground for feminist criticism. Critiquing Teresa de Lauretis's definition of experience as "an ongoing process by which subjectivity is constructed semiotically and historically," Diana Fuss claims "that there is little agreement amongst women on exactly what constitutes 'a woman's experience.' . . . 'experience' is rather shaky ground on which to base the notion of a class of women."[14] In my opinion, however, Fuss misreads de Lauretis's call for "a materialist theory of subjectivity," which would "approach the subject through the apparati, the social technologies in which it is constituted" (among which writing and reading practices are surely to be included), and which in no way suggests that there is only one woman-as-subject or one universal feminine experience to be constructed.[15] Moreover, de Lauretis's account of how subjectivity is produced through experience—one's "material, economic, and interpersonal" relations—indicates that we subjects are not merely acted upon but active, and so offers a way out of purely determinist notions of subjectivity: "[subjectivity] is produced not by external ideas, values, or material causes, but by one's personal, subjective engagement in the practices, discourses, and institutions that lend significance (value, meaning, and affect) to the events of the world" (p. 159).[16] And as Rita Felski asserts, "we may not conclude that because subjectivity is constructed, it constitutes an illusion which merely serves to reproduce the status quo"; her feminist appropriation of the work of Anthony Giddens suggests that it is in good part through subjective practices, carried out as individuals and in groups, that we make change.[17] We do this not by presuming that we—or the subjects I study here—can occupy a space outside dominant ideologies, but rather by identifying the positions within ideologies and the clashes among those positions that offer a way into critique. So that while I have refrained from making easy claims for the "revolutionary," "subversive" potential of women's texts or, alternatively, from arguing that the subject is so overdetermined that she maintains no place of her own to speak from, I am yet interested in reclaiming some ideological capital for feminist practice from the texts I study.

Understanding subjectivity in these terms requires abandoning the notion that women have had no subjectivity of which to speak, and it restores some agency to historical actors who have been represented at times in feminist criticism as wholly subject *to* rather than as subjects *of* institutions and ideologies. Experience is an important concept for my work precisely because it returns a degree of authority to those who lived and wrote. I would not wish, however, to give the impression of believing that experience can be simply read off from the texts analyzed here; an autobiography is not experience itself—"the real thing"—but a representation of experience. No "text can transmit an unmediated representation of the real" (Felski, p. 79), and autobiographical texts are not the exceptions to that rule. Yet having said that, I wish also to say that, for me, something crucial would be lost by considering autobiographies as "mere" representations. Keeping my focus on how women represented themselves enables me to honor my political, critical, and ideological investments. I believe that it is not only possible but also ideologically necessary to employ theory in feminist critical and political struggle, and I want to foreground and reconstruct women's historical experience in its representational aspect as the very basis for undertaking theoretical work.

The new refocusing on questions of women's subjectivity that I engage in here is part of the shift back to questions of authorship among feminist theorists and critics of the 1980s and 1990s. While for some poststructuralists the author may be long dead and buried, recent feminist work suggests that the woman author is yet to be born. Nancy K. Miller argues that women's "relation to integrity and textuality, desire and authority, displays structurally important differences" from men's relation to those same categories, and urges us to reopen the question of literary subjectivity for women; as Elizabeth Fox-Genovese writes in an essay on African-American women's autobiography, "there remain plenty of subjects and authors who, never having had much opportunity to write in their own names or the names of their kind, much less in the name of the culture as a whole, are eager to seize the abandoned podium" of the deceased.[18] Interest in women's authorship is directly related to a new sense of the relevance of gender to literature, politics, and history. Yet the new theory and practice regarding women's subjectivity has not quite figured out how to avoid reinscribing masculinist notions of authorship in constituting female authorial subjects. "Should we valorize the author," Cheryl Walker asks, "if such a person necessarily implies the same kind of repression we associate with patriarchy"?[19] Moreover, can we make our accounts of women's authorship particular enough, and mark them as such, so as to prevent taking a few individual examples as representative of all women's experience? Shouldn't we be talking about and writing of subjectivities in the plural rather than the singular?

Here I have followed the example of Regenia Gagnier, whose work within a wide range of Victorian texts—from the autobiographical canon to boarding-school and public-school memoirs by middle-class women and men to working-class "lifewriting"—delicately situates each body of texts within the specificities of the class and gender positions occupied by their authors.[20] I hope that my subjects are no less carefully situated: with the exception of Chapter 1, my study is largely concerned with middle-class women, and almost exclusively focused on the relationship between middle-class ideology and women's self-representations; my few working-class autobiographers can be found among the actresses of Chapter 4 and the suffragettes of Chapter 6, and when I deal with them, I am most concerned with how they embraced or rejected middle-class norms.

It is crucial to specify class here, for consciousness of class as a category of analysis has been largely absent from the discourse of most American feminist literary critics working on British texts, perhaps because class is—in its own particular ways—as difficult and as historically variable a category as gender. The problems of theorizing relations between class and gender have been all too well documented, and need no rehearsing here.[21] Only a very few feminist literary critics, working in what I identify as a feminist materialist tradition and with whose work I affiliate my own, have understood class differences and class constructions as serious matters of concern.[22] But by failing to take into account the privileged class position of writers from Austen to Eliot, many feminist critics have made a universalizing move not all that dissimilar to what they have accused masculinist critics of. Assuming middle-class experience as the unchallenged norm, and making gender the only distinctive mark of oppression, feminist readers have neglected to perceive the ways in which white middle-class women were (and are) privileged by virtue of their class and race position. While middle-class men "limited [bourgeois women's] sphere of action and marginalized them from centers of power," middle-class women, as Ruth L. Smith and Deborah M. Valenze remind us, also "participated in the hegemony"; the claim of women's essential marginality must be susceptible to qualification on the grounds of race and class as well as gender.[23]

Class and race must be brought into any analysis of subjectivity, for it would be naive to assume that class and race positions do not shape one's experience of oneself in ways as pervasive and profound as gender does. Thus, the conclusions I draw here about white middle-class women's subjectivities cannot be assumed to apply to working-class, non-white, or non-Western experiences and subjectivities. The texts and writers I analyze will be explicitly marked according to class and implicitly marked by race as part of my effort to identify specific subjectivities for writers, actresses, and suffragettes; yet I no more wish to essentialize class and race than gender, for all three categories should be conceived as contextual and, as such, subject to change. While I like to think that the method and theory herein could be useful to critics and theorists working with other discursive formations, my conclusions are limited to the historical fields of the texts I examine.

The focus of *Representing Femininity* is on women's texts, but it begins with two exemplars from the masculine canon of nineteenth-century autobiography: William Wordsworth's *Prelude* (1805) and Thomas Carlyle's *Sartor Resartus* (1832–33). I start here in order to disabuse myself and others of the notion that, for men, autobiography is a relatively unproblematic genre; to look at how cultural conditions shape the practice of autobiography for literary men; and to resolve some of my questions about the pragmatic uses of autobiography in relation to new forces of literary production as they emerged in the early nineteenth century. As a reader of nineteenth-century autobiographies by men, I had noticed that autobiography sums up a life lived as it draws to its close for Mill, Ruskin, and Trollope, while the move to autobiographical writing for Wordsworth and Carlyle comes much earlier in their careers: *The Prelude* and *Sartor Resartus* not only record the lives led, but also project forward, offering visions of what the poet-genius should and will become. These texts constitute identities yet to be fully enacted, identities that only come into being through textual production. As Nussbaum has observed of her eighteenth-century sub-jects, "narratives of 'self' make possible the definition of a gendered middle-class subjectivity" (p. xiv): for Wordsworth and Carlyle, such narratives are crucial to establishing literary and vocational identities that are intimately bound up with their positions in gender and class constructs.

I argue that the status of the literary man is very much at issue in these texts, especially when we contrast it with the changing situation of the profes-sional man in the same historical moment. Because writers' products are in-creasingly treated as marketable goods under new conditions of mass literacy and circulation, literary men lack the socioeconomic prestige of professionals, whose specialized services are neither sold directly in the market nor made available to all consumers. *The Prelude* and *Sartor Resartus*, however, contest and critique the commodification of literature by recasting the literary self as an unalienated subject whose work (and works), like the professional's, cannot be detached from the self; by writing the self into the work, both Wordsworth and Carlyle suggest, in different ways, that authorial identity is not determined by the marketplace but is rather a function of conditions internal to the self. These writers authorize themselves by announcing autobiographically their own subjective fitness for the literary and cultural work they undertake.

Looking at *The Prelude* and *Sartor Resartus* in relation to the paradigm I establish for professional identity shows that they are patterned on the middle-class narrative of vocation. I define the writer's "calling," however, not in sa-cred or spiritual terms, as M. H. Abrams has most forcefully done, but in terms of new bourgeois emphases on work, respectability, and gentlemanliness.[24] In sum, these two texts provide different but related accounts of the means by which their authors come to assume the mantle of authorship, positing it as a worthy, honorable vocation for the middle-class man; the end of each writer's "apprenticeship" is the production of the work which verifies the authenticity of his calling and the particularity of his "genius," and the process by which this end is achieved is represented in the autobiographical text. For Wordsworth and Carlyle, writing autobiography becomes a way of attaining both literary legitimacy and a desired subjectivity.

Not surprisingly, women writers rarely represent their experience in these terms, for the question of female authorship is quite differently framed. As numerous scholars have established, most middle-class Victorians believed that a woman's true vocation was marriage and motherhood; paid work belonged to the public, masculine sphere, while woman's proper place, the home, was pri-vate and feminine. And nineteenth-century autobiography has been tradition-ally understood, in George P. Landow's words, as "largely a matter of public discourse," whereas nineteenth-century women were, by ideological definition, private creatures.[25] Yet as I argue throughout, relying on those fixed ideological positions as if they tell the whole story about this culture inadequately repre-sents the actual experience of many Victorian and Edwardian women, whose practice as autobiographers is but one element of their participation in the pub-lic sphere. Those women who write autobiography enter into a discourse from which they are, in ideological terms, supposed to be excluded, yet they enter it all the same. For middle-class women autobiographers, then, the "public discourse" of autobiography has to be negotiated, at least in part, by and through the representation of the private sphere.

Chapter 2 opens by juxtaposing two contradictory discourses: literary professionalism at mid-century, which explicitly excludes women from authorship by making feminine domesticity a precondition for men's public literary work, and Elizabeth Barrett Browning's *Aurora Leigh* (1856), a text that contests the cultural ban on female literary labor by appropriating the Wordsworthian paradigm for poetic development. Barrett Browning, however, is self-consciously "exceptional" in her eagerness to engage the dominant masculine model; I devote most of my attention to how other autobiographers legitimate their entrance into "public discourse" by invoking the norms of private-sphere femininity as their warrant for undertaking literary and self-representational work. Here I move from the realm of high literary culture, and its attendant concerns with form, genre, and tradition, to works less self-consciously "literary" but more identifiably autobiographical insofar as they purport to tell the history of real lives lived. As I analyze texts by women of strong religious commitment— Mary Martha Sherwood, Charlotte Elizabeth Tonna, and Mary Anne Schimmelpenninck—I locate a reliance on spiritual authority that permits a degree of feminine individualism, for religious discourse licenses self-representation as part of the production of exemplary Christian feminine subjects. Unlike the Romantic autobiographer, who represents his work and his identity as antithetical to prevailing cultural norms, or the professional literary man, who seeks to derive his authority from the public efficacy of his labors, the subjects of these autobiographies eschew publicity and the implied values of the public sphere. The autobiographical subjects produced in these texts do not transgress their culture's prescriptive norms for bourgeois femininity; they rather assume the truth and value of those norms and become responsible for embodying them in self-representation for an audience of like-minded private readers.

For the autobiographers of Chapter 3, however, who do not rely heavily on spiritual authority, neither writing for publication nor the practice of self-representation is so readily assimilable to the ideology of middle-class femininity. The first two autobiographies I look at here, by Mary Howitt and Harriet Martineau, actively explore the conflict that attends the lives of women writers who of necessity have domestic duties of diverse kinds to perform. Their texts pit the claims that literary labor makes on writing women against the selflessness required of Victorian domestic women. In its negotiation of the conventions of "public discourse" and those of private life, Martineau's *Autobiography* (1877) in particular raises knotty questions of autobiographical propriety, taken up by Margaret Oliphant and George Eliot, but elided by the memoirists I then go on to analyze.

The memoir, a form usually considered generically inferior to autobiography proper, becomes in the hands of some middle-class women an important means of representing themselves; its self-displacing characteristics make it a form with which many seem to have felt subjective affinities. The formal properties of memoir enable its practitioners both to speak and to remain silent about themselves, almost in the same gesture, by focusing on others. Such memoirists as Camilla Crosland, Eliza Lynn Linton, and Anne Thackeray Ritchie employ this form, I argue, in order to avoid the self-centeredness that "public discourse" would seem to entail. Finally, the family memoir narrates the subject by putting domestic life into discourse. In *A Writer's Reminiscences* (1918), Mary Ward writes her family's history as a success story in which she plays the pivotal role of conveying "private" experience to the public; in Margaret Oliphant's *Autobiography* (1899), however, neither the writer's life nor familial ties can provide a linear plot, narrative closure, or personal satisfaction. In short, the texts I examine in Chapters 2 and 3 consciously situate their authors as private subjects within a domestic feminine discourse while at the same time, through the very act of publication, they publicize both that subjectivity and the context in which it is created. In this way, autobiography functions generically as a mediating realm in which both the public and the private are produced for reading consumers, not as distinct realms, but as interdependent and mutually constitutive.

In Chapters 4 and 5, I locate other sites at which domesticated feminine subjects are produced for public consumption—the late Victorian theater and a group of autobiographies written by its actresses. The large number of published autobiographies by "leading ladies" of the stage drew my attention because their sheer volume suggested that as professional performers, actresses were fully licensed to represent themselves textually; I imagined that actresses' texts would look different from writers' texts because of the differences between the media in which members of each group primarily work. Unlike writers, whose "public" identities are created only through the mediating realm of "publication," actresses have a physical, public being for their audiences. They make their identities in public and for the public, not only in the roles they play, but also in how they look and move and interact with their fellow players. A critical difference between writers and actresses is thus played out on and through the body: what separates "public" performers from "private" writers is that while actresses, like writers, are invested with the authority to represent private life, they do so on a public stage.

Yet to my surprise, I found that there are as many (if not more) resemblances as differences between actresses' and writers' texts. In Chapter 4, while continuing to develop the argument about the publicizing of the private, I use the history of professionalization in the Victorian theater as the context for my analysis of autobiographies by the actresses Fanny Kemble, Madge Kendal, and Marie Bancroft. Here I establish that the effort to "reform" the stage requires them to internalize and disseminate the standards of middle-class femininity: what licenses the dramatic and textual performances of Kendal and Bancroft is that they fit their lives to a middle-class narrative of domestic womanhood radically at odds with their own properly working-class experience. The crux of their value for me, however, lies in how they reveal middle-class womanhood to be a matter of learned behavior rather than a natural orientation, for they insist that bourgeois respectability is a goal that can be achieved through the practices of theatrical and autobiographical self-representation.

The new drama of the late Victorian theater, which stages private bourgeois life for public mimesis, remakes the actress as a middle-class lady whose private identity becomes a matter of public discourse, and it is this dynamic I trace in Chapter 5. From the domestic realism of Robertson's "cup-and-saucer" plays to Pinero's "New Woman" dramas, the actress is given the task of representing publicly what the (usually male) playwright presumes all women to feel and experience privately. As George Bernard Shaw put it, "every woman who sees [Eleanora] Duse play Magda feels that Duse is acting and speaking for her and for all women as they are hardly able to speak and act for themselves."[26] Similarly, the hatred for domestic life that Beatrice Webb could articulate only in the privacy of her diary can be publicly expressed by the actress of the 1890s in, for example, *The Second Mrs. Tanqueray* (1893).

Significantly, then, it is primarily the actress's identity, not her body, that becomes the subject of discourse and a matter of intersubjective making and remaking. In discussing texts by Ellen Terry, Stella Campbell, and Irene Vanbrugh, I show that the new conditions of middle-class theater emphasize the personality of the actress as the mark of her particular, individual power. This public identity depends on her being delivered to her audience as a commodity to whom each spectator ostensibly has an unmediated relationship. Among the texts of these late Victorian actresses, an intersubjective realm of the "private" is thus publicized, as representations of interiority come to occupy a larger place in their autobiographies, but those representations of the "true self" are themselves highly constructed, in part by identifiably "theatrical" conventions. I conclude the chapter by suggesting, in my reading of Vanbrugh's autobiography, that the subject who shapes herself as an isolated being, with problems that are wholly internal to the self, elides the socially specific material and economic conditions that make her experience of work and of her own subjectivity alternately pleasurable and frustrating.

The final chapter explores another public site for the making of feminine identities, the texts and practices of the Edwardian suffragettes, and here I work through some of the political dimensions of subjectivity formation. By exploring the complex relationships among political actors, I identify two competing forms of subjectivity in suffragette autobiographies. Adapting the Victorian ethic of feminine selflessness to their campaign for the vote, suffragette ideologists promote an intersubjective norm for collective feminine identity produced through the common experiences of imprisonment. The practices of both hunger-striking and forcible feeding—represented in texts by Mary Richardson, Sylvia Pankhurst, and Constance Lytton as instrumental in creating a shared experience of a self that transcends all differences among women in their mutual devotion to "the Cause"—make self-sacrifice a concrete reality for these and other women. Those who endure the physical force exercised against their bodies experience the material realization of suffragette ideology. Through these practices, they redefine the ethic of selflessness by bringing it into politics, where it serves as the basis for developing political community among women of different classes.

Yet the intersubjective model and the tactics of the suffragette leadership are also subject to critique, especially among working-class activists and women writers who repudiate self-sacrifice and the loss of personal autonomy enforced by the movement. Those who dissent from the Women's Social and Political Union—including Teresa Billington-Grieg, Hannah Mitchell, Cicely Hamilton, May Sinclair, and Sylvia Pankhurst—appraise their own emotional, physical, and aesthetic needs as insufficiently met by the movement, while they still count political struggle as an important constituent of personal identity. These women seek to define themselves within the political community in terms that will allow for both individual autonomy and collective action. As an important venue for exploring the relationship between subjects and their communities, and as a crucial moment in the history of middle-class women's effort to give voice to their own histories, the suffragette movement also draws my attention for its use of autobiography as a means of writing a collective women's history, a project that continues to engage many feminists today.

Reading these autobiographies, by women who were as "public" as any of their male contemporaries, has demonstrated to me that the ideology of domestic femininity persistently shaped the written lives of Victorian and Edwardian women. And the range of texts I consider enables me to argue that the discourse of femininity was something many public women consciously appropriated as a means of legitimating their public identities, of achieving professional success, of making political change. Yet I am by no means unaware of the ways in which the ideological division of spheres oppressed—and continues to oppress—many women. Capitalist culture in the nineteenth and twentieth centuries, both here and in England, has simultaneously apotheosized middle-class women's domesticity and refused to recognize domestic labor as work. Historically, middle-class women have been either prevented from working outside the home or compelled to do so, and usually directed into fields that pay them less and require of them more. Women have been dependent on fathers, brothers, husbands, lovers, and sons, and left impoverished when those supporting men died or disappeared. Marriage and motherhood have been made to seem the fitting destiny of every "normal" woman whether or not she is so inclined; women's access to education has been limited, women's political power appropriated. As a group—a multiple, diverse, irreducible group—women have not been historically self-determining or autonomous, but "relative creatures."

Yet, some women did work, write, participate in politics, play Portia in public, choose chastity and "independence" over marriage and motherhood, and some mothers managed to do the work of domesticity as well as the work of representation. And women's historical practices—multiple and diverse as they have been—have helped to produce a trenchant critique of the idea of the individual life as the primary locus of value: for many women, the liberal ideal of independence was, in the 1850s, not possible, and by the 1900s, not desirable. Women's historical experiences, as we recover them, teach us that interdependence has been and still is a basic fact for many of us, and for many men as well. My own experiences—as daughter, sister, friend, lover, student, teacher, colleague, writer—have taught me to cherish the ties that bind me to others, to institutions, and to ideas, even as I sometimes resist those ties. Insofar as what

I write contributes to what Foucault has called "the history of the present," my own contemporary concerns, my own subject positions, are as much a part of this work as those of the subjects I seek to reconstitute and they define my perspective throughout.[27] And I speak with Ray Strachey, early historian of the suffrage movement, when she abjures the snare of what Donna Haraway calls "the god trick" in positioning her work as an interested and thus ideological history:

> I feel bound to confess at the outset that in writing this book I have not been unbiased. . . . I am both open to and proud of the charge that I cannot take a wholly impartial view. I have conscientiously tried to write history . . . but my assumptions are undoubtedly feminist, and my eyes perhaps blinded to the virtues of the past.[28]

While confession is not my mode, my eyes do seek out "the virtues of the past," if only as a way of coming to terms with the present; yet I, too, "conscientiously" write this history straight from the heart.

1

Producing the Professional: Wordsworth, Carlyle, and the Authorial Self

WRITING FOR *The Examiner* in 1846 as one of the many who made his living by literature, John Forster contrasts the vagaries of a literary career with the secure course of the middle-class professional:

> For the lawyer there are many roads open to preferment; for the divine many; for the doctor some. The soldier and the sailor may have pensions in the distant prospect. Even the citizen has his gown, his dinners, and the civic chair. But the literary man is *unplaced*. His position in society lies in that vast unsurveyed region . . . in which so many of her Majesty's poorer lieges live, and breathe, and suffer, and run a long course, and die.[1]

Melodramatically phrased though it is, Forster's point accurately measures the material differences at mid-century between the "prospects" of the professional and those of the literary man. From his exalted position, the professional can see "many roads" open ahead, roads cleared by those who have traveled the path before him; the writer, wandering in an "unsurveyed region" where no paths have been broken, has no signposts to follow. "On the beaten road there is tolerable travelling," said Carlyle in his 1840 lecture on "The Hero as Man of Letters," "but it is sore work, and many have to perish, fashioning a path through the impassable!"[2] And as Wordsworth wrote in 1815, the original writer "will be called upon to clear and often to shape his own road," and not only because original genius necessarily blazes its own path; for unlike professional work, literary production lacks objective rules and standards for what constitutes quality work and workers of quality.[3]

As Leonore Davidoff and Catherine Hall have argued, the early nineteenth century was a crucial period of transformation in which socioeconomic roles were redefined with direct reference to gender: "masculine identity was equated with an emerging concept of 'occupation,' while women remained within a familial frame."[4] "The concept of work," as Clifford Siskin argues, "had to be rewritten from that which a true gentleman does not have to do, to the primary activity informing adult identity," or at least adult masculine identity.[5] Accordingly, the place of the literary man also had to be redefined in relation to new norms for middle-class labor.[6] Unlike other workers, however, artists did not keep regular hours, receive wages, or produce the necessities of life. Their work was not carried out in offices or factories, but generally within the privacy of their homes, thus symbolically aligning their work with that of the household; unless they wrote for or edited periodicals, writers had no employers or employees. This relative freedom from the strict discipline that increasingly regulated the lives of nineteenth-century workers of all classes undeniably made the literary life appealing to some men, even as it made literature one of the few paid occupations middle-class women could enter without "losing caste," but it also made literature a socially and economically unstable occupation.

Eighteenth-century writers such as Johnson and Boswell perceived "free trade" in the literary marketplace as having distinct advantages over the patronage system, which had underscored writers' socioeconomic dependence on wealthier men. Writers coming of age around 1800, however, were less sanguine about their prospects in a trade that grew more competitive and commercial every day.[7] The breakdown of older structures—in which writing had been primarily (though by no means exclusively) a pastime for the gentleman-amateur—newly complicated the writer's position. Could writing poetry really be considered a respectable occupation? Was the writer merely engaged in commodity production and thus not unlike any other small tradesman seeking to sell his wares in the marketplace? Or was he a specialist who provided, as did the physician or the barrister, a service which no one else could offer?[8]

To Forster and many of his contemporaries, the desired answers to these questions were clear: they responded to the commodification of literature by promoting their work as equal in value to any other profession's. Unlike writers, medical and legal professionals were coming to achieve a recognized social and economic position in early nineteenth-century culture which put them at the apex of the middle class, at a safe distance above trade, while the literary man directly exchanged his imaginative goods as a commodity in the marketplace. But what gives the professional man the security and opportunity for advancement that Forster envies is an elaborate system of institutional procedures developed in response to market forces: barristers and physicians had been able to negotiate the marketplace by collectively implementing institutional control over their own work. The difference between Forster's "*unplaced*" writer and the well-placed professional is that corporate professional ideology ensures a central position for professional services within the structure of nineteenth-century society; the individual practitioner finds his place in belonging to a recognized body of like members.

The primary fiction about nineteenth-century authorship, on the other hand, was (and is) that the man of genius is wholly his own product, an individual whose native abilities alone enable him to succeed; even those literary men who bemoaned the lack of institutional support for writers assumed that each individual would rise or fall in the marketplace solely on account of his own personal attributes—industry, imagination, and self-discipline. This mythologizing of the individual as arbiter of his own destiny obscures not only the social and economic factors which help to determine literary success or failure, but also the extent to which the myth is itself produced in response to those factors. "The ideology of free enterprise, in particular the notion of the 'profession,' necessarily overlooks the new relationship of the writer to the new structures of publishing" (p. 5), as N. N. Feltes has argued, and it is in response to this ideology that literary men alternately embrace and reject this way of conceptualizing their work.

That nineteenth-century literary men so consistently compare their own practice with the professions suggests that we should critically investigate the discursive underpinnings of such comparisons, and the use of the term "professional" in literary discourse provides a case in point. Used loosely to characterize all literary workers who earned money from their writing, the word "professional" has, in different historical contexts, specific connotations that twentieth-century readers and writers have tended to ignore.[9] In the eighteenth century, for example, writers who were labeled or labeled themselves as professionals were those who wrote as a full-time occupation; writing was the main source of their income, not a sideline.[10] What distinguished the professional author from the amateur writer was payment, for in theory, paid publication was the only thing that made a writer a "professional": "if a writer's work appeared under the imprimatur of a reputable man . . . ipso facto he was a member of the profession" (Saunders, p. 142).

Yet, in the first third of the nineteenth century, as the notion of what constituted a profession changed and as standards were developed to distinguish "true professions" from mere occupations, literature did not possess the attributes that characterized other professions. As Gaye Tuchman puts it, "nineteenth-century writers were not professionals . . . they did not control significant elements of their work."[11] With control over who could publish located primarily in the hands of publishers and booksellers, writers themselves had no means of determining who could enter into literary work; without the training procedures or protocols that increasingly typified other professional practices after 1800, the business of authorship took on the quality of being an easily accessible occupation requiring perseverance and perhaps a modicum of talent, but not necessarily capital, connections, or a degree. As law and medicine grew in power and status, however, some writers reappropriated the term "professional" to describe their work, for pragmatic and polemical purposes. Even though literary men could not exercise the kind of control that physicians and barristers established over the composition of their ranks or the marketplace itself, there was by mid-century an identifiable socioeconomic group of professional men of letters who consciously represented their work as equivalent in value to other professional activities.

My argument, however, is not primarily concerned with whether or not literary men achieved the corporate identity or hegemony that the professions established. Rather, I want to argue that masculine literary identity in the nineteenth century is formed in the context of a wider discourse about occupational and especially professional identity: certain correspondences between the literary and the professional affect the construction of the literary man as well as the literary woman, that anomalous figure who will be my focus in two subsequent chapters. For despite their ambivalence toward the professions and professional authors and the ambiguity of their different positions, literary men such as Wordsworth, Carlyle, and their descendents did achieve tremendous cultural power over their audiences: in their autobiographical texts, *The Prelude* and *Sartor Resartus*, Wordsworth and Carlyle establish dominant cultural models for true authorship. While I use the professions to demonstrate certain cultural analogies between literary work and professional labor, then, I am most interested in showing how the category of the literary man is redefined in the early nineteenth century and in identifying under what conditions and through what discourses it emerges.

Professional Men and Literary Men

The lack of precise restrictions on who could practice authorship irked the major Romantics: from Blake to Keats, all six castigated the sickly taste of the day, the proliferation of hack writing, and the pursuit of authorship as a trade for the many rather than a specialized art for the few. Lamenting the fact that "of all trades, literature at present demands the least talent or information," Coleridge separates the true artist from the great mass of opportunistic hacks, those "whose presumption is in due proportion to their want of sense and sensibility; men, who being first scriblers [sic] from idleness and ignorance next become libellers from envy and malevolence."[12] In Coleridge's formulation, pursuing literature as a trade is morally suspect: the professional writer is above all a money-grubber, and the literary marketplace is too open, too easily entered by those who have little of value to offer.

The problem of how to regulate the work and character of those who practiced the same craft was by no means specific to literature, for the professions confronted a similar problem of internal structure, which they resolved in accord with a traditional model for professional organization. Within medicine, for example, professional labor had been historically divided into upper and lower branches: physicians were royally endowed with a certain training and particular privileges that, by law and tradition, surgeons and apothecaries could not attain, and social distinctions and class divisions reinforced those differences in function. The eventual consolidation between branches within each profession eventually made the socioeconomic differences between individuals less of a factor in determining social status, for power and position were conferred by the profession itself: the passage of the Apothecaries Act in 1815, the first law enabling a profession to set up its own procedures and standards, marks the onset of an era of professional self-determination.[13] While the ranks still remained divided, over the course of the century the social distinctions between the branches were more or less eliminated, although some specialization of function still remained in place.[14]

In literary relations around the turn of the century, we can also discern the presence of a two-tier system. The upper branch—literati who were equipped

with private or professional incomes and thus wrote not from economic necessity, but for pleasure and fame, as Byron did (at first) and as Scott did (before
his fall)—could affect to disdain the dictates of the marketplace. Those of the
lower branch—"authors by profession" who wrote for the penny press and the
popular taste—had to make their way in an unstable literary economy frag-
mented by the growth of heterogeneous reading audiences. Whereas "professional" is an honorific to which some occupations aspire, the designation tended
in Romantic usage to draw the line separating "true" artists from "mere" scrib-
bling tradespeople, a line that few men—and almost no women—could cross.

It is crucial to realize, however, that the Romantics themselves draw this
line, or at least redraw it in such a way as to include some few while excluding
others; what separates the higher from the lower, the artist from the hack, is
itself under contestation in this period, and where the line is drawn depends on
who holds the pen. "The élite men" Gaye Tuchman studies in *Edging Women
Out* "began insistently to differentiate their literature from the literature of
others" during this period (p. 8). For example, although Coleridge's own heterogeneous literary practice as both journalist and philosopher might associate
him with either branch of literary production, he rhetorically asserts that he
belongs to the higher rank simply by assuming the authority to classify all
others as morally and intellectually inferior. This is indeed a standard move
within the discourse of professionalism: the attribution of high status to one's
own work, whether solely on one's own behalf or on behalf of a group ("literary men"), functions within Romantic and Victorian representations as a means
of making high claims for art and the artist.[15] And in making those claims for
and about their work, both literary and professional men established ideals for
middle-class men's work that connected gender identity to occupational identity
in crucial ways. Before considering the makeup of professional hegemony and
returning to literary relations, I want to look briefly at the way in which issues
of class and masculinity are intertwined in the discourse of professionalism. In
doing so, I will suggest that professional self-representations help to establish
cultural models for middle-class masculine work that have a great impact on
literary men as well.

Most historians and sociologists agree that the eighteenth century ushered
in "the rise of the professions" as part of the economic and social transforma-
tions stemming from the Industrial Revolution, which produced changes in the
structure and status of the three traditional "learned professions," medicine,
law, and the clergy. Entry into the professions, once solely the province of the
younger sons of landed families, remained contingent upon family background
and connections, but new money could also provide the necessary funds for
entry fees and material support. While the "paltry curacy" Wordsworth once
feared would be his fate might not prove lucrative, any professional position
would provide some compensatory social advantages.[16] And being a professional
worker, even a low-paid one, enabled the middle-class man to create and maintain ties to his class.

Although not all gentlemen were professionals, all professionals seemingly aspired to the status of gentlemen, and were anxious to maintain traditional connections between professional work in the higher branches and social privilege. Before standardized methods for controlling access to the legal profession were created, for instance, the sole purpose of the perfunctory examination for aspirants was to give practicing barristers an opportunity to assess the candidates' social skills and personal demeanor. For the sons of gentlemen, passing these "tests" was no problem, but by the middle of the century, highly structured systems of entry were replacing this self-selecting method. Yet even in an era of academic credentialing and more competitive examinations, standards of gentlemanliness were still firmly upheld, and gentlemanliness was, by and large, an inherited characteristic. As a writer for the *Saturday Review* asserted in the 1850s, "Clergymen beget clergymen and barristers, barristers beget barristers and clergymen": transmitted almost genetically from father to son—apparently without any maternal contribution to this particular reproductive project—professional values continued to reproduce themselves through and in respectable, gentlemanly professionals.[17]

Educational mechanisms effectively controlled and maintained the social composition of the professions, but other social forces played a part. Lower-middle-class boys who went in for professional life became members of the lower branches, being employed as solicitors and attorneys rather than as barristers, or as surgeons and apothecaries rather than as physicians. Establishing the class-related differences in occupation was essential to raising the social tone of the professions, for a gentlemanly character, as Adam Smith writes, was perceived as necessary to the delicate nature of professional work: "We trust our health to the physician; our fortune and sometimes our life and reputation to the lawyer and the attorney. Such confidence could not safely be reposed in people of a very mean or low condition."[18] Only gentlemen could be entrusted with the private concerns of other gentlemen: anxieties about "contamination" by those from a lower class position thus reinforce the representation of the middle-class professional as the bastion of all good masculine virtues—discretion, a sense of honor, self-discipline. R. L. Edgeworth, citing Blackstone's recommendation, promoted "the advantages of an academical education for barristers" over an apprenticeship, claiming that "if the practice of breeding up lawyers at attorneys' desks were persisted in, the profession would be utterly degraded, no *gentlemen* would send their sons to the bar."[19] The character of a professional is thus as important as education, and character, as these commentators imagine it, is very much linked to class position: the professional man must represent middle-class morals and standards, yet he must also be superior to the pettiness of everyday life. A profession confers certain rights on its practitioners, yet it also requires that they embody particular qualities, transmitted largely through middle-class constructs.

What a "professional character" ideally confers on the nineteenth-century man is independence: as the proprietor of his own practice, the physician or barrister works only for himself and, by extension, for his family. In contrast, the literary man of this period often found himself working for others—publishers and familial dependants—without earning very much for himself; with so many competing for readerly attention and with so little remuneration available for literary work, authorship alone did not provide a stable social or economic position, and so left its practitioners vulnerable. Only for the rare individual could literature secure an independence; for most full-time workers it could barely provide a subsistence.

In a letter of 1813 to George Crabbe, Walter Scott defines their shared poetic practice as clearly secondary to their professional work, which endows each of them with a fixed social and economic identity, and expresses a clear connection between independence and gender identity:

> I have often thought it the most fortunate thing for bards like you and me to have an establishd [sic] profession and professional character to render us independent. . . . did any of my sons show poetical talent of which (to my great satisfaction) there are no appearances the first thing I should [do] would be to inculcate upon [him] the duty of cultivating some honourable profession and qualifying himself to play a more respectable part in Society than the mere poet.[20]

Scott's security is, of course, based on class privilege and the steady income that possessing a "professional character" provides; for someone like Keats, who lacked capital and connections, becoming a writer was a more risky occupational choice than becoming a surgeon's apprentice.[21] But the link Scott makes between a "professional character" and respectability underscores the inferior condition of the literary man as compared to the professional: if dependence is the lot of the writer, then clearly no son could be advised to take that road, for the "duty" of the son, as Scott establishes it, is to become self-reliant, self-disciplined, and self-sustaining. A properly gendered, properly masculine identity is in part a function of a young man's relation to the right kind of work. And while independence is coded as a male, middle-class ideal, dependence is for children and women: men must be autonomous and self-sufficient in the public sphere if they are to support and maintain those who rely on them. In this way, professional organization is highly suited to the socioeconomic as well as gendered needs of the men whose interests it served: professional work in the nineteenth century could potentially yield both autonomy and security to the independent men on whom private women depended. And as I will establish later, this ideology had a considerable impact on literary men and on how they sought to represent their work.

As both a personal and a corporate attribute, a middle-class ideal of masculinity for the individual as well as the class, independence is the hallmark of professional organization in the nineteenth century: ruled by their own internal regulations and laws, able to devise their own standards by government sanction, professional practitioners could, in theory, exercise control over every aspect of professional entry, training, and service. Moreover, only professionals could evaluate their own work since, by definition, only they were qualified to judge themselves; because the authority for separating the good physician from the bad one rests with the physicians themselves, rather than with their clients, the profession could perpetuate its own interests without fear of external challenge to that independent authority.[22] The concentration of knowledge in expert hands gives the professions that prerogative, because the use, control, and dissemination of knowledge confers on its possessors the power to distinguish the illegitimate quack from the legitimate practitioner. Thus a profession demarcates its sphere of power and knowledge as self-contained, self-generated, and wholly insulated against all judgments it defines as "external" to it.

The sole point on which the consumer public can interrogate the physician, as Edgeworth notes, is as to whether or not his medical care satisfies his patients' needs.

> The measure of a physician's talents may be frequently mistaken; but all the world is competent to decide on this one simple, essential point, whether his patients die or recover under his care. Success is the ultimate standard, by which medical skill and learning, like all other species of merit, are appreciated by mankind; for though ignorant persons are not able to judge of the enlarged and remote views, which may lead to great discoveries, yet they are ready to reward most liberally any practical application of ingenuity.   (pp. 201–202)

Lay judgments "may be frequently mistaken," since the competence to decide the finer points of medical practice is vested in the hands of the practitioners themselves. Classed among those "ignorant persons" who lack the authority to judge and must content themselves with admiring what Edgeworth calls "the happy result of [the physician's] practice" (p. 202), the consumer occupies a very different position in the market for medical services than he or she would in buying cattle or tea. As Maureen Cain notes, professionals function as "producers who define both the needs of the consumer and how those needs should be met": patient-consumers depend on the physician-producer to shape their "needs."[23] The autonomy of a profession thus rests on its ability to convert the knowledge its practitioners collectively possess into power over those who cannot assess their "large and remote views."

In effect, professionals created a stable market for their services by creating a variety of real practices and a network of imaginary relations; by surrounding themselves with a certain aura of superior wisdom and the promise of practical success, they rallied public confidence and trust in what they had to offer. Medicine was particularly efficient at establishing itself in a position of social authority because new technologies provided a rational scientific basis for medical practice. "Other professions," Philip Elliott observes, "had greater difficulty in specifying a body of knowledge or expertise which would form a universal basis for professional practice and which could be taught as such to aspiring professionals" (p. 41).

I believe we can see Wordsworth attempting to establish literature as an independent sphere along these same lines in the "Preface" to the second edition of *Lyrical Ballads* (1800) and I want to read his manifesto in light of the professional project described earlier, for the "Preface" parallels that project in two ways. Wordsworth bases his belief in the sovereignty of the artist's judgment over his critics on another claim, that the artist possesses superior taste and knowledge; and the artist's relation to the public, as he describes it, is to instruct and edify as a superior, not an equal. On both fronts, Wordsworth defines readerly "needs" according to his own standards. Yet the difference between the literary man and the professional also reveals itself in and as a difference between the writer and the text he necessarily produces in order to authorize himself.

Literary Authority and the "Literary Character"

Wordsworth opposes the debilitating practices of literary entrepreneurs to the constructive and instructive role the poet must play: his work is an antidote to "the gaudiness and inane phraseology" (p. 70) of his contemporaries, and he lodges the responsibility for reforming the "fickle tastes, and fickle appetites" (p. 71) of the reading public with writers such as himself. The two constituents of the literary market—writers and readers—are mutually at fault: readers crave "frantic novels, sickly and stupid German tragedies, and deluges of idle and extravagant stories in verse" (p. 74) because it is "to this tendency of life and manners and literature and theatrical exhibitions have conformed themselves" (pp. 73–74). Like Coleridge, Wordsworth separates himself from other inferior practitioners and asserts authority over reading consumers; he establishes his distance from both the unqualified hack and the ignorant consumer just as the professional man does. The strategy of the *Lyrical Ballads*, both preface and poems, is to reshape the reading public in the image Wordsworth dictates for it, and so to create the readers who will be able to read his poems; "the people's" correct appreciation of his work will be "a recompense for the original work bestowed upon the text," as Kurt Heinzelman puts it, and result in the communication of the knowledge he possesses, knowledge that ideally should transform not only poetic taste, but human society itself.[24] As such, Wordsworth's implicit task is to produce better writers as well, to create those who can reproduce the lessons the poet offers.

In effect, the "Preface" provides Wordsworth, in meeting the reading public, with some of the armature the professional man assumed: it tries to establish a means of distinguishing the true poet's product from the inferior verse of the hack, a theory that justifies practice, and a program for disciplining taste so as to produce proper readers. Stripping the critic of his authority by asserting the poetic practitioner's superior claim to knowledge of his craft, Wordsworth appeals directly to the reader, advising him that "much of what is ordinarily enjoyed" (p. 89) must be given up if he is to appreciate what Wordsworth does. As the arbiter of taste, the poet, like the physician or the barrister, rests his claim to authority on his superior knowledge; by virtue of that knowledge, acquired by "long continued intercourse with the best models of composition" (p. 89), he alone can judge good from bad, unless the reader, too, willingly undertakes the task of acquiring the capacity for judgment by submitting himself to the education the poet can give. In effect, Wordsworth argues that literary value cannot be determined in the marketplace, for no buyer is qualified to judge the worth of the goods for sale, and their worth cannot be measured in shillings or pounds: literature, like medicine or law, should not be subject to the fluctuations of market exchange, but take its proper place as a specialized service that its purveyor alone can rightly evaluate.

In the "Preface," Wordsworth converts his knowledge to rhetorical power, and in this he adopts a professional strategy for achieving socioeconomic prestige by making his authority a function of his own individual character. By 1798–99, as his most recent biographer notes, Wordsworth "was clearly attempting to recover control over his own publishing. . . . he was beginning now to conceive of himself more professionally as a poet."[25] Yet to think of poetry as a "profession," to imagine this high calling in terms of "making money, establishing a reputation, marketing, and accumulating material for future volumes" (Gill, p. 164), also requires that Wordsworth begin to attend to the commodity status of the literary text, which must further complicate his strategy for achieving literary power as compared with that of the professional man.

The ideology of the professional mystifies the relations between producer and consumer by specifying knowledge, rather than a particular work product, as the commodity to be exchanged on the market; that commodity can only be produced by the professional body, be it the individual practitioner's or the corporate whole's. As M. S. Larson explains, the difference between the professional and any other producer of a commodity resides in the fact that a professional sells himself, not an alienable product, as the possessor of that specialized knowledge: "unlike craft or industrial labor . . . most professions produce intangible goods: the product, in other words, is only formally alienable and is inextricably bound to the person and the personality of the producer. It follows, therefore, that *the producers themselves have to be produced* if the products or commodities are to be given a distinctive form."[26] In short, the professional produces only himself and, significantly, in the form of a potentially unalienated subject; since the physician's individual identity can never be separated from the set of practices that produces him, his services can never be sold on the market without his full participation. The ideology of professionalism thus draws on Locke's premise that "every man has a *property* in his own person," but it refuses to allow that "property" to be alienated from its possessor in the marketplace by making it the very ground of the professional's identity.[27] What differentiates the professional from the wage laborer is that no other capitalist can appropriate the surplus value of the professional as his own: the professional cannot be alienated from his labor because his own body is literally invested with it.

Larson's point about professional self-creation illustrates both the similarities and the differences between the professional and the literary man. While the Romantics sometimes insist that literature has its source in inspiration rather than in labor, the mythology of genius as internal, inalienable, and natural is analogous to the professional's attribution of his power to a discipline undergone by the very few. In both cases, the field of activity is clearly demarcated as belonging only to those entitled to it by a special claim. No amount of industry could ever qualify the unqualified quack or the unworthy hack to perform the valuable work appropriated in the interests of a particular class. And the true author is not a hack, as Nigel Cross asserts, because he possesses this intangible, inalienable thing called genius: "Authorship was allowed to be the occupation of genius . . . but everyone else who wrote did so from base commercial motives and were scribblers, hacks, and dunces" (p. 90). Literature could not be chosen as an occupation; it had to choose you. In William Hazlitt's Romantic use of the term "professional" in the sense of "learned" or "mechanical," talent of the highest order could never be considered under the rubric of a profession: "Professional Art is a contradiction in terms. Art is genius, and genius cannot belong to a profession."[28]

Even more than the professional, the literary man must insist on his own uniqueness, his own internal difference from other writers, as the ground of his claim to true authorship, particularly in the new literary marketplace. No accident, then, that the nineteenth-century author begins to forge the illusion that he has "a personal relationship with his audience" (Poovey, p. 104) just at the moment when new technologies of writing threaten to make the author's alienation from his product an inalterable condition of literary work. For the writer, unlike the physician or barrister, does actually produce a marketable object from his labors, the literary text, and in the relationship between the man and the text lies the particular problematic of early nineteenth-century literary production.

We see, then, that the Romantics wage a double battle against the "professional" even as they adopt the knowledge-power model of self-creation: Wordsworth, Coleridge, and their peers want to rival the claims to cultural power made by the legal and medical professions while defending their own work as superior to that of other literary workers. Isaac D'Israeli's *Essay on the Manners and Genius of the Literary Character* (1795) dramatizes both aspects of this struggle, and reveals some of the inherent arbitrariness in where the battle lines are drawn.[29] Read and admired by Scott, Moore, Byron, Rogers, and others, D'Israeli's text attempts to define the "literary character" as operating independently of local circumstances or historical and social differences between writers. Its very first sentence posits the existence of a transnational fellowship of inspired artists who hover above the petty material interests of ordinary men: "Diffused over enlightened Europe, an order of men has arisen, who, uninfluenced by the interests or the passions which give an impulse to the other classes of society, are connected by the secret links of congenial pursuits, and, insensibly to themselves, are combining in the same common labours, and participating in the same divided glory" (p. 23). In this respect, D'Israeli's disinterested artists are like barristers seeking to uphold the dominion of justice or physicians striving to eradicate disease. Artists and professionals labor for the common good, not for their own pecuniary reward.

But D'Israeli goes on to separate artists from professionals by articulating in what respects they differ:

> The LITERARY CHARACTER, is a denomination which, however vague, de-
> fines the pursuits of the individual, and separates him from other professions.
> . . . Professional characters are modified by the change of manners, and are
> usually national; while the literary character, from the objects in which it con-
> cerns itself, retains a more permanent, and necessarily a more independent
> nature.   (p. 25)

D'Israeli distinguishes "the literary character," always essentially the same
wherever it appears, from "the professional character," which is "modified" by
historical circumstance and the vagaries of social life: professions are time- and
place-specific, while genius is not. The "faculty of genius," as he later calls it,
can remove the individual from his particular circumstances; it "can exist independent of education, and where it is wanting, education can never confer it"
(p. 79), for genius transcends accidents of birth. The secular professions are
thus represented as subordinate to the literary, which assumes an almost clerical function in D'Israeli's text. He represents "the literary character" as an
innate principle not to be gained by any of the methods one could use to educate oneself as a barrister or a physician; in an argument that anticipates Carlyle's subsequent formulation, D'Israeli locates a "predisposition" in each man
for a specific calling.

D'Israeli's discussion of genius as that which transcends time, place, and
social origin thus bears a close similarity to the Calvinist notion of election;
while many may be called, few are chosen. The important point about election
in terms of this discussion is, as Max Weber puts it, that "the elect differ
externally in this life in no way from the damned": similarly, identifying whether
or not that "predisposition" to literary genius was operable in any given individual, ascertaining the presence or absence of genius, could not be achieved by
ordinary human means.[30] Any criteria for judgment would inevitably prove
subjective and fallible, for on the surface, a hack and a genius might seem to
be engaged in very similar practices; as D'Israeli acknowledges, "with the mid-
dling as well as the great, the same habits must operate" (p. 69). Despite the
difficulties of making a judgment, D'Israeli yet attempts to distinguish between
works of genius and the lesser products of the inferior writer.

While the professions could eliminate this problem by pointing to the cer-
tification process and other controls that kept the unqualified out, only the reviews provided any kind of standard for literary production, and the reviews
were notoriously biased and polemical. D'Israeli resolves the issue for himself
along the lines of the upper/lower branch model by classifying the "author" as
a producer of knowledge and "the man of letters" as an acquirer or codifier of
it. "The man of letters, whose habits and whose whole life so closely resemble
those of an author, can only be distinguished by this simple circumstance, that
the man of letters is not an author" (p. 298), with the word "author" bearing
its originary sense of "maker, producer, or creator." The production of knowledge—as opposed to the man of letters' dissemination of it—is another signifier
of authorship, a distinction created and maintained in the new mass periodicals
of the era: the anonymous reviewer, subsumed by the collective editorial identity of the journal, comments on and provides copious extracts from the pub-

lished works of "original" authors.[31] In categorizing the author's work as that which produces the knowledge that motivates the man of letters' work, D'Israeli assigns the author a productive role because the author's work has the necessary surplus value to generate further labor.[32] Since the author creates a commodity that circulates—and which can be read, rewritten, and written up—he fuels other work. In the production of knowledge, then, the author exercises the independent power that runs the literary economy, in which other writers depend on his labor for their own.

In this juncture between political economy and literary taxonomy we come close to identifying Wordsworth's sense of his own generative role as an originating force in English poetry. "The mere communication of *knowledge*," in the language of the "Essay, Supplementary to the Preface" (1815), is not a sufficient task for the "original Genius" (p. 210), for "Genius is the introduction of a new element into the intellectual universe . . . it is the application of powers to objects on which they had not before been exercised, or the employment of them in such a manner as to produce effects hitherto unknown" (p. 212). The artist of genius, in other words, is truly productive, and Wordsworth's language of production here is predictably imbricated with economics; the exchanges of his thought and poetry center on what Kurt Heinzelman calls his "need to produce in all readers a disposition in harmony with [his] own understanding of poetry as a socially productive, economically pertinent labor" (p. 199).

One way Wordsworth tries to create that "disposition" is by theorizing, as in the "Preface" and the "Essay"; another is by writing poetry, and particularly autobiographical poetry. My concern is with how Wordsworth uses the autobiographical mode to represent himself as a producer of original knowledge. If, like the professional, the poet must be produced and is his own product, then his text should record the history of that process; *The Prelude* should specify the sources of the poet's power and also establish the authenticity of the line separating the producer from the disseminator, the productive writer from the unproductive one. In writing the literary text, the literary man has the opportunity to create his own identity as a working writer, to inscribe his unique signature, yet Wordsworth's poem also betrays his own implication in cultural fictions of masculine development; indeed, it is at the intersection of the unique and the universal that the masculine poet locates himself.[33] Through representing the production of the literary self as a matter of self-discipline, Wordsworth attempts to author the narrative of his own entry into productive authorship.

Wordsworth in the 1790s

Ever since Matthew Arnold, critics have tended to focus more on Wordsworth's lack of learning than on the social and cultural implications of his participation in Cambridge life. But whether or not Wordsworth learned anything at university matters less for this analysis than the fact that, like other Englishmen of his class, he was integrated into a body of elites, subjected to the same influences and ideologies, and exposed to a certain set of assumptions about the proper role of the middle-class gentleman. Even Wordsworth's negative reaction to Cambridge illustrates the extent to which he had internalized the standard notions of male middle-class development, for he subsequently conceptualizes his experience in terms of an opposition between working and not working: the independence he could have achieved through industry is continually contrasted with what he failed to achieve because of idleness.[34] I want now to look briefly at the material circumstances of Wordsworth's early life in to order to show that this lack of industry was a personal "failing" with cultural and gendered implications.

When Wordsworth went up to university in October 1787, his worldly prospects were neither particularly bleak nor especially auspicious. Entangled in litigation with Lord Lonsdale over money owed to their father, the Wordsworth sons had little inherited income at their disposal, and thus the four boys needed to prepare themselves to earn their own livings as well as to support their sister Dorothy. Through the assistance of relatives, Wordsworth's older brother, Richard, became an attorney, as his father had been; John rose to his position as East India Company captain and maritime entrepreneur through long effort and hard work; the youngest son, Christopher, became a Cambridge fellow and master, despite the fact that much of the family seemed to consider him William's intellectual inferior. As the sons of a professional with their own aspirations to gentlemanly status, the Wordsworth brothers "naturally" elected to follow their father into professional occupations that would provide each of them with an independent living and a respectable social position.

Of William himself great things were expected. Educated at Hawkshead, a prestigious northern school run by Cambridge graduates for sons of the middle and professional classes, Wordsworth received the preliminary instruction in mathematics which gave him a leg up on his less prepared college classmates; in his own words, Hawkshead provided him "a full twelve-month's start of the freshmen of [his] year" at university.[35] Family ties also helped him at St. John's, as his uncle William was a fellow of that college. Despite his family's financial instability, Wordsworth thus had the necessary entrée to any one of the traditional learned professions; even had he been completely sure of his desire to be a poet, he might still have combined a career in law, as Francis Jeffrey and Walter Scott were to do, with the pursuit of his literary interests. To choose poetry without the security of an independence or the safety net of a professional income was both socially and economically ill-advised. "When he will go into orders I do not know, nor how he will employ himself," wrote Dorothy Wordsworth in 1790; "he must, when he is three and twenty either go into orders or take pupils" (Shaver, 1:29).

But the young Wordsworth rejected the prescribed course of study for the university student, probably out of contempt for the rules that laid down a strict discipline for some, while permitting wealthy fellow-commoners to do as they pleased. "I was a freeman, in the purest sense / Was free," and he distanced himself from the life that would tie him to a routine.[36] But Wordsworth's antagonism to class privilege in the 1790s could not alter his situation: he was part of that system and he needed to maintain himself. Having ruled out law and abdicated the opportunity of an academic career, Wordsworth left himself only two viable options: as the Cambridge-educated son of a professional, he was fitted only to be a vicar or a schoolmaster, both respectable and quasi-gentlemanly professions, but of low socioeconomic standing with little or no outlet for advancement. He chose instead to follow his inclinations: in the 1790s, Wordsworth lived briefly in London, traveled on the continent, and wrote some of his earliest poems, spending little money, but earning even less. From being "an idler among academic bowers" (8.649), he became an idler at large. Stephen Gill sums up Wordsworth's "lamentable" position at the time he began writing *The Prelude*: "At 28 years of age he had neither a settled income nor the professional qualifications needed to secure one" (p. 3).

In retrospect, Wordsworth reproached himself not for having diverged from the prescribed academic course, but for having had no course at all: his "vague / And loose indifference" (3.331–32) to everything marks a lapse in self-discipline, a failure which haunts *The Prelude*. The young man who neglects the rational training of body and mind that Edgeworth recommends in his *Essays on Professional Education* (1809) runs the risk of losing his best opportunity for independence and success: "The earlier this discipline is commenced, it will the sooner become easy and habitual; and . . . the greater will be the chance that he will pursue it with ardour and perseverance" (p. 22). While parents bear some responsibility for guiding young sons, a writer for the *Westminster Review* locates the conditions for success or failure within the individual: "The education of those who are really educated, is their own work. And, being their own work, not only are all the previous time and money lost, but that period of life which ought to have been occupied in acquisition, has past, never to return, never to be compensated by after-industry."[37] In terms of masculine identity, then, to relinquish one's best chance is to arrest one's own development by failing to acquire the valuable capital no man should be without.

Wordsworth at first felt his failure to be a good capitalist, to lay up the stores of knowledge that could be converted to future profit, to be his cardinal flaw in his Cambridge years. Writing to his classmate William Mathews in 1791, he bemoans the lack of a stock to draw on: "But what must I do amongst that immense wilderness, who have no resolution, and who have not prepared myself for the enterprise by any sort of discipline among the Western languages? who know little of Latin, and scarce anything of Greek. A pretty confession for a young gentleman whose whole life ought to have been devoted to study" (Shaver, 1:62). Without "resolution" or "discipline," Wordsworth remains in his own mind a gentleman, but an idle, profitless one.

In the years immediately following his departure from Cambridge, Wordsworth did very little to advance his literary career. Unlike Dr. Johnson, who gave up a failing school for the even more uncertain fortunes of Grub Street, Wordsworth did not set out to make his mark in urban literary circles; he chose instead to remain in the country. Even in his longest sojourn in the city, he went not "to seek a fortune or a job; so he sought no introductions to persons of position or quality" (Moorman, p. 154). Plans to start a periodical with Mathews were aborted due to lack of ready funds and because Wordsworth was unwilling to move permanently to London; fitful publication did little to establish him as an author. By "early 1797," Gill rightly claims, "Wordsworth had become a poet who did not publish poems" (p. 118); he "deliberately [distanced] himself from the political centre, from publishers, and the whole professional world of literature" (p. 174). Even after the appearance of *Lyrical Ballads* in 1798, Wordsworth informed his publisher that "no motives whatever, nothing but pecuniary necessity, will, I think, ever prevail upon me to commit myself to the press again" (Shaver, 1:267). The crucial factor in determining Wordsworth against publication, at least for the moment, however, had less to do with the conditions of the marketplace than with the state of his own purse: the legacy from Raisley Calvert's will gave him a large enough (unearned) income to "secure me from want if not to render me independent" (Shaver, 1:130).[38] Calvert's money enabled Wordsworth to avoid the employments that would have made him an "author by profession"; as I have already suggested, he tried to redefine the terms of authorship rather than compete in the marketplace, and the semi-independence Calvert's money provided gave him the partial means to do so.

To reap the benefits of patronage without having to answer to a living patron: the fortuitous circumstances of Calvert's legacy allow Wordsworth to represent himself as free from the exigencies of the marketplace. "By a bequest sufficient for my needs" did Calvert "Enable me to pause for choice, and walk / At large and unrestrained" (13.357–59) so that Wordsworth could follow "the bent of Nature" (13.367). Yet despite the fact that Wordsworth represents independent authorship as his "natural" vocation, *The Prelude* is as dependent on the social structures it seems to reject as Wordsworth was on the good will of the dead patron to whom he belatedly pays tribute.

As I will demonstrate later, Wordsworth projects a disciplinary force onto nature which comes to substitute for the discipline the proper masculine subject is supposed to acquire "naturally" in the course of moving from family to school to profession. While it is not a term Wordsworth employs in the "Preface," "discipline" figures in *The Prelude* as one of the primary words used to denote the forces that produce the poet. James K. Chandler partly glosses this multivalent term as "a double-sided concept whose two sides correspond to the two primary senses of the word: firmness of mind, on the one hand, and the process by which this is achieved."[39] Clearly, one cannot exist independently of the other, for one's "firmness of mind" in the present depends on being able to plot a narrative which charts change and progression over time: "One's present discipline resides in the habitual contemplation of how one supposes oneself to have been disciplined in the past" (Chandler, p. 215). So Wordsworth could only arrive at this perspective over time, and in time:

> my hope has been that I might fetch
> Invigorating thoughts from former years,
> Might fix the wavering balance of my mind,

> And haply meet reproaches too, whose power
> May spur me on, in manhood now mature,
> To honorable toil.   (1.648–53)

By recovering "invigorating thoughts from former years" as the material for his poem, Wordsworth makes up for his own lapses. He converts a natural education to economic, psychic, and literary gain, for as Heinzelman has observed, "Memory is the true capitalist of the Wordsworthian imagination" (p. 225); in Franco Moretti's words, *"Bildung* is concluded under the sign of memory, of *mémoire voluntaire,* of the rationalization of the accomplished journey" (p. 68). Substituting a history of natural discipline for the naturalizing social discipline that characterizes proper masculine development, Wordsworth represents himself as both like other men, in that he, too, has been prepared and prepared himself for the work he is to pursue, and unlike them, in that his preparation and his practice take place outside normative disciplines.[40]

That Wordsworth attributes his own growth to natural discipline makes his education unique; engaging in self-representation enables him to establish the particular stages of his own "development." Yet in recording the narrative of development, Wordsworth himself becomes a naturalizing force; his autobiographical text creates an enormously influential cultural standard for artistic identity.[41] Wordsworthian discipline, I would suggest, thus has both an individual and a cultural dimension: *The Prelude* reenacts the process of disciplining that creates the subject-as-poet and presents that process as qualifying Wordsworth to extend his discipline over both his readership and his competitors.

"Natural Discipline" and Educational Critique

The Prelude opens with the issue of self-discipline very much at the fore, as if in beginning to write, Wordsworth must immediately establish writing as a labor freely undertaken; as David Simpson remarks, the first book "develops its argument largely through a continual scrambling of the language of honest labour with that of indolence and inertia."[42] "From yon city's walls set free" (1.7), the speaker sets out on a journey in search of a place of "rest":

> What dwelling shall receive me, in what vale
> Shall be my harbour, underneath what grove
> Shall I take up my home, and what sweet stream
> Shall with its murmurs lull me to my rest?   (1.11–14)

The release from "the heavy weight of many a weary day" (1.24) and the quest for a "dwelling" mark no pure passage into indolence, but a pursuit of the proper site for labor: "I am free, for months to come / May dedicate myself to chosen tasks" (1.33–34). In shaking off "that burthen of my own unnatural self" (1.23)—the "weight" he associates with city life—he takes up a new servitude. For Wordsworth, work can be freedom, an escape from alienation, but only if that work be freely chosen: within 100 lines of the joyful opening, when the initial mood of inspiration has passed, he characterizes poetic labor as "a servile yoke" (1.113).[43] The inconstancy of this mood is what writing itself is supposed to correct. Only through submitting himself to the work-discipline writing demands can Wordsworth control "a mind that every hour / Turns recreant to her task" (1.259–60).

The "task," as Wordsworth envisions it, is to make that discipline both productive and pleasurable, to make poetic work an activity to which his whole being consents—in short, to ensure that he will not become alienated from his own labor. The "gentle breeze" (1.1) that blows in the open air on the speaker's release from "prison" (1.8) signals liberty; the "corresponding mild creative breeze" (1.43), the internal analogue which M. H. Abrams describes as "a prophetic *spiritus* or inspiration which assures him of his poetic mission" (p. 75), stands for the liberty of labor, "brings with it vernal promises, the hope / Of active days, of dignity and thought, / Of prowess in an honorable field" (1.50–52). Poetic work, therefore, must be both pleasurable and profitable if it is to be "an honorable field" for Wordsworth to labor in.

The "glad preamble" is, of course, represented as a spontaneous outpouring of verse, the fruit of a moment of inspiration already passed, a moment in which the distinction between industry and idleness is not fully operable; however, Wordsworth's subsequent uncertainty about how to proceed, or if to proceed at all, creates the block that fictively generates the poem. His "rigorous inquisition" (1.159) into his own psyche calls him to account for both the "longing . . . / To brace myself to some determined aim" (1.123–24) and the "want of power" (1.241) that makes "the whole beauteous fabric" (1.226) of the projected work seem "shadowy and unsubstantial" (1.228).

In analyzing the relationship between the conditions of the narrative present and the yet-to-be-written history of the narrativized past, Wordsworth attempts to fuse the labor of poetry with the pleasure of idleness by recalling the twin legacy of nature, its "impressive discipline of fear" and the "pleasure and repeated happiness" (1.631, 632) it provided. Unwilling to believe that nature's ministry has produced nothing, Wordsworth proposes to trace the means that should lead him to a desired end:

> . . . not in vain,
> By day or star-light, thus from my first dawn
> Of childhood didst thou intertwine for me
> The passions that build up our human soul,
> Not with the mean and vulgar works of man,
> But with high objects, with enduring things,
> With life and Nature, purifying thus
> The elements of feeling and of thought,
> And sanctifying by such discipline
> Both pain and fear, until we recognise
> A grandeur in the beatings of the heart.   (1.431–41)

Through recollection, the poet prepares himself by reviewing his preparation, which he defines as natural, not social; in rehearsing the discipline nature imposed—both its pleasures and its "severer interventions" (1.370)—Wordsworth seeks to discipline himself for the writing the *The Recluse*. The years of apprenticeship under natural tutelage are recorded so as to mark the termination of his education and his entrance into poetic maturity.

Wordsworth defines that education directly against the cultural standard. In the fifth book of *The Prelude*, he critiques "the monster birth" (5.292) of educational theory, describing the prototypical Edgeworthian child as precocious, sophisticated, and artificial, leading "a life of lies" and "vanity" (5.350, 354): educational discipline creates mechanical progeny, a "dwarf man" (5.295) crammed with facts and "knowledge . . . purchased with the loss of power" (5.449).[44] Wordsworth thus imagines his own lack of training on the mechanistic model as a fortunate fall which gave him the freedom to follow his own "natural" path:

> . . . I was reared
> Safe from an evil which these days have laid
> Upon the children of the land—a pest
> That might have dried me up body and soul.
> This verse is dedicate to Nature's self
> And things that teach as Nature teaches: then,
> Oh, where had been the man, the poet where—
> Where had we been we two, beloved friend,
> If we, in lieu of wandering as we did
> Through heights and hollows and bye-spots of tales
> Rich with indigenous produce, open ground
> Of fancy, happy pastures ranged at will,
> Had been attended, followed, watched, and noosed,
> Each in his several melancholy walk,
> Stringed like a poor man's heifer at its feed,
> Led through the lanes in forlorn servitude . . .   (5.226–41)

Unlike the domesticated "heifer at its feed"—subjected to "servitude" so that it will produce the milk that provides its owner's subsistence, only nurtured so that it can be slaughtered and sold in the market—Wordsworth has lived (or represents himself as having lived) his wild young life outside the productive economy of practical education. Yet his natural education nonetheless has a product: it makes him a man and a poet. Thus Wordsworth's analogy between education and animal husbandry argues not merely "that social relations of production cannot touch the inner resources of man," as Gayatri Spivak would have it, but that the two are in active opposition.[45]

By extension, *The Prelude* itself is "indigenous produce," "dedicate to Nature's self / And things that teach as Nature teaches": its ambition is to teach as Wordsworth has been taught, and specifically to teach its readers to think of poetry as a natural, undivided labor that the poet cannot choose but produce. In opposing one sort of education to another, Wordsworth reaffirms the value of discipline in the making of the individual, but he insists on the priority of his natural education to the artificial systems that only foster personal development so as to insert the individual into his place in commodity production. Those "stewards of our labour" (5.378), as he describes educators, who "would controul / All accidents, and to the very road / Which they have fashioned would confine us down / Like engines" (5.380–83) ignore the beneficent presence of "a wiser spirit" (5.385) at work in the world, a spirit "most prodigal / Of blessings, and most studious of our good / Even in what seem our most unfruitful hours" (5.386–88). The creation of a fully alive human being, Wordsworth implies, should be an end in itself, but underlying his critique of the capitalist developmental model is a sense of poetic identity radically at odds with the practice of the early nineteenth-century literary marketplace.

That this natural education has no other product than *The Prelude* (since the work of maturity—*The Recluse*—never gets written) only confirms Wordsworth's antagonism to the economic logic that makes production the inevitable outcome of educational discipline. Tracing the history of *The Recluse* project, Kenneth R. Johnston notes that "all versions of *The Prelude* end at the point of *The Recluse*'s beginning; *The Recluse* could begin any time *The Prelude* could be considered finished. This is the essential reason *The Prelude* never was completed, or never left alone as complete."[46] Not proceeding with *The Recluse* illustrates that the "rigorous inquisition" became its own end, rather than a means to one; the work meant to affirm the poet *as* poet remains obsessed throughout with the issue of for what, if anything, its writing—and the life it purports to record—has prepared him. Moreover, the consistency with which Wordsworth addresses Coleridge as his intended audience signals, among other things, his own unwillingness to put the poem into wider public circulation, into the systems of distribution through which he could become alienated from the poem that insists on inalienability as the condition of poetic identity.[47] I want to turn now to the point in *The Prelude* at which Wordsworth's anxieties about the status of poetry in the new market economy and about his own identity as working poet are most clearly articulated in order to illustrate how Wordsworth confronts and "transcends" the challenge the marketplace offers.

Literary Commodities and Wordsworthian Poetic Identity

Most critics agree that the seventh book of *The Prelude*, "Residence in London," both records and provokes a crisis in identity that hinges on Wordsworth's encounter with the blind beggar near the conclusion of the book, but few have specifically considered it as a crisis of poetic identity.[48] As I see it, the content and mood of this book are directly related to the meditation on the lack of progress in writing the work with which Wordsworth begins:

> Five years are vanished since I first poured out,
> Saluted by that animating breeze
> Which met me issuing from the city's walls,
> A glad preamble to this verse. I sang
> Aloud in dithyrambic fervour, deep
> But short-lived uproar . . .
>   . . . But 'twas not long

> Ere the interrupted strain broke forth once more,
> And flowed awhile in strength; then stopped for years—
> Not heard again until a little space
> Before last primrose-time.   (7.1–6, 9–13)

In the years that had "vanished" since the "glad preamble" was composed, Wordsworth had been busy—having expanded *The Prelude* from its two-part form to five books, undertaken work on the longer version plus miscellaneous pieces for *The Recluse*, not to mention having written some of his greatest shorter poems—but he had not yet finished the task he set himself; indeed in 1804, when these lines were written, he had decided to expand further the scope of the preliminary autobiographical poem. Wordsworth's inability to complete this work of apprenticeship coincides with a crisis precipitated by an external threat in the form of London, the geographical site that typified "the increasing accumulation of men in cities" of which Wordsworth had complained in the "Preface" to *Lyrical Ballads*. London embodies not only the new urban industrialism and the exact antithesis of the rural community in which Wordsworth made his home, but also the triumph of the new market economy and the spectacular society. In this book, Wordsworth enters London to find it an unreal city, unreal precisely because, in the words of Stallybrass and White, here "differences proliferate" (p. 123) and so destabilize all the oppositions—between signs and meanings, works and authors, writers and readers—on which Wordsworth's sense of authorship depends.

Lack of confidence and the powerful seductiveness of urban spectacle induce in the speaker a mood of idle "fancy" (7.79) as he begins to catalogue the sights he saw while "a casual dweller and at large, among / The unfenced regions of society" (7.61–62):

> . . . Shall I give way,
> Copying the impression of the memory—
> Though things remembered idly do half seem
> The work of fancy—shall I, as the mood
> Inclines me, here describe for pastime's sake,
> Some portion of that motley imagery,
> A vivid pleasure of my youth, and now,
> Among the lonely places that I love,
> A frequent daydream for my riper mind?   (7.145–53)

Wordsworth here syntactically telegraphs his attitude toward his topic in using the strangely passive, conditional "shall I." "Copying the impression of the memory" is not typical Wordsworthian practice, which usually involves an active modification of what is seen by the power of the viewing eye, which "half creates" what it perceives. Giving himself over to "fancy," the subordinate power as Coleridge defines it in the *Biographia Literaria*, Wordsworth's stance as poet approximates that of the copyist he watches, a mere imitator whose whole aim is to reproduce mechanically "those mimic sights that ape / The absolute presence of reality, / Expressing as in mirror sea and land" (7.248–50). Like the hack artist who paints "some miniature of famous spots and things"

(7.268) for the urban viewer to consume, Wordsworth passively reproduces London, "with his greedy pencil taking in / A whole horizon on all sides" (7.258–59). And in doing so, he undoes the distinction between what he has been doing thus far in composing *The Prelude* and what these "mechanic" urban artists do. Despite the difference between high art and hack work on which Wordsworth insists in principle, then, he finds it difficult to distinguish his practice from the mechanical, commodified art he sees around him.

The rival power of the copyist to represent "all that the traveller sees when he is there" (7.280) threatens Wordsworth's claim to a singular power of vision by reducing the poet to the position of the spectator-consumer. As "files of ballads dangle from dead walls" (7.209), severed from their producers, whose signatures are erased at the moment their products enter circulation, Wordsworth reads the city without writing it, temporarily becoming one of the readers whose "craving for extraordinary incident" and "degrading thirst after outrageous stimulation" (pp. 73, 74) he had deplored in the "Preface" to *Lyrical Ballads*.

When Wordsworth does once again produce writing of his own as opposed to merely describing the work of others, it is, significantly, in order to relate "a story drawn / From [his] own ground (7.321–22), the tale of the Maid of Buttermere: he recontextualizes it and supplies it with its true history, a history which only he and Coleridge should, by poetic rights, have the privilege to tell. The "real" Maid, victim of a bigamist, possesses a "retiredness of mind / Unsoiled by commendation and excess / Of public notice" and "lives in peace / Upon the spot where she was born and reared; / Without contamination" (7.338–40, 351–53); London's Maid, by contrast, is a melodramatic theatrical heroine. Wordsworth tries to reclaim both her and her story, yet in the context of this book, his act only reinscribes her as one of his familiar tropes, one of his many seduced maidens and female vagrants. While Wordsworth's explicit intent is to shield the victimized woman from further "public notice" and "contamination," his memorializing of her, "more sentimental" (p. 161) in Kenneth R. Johnston's opinion that anything one might have seen on the London stage of the day, produces the opposite effect: like his London contemporaries, he fits his living subject to a preconceived model for representation.

That Wordsworth should light on a familiar figure as a subject, a figure from his own neighborhood, is not surprising, since, as Michael H. Friedman has suggested, it is the absence of an "available community in which and by which he may establish or confirm his identity" that sets Wordsworth reeling in the first place.[49]

> . . . all the ballast of familiar life—
> The present, and the past, hope, fear, all stays,
> All laws of acting, thinking, speaking man—
> Went from me, neither knowing me, nor known.   (7.604–607)

The unreal city blinds and silences not just the man, but the poet, and thus it is no accident that Wordsworth's apocalyptic urban moment occurs as he looks at a man who can neither see nor work:

> . . . lost
> Amid the moving pageant, 'twas my chance
> Abruptly to be smitten with the view
> Of a blind beggar, who, with upright face,
> Stood propped against a wall, upon his chest
> Wearing a written paper, to explain
> The story of the man, and who he was.
> My mind did at this spectacle turn round
> As with the might of waters, and it seemed
> To me that in this label was a type
> Or emblem of the utmost that we know
> Both of ourselves and of the universe,
> And on the shape of this unmoving man,
> His fixed face and sightless eyes, I looked,
> As if admonished from another world.   (7.609–23)

In the "spectacle" of the blind beggar, which the poet views through the frame of the typological tradition, Wordsworth is struck by the man's ability to represent himself by himself; the story written on his chest, which presumably solicits the charity of the passerby, locates him in the social order as the inhabitant of a certain physical and economic place. But that those few words represent the man for all who see him is, for Wordsworth, an awful prospect: he has spent six years trying to accomplish what "this label" does for this figure in a few brief lines. By reminding him of the protracted length of his own self-representing project, of his own insecure place in an economy that constantly threatens to transform the visionary poet into a species of blind beggar, this figure paradoxically becomes the means by which Wordsworth regains the power to represent.

After the initial recognition of likeness comes the affirmation of difference, as Wordsworth immediately accedes to the universalizing gesture that subsumes the specific and local identity of the beggar into a transcendental category.[50] In his subsequent description of Bartholomew Fair, Wordsworth rises above "the whole swarm of its inhabitants" (7.699) to his characteristic stance as seer:

> But though the picture weary out the eye,
> By nature an unmanageable sight,
> It is not wholly so to him who looks
> In steadiness, who hath among least things
> An under-sense of greatness, sees the parts
> As parts, but with a feeling of the whole.   (7.708–13)

What Jon P. Klancher has called "discursive colonialism" (p. 25) is clearly at work here, in that the poet who intends to write the universal poem "on Man, on Nature, and on Human Life" must create a position for himself from which he can survey the entire expanse of the human scene.[51] Wordsworth psychically and poetically accomplishes this through the saving power of natural discipline, which is reaffirmed in the next book through a comparison between the "blank confusion" (7.696) of the urban marketplace and the manageable simplicity of rural Grasmere Fair. As this non-institutional power reasserts itself, Wordsworth is able to save his poetic power by rising above the forces which nearly succeed in undoing it completely. In that movement—from implication in the marketplace to a position above and beyond it—lies the crucial constituent of Wordsworth's literary identity.

At Grasmere, Wordsworth finds—or creates—not only a home, but also a mode of social and economic relations that brings him a sense of well-being. Among the farm laborers who carry their own produce to market and exchange it for goods or cash with their fellows, he sees the firm rootedness in place and community that London merchants lack, and presents it as an ideal:

> Man free, man working for himself, with choice
> Of time, and place, and object; by his wants,
> His comforts, native occupations, cares
> Conducted on to individual ends
> Or social, and still followed by a train,
> Unwooed, unthought-of even: simplicity,
> And beauty, and inevitable grace.   (8.152–58)

Within the context of what Raymond Williams has called a "knowable community," producers and consumers participate in transactions that do not diminish their lives in the way that urban economics would; nor does the free independence of the workers occlude the fact of their interdependence, for in the world of Grasmere, the needs of individuals and those of the community are presented as harmoniously integrated.[52] Wordsworth's rural marketplace, unlike the urban, literary one, is a society of equals, its relations unmediated and its values clearly defined. What Klancher has observed of *Lyrical Ballads* is true here as well: Wordsworth substitutes a vision of "a purely symbolic exchange" among rural buyers and readers for the "degraded commodity exchanges" (p. 143) that characterize urban literary culture.

Wordsworth locates value in a mode of production and distribution that depends on the existence of a network of interpersonal relations; that such a mode was, by 1805, almost obsolete suggests that his creation of an autobiographical representation was both a futile, anachronistic gesture and an extraordinarily prescient one, both a last-ditch effort to constitute himself as "a man speaking to men" and an acknowledgment of the pressures to commodify the self-as-poet. As literature itself becomes less a matter of the private circulation of manuscripts among equals and intimates and more an exchange of texts for money between parties with no extratextual knowledge of each other, self-representation becomes the linchpin between the anonymous writer and his writing. The presence of his signature, the narrative unfolding of his history, inscribes this text as belonging to Wordsworth, who becomes "knowable" to his readers and inseparable from this text as a function of that self-representation.[53] Poems and prefaces thus contextualize the identity of their author so as to supply the biographical dimension, that necessary frame of reference, for the reading of the work.

Contextualizing the self within the writing does not automatically ensure that one's work will then be read "correctly," or according to the author's own wishes, for the possibilities of being misread, as Wordsworth knew and experienced and tried to minimize, can never be eliminated. But even misreadings and misappropriations serve some kind of publicizing function, since once the author has been put into discourse, has himself become part of what is disseminated by periodicals and reviews, what constitutes the author is presumed to be knowable, even if contestable. In other words, Wordsworth's self-representing impulse, although rooted in his engagement with an older form of literary production, fits into the new system of mass production and national distribution of literature. Even though he removes himself from the geographical centers of literary life to the Lake District, he achieves a public currency by being written up and discussed, criticized in the pages of the *Edinburgh Review* and crowned from Hazlitt's London podium. With the rise of mass media come manifold new possibilities for establishing what we might call a disembodied public identity, possibilities that may be open to women writers as much as to men.

Wordsworth's relation to these new structures of publicly representing the author is complicated, as I have pointed out, by his own hesitation about disclosing himself to the world's eye; by 1850, however, when *The Prelude* was published posthumously, social and literary conditions had changed such that the poem's autobiographical character startled no one.[54] For however much Keats may have kicked against "the egotistical sublime," Wordsworth's creation of the poetic self underwrote Keats's own conception of authorial identity; however much Arnold lamented the "wintry clime" upon which the dead Laureate had fallen, Wordsworth's vision of what the poet and poetry should be helped to shape Arnold's own. And in *Aurora Leigh* (1856), Elizabeth Barrett Browning accepted, without the critical questioning that characterizes her other uses of his work, Wordsworth's account of how the poetic self comes to be produced outside social systems, signifying that even across gender lines Wordsworth's paradigm could be appropriated. By the publication of *The Prelude*, that is, poets had so completely internalized Wordsworthian autobiographical style and its uses in the marketplace—as in Tennyson's *In Memoriam*, the best-selling poem of that year—that *The Prelude* itself seemed rather passé by comparison. Yet *In Memoriam* could never even have been written, never mind read, without the precedent of *The Prelude* and the poetry associated with it, regardless of the fact that the two poems were published at almost the same moment. For as Clifford Siskin puts it, locating "the culmination of English Romanticism" in the 1830s, "the constructs and strategies of Romantic texts became 'normal' within and for the very culture that had produced them."[55] Tennyson's self-representation was made possible as a poetic gesture because it had the precedent of half a century of Romantic theory and practice of autobiographical representation behind it: what Wordsworth takes fourteen books to accomplish, Tennyson can telegraph in a few short verse paragraphs, because by 1850, readers of poetry know how to read the familiar, conventional signs of poetic self-representation.[56]

At the conclusion of this chapter, I will return briefly to the legacy Wordsworth left to those men and women of letters who followed him, but now I would like to take up the autobiographical work of another writer who shaped the nineteenth-century discourse of literary identity. In the early career of Thomas Carlyle, we find an obsession with representing the self, most often in the guise of others, that is matched in intensity only by the extreme antagonism Carlyle felt for everything that constituted the literary marketplace as it came to be defined in the 1820s and 1830s.

Carlyle and Professional Discipline

Like Wordsworth, Carlyle began on the margins of literary culture and wound up at its center. His original connection to the world of letters was even more tenuous than Wordsworth's, for Carlyle was a Scot, and thus an alien in London, the son of a stonemason, a man with no inheritance other than a lived experience of Presbyterianism, which remained with him all his life, and a zeal for proselytizing. Unlike Wordsworth, he was not given a legacy or educated at Oxbridge, and so in a sense he was "disadvantaged," to use a modern term; some of the bitterness we will see him expressing can be attributed to the facts of his class background. Carlyle's distance from social and economic power, however, gave him the advantage of a critical outsider's perspective on literary and professional matters. Forced by economic necessity to take up his pen as a reviewer—as Wordsworth was not—Carlyle conceived a deep disgust for the hackdom to which he was condemned for more than ten years, but during this period he developed as well an elaborate notion of the nature of "true" authorship: as David Riede describes it, Carlyle "wanted to speak from a pulpit outside of the contentious, partisan journals, wanted to remain unsullied by the review business as a mere trade and to speak from an independent position befitting the high romantic ideal of the author."[57] His *Sartor Resartus* (1833–34) thematizes and ironizes the dichotomous distinction between the man of letters and the man of genius.

As his letters from the 1820s and 1830s illustrate, Carlyle was centrally concerned with the issues that also preoccupied Wordsworth—the idleness/industry polarity, the need to represent literary work as useful labor, the difficulties of establishing oneself in a secure position beyond the marketplace—yet he also had a keen sense of the ironies of his situation, and a keen sense of parody as well. While Wordsworth's central concern is with making his claim to authorship impregnable, Carlyle's self-representations, forged out of the materials of his engagement in the marketplace, question the fictions of authorship itself; *Sartor Resartus* continually re-poses the problem of the author's relation to his text by presenting the reader with multiple ways of thinking about that relationship. In examining the years that made up Carlyle's long "apprenticeship," the years in which cultural, economic, and personal imperatives were shaped into the characteristic Carlylean vision, I will show how the dynamics of his particular position in relation both to professionalism and to literary production make *Sartor Resartus* a central touchstone for understanding the place of the author in Victorian culture.

One of the first "facts" we learn about Diogenes Teufelsdröckh concerns what he does, or more precisely, what he does not do for a living: "though, by title and diploma, *Professor der Allerley-Wissenschaft*, or as we should say in English, 'Professor of Things in General,' he had never delivered any Course."[58] Carlyle directs his mild irony, biographically based on his first two unsuccessful attempts to obtain professorships, as much at himself as at the system; though he wanted and needed a job, he recognized that an academic position would confer upon him only spurious status.[59] "Teufelsdröckh, 'recommended by the highest Names,' " as Carlyle was by Jeffrey and Goethe, "had been promoted thereby to a Name merely" (p. 19): the title of "Professor" might signify cultural power and prestige, but to Carlyle it would have reflected only the power of the connections that he had forged by 1828, and the illusory nature of professional preferment itself. To be "a Name merely" was never Carlyle's goal; he sought to make that name on the basis of authentic visionary power, to be the "Hero as Man of Letters" that was missing from the British literary scene.

Carlyle's desire to make a name for himself was an early dream: as he wrote at age eighteen to an Edinburgh school friend, "since I have [been] able to form a wish—*the wish of being known* has been the foremost," but the adolescent aspiration to fame soon took a more pragmatic shape.[60] As an eldest son, he was educated by his parents with funds they could little afford to spend yet never grudged him; his sense of filial duty, particularly to his mother's religious values, made a clerical career the obvious and acceptable choice, yet it was not a choice Carlyle could square with his conscience. Nor would it have fulfilled his thirst for a wider life than the one he had known, for in starting at the bottom of the ladder, he would have had to climb for many long years to attain the kind of position that would have given him the freedom to pursue other interests. "To be obliged after all to flatter and wheedle [a country squire's] piques and prejudices in order to obtain—a country parsonage" (*CL*, 1:60) was not a fitting conclusion to the narrative he and his mother had already written for him; her Calvinist sense of his predestined vocation, combined with his own more secular longing for worldly advancement, singled him out as born for better things.

Teaching proved an ever worse alternative, not surprisingly, for pedagogues were poorly paid and notoriously ill-treated. Although Carlyle worked as a schoolmaster and then mostly as a private tutor for several years, he thoroughly despised it almost from the beginning. He wrote to Robert Mitchell in 1818, "I continue [to teach] (that I might subsist thereby), with about as much satisfaction as I should beat hemp, if such were my vocation" (*CL*, 1:118–19). Law as well was quickly "renounced" as "a shapeless mass of absurdity and chicane"; "the ten years, which a barrister commonly spends in painful idleness before arriving at employment, is more than my physical or moral frame could endure" (*CL*, 1:231, 231–32).[61] Literature, it seemed, was Carlyle's only alternative, yet he initially shied away from it, for "the road to subsistence in that direction . . . is not very clear" (*CL*, 1:158). Having abandoned more than one profession in the search for congenial labor, Carlyle highlights the ironies of being a man without a vocation in representing himself to others. Resigning himself to await "that distant day, when some profession may present itself, which my inclination and my faculties may concur in inviting me to engage in" (*CL*, 1:164), he invokes the language of the calling even as he parodies the notion that "that distant day" will ever just happen to arrive.

What Carlyle failed to realize until after he had forsworn the steps that would have led to a professional career were all its advantages, the fixed goal and certain course a professional education prescribed, the steadying ballast it might have given an unsteady spirit. While he had dismissed the barrister's apprenticeship as ten years of idleness, he later came to feel that training in a professional discipline would have provided the stability that he lacked throughout the 1820s. Before he unwillingly assented to periodical writing and translation as the only means available for earning a subsistence, he figured his existence as that of the wanderer, unfixed and unhoused, searching only for "something stationary—some 'local habitation and some name' " (*CL*, 1:292); he sought the security of "some permanent employment, so that I may no longer wander about the earth a moping hypochondriac, the soul eating itself up for want of something else to act upon" (*CL*, 1:330).[62] Like Wordsworth, Carlyle associated the idea of a home with everything that he lacked: "The wretch that has no home, no fixed status among men, too light a purse and too keen a soul" (*CL*, 2:43) lacks the primary constitutive marks of male adult identity.

Again like Wordsworth, Carlyle plays out the ramifications of this lack by attempting to impose a self-discipline that would give him a structured work routine, writing in 1826 that without "a more self-regulated existence I must soon sink to utter destruction both of soul and body" (*CL*, 4:40). The imperative to " 'Produce! Produce!' " (p. 197) that sounds throughout *Sartor Resartus* clearly echoes the letters of the 1820s, in which Carlyle frequently castigates himself for his own failure to follow that imperative, as seen here in a representative letter to Anna Montagu of 1825:

> If ever mortal was possessed by the very Genius of Indolence, it must be your unhappy correspondent. . . . Surely there is not in the British Islands such a peasant slave as I. Work, labour, toil according to your strength! is the rigid mandate Nature gives to all men; to me too she speaks with a voice sharp as a two-edged sword; I listen, and tremble, and turn round and then—compose myself again to rest. . . . The currents of my activity are stopt and stagnating; my mind is growing flat and rude and barren as an Irish bog: woe to me if I make no effort to clear it and recover it!   (*CL*, 3:348–49)

Like Wordsworth, Carlyle locates the voice of discipline in Nature, and posits his own internal condition as subject to another external force, the "Genius of Indolence." At the same time, he allies himself with the forces of discipline by making an effort to cast out the bad demon and replace it with a good angel.

As his chosen medium for labor, writing is the means of accomplishing this, and he depicts writing as a form of improvement: "to clear" and "recover" the wasted "bog" of his mind would be to undo the damage of the past. And the discipline of writing extends not only to producing work for the press, but also to the writing of letters. In the correspondence between Carlyle and Jane Welsh—individuals whose lives are unregulated by the industrial or professional clock—each continually exhorts the other to "commence a meditated plan of life and labour" and to "send a thousand thoughts and warmest wishes daily, and long letters every week" (*CL*, 3:199).[63] Any and all writing can thus be constructed as labor of a sort, for if nothing else, composing love letters to Jane documents the time that would otherwise be irrecoverable.

The writing of letters alone, or even of periodical essays, did not further Carlyle's career, and he certainly did not wish the writing life on anyone who had the possibility of taking a more certain road to success. In the letters he wrote to male friends and relations in the 1820s, Carlyle continually encouraged them to persevere in their professions, presenting himself as a negative example of what happens to the man who strays from the avenues of established professional procedure. To Robert Mitchell, who became a teacher, he extols the value of "having a fixed object in life, a kind of chart of the course you are to follow. . . . None but a wandering restless pilgrim, who has travelled long and advanced little, anxious to proceed on his destined journey, but perpetually missing or changing his path—can tell you how fine a thing it is to have a beaten turnpike for your accom[m]odation" (*CL*, 2:78). To his brother John, he expresses his regrets over the time and money he had wasted without achieving any material end: "I cannot help seeing that with half the expence, and one tenth of the labour which I have incurred, I might at this time have been enjoying the comforts of some solid and fixed establishment in one of the regular departments of exertion" (*CL*, 2:145–46).

Carlyle's letters to John, who trained as a doctor but wanted to pursue literature as a career, are particularly explicit on the value of having a profession, framing it as a duty for John to equip himself with a professional character.[64]

> To conquer our inclinations of whatever sort is a lesson which all men have to learn; and the man who learns it soonest will learn it easiest. This Medicine your judgement says is to be useful to you: do you assail it and get the better of it, in spite of all other considerations. It is a noble thing to have a profession by the end: it makes a man independent of all mortals; he is richer than a lord, for no *external* change can destroy the possession which he has acquired for himself. . . . It appears to me that a man who is not born to some independency, if he means to devote himself to literature properly so called, even *ought* to study some profession which as a first preliminary will enable him to live. It is galling and heartbreaking to live on the precarious windfalls of literature: and the idea that one has not time for practicing an honest calling is stark delusion.   (*CL*, 4:4)

In language that recalls Edgeworth's injunction to parents on instilling discipline in their would-be barristers and physicians, Carlyle urges his brother to submit his "inclinations" to the yoke of a useful, "honest calling"; like Scott, he insists that literary pursuits should be subordinated to the necessity of making an honorable living.[65] Echoing the discourse of professionalism, Carlyle claims that a "professional character" makes the individual invulnerable to changing fortunes, "for no *external* change can destroy the possession which he has acquired for himself." As a safeguard against the vagaries of economic life, professional knowledge constitutes an inward store of capital that can be continually drawn on and converted to social currency, thus protecting its possessor from bankruptcy. Figuring the same advice to his still-recalcitrant brother six years later, Carlyle writes that "the voice of all Experience seems to be in favour of a Profession: you sail there, as under convoy, in the middle of a fleet, and have a thousandfold chance of reaching port" (*CL*, 5:128). The literary life, by comparison, is a ceaseless solo journey over uncharted waters, with no destination in sight: "any professional gain is far surer and more easily got" (*CL*, 5:189).

Teufelsdröckh, too, asserts the worth of a profession to the adult male, for it will provide direction, discipline, and purpose, as it supplies the young man's hunger with food, but Teufelsdröckh's perspective suggests an underlying irony in all of Carlyle's claims about the value of a profession. No worldly profession can satisfy Teufelsdröckh's own hunger; he lambastes the logic that assigns each individual his productive social place.

> ". . . . hence have we, with wise foresight, Indentures and Apprenticeships for our irrational young; whereby, in due season, the vague universality of a Man shall find himself ready-moulded into a specific Craftsman; and so thenceforth work, with much or with little waste of Capability as it may be; yet not with the worst waste, that of time. . . . is it not well that there should be what we call Professions, or Bread-studies (*Brodzwëcke*) preappointed us? Here, circling like the gin-horse, for whom partial or total blindness is no evil, the Bread-artist can travel contentedly round and round, still fancying that it is forward and forward; and realise much: for himself victual; for the world an additional horse's power in the grand corn-mill or hemp-mill of Economic Society."   (p. 120)

According to Teufelsdröckh, the worth of a profession is that it gives the "vague" young man something to do, something to work at, so that "the worst waste, that of time" may be avoided even as he attains the means of supporting himself and of contributing to the growth of "Economic Society." But in using the language of "Indentures" and "Apprenticeships," Carlyle compares professional training to the process of becoming an artisan or craftsman, and so directly and sardonically reveals the economic motivation for pursuing "Bread-studies."

By avoiding such terms as "vocation" and "calling" in characterizing the professions, Carlyle also reveals the nature of a social illusion: like a horse wearing blinkers, "the Bread-artist" sees neither to the right nor to the left, unable even to discover that what seems like forward movement is merely the tracing of a circle. To recall Forster's observation, the professional follows the road many have traveled before him, and for Carlyle, this "is no evil" in and of itself. But it is a course neither he nor Teufelsdröckh can emulate: " 'For me too had such a leading-string been provided; only that it proved a neck-halter, and had nigh throttled me, till I broke it off' " (p. 120). As for Wordsworth, the Carlylean genius must shape his own road, for as Carlyle wrote in his first essay on Jean Paul Richter, "Genius has privileges of its own; it selects an orbit for itself"; the professional has the advantage of the historical experience of his predecessors, but "the new man is in a new time, under new conditions; his course can be the *fac-simile* [sic] of no prior one, but is by its nature original" (*Sartor Resartus*, p. 119).[66]

For both Carlyle and Wordsworth, genius is an internal faculty that must be externally realized in the form of work, or in *a* work. As Teufelsdröckh puts it, " 'Not what I Have . . . but what I Do is my Kingdom' " (p. 119). Until that work has been performed, as D'Israeli's text suggests, the presence of genius in an individual cannot be verified, even to himself : " 'A certain inarticulate Self-consciousness dwells dimly in us; which only our Works can render articulate and decisively discernible. Our Works are the mirror wherein the spirit first sees its natural lineaments' " (p. 162).

Thus Carlyle's critics consider his autobiographical text as the work in which he first renders articulate that " 'inarticulate Self-consciousness' "; following Carlisle Moore, Walter L. Reed claims "that it was only in the writing of *Sartor* itself that the sense of affirmation was fully achieved."[67] It seems to me that this is undoubtedly so: it was absolutely necessary for Carlyle to write *Sartor* so as to confirm his identity as an author. But this way of formulating the issue elides the question of why it was so, why producing this particular text in the particular form that it takes creates a "sense of affirmation" rather than a sense of despair, given the history of the text's early unfavorable reception by the publishers who rejected it and the readers who could not understand it. Carlyle's triumph in finishing *Sartor* depended not on public acclamation of the work, but on his own (and his intimates') estimate of its value; the "sense of affirmation" initially represented only a willed private response, not a shared public one.

A statement such as Reed's reflects what Jerome J. McGann has called "an uncritical absorption in Romanticism's own self-representations," self-representations that have come to achieve academic currency over the past century and a half; if we see *Sartor Resartus* as the culmination of Carlyle's "protracted apprenticeship," to use Fred Kaplan's term, it is only because Carlyle and his interpreters have succeeded in dictating the terms under which he and his text are to be read, largely through the aid of words such as "apprenticeship" and "vocation."[68] But the underrepresented or suppressed term in most analysis of *Sartor Resartus* is, I will be arguing, as intrinsically necessary to understanding Carlyle's text in its social and literary contexts as the heretofore primary term; thus my discussion will center less on Carlylean genius than on its complementary category, the Carlylean hack, and on the interrelation of the two in *Sartor Resartus*.

Because Carlyle sometimes plays one part, sometimes the other, and sometimes both simultaneously, the relationship between these two poles is seldom stable. Many readers believe that by the conclusion of *Sartor*, Carlyle sees himself more as Teufelsdröckh than as the editor by virtue of having produced that mark of genius, an "original" work; I argue instead that the text itself continually readdresses the issue of the connection between the producer and the text produced, usually via the trope of the paper bags filled with those fragmentary "Biographical Documents." To claim, as G. B. Tennyson does, that "Carlyle's own literary experience dictated the materials and the form of *Sartor*" is an important first principle to establish, but the implications of that experience for the writing of *Sartor* have not been fully explored, even by Tennyson himself.[69] Carlyle's engagement in literary production during the 1820s and 1830s should be read not only as background to *Sartor*, but also in dialogue with it; the two are mutually determining.

Teufelsdröckh and the Editor: the Genius and the Hack

Sartor begins, appropriately enough, by anticipating its own reception in reciting the conditions of its publication:

> The first thought naturally was to publish Article after Article on this remarkable Volume, in such widely-circulating Critical Journals as the Editor might stand connected with, or by money or love procure access to. But, on the other hand, was it not clear that such matter as must here be revealed, and treated of, might endanger the circulation of any Journal extant? If, indeed, all party-divisions in the State, could have been abolished, Whig, Tory, and Radical, embracing in discrepant union; and all the Journals of the Nation could have been jumbled into one Journal, and the Philosophy of Clothes poured forth in incessant torrents therefrom, the attempt had seemed possible. But, alas, what vehicle of that sort have we, except *Fraser's Magazine*?   (pp. 10–11)

The editor's quandary over where to publish is also a quandary over whether or not to publish at all: the existence of multiple reading audiences, each aligned with a different political constituency, makes *Fraser's*, the periodical in which *Sartor* was actually published, the best (albeit an imperfect) medium for reaching the largest possible readership. The radicalism of the Clothes Philosophy debars it from the pages of the most "widely-circulating" middle-class journals—the *Edinburgh*, the *Westminster*, the *Quarterly*, and *Blackwood's*—for various reasons, or so the editor implies; partisan readers are thus warned that they may be offended, even outraged, by what will follow. In the editor's best of all possible worlds for readers and writers, in which "party-divisions" would not exist, Teufelsdröckh's work could flow "forth in incessant torrents," undivided and undivisive; instead it must be submitted to the fragmentation of the periodical press, where ideological differences hold sway and where the Clothes Philosophy must literally be divided into irregular monthly parts. *Sartor Resartus* thus reproduces, at the level of form, the culturally and economically determined structures that make writing and publishing in early Victorian society operations that take place between and across divisions and distances; in its internal fragmentation, its alternation between one voice and another, and its refusal of genre and linear narrative, it negotiates the contradictions of periodical publication and the literary marketplace.

Without the existence of a periodical trade, of course, *Sartor Resartus* "might never have appeared in Carlyle's lifetime," as Walter E. Houghton notes. "After James Fraser's demand for prepayment of 150 pounds was indignantly rejected and the manuscript was refused by Longmans, by Colburn and Bentley, and by John Murray . . . Fraser finally agreed to print it in his Magazine."[70] As Carlyle's only means of circulating *Sartor*, *Fraser's* was a boon, but more periodical publishing was precisely what he wanted to avoid, particularly for the first work that was to be wholly his own, rather than a review essay, a translation like *Wilhelm Meister's Apprenticeship* (1825), or a compilation of translated extracts from the works of others, like *German Romance* (1827). Carlyle associated miscellaneous piecework and periodical publication with hackdom, and hackdom with effeminacy:

> Good Heavens! I often inwardly exclaim, and is *this* the Literary World? This rascal rout, this dirty rabble, destitute not only of high feeling or knowledge or intellect, but even of common honesty? The very best of them are ill-natured weaklings: they are not red-blooded *men* at all; they are only *things* for writing "articles." (*CL*, 3:234)

His disgust at those *"things"* who write articles simultaneously establishes his distance from the ordinary ranks of literary men and masks his fear at the possibility of becoming one of them. The problem for Carlyle throughout the 1820s is how to do the hack work he must do in order to earn money and still remain a "red-blooded *man*" without becoming a hack in his own mind, to himself: "A miserable scrub of an author sharking and writing 'articles' about Town, like Hazzlitt, Dequincey [sic] and that class of living creatures, is a thing which as our [Fa]ther says, I *canna* be" (*CL*, 3:161).

For Carlyle, the only honorable literary work was the truly original work of genius, like the first part of *Faust*. While literary historians have bestowed a similar distinction on *Sartor Resartus*, its claim to originality, if we examine it critically, really rests in how Carlyle combines his materials into a new form rather than in the materials themselves, for all the elements of his prior literary work—editing, translating, compiling—are present in *Sartor*, parodically represented as the skills that make up the man of letters. Moreover, as Tennyson has shown, the things that seem most strange and original about the text to a modern reader—particularly its use of narrative personae—were utterly conventional for early Victorian periodicals such as *Fraser's* and its ancestor, *Blackwood's*. "That *Sartor* was begun as an article for *Fraser's*" is "not surprising" (p. 141), as Tennyson notes, but is is undeniably suggestive. That "a work of genius" should begin as "taskwork," "a string of magazine articles" (*CL*, 5:171) written for a periodical, points out the tenuousness of the distinction between genius and man of letters on which so much of nineteenth-century literary production depends, including Carlyle's own.[71] His exploitation of the conventions of *Fraser's*, however, enables him to make use of his whole range of literary experiences while also challenging the structuring principles of the literary economy. By using two personae and playing both parts, he establishes a place to speak from, the pulpit he had been looking for, yet he creates that place as one by which his own literary identity cannot be fully determined: whether Thomas Carlyle is author or hack, genius or man of letters, remains indeterminate within the context of the periodical text.

Like other magazines of its kind, *Fraser's* maintained a nominal policy of anonymity. This policy gave its contributors the freedom to speak out, sometimes in nearly libelous satires, as well as the liberty to transgress the boundaries of authorial identity itself by blurring the line between fictional narrator and actual writer: the fictive Oliver Yorke, elected Editor of Regina in a two-part feature that sent up nearly every working writer of the day, was licensed to speak in ways that William Maginn, who never signed his real name to an article and was not even officially known to be *Fraser's* editor, was not. In patterning his style after this mode, Carlyle gained the opportunity "to speak fearlessly" (*CL*, 5:216) about his most deeply held beliefs; as George Levine notes, he "used fictional characters for the expression of his most radical ideas in order to protect himself from the public disapproval he expected."[72] Yet he also valued the cloak of secrecy that the corporate periodical text provided for another reason: it soothed his qualms about circulating a too-public, too-commodified self. Publication, he claims in a letter to his brother, includes "some degree of prostitution" (*CL*, 5:237) unacceptable to the man who would be an author; in selling his wares in the marketplace, Carlyle felt he was also selling himself. This ambiguity in Carlyle's attitude toward publicity remains to be explored in terms of the text of *Sartor* itself, the text in which Carlyle endeavors at last, as he put it in a letter to his brother John, "to be my own Editor" (*CL*, 5:144).

The fictive account of the genesis of *Sartor Resartus* draws directly on its author's own experience. Just as Carlyle had written the life of Schiller and translated numerous German texts, the editor is charged with bringing the life and work of Diogenes Teufelsdröckh to an English audience. His initial assumption is a commonplace of his time, that the work cannot be known without knowing something of the writer as well: "To state the Philosophy of Clothes without the Philosopher, the ideas of Teufelsdröckh without something of his personality, was it not to insure both of entire misapprehension?" (p. 11).[73] The question of the relation between author and work also animates Teufelsdröckh. As he writes in one of his fragments, " 'it was my favourite employment to read character in speculation, and from the Writing to construe the Writer' " (p. 113). Since, in Romantic terms, the character of the writer determines the character of the work, the two are mutually illuminating; within this scenario, everything is autobiographical.

The editor thus comes to conceptualize his task as piecing together the puzzle that makes up the man and the work. And in this the editor takes his cue from Teufelsdröckh, who claims that " 'till the Author's View of the World (*Weltansicht*) and how he actively and passively came by such view are clear: in short till a Biography of him has been philosophico-poetically written, and philosophico-poetically read' " (p. 75), no right estimate of either his philosophy or his personality can be determined. Carlyle had first formulated this view for himself and his readers in his essay on Jean-Paul Friedrich Richter of 1830:

> It is Biography that first gives us both Poet and Poem, by the significance of the one elucidating and completing that of the other. That initial outline of himself, which a man unconsciously shadows forth in his writings, and which, rightly deciphered, will be truer than any other representation of him, it is the task of the Biographer to fill-up into an actual coherent figure, and bring home to our experience, or at least our clear undoubting admiration, thereby to instruct and edify us in many ways.[74]

Carlyle might easily be describing the assignment of the editor in *Sartor Resartus*, for this is precisely the editor's original attitude, yet the statement also says something more: it foreshadows Carlyle's method of composing a pseudobiography which contextualizes the biographer by making him a character in his own work.

Teufelsdröckh's biographer attempts to catch the "initial outline" of his subject and decipher it for his readers; in doing so, he also "unconsciously shadows forth in his writings" a representation of himself, a representation that Carlyle consciously creates. So, too, Carlyle, as Schiller's biographer—or as Goethe's, Frederick the Great's, or John Sterling's—also inevitably represents himself in the process of representing someone else, whether that biographical subject be real or wholly fictive. The editor thus reenacts an aspect of Carlyle's relationship to his literary materials by searching for the key that will unlock the mysteries of the biographical subject as well as by representing himself in the process of doing so. Yet Carlyle's own skeptical, defensive posture toward biographical and autobiographical reading and writing undercuts the viability of such a search and of the self-representations it spawns.

Within the fiction of *Sartor Resartus*, however, this skepticism is only reached experientially, as the editor struggles to remain true to his convictions about what his role should be. As a man of letters, he bears the responsibility for creating Teufelsdröckh's biography, and thus for creating the conditions under which it can be read. The irregularities of genius, however, frustrate him in this task:

> Considered as an Author, Herr Teufelsdröckh has one scarcely pardonable fault, doubtless his worst: an almost total want of arrangement. In this remarkable Volume, it is true, his adherence to the mere course of Time produces, through the Narrative portions, a certain show of outward method; but of true logical method and sequence there is too little. . . . each Part overlaps, and indents, and indeed runs quite through the other. Many sections are of a debatable rubric, or even quite nondescript and unnameable; whereby the Book not only loses in accessibility, but too often distresses us. . . . To bring what order we can out of this Chaos shall be part of our endeavor. (p. 34)

Genius obeys only its own laws, not the rules of polite discourse, and thus the man of letters is a necessary mediator of the inspired text: he creates order out of chaos, brings method, logic, and sequence where once there was a sublime but unreadable disarray. The editor's labors, not quite heroic in their own right, are very necessary ones, justifiable in that they bring a measure of reason to what would otherwise seem inaccessible to reason, the outpourings of genius.

Carlyle's irony here, of course, is that the editor's work, *Sartor Resartus* itself, can hardly be considered the model of "true logical method and sequence" the editor represents it as being; the occasional indistinguishability of his prose from Teufelsdröckh's own, as well as his unfortunate "want of arrangement," further confuses the line that ostensibly separates the two writers. As the narrative moves on, in fact, this line becomes less and less rigid, as the editor makes larger claims for his own skills. The work of the hack, if undertaken in the right spirit and with an eye toward the diffusion of knowledge, is no contemptible occupation, although not truly as seminal and productive as the author's. In the editor's words, "What work nobler than transplanting foreign Thought into the barren domestic soil; except indeed planting Thought of your own, which the fewest are privileged to do?" (p. 80). In context, the editor's self-effacement, at this point, is not quite as complete as at the outset, when he posited his own identity as irrelevant to the text he transmits: "Who or what such Editor may be, must remain conjectural, and even insignificant: it is a voice publishing tidings of the philosophy of Clothes; undoubtedly a Spirit addressing Spirits" (p. 13). As handmaiden to a power greater than himself, the editor achieves a certain reflected glory from working on his subject, and he also emerges as a personality. At first just a voice, like any anonymous reviewer or translator, he becomes, like almost every other writer for *Blackwood's* and *Fraser's*, a fictive figure in his own right, subject to the same independent analysis as one would accord Christopher North, the Ettrick Shepherd, or Oliver Yorke.

Thus the distance between the producer of original thought and the disseminator of its translation decreases as the editor comes to question more and more the validity of his first assumption. From an initial impatience that the "Biographical Documents were come" (p. 52) to supplement his own efforts, he becomes increasingly impatient with the documents themselves, and simultaneously elevates his value as their interpreter: "Biography or Autobiography of Teufelsdröckh there is, clearly enough, none to be gleaned here: at most some sketchy, shadowy fugitive likeness of him may, by unheard-of efforts, partly of intellect, partly of imagination, on the side of Editor and of Reader, rise up between them" (p. 79). While the project of writing a biography has not been abandoned, its focus has changed. The text to be produced is one that exists only through the "unheard-of efforts" of reader and editor; their "imagination" and "intellect" must create and inform it.

Once the idea of composing a complete, true, factual biography has been discredited, the editor surrenders any notion of arriving at a fixed point of reference between life and work, man and text:

> Here, indeed, at length, must the Editor give utterance to a painful suspicion, which, through late Chapters, has begun to haunt him. . . . It is a suspicion grounded perhaps on trifles, yet confirmed almost into certainty by the more and more discernible humouristico-satirical tendency of Teufelsdröckh, in whom under-ground humours, and intricate sardonic rogueries, wheel within wheel,

defy all reckoning: a suspicion, in one word, that these Autobiographical Documents are partly a mystification! What if many a so-called Fact were little better than a Fiction; if here we had no direct Camera-obscura Picture of the Professor's History; but only some more or less fantastic Adumbration, symbolically, perhaps significantly enough, shadowing-forth the same!   (p. 202)

Through the process of writing Teufelsdröckh's biography, the editor comes to realize the futility of such an endeavor or, at least, its futility in the terms he had initially defined for such a project. If the "Autobiographical Documents" are "a mystification," not to be trusted as fact but rather treated as fiction, then his own work, too, can only be a fiction, a "shadowing forth" of something already shadowed forth by Teufelsdröckh himself.

The logical outcome of this radical epistemological doubt finds expression in one of Teufelsdröckh's famous maxims " 'Hence, too, the folly of that impossible Precept, *Know thyself*; till it be translated into this partially possible one, *Know what thou canst work at*' " (pp. 162–63). The force of this carefully delimited statement has its resonance for the editor as well, for it ultimately renders irrelevant the difference between the man of genius and the man of letters. Insofar as all the editor or Carlyle himself can do is to work at writing, without knowing whether anyone will read it or even if what is produced will be worth reading, his only option is to write, or else to "stand idle and despair" (p. 156). How one's work will be received by unknowable readers, how one will appear to a world that consumes the periodical as it would any other commodity, is a matter over which even the ever-vigilant Carlyle can have but little control, for speak and write he must in order to live.

His hero, however, achieves an altogether more Romantic destiny. What Teufelsdröckh can work at is established in the tenth chapter of Book Two, which the editor glosses as an account of the genius's "Conversion. . . . Teufelsdröckh accepts Authorship as his divine calling" (p. 198). Teufelsdröckh describes his "vocation" in a voice that approximates Carlyle's own:

"By this Art, which whoso will may sacrilegiously degrade into a handicraft . . . have I thenceforth abidden. Writings of mine, not indeed known as mine (for what am I?), have fallen, perhaps not altogether void, into the mighty seed-field of Opinion; fruits of my unseen sowing gratifyingly meet me here and there. I thank the Heavens that I have now found my Calling; wherein, with or without perceptible result, I am minded diligently to persevere."   (pp. 199–200)

Whether or not anyone else hears the voice that summons Teufelsdröckh to authorship matters little to him; indeed, his whole description of what comprises his art, labor, and identity is so full of qualifiers as to render the rhetoric of divine vocation almost wholly ironic. Yet Teufelsdröckh, and through him Carlyle, still wishes to distinguish the seminal, productive work of the artist, which he considers sacred, from the "handicraft" of other writers: the difference within determines the worth of the work produced.

The editor summarizes the position to which Teufelsdröckh is brought: "He has discovered that the Ideal Workshop he so panted for is even this same

Actual ill-furnished Workshop he has so long been stumbling in" (p. 199). Even the man of genius must work out his destiny in the here and now, in this imperfect world, but Teufelsdröckh, like Wordsworth, can afford the luxury of silence. While Teufelsdröckh happily fades out of existence altogether, into an impenetrable solitude and an ultimate disappearance at the end of the text, the editor, like Carlyle, must continue to work on in that "Actual ill-furnished Workshop"; there is no place outside the market or beyond the periodical trade for the writer who would be a public, working man, for "no man works save under conditions" ("Hero as Poet," p. 110).[75] If this attitude toward literary work does partially represent Carlyle's own position during the composition of *Sartor* and afterwards, as I believe it does, then it amounts to an acceptance on his part of what he could not escape, an acceptance of the conditions of literary production that would, unforeseen by him, eventually make him one of the most celebrated men in England.

Teufelsdröckh's silence was precisely what Carlyle knew he could not afford, and the periodical press, as he wrote to John Stuart Mill in October 1832 after the completion of *Sartor Resartus* but before it appeared in print, was the only medium through which he could make his voice heard:

> I had hoped that by and by I might get out of Periodicals altogether, and write Books: but the light I got in London last winter showed me that *this* was as good as over. My Editors of Periodicals are my Booksellers, who (under certain new and singular conditions) purchase and publish my *Books* for me; a monstrous method, yet still a method. . . . Often I think, it were delightful could I have leave to sit wholly silent for some three years from this date, till I had got to the bottom of many things! But that too was not appointed.   (*CL*, 6:241)

With " 'Journalists . . . the true Kings and Clergy' " (*Sartor Resartus*, p. 45) and authors in the old sense nowhere to be found, Carlyle refused to sit idle and silent.

In his second and most popular series of lectures, "On Heroes and Hero-Worship" (1840), Carlyle located the age of honorable writing and publishing in the distant past:

> Never, till about a hundred years ago, was there seen any figure of a Great Soul . . . endeavouring to speak-forth the inspiration that was in him by Printed Books, and find place and subsistence by what the world would please to give him for doing that. Much had been sold and bought, and left to make its own bargain in the marketplace; but the inspired wisdom of a Heroic Soul never till then, in that naked manner.   (p. 154)

His own experience had brought him to assent to sell, buy, and bargain, although not without regret and not without a struggle. Carlyle stands as the first of the Victorians who made names for themselves by doing the same, and who were transformed in the crucible of the marketplace: Carlyle's heroic author is reborn as the literary professional.

Wordsworth's and Carlyle's fictions of authorial identity and development represent alternative paradigms for the men of letters who were to follow them.

Wordsworth's desire to place himself and his work at a distance from the necessities of the literary marketplace, even as he claims the centrality of the literary man to English culture, inaugurates an important mode for nineteenth-century self-representation. We could trace it in Victorian writers as diverse as Arnold, Gosse, and Butler, all of whom privileged the aesthetic as the finer realm of human existence and who helped to shape the bent toward interiority that dominates nineteenth-century literature. While Wordsworthian withdrawal from the social is as much mythos as reality, as I have tried to suggest, and is subject to criticism as well as imitation by his later readers and revisers, his persona and his practice provided a model to which other writers, novelists as well as poets, returned again and again.

Carlyle, on the other hand, achieved equal if not greater status as diagnostician of the ills of his culture without retreating from a public stance: unlike Wordsworthian "wise passiveness," Carlylean activism always promotes an engaged position for the author in culture, and a strenuous readiness to turn the hand to whatsoever it findeth to do. But Carlyle's willingness to specify autobiographically, though in disguise, the grounds of his engagement finds few imitators among high-culture authors: Trollope's far more prosaic account of his practice, for example, was rejected by his contemporaries as vulgar precisely because it too readily demystified the author's position, leaving out the heroic element that had generated the Carlylean dialectic between genius and hack. While I hesitate to claim, then, that either Wordsworth or Carlyle initiated a definite "tradition" of autobiographical writing for subsequent male autobiographers, I do want to suggest that the terms of their self-representations reappear in different guises as part of the Victorian discourse on authorial identity.

They reappear as well, in different ways, in the texts by women writers to which I will turn in the next two chapters, for despite some feminist claims to the contrary, a few women writers sought to appropriate masculine fictions to explore and express their own literary subjectivities. Elizabeth Barrett Browning, for example, seems not to find Wordsworth's account of the development of poetic subjectivity so gender-specific as to debar her from employing it; nor does Harriet Martineau hesitate either to represent herself as a public figure or to demystify Romantic genius. More significantly for my purposes, however, the splitting of authorship into primary and secondary functions, as practiced by the Romantics and ironized by Carlyle, also shapes women's understanding of literary identity in ways that prove painful to some, as in the case of Mary Howitt and Margaret Oliphant, who internalized the distinctions that relegated their work as writers to the second rank. But just as male writers faced the market and devised strategies of self-representation to negotiate it, women writers also produced a variety of discursive responses and positions that involved and enabled their visions of writing and of gender. From within a field of very different imperatives for women writers, I will now look at those texts which, taken as a group, collectively undertake the task of articulating female authorship.

2

"My Authorship Self":
Public and Private in
Women Writers' Autobiographies*

ONE OF THE critical distinctions between the professional man and the writer, as traced in Chapter 1, lies in the way each demonstrates his expertise. The physician or the barrister has no product other than himself to sell, making him "unproductive" by Adam Smith's standards, but endowing him with a social and economic position comfortably above the ungentlemanly merchant classes. The artist, by contrast, appears to generate his poetic authority entirely from within, but his "genius" can only be realized and confirmed in the material product he makes. It is the stigma of being a mere tradesman, whose "files of ballads dangle from dead walls," that the nineteenth-century literary man with aspirations to high status seeks to avoid: the artist combats the separation of product from producer that occurs in the capitalist literary marketplace by insisting on the identity between who he is and what he does, in Wordsworth's case, or, in Carlyle's, by self-consciously assessing the relation between the self and its work, and ultimately reaffirming their interdependence. Thus Romantic literary subjectivity has as one of its internal necessities an autobiographical impulse everywhere expressed as constitutive of writing itself: in effect, the artist must keep announcing his own centrality to the written text, his position as writing subject, by textualizing himself as the subject of all he writes.

For the nineteenth-century literary man, becoming an author depends in part on being able to express and maintain a continuity between producer and product; it is alienation from his own labor, his own text, that these authors fear. But can the same be said of women writers, for whom we might imagine the literary marketplace to be differently problematic? As Gilbert and Gubar were the first to argue, women writers from Fanny Burney to Mary Shelley to George Eliot all express a pervasive anxiety about authorship. In their recourse to anonymous or pseudonymous publication, many writing women put their own work at a distance from themselves, from their private lives and private identities.[1] Yet at the same time, as in the spiritual autobiographies I will ex-

---

*The quotation is from a letter of 1816 from Maria Edgeworth to her friend Mrs. Ruxton, quoted in Marilyn Butler, *Maria Edgeworth* (Oxford: Oxford University Press, 1972), p. 278.

amine later, women writers can create that necessary connection between life and work, writer and text, if they configure their authorship as congruent with the norms of domestic femininity. I would like provisionally to claim that middle-class women do have a different relation to the issues I have examined vis-à-vis *The Prelude* and *Sartor Resartus,* and to argue that differing norms of publicity and privacy for the sexes is what makes that difference, however, I also want to suggest that women's self-representational strategies may differ from those of the male authors I have already analyzed in the means they use, but perhaps not in the end they have in view. Women writers also fear the alienation of the marketplace and seek to circumvent it, but the cultural prohibition against public female labor makes for an additional stumbling block in their path.

In a letter of 1856, Elizabeth Barrett Browning outlines the implications of representing private experience for public consumption. Her correspondent is Mary Howitt, a writer who fed the popular taste for information on the private lives of literary people and one of the autobiographers considered in Chapter 3, whom Barrett Browning gently reprimands for seeking to exploit their epistolary friendship:

> It will be best to tell you at once frankly, that my husband & myself have the . . . peculiarity of objecting *extremely* & *earnestly* to being offered up to the public during our lives, in any possible form of the fashionable diet, . . . "memoirs," "ana," or "personal sketches" . . . in fact we have made up our minds long ago never to provide a hint of information of this kind. . . . I will ask you & yours to prove your cordiality of feeling to me . . . by leaving me & mine in the personal obscurity we covet. Dear Mrs Howitt, because our books belong to the public . . . do our persons? do our lives? I have a right to my life, I think, till I am dead. Afterwards, if people dont forget us, they lay us on the anatomizing table, & we dont shrink . . . usually. Though *I,* even in that position, mean in the spirit, to rap loudly, protesting.[2]

Barrett Browning refuses to be served up as a choice dish for "the fashionable diet" on the grounds that publicly representing her private life without fictionalizing would be equivalent to selling herself and her family; readerly curiosity about the lives of the famous, which feeds on and is fed by the literary establishment, would bring what should remain private into the sensationalizing glare of publicity. Moreover, she objects not only on her behalf, but on Robert Browning's as well, suggesting perhaps that the gender of the author to be "consumed" is not a relevant factor in this instance.[3] Yet her attention is focused less on herself than on the interests of "me and mine," the domestic circle of which she is part and which she wants to protect; she speaks not only or even primarily as author, but also as wife and mother, as the representative of feminine concerns. Distinguishing between "our books," the commodity she and her husband produce, and their private "persons" and "lives," which they neither sell in the marketplace nor sanction others to sell, Barrett Browning defends the privacy of the domestic sphere in order to maintain its integrity as a realm in which the public has no business.

In that division between "our books"—proper inhabitants of the public sphere—and "our persons," "our lives," Barrett Browning differentiates her way of representing herself from Wordsworth's use of the private self as a necessary component in shaping a public authorial persona. While both Wordsworth and Carlyle are at some pains to identify the sources of the publicly represented self in private experience, Barrett Browning wants to insist on a radical division between the two. In her own autobiographical poem, *Aurora Leigh* (1856), she adopted only the form of first-person narrative; the assumptions of contemporary reviewers notwithstanding, Barrett Browning did not wholly identify herself with her heroine or freight Aurora with much autobiographical baggage. Her aversion to publicity made her acutely sensitive to the implications of using a narrating "I," and when given the option of "going public" with her own story, or her family's, she firmly rejected the opportunity.

The language of Barrett Browning's defense here reveals more than a passing dread of publicity. Her anxiety about being represented is strangely visceral, expressed in metaphors of consumption ("diet") and dissection ("anatomizing table"), as if the passage to the public realm from the private one implied a threat to bodily integrity; she resists putting any part of her private "person," or the persons of those she loves, into public circulation. Barrett Browning draws about herself and her family what Fanny Burney called "a mantle of impenetrable obscurity" even as she simultaneously engages in the public process of being a writer, whose name (if not her body) circulates at large within public discourse merely by virtue of publication.[4] And here we see a motif that continually emerges in many literary women's autobiographies, an anxiety about literature and literary production itself, about how texts function in the world and how their circulation affects their producers.

While I do not want to suggest that this anxiety about publication is felt only by women or only about femininity—for Barrett Browning's alarm includes a perceived threat to her entire family—I believe that there is a specifically feminine anxiety expressed here about public authorship, and that it is linked to the cultural division of masculine and feminine spheres. For the bodily terror about publicizing the self that Barrett Browning's letter registers indicates a gendered discomfort with public exposure that professional literary men, always already members of a legitimate public body that has its "home" in the public world, do not explicitly represent even if they may experience it. And that Barrett Browning feels the threat of the public to be directed not only at her, but also at her husband and son, suggests a problematic relationship between her status as writer and her position as domestic woman, as wife and mother.

The anxiety among women writers about going public is linked to women's cultural positioning on the inside, at the center of the domestic circle, which is itself circumscribed by the larger circle of the public world. Because nineteenth-century middle-class women derive their primary social and cultural self-definitions from their identification with the private realm, for writers to maintain their placement in that realm even as they symbolically move outside it through writing requires, above all, tact: knowing themselves to be divided between the privacy of the domestic and the publicity of the market, they may yet minimize the effects of their rupture with conventional femininity by not calling attention to it. From this perspective, Barrett Browning might abhor publicity because it necessarily exposes that she has already consented to divide her identity by working and thus breaching the unwritten rule that prohibits middle-class women from being workers. The metaphorical disintegration that she fears may itself mimic the division she already experiences by being both a Victorian woman and a woman writer.[5]

As Mary Poovey argues in her discussions of *David Copperfield* and *Jane Eyre*, middle-class women who work challenge the stability of the domestic ideal by exposing the gendered separation of spheres to be a social construct, not a natural fact; the binding of women to domesticity rationalizes their exclusion from the public sphere and paid work by constructing the private sphere as "an arena where [women's] work is performed as selflessly and effortlessly as love is given," "as immune to the alienation of work."[6] For while the middle-class man makes himself through his work in the public sphere, he also depends on the material and emotional support of the private realm for sustenance; although the private home might be "woman's sphere," men also experience it as the domain of personal life in which one's "true self" is shaped in childhood and nurtured in adulthood.[7] Thus the stability of both public and private spheres depends on domesticity for women: the rigid ideological divisions between masculine and feminine realms in Victorian culture underwrite oppositions that depend in part on separating women from public life, and especially economic activity.

Gendered ideological discourse thus threatens to make of women writers precisely what no middle-class women are supposed to be—divided subjects whose participation in public work undermines the integrity of the private sphere. Yet women did write, and in that practice, that experience, they undid the ideological division of spheres in their own persons. My task here is to represent how my subjects represent themselves in the face of this ideology: on what basis do writing women establish themselves when their doubled position—as workers, as middle-class women—makes constituting their subjectivities threatening and threatened acts?

This chapter has three different locales: first, the emerging discourse of professionalism among mid-Victorian literary men; second, Barrett Browning's *Aurora Leigh*, that bold fictional effort to represent a writing woman which appropriates Romantic discourse yet is also constrained by it; and third, a set of autobiographies by spiritual women writers that mark a kind of collective feminine counterpoint to professional discourse. Men of letters sought to establish literature's public function as the justification for according their work professional status, and excluded women from the discourse of literary professionalism by making women's private standing one of the conditions for men's public labor. As if in response, religious women paradoxically justify their entry into public discourse by representing their work as private and domestic, thus rhetorically maintaining an identification with the private sphere that preserves them from the alienations—economic and gendered—of the marketplace.

In this way, they avoid the problem of writerly alienation traced in Chapter 1 by refusing to conceptualize their own work as part of the public sphere.

While the rhetoric of male professionalism attempts to cast literary work as exclusively masculine, *Aurora Leigh* and these autobiographies stake out the place of women as writers, but not without raising problematic issues about the relation of public to private, the domestic to the world outside it. Thus what I am tracing here above all are discursive strategies among middle-class women's texts for representing literary work and literary workers; how each of the writers I consider experiences and articulates the relationship between writing and gender in constructing an "authorship self" will be the central concern in this chapter as in the one that follows.

Professional Men and Amateur Women

In the 1840s and 1850s, men writers began making self-conscious claims to professional status.[8] Considering the condition of authors in England and on the continent, George Henry Lewes opens an 1847 essay in *Fraser's* by asserting that "literature has become a profession. . . . Bad or good, there is no evading the 'great fact,' now that it is so firmly established."[9] Lewes allows that this new state of affairs might be "bad" instead of "good," first, because he thinks it possible, à la Coleridge, that literature might be corrupted by profit-seekers, and second, because he fears that unsuitable people might attempt to enlist in the ranks of the literary army:

> If we reflect upon the great aims of literature, we shall easily perceive how important it is that the lay teachers of the people should be men of an unmistakeable vocation. Literature should be a profession, not a trade. It should be a profession, just lucrative enough to furnish a decent subsistence to its members, but in no way lucrative enough to tempt speculators. As soon as its rewards are high enough and secure enough to tempt men to enter the lists for the sake of the reward, and parents think of it as an opening for their sons, from that moment it becomes vitiated. Then will the ranks, already so numerous, be swelled by an innumerable host of hungry pretenders. It will be—and, indeed, is, now fast approaching that state—like the army of Xerxes, swelled and encumbered by women, children, and ill-trained troops. It should be a Macedonian phalanx, chosen, compact, and irresistible.   (p. 285)

In representing the literary profession, Lewes draws on two concepts: Coleridge's clerisy, the disinterested "lay teachers of the people" who have a "vocation" for their great public-spirited work, and the professional rhetoric of the military as a cadre of well-trained, well-disciplined soldiers—"chosen, compact, and irresistible"—who protect the literary commonwealth from enemies within and without. Through analogy, he establishes literary men as a public body that supports, and should be supported by, the state.

When Lewes opposes "profession" to "trade," he invokes the specter of the marketplace, which always shadows the professional ideal and threatens to expose its mystifications, particularly in the case of literature. Art should not provide a field for "speculation," that most dangerous practice of trading on what one does not actually possess; it should rather inhabit a sphere in which, as Wordsworth would have it, values remain stable because they transcend the competitive exchange that characterizes all other market activities. But Lewes's language is also gender-specific: only men can have this "unmistakeable vocation," whereas women are explicitly grouped with the "speculators," the "hungry pretenders," and the "ill-trained troops."

In an essay published three years later, Lewes restates the case even more baldly, and directs his complaint against "the group of female authors [that becomes] every year more multitudinous and more successful. . . . they are ruining our profession. Wherever we carry our skilful [sic] pens, we find the place preoccupied by a woman"; like a guerilla army, "the women have made an invasion of our legitimate domain."[10] In this context, Robert Southey's famous rejoinder to Charlotte Brontë's query as to whether or not she should pursue a literary career—"Literature cannot be the business of a woman's life, and it ought not to be"—expresses an explicitly male and thoroughly professional attitude. Women are not only debarred from the practice of high literature, but also warned not to make a male vocation the *business* of their lives.[11]

Since making literature a profession depends on severing its connection to trade, and since the literary trade at mid-century is carried on in equal if not greater part by women, the professionalization of literary men seems to be contingent upon keeping women entirely out of the business. As Julia Swindells observes, "The nineteenth-century history of the professions is largely about safeguarding careers for gentlemen, and defining and redefining . . . structures of work in relation to male power" (p. 24); the literary profession, in the process of constituting itself as such, is no less devoted to the same proposition. Despite Lewes's dire words, women continued to work in literature, of course, and developed particular strategies for legitimating their authorship, some of which will be considered later. Yet the work women did was rarely accorded the cultural status of men's literary production, except in the case of an "exceptional woman," such as George Eliot, who transcended the norm.[12] Moreover, middle-class women who engaged in the public work of writing—except for those with an overtly religious perspective—inevitably experienced conflict as women workers; without the formal and informal sanctions that authorized men's work, women who wrote lacked cultural support for their labor.

In a sense, women writers were doubly excluded: they had breached norms of domesticity by taking up paid work, and they were also left out of the discourse on literary professionalism, which emphasized the public function of literary men. Claims to professional status at mid-century were based on advocacy of literature as a public organ of opinion, education, and ideology; like barristers or physicians, literary professionals ministered to the needs of a national community. "Services done to the State," one commentator begins, "by distinguished efforts in art, literature, and science, are as unequivocal, and at the least as important, as services done by professors of arms, law, divinity, and diplomacy." Like their brethren in other fields, professional literary men derived value and standing from their public function, which was intimately linked to their dissemination of values that advanced the interests of the nation. Thus the literary profession as a whole earned its reward. "The claims of literature and science are for a due recognition and recompense of such valuable service rendered to the State. They are advanced, not in behalf of individuals, but of the class."[13] Defined as a member of a class of public figures, an atom within a larger institutionalized network who plays his role in constituting public discourse, the professional author is part of a discrete, identifiable, representable group; he is not merely a private individual competing in the marketplace, but a public functionary with a specifiable social role.

By constituting themselves as a class, at least rhetorically, and by defining their work in terms that explicitly excluded women, male professionals denied membership in that class to all middle-class married women, and to most of the single ones as well. Indeed, until feminists first began to organize oppositionally in the 1850s, middle-class women could not constitute themselves as a visible social group at all: without access to the formal and informal networks that male professionals established in order to advance their claims on a more powerful collective basis, middle-class women could not effectively represent or address their own interests, nor were they even supposed to have interests separate from those of men. Lacking basic constitutive legal and economic rights, the rights that would grant them equality of status, women writers were theoretically debarred from public discourse and professional identification. Such women as Harriet Martineau, who engaged in public debate and who sought to appropriate a masculine model for representing herself, ran the risk of being attacked as "unfeminine" for doing so.

Middle-class women were excluded from the class of professional authors on two seemingly distinct but ideologically related grounds. According to an essay of 1864 in *The London Review*, their lack of access to the experiential and educational opportunities afforded men prevented women from attaining a public character. Without the "long experience [of] the meannesses of the world," without the "literary education" in classical models that imposed its necessary "severe discipline" on aspirants, even "the best women exhibit their deficiency."[14] Just as literary men embodied the values of their sphere, literary women derived their distinctive talents from their position within the family. "Like children," women "have a keen perception of what is noble and ignoble in character, and an unlimited power of appreciating nicely fine traits and symptoms of what is evil as well as of what is good"; they "feel strongly and acutely . . . and are commonly fluent in expression" (p. 328). The writer implies that so long as spheres remained separate, differences in opportunity would produce differences in character that made men public, women private, and their roles distinct. And although this reviewer does not say so, we might adduce from other evidence—such as Ruskin's *Sesame and Lilies* (1864), to take the most notorious example—that some Victorians believed that those differences in character were naturally ordained rather than socially constituted.

But these claims are descriptive rather than prescriptive, and liberal feminists at mid-century might have refuted them by arguing that greater educational and economic opportunities for women would necessarily alter the way in which gender and gender roles were constituted; however, as this essayist goes on to assert, the separation of women from professional authorship is not merely a matter of custom or prejudice, but necessary to the very existence of a class of professional authors. Women should not write because the true work of women, "a mission quite as grand as that of literary authorship," is to "[keep] alive for men certain ideas, and ideals too, which would soon pass out of the world in the rush and hurry of material existence if they were not fed and replenished by those who are able to stand aloof from the worry and vexations of active life" (p. 329). Men must be "fed and replenished" in more ways than one, with tea and dinner as well as with love and affection, but this writer represses the materiality of women's domestic labor and replaces it with a wholly spiritualized function. Men who work with "ideas, and ideals" require women to protect and transmit culture, virtue, and private values; women reproduce the material and ideological conditions of (private) domesticity in order to en-sure that (public) art will be produced. Like Conrad's Marlow at the conclusion of *Heart of Darkness*, this reviewer posits women's continuing self-sacrifice as essential to the advance of imperial civilization.

Thus men's and women's spheres are not truly separate in either ideology or experience, but interdependent, in that masculine authorship requires wom-en's domestic labor, while women depend on men for financial support; each sphere relies on the other to define it as what it is not as well as to support it for what it is. The force that counteracts men's alienation in the marketplace, domestic femininity, must not itself be subject to the division of self that paid work produces, so that "agitation for equal rights"—which, as Catherine Gal-lagher asserts, "rested on an assumption of disparate interests"—threatened to undo the family's force as a counter to "the competitive ethos" of the public sphere.[15] (If I have here emphasized masculine dependence on private feminin-ity, I do not mean to suggest that the dependency works in one direction only. The legal doctrine of coverture had long institutionalized women's need for "protection" by—and from—men.[16]) Women who work for money threaten the structure of that mutual dependence by asserting their claim to indepen-dence and autonomy, so-called masculine prerogatives. "If women were to be-come as men" (p. 329), which they most assuredly would if they sacrificed their femininity for masculine goals, "the sacred fire" of ideas, ideals, and inspiration "would soon become extinct" (p. 329); only "by undergoing a defeminizing process" (p. 328), only by herself becoming a worker could a woman become a great artist. Women who work thus potentially injure men's interests by com-peting with them in the public sphere and by revealing women's "natural" condition of "dependence" to be a cultural and economic fiction.

While the professional text of the literary man barely acknowledges the ways in which it undermines its own arguments about the separation of spheres, *Aurora Leigh* foregrounds the interdependence of private and public realms by its thorough inquiry into ideologies of feminine domestic dependency and mas-culine aesthetic autonomy. Barrett Browning represents her writing heroine as pulled in contradictory directions by what seem to be mutually exclusive alter-natives, the life of writing and the life of the "common woman," yet over the course of this narrative, she attempts to reconcile them. The poem contests the separation of spheres in making its heroine both artist and woman: throughout *Aurora Leigh*, Barrett Browning argues against the polarity between female dependence and male independence as an inadequate representation of personal identity and attempts explicitly to substitute a vision of interdependence in its place. In doing so, she seeks both to counter the professional's prohibition against female labor and to rewrite Wordsworth's narrative of poetic development from her own standpoint; her effort is not without its own problems, but those, too, are of definite interest here.

Aurora Leigh *and the Problem of Wholeness*

In describing the education Aurora receives at the hands of her English aunt, Barrett Browning attacks the feminine curriculum that dooms most women to be mere dilettantes. Aurora's aunt prefers "instructed piety" to theological controversy, supplies "a little algebra" and just enough science to prevent her charge from turning out "frivolous."[17] Her niece learns "tongues, not books" (1.402), geographical trivia—to provide "a general insight into useful facts" (1.414)— some music, some drawing, some dancing; she "spun glass, stuffed birds, and modelled flowers in wax" (1.425). To Aurora, this is severe discipline, but her aunt has no vocational aim in sight, unless we consider domesticity itself a vocation. For Aunt Leigh intends to produce a proper English girl who will become, in time, a proper English wife: to that end she assigns her niece "a score of books on womanhood" (1.427). They preach women's "general missionariness" (1.435) and praise "their angelic reach / Of virtue, chiefly used to sit and darn, / And fatten household sinners" (1.438–40). In those books— which closely resemble not only the professional man's vision of domesticity, but also the conduct manuals Sarah Stickney Ellis published for and about the women, wives, and daughters of England—Aurora reads and rejects the cultural norms for femininity that cultivate women's "potential faculty in everything / Of abdicating power in it" (1.441–42). She correctly realizes that women's education is designed to keep them in their place, to enforce their dependence on men, and discerns the ideological intent of her aunt's vision.

Although Aunt Leigh and the authors she favors are the instruments of this ideology, Aurora believes that such training for women serves only men's interests:

> We sew, sew, prick our fingers, dull our sight,
> Producing what? A pair of slippers, sir,
> To put on when you're weary—or a stool
> To tumble over and vex you. . . .   (1.457–60)

Aurora sees women's domestic labor as entirely devoted to men's comforts; that women sometimes go astray in their efforts, as when they make a footstool a drawing-room obstruction suitable for tripping over, is ironically "symbolical" (1.456) of the wasted energy they expend on trivialities. Aurora is ambitious to do some "real" work in the world, and the model for identity she initially adopts requires her to ally herself with the masculinist rhetoric of individualism. She wants to be an independent producer of poetic works, and to do so she must identify with male prerogative and reject the norms of the feminine sphere.[18]

In Wordsworthian fashion, Aurora locates in nature the force that counters her aunt's artifice:

> I had relations in the Unseen, and drew
> The elemental nutriment and heat
> From nature, as earth feels the sun at nights,
> Or as a babe sucks surely in the dark.   (1.473–76)

Receiving her true nourishment from the elements, Aurora outwardly complies with her aunt's strictures, but makes an internal world for herself:

> I kept the life, thrust on me, on the outside
> Of the inner life, with all its ample room
> For heart and lungs, for will and intellect,
> Inviolable by conventions.   (1.477–80)

In opposing "the inner life" to the "conventions" of feminine character, Barrett Browning aligns her heroine with Wordsworthian poetic subjectivity, which values "a poet's individualism" (2.478)—and not the social relations in which the poet lives—above all else.

Aurora's aunt attempts to crush that "individualism," that Romantic self (also coded as masculine) which transcends the everyday, the ordinary, and the material, for "individualism" functions as the sign for self-assertion and independence, everything from which women are debarred.[19] For Aurora and Barrett Browning, the Wordsworthian account of how the poet is produced here proves to be a useful counter to cultural myths of women's incapacity for poetry and their disposition to domesticity. But in appropriating Wordsworth's model for poetic subjectivity, Barrett Browning inherits as well its ideological underpinnings: Aurora's exceptionality, her difference as a poet, separates her from other women and isolates her.

Within the fiction of the poem, which is less a Wordsworthian retrospective of the past than a "novel-poem" of education which attempts to make sense of events as they are being both lived and remembered, we are meant to see Aurora as an individual-in-process, who learns from experience and is indeed misled at times. From her aunt's example, she falsely identifies all that is conventionally feminine as negative; from the story of Marian Erle, however, she comes to understand the value of selflessness and to celebrate what is truly good about women, their capacity to love selflessly. It is possible, then, to read the poem as a partial revision of Wordsworthian poetics in a new feminine key: Aurora's "masculine" egotism comes to be modified by her embrace of the world of women, and specifically a working-class woman, whom Wordsworth would probably objectify rather than invest with something that approximates a voice of her own. But before she lives in the world, when she "[discourses] of life and art, with both untried" (8.303), Aurora sees life as an either/or proposition: art and love seem mutually exclusive for women, and so she chooses "the inner life" and poetry over the conventional woman's life, the one that her aunt prescribes for her, without even attempting to imagine some alternative to heterosexual pairing that might provide her with satisfying affective ties.[20]

When Romney asks her to be his wife, after he has disparaged all poetry as useless and her poetic ambition as unfulfillable, she replies in terms that reveal the contradiction that makes women both dependent and depended on:

> ". . . am I proved too weak
> To stand alone, yet strong enough to bear
> Such leaners on my shoulder? poor to think,
> Yet rich enough to sympathise with thought?
> Incompetent to sing, as blackbirds can,
> Yet competent to love, like HIM?"   (2.359–64)

With this critique, Aurora reacts against the whole tenor of her English education as she reveals the doubleness of women's position. Instead of choosing wifely submission, she will pursue her own work: "'I, too, have my vocation,—work to do, / The heavens and earth have set me'" (2.455–56). And when Romney attempts to endow her with the fortune her aunt's will has denied her, she similarly rejects the fiction of women's need for male support: "'You face, to-day, / A man who wants instruction, mark me, not / A woman who wants protection'" (2.1072–74). She believes art and marriage cannot be combined, in that one requires independent "individualism," the other dependent selflessness, and opts for the poet's life.

Ultimately, Aurora's "experience" proves her youthful understanding of the world to be incorrect. In Barrett Browning's fiction, art does not turn out to be the realm of autonomy that Aurora had imagined it, and marriage need not be a wholly compromised ideal. She learns that private feminine values and public masculine aspirations—the "heart" and the "head" in the metaphorical shorthand—must be combined because each is incomplete in itself. Romney has failed in his work because "it takes a soul, / To move a body" (2.479–80); Aurora has almost failed in her life because she "'would not be a woman like the rest, / A simple woman who believes in love'" (9.661–62). When Aurora's experience of herself as a gendered subject begins to impinge on her consciousness, she begins to find the value in what she has rejected.

In bringing the two lovers together at the end of the poem, Barrett Browning figures human wholeness in terms of a marriage metaphor, a familiar trope of Romantic discourse, but far more literal in *Aurora Leigh* than it is in *The Prelude* or *Prometheus Unbound*. She makes the split within the female poetic self—between the feminine desire and aptitude for love and domesticity and the masculine ones for poetry and public engagement—resolvable through marriage. In marrying Aurora to Romney, Barrett Browning reverses the gendered positions of the Romantic metaphor—or, as Dorothy Mermin puts it, "she switches the locus of power within them" (p. 215)—but retains the split that metaphor implies between different spheres of experience.

As Margaret Homans has most cogently argued, Wordsworth's marriage of mind and nature exemplifies the Romantic vision of the feminine as empowering to the male artist: consummated in "spousal verse," this union binds the masculine self to a feminized landscape and thus heals the wound of separation and alienation within, enabling the male poet to produce the poem that celebrates that consummation.[21] For a woman poet to figure her relation to the world in Romantic terms should, then, be difficult, for if she takes the feminine position, she can produce nothing of poetry; if she wholly identifies with the masculine, she threatens the stability of gender and subjectivity. But her creator's embrace of the masculine position does not seem problematic for Aurora as a poet. Barrett Browning, "self-tutored in a conventionally male classical education . . . affiliated herself with a corpus of male poets," as Deirdre David reminds us, establishing "a firm identification with male modes of political thought and aesthetic practice."[22] While Aurora questions herself as poet throughout the work, she does so in a spirit of self-criticism that ultimately leads, in her own estimation, to better work: she doubts her own worthiness, not the authority of the Romantic standard she aspires to imitate. Barrett Browning fully accepts the ideals of Romantic subjectivity, for "the romantic theory of the subject," as Cora Kaplan notes, was "so firmly entrenched within the discourse" of high literary culture that to challenge it, she would have had to leap outside the ideological conditions that gendered poetic and political authority as masculine. "As a woman poet," Mermin notes, "she would have to play two opposing roles at one time."[23] But the poet-heroine's plight within the poem hinges on just this distinction between the roles assigned the male poetic subject and his female object. Although Aurora rejects the economic dependence marriage entails for women, she comes to recognize her own Romantic need for the wholeness of experience that poetic work alone cannot provide, and identifies that need with her own previously rejected identity as a woman. Through a new marriage, Barrett Browning refigures the interdependence of masculine and feminine spheres.

While Aurora eschews conventional femininity, she finds she cannot do without love: she envies her successful fellow (all male) poets not for their "native gifts or popular applause" (5.517), but for their wives and mothers (5.518–40). Her lack of affective ties makes her identify herself to a male friend as one of the boys, as something other than womanly, as she had in speaking to Romney:

> ". . . my dear Lord Howe, you shall not speak
> To a printing woman who has lost her place
> (The sweet safe corner of the household fire
> Behind the heads of children) compliments,
> As if she were a woman. We who have clipt
> The curls before our eyes, may see at least
> As plain as men do: speak out, man to man;
> No compliments, beseech you."   (5.805–12)

"A printing woman who has lost her place" at the domestic hearth through taking a place in the world of work must return to that domestic place even as she and her beloved must redefine it, as Aurora and Romney will. For the woman poet, then, as for the man, work alone cannot suffice, for the feminine self also requires the affirmation that only love can provide, but the woman poet experiences and represents this need explicitly. Unlike the male professional, who takes for granted women's emotional sustenance and reproductive labor, the woman writer finds herself in the contradictory position of having to reject the conventions of femininity even as she reinscribes marriage, the institution that guarantees women's subordination, as a cultural and personal ideal.[24]

Aurora begins to reconcile the split between "the inner life" and the external world, between art and love, when she recognizes that in accepting the inevitability of that split, she has impeded the progress of her poetry and undermined her own personal happiness. Addressing Romney, she attributes each of their particular errors to the same cause, their mutual incompleteness as individuals:

> ". . . You only thought to rescue men
> By half-means, half-way, seeing half their wants,
> While thinking nothing of your personal gain.
> But I who saw the human nature broad
> At both sides, comprehending, too, the soul's,
> And all the high necessities of Art,
> Betrayed the thing I saw, and wronged my own life
> For which I pleaded. Passioned to exalt
> The artist's instinct in me at the cost
> Of putting down the woman's—I forgot
> No perfect artist is developed here
> From any imperfect woman. . . ."   (9.638–49)

Within the self, the two "instincts"—for Romney, the reformer's and the man's; for Aurora, the artist's and the woman's—must be brought into balance and harmony, with each faculty "developed" to its fullest potential. This internal reconciliation also requires—or sanctions—an external social union of different beings: Barrett Browning thus revises the content of the ideal of complementarity between genders even as she retains it as her ideological framework for gender identity.

Through her poetic persona, Barrett Browning acknowledges that conflicting claims on the woman writer deconstruct the fiction of Romantic autonomy. Aurora cannot maintain the position of the independent, isolated poetic subject who transcends all human desires, while Barrett Browning presents a woman's need for love and family as an essential and ahistorical "instinct," something enduring rather than something culturally conditioned. Yet she also begins to imagine—within the terms, set out by Tennyson in *The Princess* (1847), that structured most mid-Victorian discussions of gender distinctions—a woman writer who would be subject to neither that paralyzing split consciousness nor that separation of the feminine world of loving familial ties from the masculine world of poetic and political activity. *Aurora Leigh* points up the basic insufficiency of Romantic self-representation and subjectivity and all that they connote, for men and for women, by positing another possibility: transforming the structures of an inherited literary and cultural tradition so as to produce a new subject that could unite both public and private, poetic and personal experience.

Ideology and Contradiction in Women's Writing

Among nineteenth-century British women's texts, *Aurora Leigh* comes closest to enacting from a woman's standpoint a cultural paradigm previously employed only by men. Barrett Browning represents Aurora as the possessor of an authentic poetic vocation, and it is a calling with a distinctly public element: with Romney, Aurora will participate in the making of a terrestrial New Jerusalem. Together Barrett Browning and Aurora reject the notion of female dependence promulgated by the professional discourse and assert women's right to be artists on the same terms as men. Because it is a woman's story, however, neither Aurora nor Barrett Browning undervalues the importance of (stereotypically) feminine attributes to the new society, for the poet who is also a woman combines in her person significant powers for social good. And Barrett Browning certainly does not hold with the male professional desire to keep women out of public life, since she seems to believe, as other contemporary feminists did, that women's particular "natural" aptitude for caring nurturance could be of use in ameliorating public ills. But Aurora's story clearly elides some of the more problematic issues women writers, and other middle-class working women, faced in going public. In challenging the ideological boundaries of women's role by affirming Aurora's right to work, while simultaneously returning her to a domestic configuration at the end of the poem, Barrett Browning situates her heroine as part of both spheres, and so suggests that the woman writer can establish her identity at their nexus; however, in doing so, she implies (misleadingly, I think) that marriage and career, family and authorial vocation, can be an unproblematic combination for a Victorian woman writer, be she fictive or actual.

Many feminist critics have taken this double positioning as a sign of women's power to cross ideological boundaries and have thus understood women's writing as a privileged site of transgression. The woman author is said to disrupt the separation of spheres, to blur the line between men's productive work in the marketplace and women's reproductive labor in the home, by creating texts that embody her transgression and extend it into a public arena of reading, where its (usually hidden) meaning may be deciphered. By writing at all, Barrett Browning is said to achieve a voice despite the general ideological silencing of women.

Yet this way of looking at female authorship too often overlooks the possibility that an underlying adherence to the ideologies she presumably contests is what sanctions "transgression" as an available stance for the woman writer. In Barrett Browning's case, it is important to note the ways in which she fails to challenge dominant models. Her appropriation of a Romantic idiom, for example, leads to the reproduction of elitist norms of literary values: Aurora's privileging of poetry over prose draws on a high Romantic disdain for "vulgar

needs" and "common grain" (3.303–29) that links her more closely to Wordsworth than to Felicia Hemans, reinscribing the genius/hack distinction. More
dramatically, as Deirdre David has persuasively argued, "women's talent is made
the attendant of conservative male ideals" (p. 98) of the political and social
order in *Aurora Leigh*. The poem and the poet look "transgressive," then, only
if we have bought the idea that all women's speech is inherently liberatory, no
matter what women have to say; yet knowing as we do that women *did* have
voices in the nineteenth century must make us attentive to what they were
saying and how what they said affected their ability to speak and to be heard.
I find it crucial to remember here that women's speech, like women's silence,
can also be a product of their ideological positioning; to assign a univocal meaning to either one—all speech is "good," all silence is "bad"—is to oversimplify
the operations of both domination and resistance.

The political theorist Carole Pateman's analysis of working married women
as both individuals and *not* individuals provides a relevant case in point here,
for it establishes that ideology can structure experience in determining ways,
yet also contradict itself internally. The married woman, "civilly dead" in that
she was her husband's legal property and thus unable to make contracts in her
own person or to control her own money, "stood to him as a slave/servant to
a master."[25] Yet the legal prescription against women's autonomy was undercut in practice when "wives entered the employment contract" (p. 131): women
could make terms with an employer and execute their work faithfully—even if
their wages ultimately came under their husbands' control—and so affirmed
that they possessed the capacity to be legal subjects in the same sense as men.
Pateman's analysis thus suggests that we should not be bound to see middle-
class women who wrote for money as only private and domestic but—sometimes and in particular cases—as participants in both spheres and as such conscious of and subject to contradictory cultural forces.

For women writers, this may mean that their subjective experience of being
simultaneously public and private, workers and women, appears to them less as
a desirable "transgression" and more as a contradiction to resolve or minimize
in accord with hegemonic discourse. So if Barrett Browning is "transgressive"
in her appropriation of masculinist discourse, and genuinely insightful in identifying a need to resolve the cultural tension between "masculine" artistry and
"feminine" affectivity, then she is also cautiously conservative in her vision of
gender. Rather than wishing away the contradictions of her position as a woman
who empowers herself by speaking the language of the fathers, we have to see
that doubleness as itself a product of ideological contradiction.

Those women who were and were not individuals also wrote autobiography,
and so entered into an individualist discourse with which some, but not all, of
those capacities culturally designated as feminine were in tension. The spiritual
autobiographies to which I will turn next offer prime examples of how some
women's self-representations negotiate the relationship between public and private: they employ the idiom of domesticity to sanction their entrance into publicity, yet simultaneously redefine their reading public in terms of the norms

of privacy. Along the same lines as the reading of *Aurora Leigh*, the discourse of Evangelical religion both affirms and denies women's positions as individual subjects by granting them voices but putting them in the service of a conservative ideology of femininity. Yet unlike Barrett Browning's fictive autobiographer, who at first perceives the demands of Victorian domesticity as an obstacle to her aesthetic quest, the spiritual autobiographer constructs her "authorship self" as complementary to—and indeed dependent on—her "domestic self," and in doing so, she tactfully refrains from calling attention to the ways in which the very fact of her working might make her, by some ideological standards, unfeminine. The discourse of Christian piety also invests religious women with an authority defined quite differently from the male professional's even as it minimizes the risks of their engagement in autobiographical discourse; they negotiate the crossing from the inner circle to the outer one by always representing themselves in their texts through the signifiers of domesticity and by refusing to locate themselves or their work in the public realm of exchange.[26]

Within certain patriarchal constraints on what they can represent, the Evangelical emphasis on individual authority enables women writers to invoke a system of values that sanctifies their work as useful and important and designates their self-representations as exemplary. Acting in conjunction with the economic logic that assigns women to the domestic realm, religious discourse gives women authority over that interior space, which is redefined as a new locus for cultural and even literary value. While Barrett Browning maligns the "general missionariness" that Aunt Leigh's books try to instill in their readers, we will see that representing authorship as a moral mission provides middle-class women writers with one of the very few legitimate poses they can assume as literary subjects within Victorian culture. Just as other such middle-class women workers as Florence Nightingale repeatedly justified their work on the grounds that they had been divinely "called" to perform it, religious women writers naturalize their unnatural acts by invoking a higher law as the sanction for their work.

There are two ways in which we can read this conservative strategy for writing and self-representation as a challenge to the dominant ideology of the professional literary man. First, the spiritual work of the writing woman inevitably criticizes the public sphere and secular literature as corrupt and inauthentic; in the years that followed, feminists as diverse as Josephine Butler and Christabel Pankhurst would do the same in making their claims for women's equality with, and even superiority to, men. Second, and more importantly for my purposes, these texts demonstrate that women who write autobiography necessarily confront contradictory paradigms for identity within their own experience of writing autobiography, as Aurora Leigh does: self-representation is not the founding step in a literary career or the literary act that seals authorial identity, as it is for Wordsworth or Carlyle, but rather an extension of women's selflessness into a self-centered form. Thus these autobiographies implicitly critique the male professional's appropriation of all literary value to the public sphere in delineating the private sources of morality and spirituality.

Tactful Silences in Religious Women's Autobiographies

The women autobiographers considered here are unfamiliar to today's readers, but in their own time, they were all widely read and extremely productive writers. Mary Martha Sherwood (1775–1851), author of *The Fairchild Family* (1817) and the "Henry Milner" tales, was among the most popular writers of children's stories in the century. "Well-born, well-informed, and well-meaning," in the words of one biographer, she was the daughter of a country clergyman and converted to Evangelicalism while living in India.[27] In the 1830s and 1840s, Charlotte Tonna (1790–1846), whose autobiography Vineta Colby describes as the story of "a real life evangelical Dorothea Brooke," published tracts and novels of the strictest Evangelical tenor for a burgeoning readership. She also served for fifteen years as the editor of the popular *Christian Lady's Magazine*.[28] By the time these two came to write their life stories, then, they were well known as "authors" even if they lacked the glamour of their most illustrious male and female contemporaries. But in their autobiographies, where we might expect them to represent themselves as professional authors, they do not lay claim to that authorial status; rather, they constitute appropriately decorous female autobiographical personae through which they differentiate themselves and their work from those who labor in the public sphere.

Their different rationales for working in this genre, as they explain them, do not express the wish to capitalize on their popularity: publicity is the last thing the spiritual woman writer cares to seek. Their explicit intention in representing themselves is to control the way in which their readers, contemporary and future, will read them. In her *Personal Recollections* (1842), Tonna attempts to seal off what she has constituted as her private self from public view. Asserting the sanctity of "private domestic history" and "the sacredness of home," and defending the absence of any remarks on her "private life," she yet acknowledges what Barrett Browning would not, "that when it has pleased God to bring any one before the public in the capacity of an author, that person becomes in some sense public property; having abandoned the privacy from which no one ought to be forced."[29] Writing about ten years later, and commenting on "the propensity of the age for writing and recording the lives of every individual who has had the smallest claim to celebrity," Sherwood presents *The Life of Mrs. Sherwood* (1857) as a necessary defense against what others might write of her if she were to leave it unwritten: "Could I be quite sure, that when I am gone, nobody would say anything about me, I should, I think, spare myself the trouble which I am now about to take."[30] She, too, assumes that the text of her life can be appropriated, and defends against that possibility by writing autobiography, by telling her story in her own terms. Their texts function in part, then, as public means of shaping and controlling their selves, as they would for male autobiographers, yet these women also express a distrust of the public sphere and its norms.

In explaining their motives, the spiritual autobiographers also signal a particular conception of the relation between the private and the public spheres, viewing them not as separate realms, but as concentric circles: in a different context, Catherine Gallagher suggests that "families [form] a series of enclaves that are at once a part of and separate from the larger society."[31] While Tonna realizes, for example, that her rhetorical representation of her "person" will become "public property," she posits some familial, interpersonal experience as prior to and privileged over public discourse. By omitting certain details of her marriage, for instance, she retains a degree of control over what she has tactfully constructed as her own private "person," the interpersonal relations that involve her husband and her family. The "sacredness" of the private realm, its integrity as a space that is contained by yet theoretically sealed off from the public world, must be preserved inviolate, for as we shall see, it is in maintaining the sanctity of the interior that spiritual woman writers are authorized to represent themselves publicly. That something of themselves remains private and goes unrepresented—the intricacy of family life, for example—marks them as proper inhabitants of the domestic sphere, where neither self nor others should be commodified.

In sharp contrast to Barrett Browning's or Harriet Martineau's experience of authorship, it is imperative for spiritual autobiographers not to be (or not to feel themselves to be) extraordinary or exceptional women: to establish and maintain their authority to write, they must observe the norms that constitute appropriate feminine behavior and avoid the eccentricities displayed by those who exceed the prescribed bounds of middle-class femininity. Asserting her own claim to be considered representative of the norm, Sherwood expresses her desire not to be thought exceptional (and thus unwomanly) mainly in terms of her distaste for the stereotypical literary woman. The "bluestocking" who forfeits femininity in her quest for publicity is an eccentric female rather than a conventional, unexceptionable one, and Sherwood seems not to have any other model available for identifying herself as a literary woman, and certainly not a professional one. Recalling her father's repeated claim that she "was to grow up a genius," Sherwood asserts that back then, as at the time of writing, to be "a celebrated authoress" was not her wish: "Even then I felt, if it were necessary to be very singular, I would rather not be a genius" (pp. 51–52). While "it was a matter of course to me that I was to write, and also a matter of instinct . . . I had a horror of being thought a literary lady; for it was, I fancied, ungraceful" (p. 118). When "forced into public" (her father suggested that she should help an impoverished family friend by publishing her first work and donating the proceeds to him), "my heart sunk at the proposition": "to be set down so soon in that character which I had always dreaded," to feel "the mortification which I felt at being thus dragged into public," made her wish "that I had never known the use of a pen" (p. 119). Her distaste for "that character" indicates her unwillingness to frame her own authorship along the lines of the "learned lady"; moreover, it does not even occur to her to make the kind of claims to aesthetic vocation that Aurora Leigh does.

Like a proper heroine from a Burney or an Austen novel, Sherwood expresses the fear that public exposure will bring "mortification." Alongside Barrett Browning's fear of being consumed and dissected, Sherwood's anxiety reminds us that this dead metaphor connotes a real anxiety: women writers who enter the public world, even through the impersonal medium of print, risk social or moral death and incur a threat to the stability of their identities. Because the entry into authorship potentially entails "a defeminizing process" in making workers of women, the religious writing woman constructs her writing self as firmly anchored in the norms of the private sphere in order to retain the security of obscurity; in the absence of certain kinds of information, the text of her life appears to fit the feminine norm. In the very act of being tactful, however, women autobiographers reveal the division they wish to cover up, for the need for tact signals the gap between what can and cannot be represented: they efface their own position as writers even as they write the stories of their lives.

Not surprisingly, given their concern with maintaining feminine decorum, these texts emphasize their authors' positions as creators of home and family life, and not their paid work as participants in the literary economy. While women autobiographers may admit that writing for publication earns them money, they tend to represent the financial rewards of literary labor as subordinate to some other, more communal purpose. After her husband's financial reverses, Mary Sewell published "my first little book . . . to earn money, if I could, for the purchase of books to help me in the children's education"; when Tonna's separation from her husband "rendered it needful to turn the little talent I possessed to account," she did so, but "still keeping in view the grand object of promoting God's glory" (p. 189).[32] Recasting their writerly labor as an integral part of women's domestic work, the religious autobiographers rarely mention literary production apart from its domestic and domesticated ends. In this fashion, they, too—like Wordsworth—cover over their participation in the marketplace, but in a decidedly different way: whereas the Romantic author asserts his distance from the economic by insisting on his labor as vocation, spiritual women writers represent their literary work as a component of their domestic calling as mothers, daughters, and children of God.

The silences imposed about the actual activity of writing by this ideological positioning of women can be quite maddening. We can juxtapose Sherwood's *Life* with Mill's *Autobiography* (1877) (the classic case of the life that, without Harriet Taylor, would have consisted almost solely of readings and writings), or Tonna's text with Trollope's *Autobiography* (1883) (with its detailed description of all aspects of his literary work, including the ledger that sums up the total of his emoluments), and see by the comparison that these women's texts hardly seem to be by writers at all, so thoroughly do they suppress the signs of literary production. But this silence, too, supports the domestic status of the author-autobiographer: even the most minimal engagement with publishers, editors, and printers goes unrecorded, for these writers never trespass on male territory. Keeping both her discourse and her body within the limits of the feminine sphere ensures that the religious woman writer will not be subjected to the kind of criticism Mary Sewell leveled at a mid-Victorian woman evangelist who took her message to a public audience: a public proselytizer, unlike a private didact, is cut off from the legitimating power and protection of the family, for "'a lone women who speaks in public,'" Sewell intones, "'is a very lone *creature* indeed'" (quoted in Bayly, p. 179).[33]

Remaining private empowers the religious woman writer; keeping silent on certain subjects maintains that power, and politics is thus one topic these texts do not speak of. Tonna, for instance, does not refer at all to her political beliefs, even though they deeply informed the rhetoric of her industrial novels; while she admits to being "often charged with the offence of being too political in my writings" (p. 20), the autobiographical text reveals nothing that would substantiate such a charge.[34] Although Mary Anne Schimmelpenninck (1778–1856) was an adolescent at the time of the French Revolution, contemporary public discourse never enters her self-representation: she does not write about "public events, with which I have nothing to do" in her *Life* (1858), promising instead to trace "the effects which they produced on the domestic sphere with which I had experience," but she never fulfills that promise.[35] Although she has lived during "years [that] . . . have been some of the most interesting in our country's history" as an observer of "the grand march of commerce, science, and invention, including the lives of some of the first historical characters," Sewell ventures "nothing but family scraps—odds and ends—to set them down as they link together in my memory" (pp. 1–2). In all three texts, the actuality of "public" history is invoked only to be dismissed according to the implicit dictum that confines these Victorian women autobiographers to writing solely about what is proper to their sphere: unlike some of the Victorian memoirists introduced in Chapter 3, who legitimate their acts of self-representation by situating their lives within an historical framework, these women, who refuse to construct themselves as "authors," also refuse to discuss public events.

The Exemplary Text

By contrast, these autobiographies document fully the ostensibly more private world of religious experience, as their writers give voice to all the pains and pleasures of the Christian subject. Although most twentieth-century feminists have tended to view religion as a primary instrument of the patriarchal ideology that consigns women to silence, recent revisionist work has begun to challenge the monolithic view that casts all religious discourse as inherently oppressive. As Gail Malmgreen puts it, "It is surely neither possible nor necessary to weigh up, once and for all, the gains and losses for women of religious commitment. . . . the dealings of organised religion with women have been richly laced with ironies and contradictions."[36] If religion helped produce and enforce the ideology that assigned middle-class women to the domestic sphere, it also enabled them, within that realm, to write in ways that those who sought access to literary authority on secular grounds could not.[37] Most importantly, Evangelical practice licensed women to think and interpret for themselves, if not wholly without male mediation, for "the religion of the heart" invested its believers with "the onus of interpreting God's Word." As Elisabeth Jay argues in her study of Evangelicalism and the Victorian novel, "no appeal to any authoritative body of dogmatic pronouncements" could relieve individuals of their responsibility for establishing their relation to the Bible and to God, for the eternal welfare of souls ultimately depended on that relationship.[38] A religious discourse was one of the very few that could potentially allow its female agents a degree of individualism, even if here, as everywhere else in the nineteenth century, gender plays its part in determining the possible limits and acceptable range of feminine self-writing.

The cultural prohibition against public activity, for example, does not absolutely prevent middle-class women from writing even if it dictates the style and content of their work: adhering to the unwritten laws of decorum, in fact, keeps writing women from the spiritual and moral death Sherwood fears. Tonna invokes the religious bent of her works as a safeguard against the ever-present temptation of taking too much satisfaction in her own literary abilities:

> the literary labour that I pursued for my own sustenance was perfect luxury, so long as my humble productions were made available for the spiritual good of the people so dear to me. My little books and tracts became popular; because, after some struggle against a plan so humbling to literary pride, I was able to adopt the suggestion of a wise Christian brother, and form a style of such homely simplicity that if, on reading a manuscript to a child of five years old, I found there was a single sentence or word above his comprehension, it was instantly corrected to suit that lowly standard.   (p. 145)

In a move that oddly recalls Wordsworth's transvaluation of work in the opening lines of *The Prelude*, Tonna's "labour" is reconfigured as "luxury"; in Nancy Armstrong's terms, "self-regulation [becomes] a form of labor that [is] superior to labor."[39] Tonna's "literary pride" is tamed into a "homely simplicity" of both style and self once she orients her writing toward a correct spiritual end. The "wise Christian brother," figure of patriarchal authority, is to Tonna not an oppressor but a benefactor, for it is his warning that keeps her on the appropriate path for righteous Christian women. All in all, literary individualism is subordinated to the needs of a collective Christian readership; the stylistic sign of the unique author is suppressed in favor of a higher design.

In these terms, moving from private femininity to public writing entails not public "mortification" in Sherwood's sense, but the private mortification of the self before God, who can read even the unwritten; Christian self-disclosure leads to eternal spiritual life, for the writer herself and even for her readers. Unlike Wordsworth or Carlyle, who must construct the ideal readers they cannot actually locate in the real world, Tonna can relate to her readers because they share a system of values and beliefs. Moreover, by erasing all traces of art and artfulness, by bringing the self into line with the ideal, exemplary self she wants to be, she shows herself willing and able to mortify her "literary pride" before those readers in order to maintain a reading community of comprehending converts. While writing demands that she present herself to the world, Tonna reduces the risk of entering discourse by appealing to specifically religious values that require her self-effacement even as they invest her with a voice to which other Evangelical Christians will listen.

Within this system, religious autobiographers present their lives as exemplary: though by nature imperfect and sinful, they tell human stories that illustrate the workings of God's goodness and Satan's evil. As living examples, useful and beneficial to others who are working out their own salvation in their personal lives, they are not fictitious, but real: autobiographies are not unique but particular, and as such they are powerful texts for others to read.[40] In showing "what the Almighty has done for me, and those most dear to me, in leading us on in the way of salvation" (p. 2), Sherwood makes her *Life* reflect and embellish the didactic purposes of her literary works. Similarly, Tonna's narrative also seeks to influence the moral life of its readers, not through the filter of fiction, but by the authority of its subject's true experience: once we know what the word of God has done for her, we "will be ready to echo with increased earnestness that emphatic declaration, 'The Bible, the Bible alone, is the religion of Protestants;' and not only to echo, but also to act upon it" (p. 25). While Tonna's text formally approximates the Pauline conversion narrative, it also adopts its rhetorical mode in actively attempting to convert its readers to the way of Christ by invoking the authority of personal spiritual experience.[41]

That writing itself amplifies and extends woman's sphere proves to be the ultimate good to which these autobiographies attest, as they celebrate womanhood for its disinterestedness. "'Remember, it is a privilege to be a woman instead of a man,'" writes Schimmelpenninck, recording her mother's words. "'Men, heroes, and others, do things partly to do good and partly to gain a great name; but a woman's self-denial and generosity may be as great, and often greater, while it is unknown to others, and fully manifest only to her own conscience and to God: to work for this, and for this alone, is the highest of all callings'" (1:204). But invoking the language and concept of calling to define and deify womanhood, as conservative writers from Hannah More to Sarah Ellis repeatedly do in their writings, does not strictly determine the ways in which that vocation may be expressed. It rules out only the love of fame as an end while presenting as the paramount object the necessity of making one's conscience fit for God's sight.

The way to keep that conscience clear is, paradoxically, to make its workings readable, not only to God, but also to other readers: the Christian woman's self-examination, conducted through her text, externally expresses what would otherwise remain hidden from all eyes but God's, the subject's heart and mind. While the interpersonal and the political fall beyond the circumscribed area of what the religious woman writer can represent, the most personal experience—the writer's relation to God—is made legible in her text. Reversing the logic of inside and outside, private and public, spiritual autobiography makes what is ostensibly most private, the inner self, the substance of the public representation.

As Carol Edkins's essay on eighteenth-century American women's spiritual autobiographies establishes, the religious woman can publicly represent this individual, but not unique, experience because her readers understand the conventions of religious discourse: the shared values held by autobiographer and readers "[create] a symbolic bonding with the group" such that her exemplary spiritual progress can be read and imitated by others.[42] Spiritual autobiography, then, not only permits but demands of its writers an excruciatingly thorough self-inquisition, and particularly on the issue of writing itself. For those who produce literature and self-representations are responsible not only to God, but also to other Christian readers, as a crisis of authorship reported in Tonna's text illustrates. Caught between the need to make a living and the demands of her first husband, who apparently tried to annex her earnings as his own even after they separated, Tonna must decide whether to continue writing her religious works under her own name, thereby forfeiting the income garnered by her pen, or to begin writing secular fiction under a pseudonym, which would disguise her identity and thus protect her income. She submits her case not to a court of law, but to God's will:

> The idea of hiring myself out to another master—to engage in the service of that world the friendship of which is enmity with God—to cause the Holy One of Israel to cease from before those whom by the pen I addressed—to refrain from setting forth Jesus Christ and Him crucified to a perishing world, and give the reins to an imagination ever prone to wander after folly and romance, but now subdued to a better rule—all this was so contrary to my views of Christian principle that, after much earnest prayer to God, I decided rather to work gratuitously in the good cause, trusting to him who knew all my necessity, than to entangle myself with things on which I could not ask a blessing. (p. 190)

To serve "another master"—the world or Mammon—is no option at all, since it is only her dissemination of God's word "to a perishing world" that authorizes her writing in the first place; by prayerful, conscientious self-examination, she arrives at the correct spiritual and moral decision. Moreover, to write for the secular world would entail a personal fall as well: by losing the audience of converts and believers already constituted for her, by "[giving] the reins to an imagination ever prone to wander after folly and romance," and thus undoing the labor to submit all human desires "to a better rule" which the autobiography records in painstaking detail, she would feed her body while starving her soul and the souls of others.

Again we see that writing must come under God's rule, but we see as well the way in which Tonna conceptualizes her self, God-given but marred by "indwelling sin" (p. 29), as a battleground between opposing forces of good and evil, strictly defined as the sacred and the secular. Her duty, then, is to overrule the depravity of the self, including the innate tendency of the imagination to focus on vain and worldly things, by subjecting it to the intense scrutiny of God's light, and her readers' eyes, and by keeping careful watch over herself. In Schimmelpenninck's extended metaphor, which nicely illustrates the spatial relation between inside and outside and the permeable barrier which separates them, the self is a tabernacle and "an efficient company of porters and door-keepers should guard every gate of access into the temple" (1:65). Only a constant self-surveillance can ensure that one's soul and one's writing will not be invaded by God's enemies, but that policing of the temple only restricts access; it does not prevent the autobiographer from representing the inner sanctuary. Because these exemplary texts offer models of female adolescent development and adult maturity for the Christian girl and woman, models not reserved for the few who would be writers, but for the many who will be daughters, wives, and mothers, they must instruct their readers in the way of Christian conscience. In order to be an exemplar to others, the religious autobiographer must first be a pattern to herself.

Domesticating Literature

Within the context of the literary marketplace, by contrast, the woman writer can never be an exemplary figure, for the true womanly ideal as configured by patriarchal ideology requires silent knowledge and respectful submission. "My idea of a perfect woman is of one who can write but won't," George Henry Lewes comments sardonically in 1850; one "who knows all the authors know and a great deal more; who can appreciate my genius and not spoil my market."[43] Mary Russell Mitford portrays her ideal woman in similar terms:

> The very happiest position that a woman of great talent can occupy in our high civilisation, is that of living a beloved and distinguished member of the best literary society . . . repaying all that she receives by a keen and willing sympathy; cultivating to perfection the social faculty; but abstaining from the wider field of authorship, even while she throws out here and there such choice and chosen bits as prove that nothing but disinclination to enter the arena debars her from winning the prize.[44]

The ideal woman Lewes and Mitford construct is the amateur *par excellence*: she provides the still center of the domestic sphere, defined less by what she produces than by what she reproduces—the cultured, leisured middle-class existence that approximates the anachronistic aristocratic ideal of unproductive gentility. As already noted, the secular model for professional authorship founds male artistry on female subordination: the ideal woman is confined to the home, where she carries out the unpaid labor of biological and cultural reproduction. Yet the religious woman who writes, whether or not she does so, as Mitford did, from financial necessity, makes up for what she might appear to lack in perfect womanhood by widening that domestic circle to spread what she can offer—moral Christian values—through a literary medium. She uses literature itself as her means of reproducing and exchanging domestic virtues.

Her own self-examination and knowledge of character license this use of literature. For all those middle-class women invested with the responsibility for the moral life of children (and even of adult men), interrogating the self is particularly crucial, since women mold and shape the character of all who inhabit the private sphere; as Judith Rowbotham remarks, "Mothers and elder sisters were expected to pass the benefits of their Christian experience on to all members of their household, regardless of sex or rank" (p. 71). For women who write, self-examination is even more important. By writing and publishing, and thereby extending their influence over like-minded middle- and working-class Christians, they could as easily become forces for evil as for good, particularly since their positions make them so much more susceptible to the "temptations" and "mortification" of the public sphere. In order properly to mold the character of others, their own characters must be scrutinized, continually interrogated for signs of moral and doctrinal failure. Examining the self throughout one's life—in letters, journals, and, as one's earthly life draws to its close, autobiography—thus maintains the fiction of authority that enables these women writers to begin writing in the first place. God's sanction allows them to write, and to write the self is to test and retest the validity of that sanction.

Knowledge of self and others is indeed precisely what spiritual autobiographers trade on in the marketplace. Like middle-class women novelists at mid-century, these women are presumed to know character best and encouraged to confine their attention to it, especially to female character. They believe themselves to have the best vantage point on character because of their connection with domesticity: it is "in the private lives of the children of God," as Sherwood puts it, "that we are enabled best to discern the wonderful beauty of the Divine influence . . . in the most private intercourse with the humblest and feeblest persons . . . [that] we find the best and most lively exhibitions of the Christian graces" (p. 427). Women are the purveyors of character, but also its creators, shapers, and best exemplars. Like Sarah Ellis, who conceived the influence of a woman's "individual character" as "operating upon those more immediately around her, but by no means ceasing there; for each of her domestics, each of her relatives, and each of her familiar friends, will in their turn become the centre of another circle," Sherwood sees developing and forming individual character as woman's special province.[45]

Middle-class women's school for producing personality is the home, the realm of affective ties which is ideologically counterposed to the heartless world; the Christian home, in Nancy Armstrong's words, "[detaches] itself from the political world and [provides] the complement and antidote to it" (p. 48) as the place where private virtue arms family members against public vice. Endowed with the responsibility for molding moral character through their writing as an extension of their private roles, private-sphere writers must protect themselves from "the danger of celebrity" (Sherwood, p. 509) and avoid all traffic with the public world; their sphere is located on the inside, in the home and the heart, and their place is at the center. By eliminating everything external to the domestic, they both accede to and reinforce the limits on the range of possible discourse, and so establish their right to instruct their audience within their own realm, in the formation of everyday private-sphere virtues.

Religious autobiographers clearly see literature's role in forming these virtues as central. Tonna, Sewell, and Sherwood all assume that their writing advances "the spiritual good of the people," and they also assume that secular literature, which Schimmelpenninck calls "pestilential" and of "evil influence" (1:124), does the devil's work in the world. These women thus construct their writing as one of their womanly duties: by disseminating the light of truth and salvation, they push back the powers of darkness. And middle-class women may carry out this duty in print along the same lines as they do in their homes and in their personal relations with others. Putting the values of the domestic into a public form for public circulation, spiritual woman writers project what they represent (which is equivalent to who they are) into books, tracts, or self-representing texts, which pass through the public world en route to other middle-class homes. To adopt Ellis's terms, exemplary women's texts spawn other domestic circles, other moral centers; that task, however, is not accomplished by women's "[entering] the arena," or "the wider field of authorship," but rather through reconstituting literature, and the scene of reading, as a private-sphere activity—religious women do not go out, but literature comes in. Redefined as a private agent of private values, the religious woman's work exemplifies the powerful moralizing force of private femininity, which textually combats the influence of secular novels, those "gin-palaces of the mind," in Schimmelpenninck's words, and "all that stimulates unproductive sensibilities" (1:131). By making literary work part of a domestic calling, religious women practically redefine the ideological separation between public and private.

In appropriately circular fashion, Schimmelpenninck argues that women have both shaped and been shaped by literature, and that the mutual interchange has altered both agents in the process. Casting the history of literature from her youth to the time of writing as the history of its feminization, she asserts an identity between women's role and literature's purpose:

> The great increase of literary taste amongst women has wrought a wonderful change, not only in collections of books, but in their composition. Books were then written only for men; now they are written so that women can participate in them: and no man would think of forming a library in his house, without a thought that its volumes must be the companions of his wife and daughters in many a lonely hour, when their influence must sink into the heart, and tend to modify the taste and character. Thus, in literature, as in other things, and especially in domestic life, has the mercy of God bestowed on women the especial and distinguishing blessing of upholding the moral and religious influence, that spirit of truth and love by which man can alone be redeemed from the fall she brought upon him.   (1:125)

Women's education in the principles of "literary taste" changes the structure of the domestic library, the physical locus for reading, and alters how each of its constituent parts, each book, is composed: the fact that more women read requires the production of books that will allow "feminine participation" in them. While the patriarch still determines the shape of the collection, he must choose more judiciously now than he did at some earlier point in time when books were "written only for men," for books are, anthropomorphically, "companions" for women, capable—as women in particular are—of molding human lives. "Their influence must sink into the heart," the innermost center of the reading subject, "and tend to modify the taste and character."

Books become, in short, like women, moral agents whose influence shapes the interior life of their readers. And in shaping readers, books also prepare women to become writers who will send back into the world the lessons they have learned from reading the primers of the heart. Schimmelpenninck projects feminine moral force into a material object that can save all readers—and the woman writer—from the consequences of the first woman's sin, the desire for knowledge, for if the world fell through Eve's weakness, then it can only be "redeemed" through her stronger daughters' labor as readers and writers: Adam's curse is women's "especial and distinguishing blessing."[46] And literature shapes the character of its readers within the confines of the gentleman's private library as women themselves do in their private roles as wives and mothers; it acts as an agent of that "moral and religious influence" which few men, because of their role as public beings, can supply.[47] Thus the religious woman writer need never even leave the home to do her work, which is spatially, spiritually, and socially centered in her father's house.

In the moral economy of the middle-class Christian Victorian household, domestic women produce and reproduce the spiritual food necessary for the whole family's consumption: in its self-sufficiency and autonomy from the public world that surrounds it, woman's sphere appears to constitute itself as the realm that saves the fallen public world from its own sins. And so we see in these autobiographies that within a conservative ideological framework, writing need not be constructed entirely as a threat to the feminine self, for writing itself is made private and feminine by women's influence, transposed from the public world to the private one. Nor does women's writing undermine the naturalness of the public/private split: the confluence of Christian and feminine norms produces a powerful ideology of the private sphere which simultaneously legitimates women's writing and puts it in the service of bourgeois hegemony. The exemplary autobiography elides the differences between lives and texts, realities and representations, and so presents writing women's moral role as a natural and appropriate one. When religious women represent their lives as exemplary texts, those texts also testify to the ideological importance of women writers' leading exemplary lives.

3

Literary Domesticity and Women Writers' Subjectivities

IN EXAMINING THE spiritual autobiographies, I have argued that authorship and womanhood can be ideologically and experientially compatible when both are aligned under the sign of religious authority. And I have suggested as well that no secular model for authorship can be drawn on or produced as equivalent justification for literary work. As will be demonstrated later in texts by Mary Howitt and Harriet Martineau, the demands of middle-class domesticity and the emphasis on womanhood as a vocation unto itself create splits within writing subjects who attempt to represent both domestic and literary labor as constitutive of their identities. In trying to do justice to their dual experiences of domesticity and literary production, these autobiographers find that writing and femininity—ideologically represented as mutually exclusive and subjectively experienced as in conflict—are not necessarily incompatible, but that negotiating the claims of both make them divided subjects.

As I continue in this chapter to look at how middle-class women writers experience and represent themselves as both women and workers, I explore the tensions that tend to disrupt both lives and texts as the conflicting claims of authorship and womanhood are balanced, evaluated, and adjudicated. Responses from George Eliot and Margaret Oliphant to Harriet Martineau's *Autobiography* (1877) provide useful points of entry into cultural expectations for autobiography and their gendered implications. And in analyzing memoirs by Anne Thackeray Ritchie, Mary Ward, and Oliphant, I mean to show how a change in the relationship between the private and public spheres at the end of the century enables these women to establish public autobiographical personae as their task becomes the representation of familial experience.

Writing, Authority, Femininity

In representing their first attempts to write, Mary Howitt (1799–1888) and Harriet Martineau (1802–76) differently enact the problem of establishing secular literary authority. Howitt's "seduction" by romantic fiction, as reported in her *Autobiography* (1889), is accomplished through a nursery maid; "captivated by her talk" of romance, Howitt writes "a letter about love and marriage at her dictation." In this, her first unoriginal composition foreshadows her later work as a "hack" writer: she begins writing by copying a copy, reproducing a love story that reproduces the conventions of the secular romance. She hides her "unholy letter" between the pages of a book by Madame Guyon (an exemplary French spiritual autobiographer) where her disapproving father finds it: "he himself had taught me to write, and this was the fruit of that knowledge." Like the "first parents" to whom she explicitly compares herself, she misuses the "knowledge" her father has graciously bestowed on her, putting it in the service of evil and betraying the implicit paternal command to use it for divine ends.[1] Unlike Schimmelpenninck, who redeems literature by employing it as a medium for correcting Eve's error, Howitt commits the sin of secularity against religious and patriarchal authority over and over again in her literary career. From the first, she frames her writing as conflicting with the womanly role her culture assigns her.

In her *Autobiography* (1877), Harriet Martineau also records her first try at composition and its far different result. She writes an essay, accepted by *The Monthly Repository*, in response to her younger brother's urging her, before he leaves for college, "to take refuge" from loneliness "in an attempt at authorship." Since "what James desired, I always did," "I wrote away . . . feeling mightily like a fool all the time." When to her surprise the story comes out in print, she tells no one about it, but one day her eldest brother "held out his hand for the new 'Repository'" and noticed her "confusion":

> "Harriet, what is the matter with you? I never knew you so slow to praise any thing before." I replied, in utter confusion,—"I never could baffle any body. The truth is, that paper is mine." He made no reply . . . then laid his hand on my shoulder, and said gravely (calling me "dear" for the first time) "Now, dear, leave it to other women to make shirts and darn stockings; and do you devote yourself to this." I went home in a sort of dream, so that the squares of the pavement seemed to float before my eyes. That evening made me an authoress.[2]

Martineau's aspirations, unlike Howitt's, receive a double sanction. One brother encourages her to write to relieve herself from loneliness; the other praises her work and encourages her to look beyond the usual sphere of womanly pursuits, which he implicitly defines as work different in kind from writing that she need not do. By separating writerly labor from domestic work, he makes her "an authoress." Unlike Howitt, then, Martineau experiences writing as a source of power, pleasure, and subjectivity that does not bring her into conflict with those whom she loves and honors, yet embracing writer's work seems nonetheless to separate her from woman's work.

In juxtaposing these two stories of literary origin, I find what appear to be two different destinies writ large. True to her initial position as copyist and imitator, Howitt went on to become the quintessential female "hack," turning out secular fictions and sentimental poetry for the popular press, all the time believing she had fallen from some high standard for both writing and femininity. Meanwhile, Martineau became the premier "authoress" of her day, achieving a public reputation in her lifetime that surpassed even Fanny Burney's in hers, "the first of her sex," as an 1890s advocate for women's professional work proudly if inaccurately claims, "to enter upon the routine every-day work of literature."[3] But that both stories are framed by encounters with masculine authority makes them more similar than different: even though the male figure in one case prohibits a certain kind of writing while those in the other allow it, each woman carries out her writing under that sign of subordination to an earthly—not a heavenly—father. And in both cases, the representative of masculine authority perceives writing as something other than a woman's proper role.

Each woman experiences her first attempt to write as mediated by men's power, and this may be explained in part by the fact that both women were born into religious families—Howitt's Quaker, Martineau's Unitarian—and spent a great part of their lives searching for spiritual centers to replace the ones they had abandoned.[4] Both needed something to believe in and some standard of belief: as Martineau writes of her adolescent years, "I even then felt something of the need which long after became all-powerful in me, of a clear distinction between the knowable and the unknowable,—of some available indication of an indisputable point of view, whence one's contemplation of human nature, as of everything else in the universe, should make its range" (1:106–107). While the felt conviction of the spiritual autobiographies discussed earlier provides a primary structure for their writers, the search for belief does not occupy an equally important place in these texts; their works have a spiritual dimension, but Martineau and Howitt are far more dedicated to recording the data of everyday secular experience, both literary and domestic, than to tracing the way of the soul. Yet as women who were not writing under the sign of the spiritual, each of them also lacked the sanction for authorship that Evangelical discourse provided. Unable to represent their writing as part and parcel of their feminine mission, both Howitt and Martineau represent authorship as in tension with femininity.

That they represent their struggles in somewhat different terms has much to do with the material differences between them, as women and as writers. Howitt left home to marry a man with literary and political aspirations and raised a family with him while also pursuing literary work, sometimes in collaboration with William, sometimes independently. Being a married woman and a mother as well as a writer subjected her to intense pressures, for her literary work was necessary to support the family even as it interfered with the unpaid work of domesticity. Conversely, Martineau never married and continued to live with her mother and an aunt, eventually settling in the Lake District as an independent woman for the last twenty-five years of her life. But despite her unmarried state, she, too, measured herself against a standard of ideal femininity.

In addition, their particular relationships to the marketplace also conditioned their different views of their work. Although Howitt was one of the best-selling poets of her day, "second in popularity only to [Felicia] Hemans by 1835, and to none by 1845" in the United States, recurring economic instability continually dogged her and her family.[5] By contrast, Martineau, whose family went bankrupt in the 1820s, achieved financial security on the basis of the proceeds from *Illustrations of Political Economy* (1832–34), which also made her reputation as a literary woman. Like the differences in their marital status and familial circumstances, their economic differences must be taken into account when considering the alternate emphases of their autobiographical texts, for while both self-representations express the conflict between middle-class femininity and literary work, the married "hack" presents that conflict differently from the way in which the single "authoress" does.

Mary Howitt: Marriage, Motherhood, Writing

In her autobiography, Howitt uses letters she wrote to her sister Anna over a sixty-year period, rather than the narrative proper, to set out the terms of her double vocation, as in this extract from a letter of 1836, in which she attempts to justify her work as womanly:

> I want to make thee, and more particularly dear mother, see, as I have done long, that I am not out of my line of duty in devoting myself so much to literary occupation. Just lately things were sadly against us. Dear William could not sleep at night. The days were dark and gloomy. Altogether I was quite at my wits' end. I turned over in my mind what I could do next, for, till William's "Rural Life" was finished, we had nothing available. Then I bethought myself of all those little verses and prose tales that for years I had written for the juvenile annuals. It seemed probable to me that I might turn them to account. . . . I am to have a hundred and fifty guineas for them. I must call this a signal interference of Providence for us. Is it not a cause of thankfulness, dearest sister, and have I not reason to feel that in thus writing I am fulfilling my duty?   (1:249–50)

For Howitt, literature is as much a business as a "duty," and a very necessary one: throughout her career, she often had to produce work very quickly so that her husband, engaged in such longer projects as *The Rural Life of England* (1838), could "in the study of Nature and the pursuit of general literature," in her deferential idiom, "laudably satisfy his intellect and his affections" (1:252). Howitt's work is thus a duty in that it helps provide for her family, but it also underwrites an unequal and gendered difference between her writerly identity and her husband's. For while Howitt identifies both William and herself as authors, only William's work must be uninterrupted, sustained over time as his proper occupation; she fulfills her wifely, maternal duty in making possible the conditions for his work, even though she, too, is a working writer. Thus while the writing Howitts practically collapse the boundary between the public world of work and the private one of domesticity by both being wage workers, an important aspect of the gender division of labor still prevails: his, she suggests, is the actual literary work of the family, while hers fills in the gap between what the family needs and what the male breadwinner earns. Howitt thus reproduces the split between artist and hack in gendered terms. Her turning out work for publication, or revising old texts to turn "to account," cannot be represented as valuable in its own right; while obviously necessary to the family economy, it is, like other women's work within the family, ancillary to the labor of the man.

Howitt constructs her hack writing as part of her wifely duty as a helpmeet, simultaneously legitimating it and undercutting it. She does not claim high literary status for her work; nor does she deconstruct the border between men's labor, which is intrinsically important, and women's labor, which is supplementary to men's. Thus she can represent her literary labor as a duty, as the religious autobiographers do, but only in terms of her domestic role as wife, mother, and family caretaker. While literary men argue for the public, professional status of their work, women writers of secular fiction lack the religious autobiographer's license to represent her work as serving the public good and can offer in its place only the "inferior" justification of material and maternal necessity.

Howitt envisions her life of writing not as at odds with her prescribed role, but rather as an extension of her domestic function within certain definite limits. Yet the double work load strains her relation to both literature and domesticity. The need to perform each kind of work leaves her no time for middle-class leisure, as she notes in a letter of 1843: "My week consists generally of seven working days, or, speaking more correctly, perhaps, because my employment is very much to my mind, my week is made up of seven active Sabbaths" (2:3). The life of the writer who is also a mother and a wife is one long, continuous labor, sanctified because performed out of her dedication to sustaining the family, if not wholly satisfying in other terms. When her "employment" (which could potentially refer to either literary or domestic work) makes fullest use of her mind, Howitt portrays herself as content and fulfilled, but this cannot always be the case. Of her job as editor of an annual in 1838, she recalls that she "was not proud of the work" (2:22), betraying her internalization of the prevailing literary standard that branded the annuals, largely produced by and for women, as "a chaffy, frivolous, and unsatisfactory species of publication" (1:205–206). A letter of 1845 finds her entirely disenchanted with literary drudgery: "I seem to have done very little this year. I have translated nothing, written nothing of any length, yet I never in my life felt so completely occupied. Sometimes, indeed, I have been so sick of writing and of the sight of papers and books that I have had quite a loathing to them" (2:33). A few years later, she renews the complaint: "I have been very busy. Besides that, I am so deadened and stupefied often, that I can hardly rouse myself to get out of the regular jog-trot routine of the day. I sit down after breakfast and work, work, work; then when the usual stint is done, I only want to be quiet and sleep" (2:46).

Through these letters, which speak against the grain of the narrative line in which her literary work is invariably represented as stimulating and pleasurable, we hear another counterpoint to the professional text of literary men.

Howitt never discusses her high aims or disinterestedness or "services rendered to the State," but rather represents writing as labor, one labor among many in the life of a very overworked woman: "I have not only to do what I can," she writes in apology to her sister for not writing sooner, "but . . . I must also sew for the family" (2:48).[6] For Howitt, writing has none of the Romantic mystique that Barrett Browning assigns to it. She takes a rather more Carlylean attitude toward her work, as the paean to labor in one of her short stories, "Margaret von Ehrenberg, The Artist-Wife" (1853), suggests: "'the dreams of pleasant morn must give place to the sternness of labour and noontide. Let me work truly whilst it is day, toiling for my bread, spiritual and material, in the sweat of my brow.'"[7] Another passage from this story has the ring of the editor's description of Teufelsdröckh's life, but without any apparent irony, even as it also verbally echoes one of Howitt's justifications for her own work: "Days and nights ever were devoted to study and to daily bread-winning toil—for whatever she learned must be immediately turned to account: all was severely earnest—it was a life and death struggle" (p. 14).

Within the story, this last statement is literally so, for Margaret's mother dies despite her daughter's best efforts to keep her alive in a situation that precisely reverses an event from Howitt's own life, the death of her son:

> To-morrow I intend again to commence my regular avocations. Poor dear Claude!
> at this very moment I see the unfinished translation lying before me, which
> was broken off by his death. Alas! I could have shed burning tears over this.
> How often did he beg and pray of me to put aside my translation just for that
> one day, that I might sit by him and talk or read to him! I, never thinking
> how near his end was, said, "Oh no, I must go on yet a page or two." How
> little did I think that in a short time I should have leisure enough and to spare!
> (2:17–18)

In both the fictional and the autobiographical accounts, the work of writing, necessary as it may be, cannot be sufficient to human needs. And whereas the fictional Margaret ultimately has the consolations of art to support her through all her trials (including her desertion by a mercenary husband), Howitt herself has no such solace.

We can read this last passage as Howitt's self-critical confession of a failure in mothering, as a moment in which the conflicting demands of literary domesticity reveal themselves: she must return to the hack work that helps to feed her children even though it severely limits the time she has at her disposal to mother them. Howitt represents perfectly the contrary pulls of her position as domestic woman and writer in her description of where and how she writes:

> I am obliged to do my writing in the dining-room, and thus I am exposed to
> constant interruption. But even this has its bright side, because I can bear
> interruptions better than either William or Anna Mary [her daughter, also a
> writer]. It would drive them mad; the poor mother of a family learns to be
> patient; that is one comfort.   (2:46).

"Exposed to constant interruption" while at work, interruptions from which she selflessly protects both husband and daughter, Howitt subordinates her writing to her woman's role, which is itself defined as subordination to the needs of others.[8] And her selflessness makes her simultaneously central and marginal to the household in physical, emotional, and economic terms. She is the mediatrix of any number of relationships, and this mediation defines her position in relation to others: defining herself as a unitary subject is not an option, because the discontinuity of her experience, as the formal mix of letters and narration illustrate, is always apparent to her.

Harriet Martineau: Engendering Authorship

By contrast, Martineau's representation of herself as a writing woman posits a unity of experience, which she attributes to being unmarried, and thus immune from being interrupted in her work:

> I have ever been thankful to be alone. My strong will . . . makes me fit only to live alone; and my taste and liking are for living alone. The older I have grown, the more serious and irremediable have seemed to me the evils and disadvantages of married life, as it exists among us at this time: and I am provided with what it is the bane of single life in ordinary cases to want— substantial, laborious and serious occupation. . . . My work and I have been fitted to each other, as is proved by the success of my work and my own happiness in it. The simplicity and independence of this vocation first suited my infirm and ill-developed nature, and then sufficed for my needs, together with family ties and domestic duties, such as I have been blessed with, and as every woman's heart requires.   (1:133)

Being "alone" secures Martineau from the demands to which Howitt is always subject, and it enables her to carry out "substantial, laborious and serious occupation," an opportunity that Howitt is denied. It also allows her, I would suggest, to represent her literary labor in terms usually reserved for men's work, to appropriate them for her own uses against the stereotype of women's writing as "chaffy, frivolous, and unsatisfactory": since she must have a "vocation," and does not fulfill the ordinary one of marriage and motherhood, she adopts a masculinist literary stance. But taking up this "vocation" and its idiom does not cancel out the power of the feminine model, for Martineau accepts that "family ties and domestic duties" (although not necessarily marriage) are what "every woman's heart requires" even as she presents herself as unsuited by her "infirm and ill-developed nature" to meet those duties in the way the "common woman" would. Despite her assertive defiance of feminine conventions, then, Martineau continues to measure herself against the normative middle-class standard of women's sphere, and finds herself wanting; the infirmities of her nature make her implicitly unwomanly, not only in the eyes of the world, but also in her reading of herself. As Sidonie Smith notes, "The other story of [Martineau's] life, the muted drama of repression, disrupts the evolutionary line of 'masculine' identity."[9] Martineau's identity as a literary woman is thus, like Howitt's, predicated on a radical discontinuity, for to maintain coherence between fictions of authorship and what Adrienne Rich might call "compulsory femininity" presents a series of problems.[10]

Martineau's transgression of gendered categories certainly did not go unremarked in her own time. *Fraser's* wielded its satirical pen against her in its "Gallery of Literary Characters" for November 1833, providing a visual illustration of the literary woman at home, feet on the fender, inkwell at hand, with a witch's feline familiar arching over her shoulder. The accompanying text proposes that "her countenance, figure, posture, and occupation," as represented in the illustration, make it "no great wonder that the lady should be pro-Malthusian"; given how she looks, no sensible or sensitive man would be "likely to attempt the seduction of the fair philosopher from the doctrines of no-population."[11] "Doomed to wither in the cold approbation of the political economists" (p. 576), Martineau is one of the originals for the "redundant woman," a category W. R. Greg would later create to embrace all superfluous—because unmarried—ladies.[12] Similarly, the *Quarterly Review* pulls no punches in its criticism: the tales are bad, but the author is far worse. "A *woman* who thinks childbearing a *crime against society!* An *unmarried woman* who declaims against *marriage!!*" is not far from being a monster.[13] In taking political economy as her topic, and particularly in daring to defend Malthusian principles of population control, Martineau becomes, as a misogynist of the 1790s had termed Mary Wollstonecraft, an "unsex'd female."[14] In Martineau's reception, then, we see the realization of Sherwood's and Tonna's worst fears about feminine authorship.

What misogynist contemporaries abhorred, twentieth-century feminists also find perplexing, if for different reasons. As Margaret Walters puts it, grounding her critique in her antipathy for the "impassable division" Martineau sets up between masculine reason and feminine passion, "Martineau saw her career as a writer in terms of a masculine choice, a masculine persona"; Valerie Sanders, more sympathetic than Walters to her subject, also notes that Martineau's "lifelong double-vision as a feminist" created a fixed perspective from which she could "[commend] only exceptional women who attained distinction without deviating from the accepted household norm, or losing their rationality."[15] Feminists have criticized Martineau, then, for uncritically internalizing the prevailing constructions for femininity and masculinity; although she herself escaped them as an "exceptional woman," she continued to support their validity and to measure other women's behavior against them. Her lack of support for other women makes her unwomanly.

The extent to which the twentieth-century critique repeats the terms of the early Victorian one should be clear: both assume certain standards for what constitutes appropriate feminine (or feminist) and masculine behavior and make their arguments on those grounds. Those standards are so deeply ingrained ideologically, as they were for Martineau, that moving beyond them seems impossible. Yet Martineau's "double-vision" not only gives her a bifurcated perspective on femininity, but also enables her to see through some of the blinds and fictions about literature and literary production that Howitt, by contrast, takes wholly for granted. Although she does indeed see her career as "a masculine choice," Martineau never loses her sense of that choice as designated so by cultural authority; her distance from that persona often enables her to define and represent herself in partial opposition to it.

Martineau depicts her professional beginnings as a fortunate fall into the necessity of labor which frees her from the stifling constrictions of the ladylike. When the last remnants of her family's capital are lost, she experiences it not as tragedy, but as liberation: "In a very short time, my two sisters at home and I began to feel the blessing of a wholly new freedom. I, who had been obliged to write before breakfast, or in some private way, had henceforth liberty to do my own work in my own way; for we had lost our gentility" (1:142). When she gets a job reviewing for Fox's *Monthly Repository*, she gains "literary discipline" under an experienced editor and money that "would buy my clothes. So to work I went, with needle and pen" (1:145). Defining her goals as "usefulness" and "independence" (1:171), she struggles with her writing, "yet I was very happy. The deep-felt sense of progress and expansion was delightful; and so was the exertion of all my faculties; and, not least, that of will to overcome my obstructions, and force my way to that power of public speech of which I believed myself more or less worthy" (1:147). In her era, of course, these are all, by definition, "masculine" aspirations, ones that Wordsworth and Carlyle would have shared, goals predicated on individualistic values that set the terms for success. And Martineau does not question these values and goals; she merely sets about meeting them.

Her way of meeting them, however, is not Wordsworth's or Carlyle's. With no investment in fictions of genius or inspiration, and with little tolerance for the critics who "warned [her] against 'excitement' " (1:188) as a danger to the psychological and emotional welfare of the woman writer, Martineau deconstructs the Romantic opposition between literary labor and other kinds of work:

> enormous loss of strength, energy and time is occasioned by the way in which people go to work in literature, as if its labours were in all respects different from any other kind of toil. I am confident that intellectual industry and intellectual punctuality are as practicable as industry and punctuality in any other direction. I have seen vast misery of conscience and temper arise from the irresolution and delay caused by waiting for congenial moods, favourable circumstances, and so forth. . . . I can speak, after long experience, without any doubt on this matter. I have suffered, like other writers, from indolence, irresolution, distaste to my work, absence of "inspiration," and all that: but I have also found that sitting down, however reluctantly, with the pen in my hand, I have never worked for one quarter of an hour without finding myself in full train.   (1:189–90)

The male writer, who must justify his decision to write against the other possibilities open to him, finds that the agonistic mode enables him to represent his struggle as an interior battle that he fights with himself; for Martineau, whose "vocation" is based as much on necessity as on inclination and who is not free to choose among numerous different kinds of work, there is no need to fight that particular battle. To the woman writer, who must "force [her] way to that power of public speech," hesitation, delay, and deferral all look like self-indulgence. Without devaluing her own work, she places it in the context of other kinds of labor—sewing, for example, seems as pleasurable to Martineau as writing—and thus demystifies it.

While Martineau takes her work quite seriously, then, she does not represent herself as ennobled by it. Instead, her "conception of the life of the literary adventurer as a vocation" reworks Lewes's antagonism to literary "speculators" by positing a distinction between two kinds of writers. "One has something to say which presses for utterance, and is uttered at length without a view to future fortunes"; "the other has a sort of general inclination toward literature, without any specific need of utterance, and a very definite desire for the honours and rewards of the literary career" (1:422). While she clearly classes herself with the former, and seems to find the latter contemptible, as Lewes would, her concept of herself and of all writers as "adventurers" suggests her willingness to dare saying that "which presses for utterance." It is this distinction, rather than a more rarefied discourse on the professional ethos and the public function of literature, that Martineau upholds in refusing to accept a pension offered to her during a long illness and that leads her to condemn "speculating publishers" who "try to make grasping authors, and to convert the serious function of authorship into a gambling match" (2:100).

Seeking independence both from her family and from the constraints under which even the honorable "literary adventurer" labors, Martineau simultaneously plays the game and attempts to change the rules in her own interest, and in the interests of other women. Writing about an offer to edit a new journal in 1838 (a post she turned down at the request of her brother James in a dispute that may have contributed to their subsequent estrangement), she uncharacteristically goes to her journal for a record of her response to the proposal:

> "It is an awful choice before me! Such facilities for usefulness and activity of knowledge; such certain toil and bondage; such risk of failure and descent from my position! The realities of life press upon me now. If I do this, I must brace myself to do and suffer like a man. No more waywardness, precipitation, and reliance on allowance from others! Undertaking a man's duty, I must brave a man's fate. . . . The possibility is open before me of showing what a periodical with a perfect temper may be: . . . also, of setting women forward at once into the rank of men of business. But the hazards are great." (2:110)

As Nancy K. Miller has written of Daniel Stern, "An exceptional woman, by virtue of that exceptionality, becomes subject to a double constraint: masculine responsibilities and feminine sensitivity"; "to do and suffer like a man," Martineau must put away feminine weakness, indecision, and dependency, and herself demonstrate "a perfect temper."[16] Martineau's afterthought about advancing women's claims is just that, but significant nonetheless, for it precisely illustrates the burden of the "exceptional woman" in a man's world. In playing a game on masculine terms, she comes in some way to represent her entire sex; her task is to prove that women have the capacity to learn the rules and play by them. To show herself as masculine will, paradoxically, reveal the strengths of femininity as well, and so expose the arbitrariness of gender distinctions. And that Martineau should represent this in her autobiography by abandoning narrative and opting instead for the "private" testimony that her journal provides nicely encapsulates the strategy for self-representation that both she and Howitt adopt: in their texts, as in their lives, they work toward combining the public and the private facets of their experiences, the literary and the domestic, to represent the doubleness of their perspectives and their positions.

Truth, Fiction, and Silence in Autobiography

Not published until 1877, twenty-two years after Martineau had finished writing it at breakneck speed in false anticipation of approaching death, the *Autobiography* provoked a harsh review from Margaret Oliphant, who was later to write a very different autobiography of her own (discussed in the final section of this chapter). Oliphant's attack includes a Fraserian suggestion that Martineau's lack of physical beauty "[affected] both her character and habits of thought" (negatively, one presumes) and an overall judgment on her character: "She was a very sensible woman, yet not very much of a woman at all."[17] Directing her criticism as much at the person as at the text representing the person, Oliphant does not construct a boundary between the two, as twentieth-century academic readers tend to do even in considering an autobiography. Instead, she assumes transparency between writer and text, and deems both guilty of failing to meet Victorian standards for true womanhood. And as her judgment on the character of the person writing shades into a judgment on the text, Oliphant may mark any textual deviation from the implied model for self-representation as a sign of deviance in the person as well; both the text and the life can then be dismissed in a single gesture.

Oliphant grounds her attack on the woman and the text in the allegation that Martineau has offended against "good taste, as well as against all family loyalty and the needful and graceful restraints of private life" (p. 478) in revealing the faults and foibles of the Martineau clan to public view.[18] Such candor, she implies, whether or not it has a basis in fact, is unseemly, particularly when the autobiographer has been a citizen of the world and her victims private beings: "There is no meaner and more unpardonable social crime, especially when the persons thus assailed are picked out from the gentle obscurity of private life, and have neither public record nor well-known history to be brought forth in their favour; and worst of all when the assailant has all the intimacy of family knowledge and that embittered recollection which tenacious memories preserve of petty wrong" (pp. 472–73).[19] Exposing one's private grievances to public view is thus one of the worst autobiographical vices Oliphant can imagine. It breaches the implicit rules for appropriate behavior and ignores the hold that the "needful and graceful restraints of private life" should have over everyone, even—or especially?—over a "public" woman. Martineau is guilty, in other words, of a failure in the tact so prized by the spiritual autobiographers when she disregards the precepts of private-sphere morality.

Oliphant's vitriol seems out of all proportion when we recognize that Martineau's text remains silent about a major family contretemps, her estrangement from her brother. While Martineau does not gloss over her ambivalence toward her mother or her dislike for some of her more illustrious contemporaries, she was remarkably respectful of those "needful and graceful restraints" in dealing with brother James's very public condemnation: although he had published a scathing review of the work in which she made her definite break with Christian orthodoxy, *Letters on the Laws of Man's Nature and Development* (1851), she said nothing publicly about his criticism.[20] According to Oliphant's logic, the Martineaus' feud could have been represented in the autobiography because James himself had both a "public record" and "well-known history." He had initiated the controversy by publicizing it in his review; moreover, he survived his sister's death and thus would have had an opportunity to respond to whatever textual countercharges she might have made. But Martineau clearly saw it differently: her omission of any reference to her brother's attack suggests that she identified this experience as one that could not and should not be—for whatever reasons—publicly represented.

Another contemporary reader of the *Autobiography* makes a more measured critique than Oliphant's of Martineau's excessive candor, and even praises her domestic tact in the matter of James: "One regrets continually that she felt it necessary not only to tell of her intercourse with many more or less distinguished persons—which would have been quite pleasant to everybody—but also to pronounce upon their entire merits and demerits. . . . But I rejoiced profoundly in the conquest of right feeling which determined her to leave the great, sad breach with her once beloved brother in almost total silence."[21] Coming from George Eliot—whose "right feeling" dictated that she disguise "the great, sad breach" with her own brother under the cover of fiction in *The Mill on the Floss* (1860)—this judgment has the ring of cultural authority. If the autobiographer writes about her peers, she should do so with restraint and diplomacy; if she writes of her intimates and relatives, she must be careful not to disclose anything the least bit uncomplimentary, and certainly nothing downright personal or private. Eliot's criteria for what is acceptable in an autobiography, then, are fairly close to Oliphant's: both insist that Martineau has no business in representing potentially controversial private affairs in a public form. Autobiographers should reproduce the sociocultural split between the public and the domestic spheres even if in doing so they must perform their own oppression and repression.

While Martineau's willingness to speak out directly, even on matters that should be kept "private," resists the dogma that women's autobiographies should observe the decorums of private-sphere femininity, Oliphant and Eliot suggest that the norms that define and guarantee women's place in the private realm should also operate in exactly the same way when they present themselves publicly. The ideology of private familial experience on which they draw posits every middle-class woman as daughter, wife, mother; the three roles constitute a continuous series of prescribed behaviors, attitudes, and norms with which every middle-class woman should unproblematically identify—as of course neither Eliot nor Oliphant did in her own life. Any questioning of these roles tends to unsettle the divisions that structure Victorian culture by casting doubt on their naturalness. In failing to profess deep devotion to her mother, for example, Martineau not only transgresses the code of daughterly duty, but also implicitly threatens a system of values that keeps women in their place by continually reminding them that it is their only proper place.

Martineau's *Autobiography* instead calls attention to the ambiguities of its writer's position as a female figure at the intersection of the public and the private; it openly flouts convention by suggesting that the domestic order, like public life, is socially constructed rather than naturally ordained. And so the *Autobiography* reminds Oliphant and Eliot, on the one hand, that in their own experience as public women they run the risks Martineau takes merely by putting pen to paper. On the other, it serves to open up questions about one's relation to those prescribed roles and to other people, particularly family members, questions which have tremendous emotional and psychological implications.

Ironically enough, Martineau had herself already partially argued the Oliphant-Eliot case in the *Autobiography*, claiming the necessity of separating the personal from the public in its introduction. In explaining why she will forbid the posthumous publication of her private letters, however, she invokes "the sanction of the law, [which] reflects the principles of morals" (1:7), as granting her the right to privacy rather than basing her claim solely on the sanctity of relations in the private sphere. The distinction she makes, then, between her private letters and her public autobiography is that the letters constitute an interpersonal exchange with its own internal rules and laws; like the middle-class Victorian household, which is created as a separate realm by political authority, that epistolary exchange is not subject to public regulation or intervention. While the letters properly belong to the private sphere, the *Autobiography* was prepared expressly for public consumption. It is thus subject to another set of codes and norms for public discourse within which the autobiographer yet retains certain rights granted to all public figures. Martineau presupposes two separate spheres, with the public actively and visibly governed by legal and cultural authority, and the private governing itself with the state's unspoken blessing.[22] In her thinking, when women—by definition, private creatures—emerge into a public space of discourse and representation, they can no longer justify themselves by the norms of private domesticity, as religious autobiographers would. Martineau appropriates the status of citizen, which the law in fact denies to her, and justifies herself according to the logic of the liberal public sphere.

Martineau's morality, however, is not wholly disengaged from a domestic model, for she continues to respect the integrity of private life: the "privacy guaranteed by principles and feelings of honour" precludes complete exposure of self and others, a tenet also adhered to by the memoirists whom I will next consider. As an autobiographer, Martineau has a virtually unlimited stockpile of potentially usable material for her text, yet she will not put all of it into public circulation; while there is nothing intrinsically unrepresentable about "confidential talk" (1:5), she will not make it available for public consumption, will not sell it, for a different set of rules and norms govern interpersonal relationships within the private realm. Like Barrett Browning, Martineau believes that some part of one's private experience should not be commodified.

The complex of responses surrounding the issue of publicizing the private suggests that Victorians conceptualize the autobiographical act in ways that our contemporary practice of the genre and our critical discourse on it do not. Oliphant and Eliot seem to understand self-representation as a dangerous literary act, far more dangerous than novel-writing because, theoretically at least, potentially far more self-revealing in that autobiography is supposed to take the self as its central subject. As Mary Poovey notes, an "objective text," such as a novel, can be a "mediator between self and public"; the avowedly "subjective" text the autobiographer composes may present itself, by contrast, as neither mediated nor mediating, as a window that opens directly onto the soul.[23] In theory, then, autobiographies should be transparent, as Oliphant assumes; in practice, however, they generate their own strategies of mediation.

In his essay on "The Lady Novelists," Lewes codifies the distinction between "writing out your actual experience in fiction" and "using fiction as a medium for obtruding your private history" on the public in a manner directly relevant to the Oliphant-Eliot position. The novelist must "use actual experience as his material," but not "in such form that the public will recognise it, and become, as it were, initiated into the private affairs of his characters."[24] In these terms, fiction must be both true and untrue to life: as in *The Mill on the Floss* or *David Copperfield*, the realist novel has its mainspring in experience and purports to represent "real life," but it is life altered in part (by "imagination") in the interests of preserving a certain relationship between public and private, a relationship that depends on disguise, or on some things not being said. Private experience can be represented in fiction, indeed must be, but only if it does not represent itself as such. In this sense, there are things that can be represented more tactfully in fiction than in autobiography because novelists are given more license—both to fictionalize and to tell the truth—than are autobiographers. If fiction should not "initiate" the public into "the private affairs" of characters whose experiences are drawn from or otherwise reproduce the author's own, then autobiography—which represents itself as the true history of its author's experience of self and others—has an even more problematic relation to the categories of "truth" and "experience."

A further complication arises in establishing the social context of the Victorian autobiographical act when we resituate the autobiographical text in the marketplace. Like the novel, the self-representing text is subject to circulation as a commodity: when one writes, prints, publishes, and markets an autobiography, one effectively sells oneself, one's own experience. Inserting oneself into that network of public circulation is as threatening in its way to Wordsworth and Carlyle as it is to Sherwood and Tonna. Those autobiographers, however, can report their experiences as a narrated history in which the "I" has an important, centering role, partly because of their different relation to commodity production, partly because literary and religious authority provide the necessary legitimation for self-representation. But with Martineau the exception to the rule, most secular woman autobiographers, who generally lack these two reference points, can master their anxiety about being circulated, read, and interpreted only by carefully shaping the personae they present and, more especially, by subordinating their histories of themselves to others' histories.

In this way, the middle-class woman writing autobiography both avoids self-exposure and attains a narrative stance closer to the fiction writer's: it is not her story she represents, but the story of others as she sees them. Underlying this strategy is a fundamental cynicism or pragmatism (depending on your point of view) about the way in which public representation operates: as Eliza Lynn Linton asks in *My Literary Life* (1899), "could, indeed, any public man's life be transacted without myths and masks?"[25] Probably not, if one conceives of the public sphere, as Oliphant and Linton do, as the realm of inauthenticity and compromise. In their terms, self-representation becomes its writer's last performance of a role she writes to protect herself against the deformations of publicity and celebrity, the final mask that will survive her, a mask that can shield the private individual from public view.

Some middle-class women writing autobiography minimize their risk by laying little or nothing on the line, suppressing what they construct as the private feminine self. And as we will see in Oliphant's own autobiographical practice, even the knowledge that what they write will be read by strangers need not prevent them from representing intimate experience. But whether the autobiographer represents herself indirectly through reference to a familial network and a literary-historical context largely emptied of affective content, as some of the memoirists I will next consider do, or directly and personally, as Oliphant unexpectedly does, the sense of negotiating the boundary between public and private is particularly strong in these late-century texts even as that boundary begins to show signs of being constituted in new terms.

Subjectivity in Memoir

Like Martineau, Camilla Crosland (1812–95) begins her text, *Landmarks of a Literary Life 1820–1892* (1893), by offering a rationale for writing and publishing it, but her justification depends less on a sense of her own importance as a literary woman than on her position as a historian of the everyday:

> Probably no observant person ever reaches even middle age without being conscious of those changes of manners and modes, which taking place apparently but slowly, do yet, in the course of a decade or two, bring about silent social revolutions. It is for this reason that the recollections of *any* truth-loving, truth-telling individual who has passed the allotted three-score years and ten of life, mixing in the society of a great metropolis, ought to be worth recording. Swiftly the seasons pass by; old men and women drop into their graves, taking with them memories of the past which would be precious to historians and artists; and the young spring up to mount with measured steps or rapid

strides to the world's high places, or to glide into the ranks of obscure workers.[26]

As one century passes into the next, the past as experienced by the individual
can and should be conserved for future generations; this documentary record,
Crosland asserts, plays a role in transmitting history from one age to another.

We see in this rationale for self-representation new concepts of history and
subjectivity. Unlike Carlyle and his contemporaries, who saw history as the
collective biography of great men, Crosland sees history happening in and through
all individuals, each of whom has some story to tell. As Valerie Sanders puts it
in describing this mode, "Everybody has 'recollections,' and even the humblest
have their share of interest."[27] By conferring on everyone the potential capacity to tell life stories from particular points of view, Crosland suggests that the
history of each individual, whether elite or obscure, has some value for readers.
Every person is presumed to possess a distinct subjectivity, a particular vantage
point depending on where that person stands in the world. Hence "the recollections of *any* truth-loving, truth-telling individual," and not only the story
of the great man or the exceptional woman, "ought to be worth recording."
Like Virginia Woolf, who wrote forty years later about her longing to read
"the lives of the obscure," Crosland invests the record of ordinary experience
with a historical value; she calls for life histories that will edify and represent
both high and low.

The "democratic" impulse at work here does not imply, however, that sociocultural differences among individual subjects have disappeared: some readers will reach "the world's high places," while others will join "the ranks of
obscure workers," just as the writer has occupied a particular place in the hierarchy. Gradually extending the legal and social status of the individual subject
to include all men without respect to class position, liberal ideology in the nineteenth century thus creates a nominal equality among men which masks struc-
tural inequality, for high and low remain operative categories. Within the genre
of autobiography, this means that all have access to writing the self, but that
their contributions are differentially valued. Autobiography thus becomes the
literary province of the great and the not-so-great alike: in an era in which
the ideology of liberal individualism provides—as it continues to provide for
the great many—the dominant model for middle-class subjectivity, the idea
that "the thoughts and opinions of one human being," as Mary Ward puts it,
"must always have an interest for some other human beings" makes the self-
representing text a monument to the triumph of bourgeois ideology.[28]

Those who write autobiography, however, have particular relations to the
liberal individualist model and those particularities depend in part on their positions in class and gender. By the end of the nineteenth century, middle-class
women, too, formed a social group, each member of which could legitimately
claim, as Crosland does, to be a participant-observer in and of public history.
With the rise of fictional and actual "New Women" liberated from the domestic
sphere and bent on taking their place in the public world—a place that had been
partially prepared for them by the women's movement of the previous forty

years—women were more able to position themselves textually as subjects in and of their histories. Middle-class women's autobiographies, then, underwent significant mutations once middle-class women's roles had been redefined to include possibilities for work outside the home, as autobiographies by Beatrice Webb, Annie Besant, and Frances Power Cobbe all testify; however, the dominant mode of autobiography among late Victorian literary women—the memoir—formally and thematically reflects the distinct historical experience of women as unequal and selfless subjects. In their practice as literary memoirists, Crosland and Eliza Lynn Linton (1822–98) exemplify this paradigm for autobiographical subjectivity.[29]

As shown in Oliphant's censure of Martineau and her text, generic expectations for autobiography were set in relation first, to conventions about what authors should and should not represent, and second, to a sense of autobiographies as commodities to be sold, bought, and consumed: that one's "recollections . . . ought to be worth recording" presupposes that they are also worth buying and reading. They find their value not only in the marketplace, where personalities, experiences, and self-representations are all accorded their price, but also in an emerging concept of literary history. Crosland herself takes great pains to fix the literary value that her story will have for her readers as a source for the edification of disinterested historians and, more centrally, as raw material that could be used, circulated, and reproduced in new literary productions. "I am endeavouring to depict the London life of the cultivated middle class as I remember it to have been from my early childhood," she notes in passing. "It would indeed be gratifying if I could think that my recollections could afford hints for character-drawing to any future novelist" (p. 17). Her text provides a handbook to the literary life of her day, glimpses of the everyday figures who populated contemporary coffee houses and ran the minor journals; she imagines her ideal reader as the producer of a new *Pendennis* or, better still, a new *New Grub Street*, novels which opened the "ordinary life" of the London hack to public view, putting it into discourse as the definitive representation of the literary underworld.

Crosland's recollections, then, derive their worth from their use value, from their potential utility for some writer yet-to-be. She devotes the body of her text to representing other writers, such relatively obscure figures from the not-yet-distant past as Dinah Mulock Craik, Samuel and Anna Hall, Mary Russell Mitford, and the Howitts, whose place in her text justifies its production. Crosland includes her cursory memories of Lady Blessington, Count d'Orsay, and the celebrated Gore House Circle, not because her interactions with those notables were of any particular significance to her life, but because those people's lives have come to achieve a certain public, cultural value to which her reminiscences contribute and from which her text draws some of its own value. By placing her experience in the context of a world that has vanished, a past in danger of being forgotten by a world in which she no longer plays an active part, Crosland shapes her story in accordance with what she presumes will be of widest general interest. Her textual life acquires its relevance, its value, from what use others can make of it. Yet it is important to recognize that she assigns it relevance and value in terms of a new market for the inside story on the private lives of public figures; her text, like the actresses' texts being written at the same moment and countless Hollywood memoirs written since, could accurately have been subtitled *Celebrities I Have Known.*

Other Victorian women writers also write memoir rather than more self-centered narratives, perhaps because it allows them, as it does Crosland, to tell their stories between the lines, to narrate their histories as part of a larger story; the memoir legitimates the telling of their own lives without demanding that they commit full disclosure. As Valerie Sanders writes of such texts, "The speaker is often no more than a reporter of outmoded practices, funny experiences, or impressions of the great and famous," as in Crosland's *Landmarks;* "her audience's attention is focused on the told, rather than on the teller" (*PL* p. 6). Writing the memoir can thus signify an utter unwillingness on the writer's behalf to speak of the self at all. The narrator must have a certain "name" (readers are unlikely to buy or read the recollections of someone they have never heard of) and convey an intimate look at celebrated public figures, but the memoir does not require that its narrator explicitly reveal herself.

For example, we can discern the textual presence of Eliza Lynn Linton only in the occasional aside; *My Literary Life* (1899) consists almost wholly of her impressions of Dickens, Thackeray, and Walter Savage Landor. She preserves a kind of anonymity in discourse wholly consonant with the vehemence of her response to her biographer's plea that she write her own "real" story: "My dear, I dare not! I know too much; I dare not!"[30] We know that this is her text solely by the fact that her name appears on the title page, and the text sells precisely because that name appears there. Because telling "too much" is construed as too daring, telling next to nothing is the safe course for a woman who seeks to remain outside the discourse she produces, the discourse that publicizes the private. But what she does reveal is sure to sell: as the friend and companion of some of the century's most eminent literati, and as a famous figure in her own right, Linton is well-qualified to satisfy readers whose desire for the inside story has already been fully constituted by the Victorian mass media.

With the massive Victorian expansion of the popular press, which generated a bountiful supply of "private" information on "public" figures, personality became a marketable commodity on a scale that had never before been approached. The success of a work such as Edmund Yates's *Celebrities at Home* (1877–79) (a three-volume collection of vignettes that portrays an assortment of literary, artistic, and political figures *en famille*), the astounding circulation figures for papers such as the *Illustrated London News* and *Tit-Bits,* the popularity of autobiography itself, all testify to the extraordinary transformation of the relation between the private individual and the public world. Publishers consciously created and exploited the mass appeal that "sketches from the life" held for Victorian reading audiences. As early as the 1850s, for example, Mitford had been pressured by her publisher into giving her text its misnomer (*Recollections of a Literary Life*) because Richard Bentley believed, probably with some justification, that the titular suggestion of autobiography would sell more copies than the more accurate and less glamorous titles *(Readings of Po-*

etry and *Recollections of Books)* that she preferred.[31] The power of the celebrated name, Mitford's or Linton's, thus translates directly into market value.

The memoir, then, becomes a popular form because it purports to offer an insider's perspective on a sphere to which the common reader ordinarily has little access. It can also be a peculiarly appropriate form for a woman because it allows her either to be silent about herself, as in the case of Crosland or Linton, or to narrate the self by indirection, as Anne Thackeray Ritchie (1837–1919) did. Her familial positioning as Thackeray's daughter and her own literary work make Ritchie an exemplary memoirist. Just as Linton's text rarely ventures to assert a textual "I," Ritchie's *Chapters from Some Unwritten Memoirs* (1895) suggests by its very title an absence of the putative autobiographer. Ritchie does not narrate her story by making herself the central character who stands out against the "background'" provided by her family and her era. She instead establishes her place in the text as the observer who takes all the different pieces of which lives are made and by writing makes them cohere. As Winifred Gerin states, "It is not that she seeks to put herself in the picture, rather that without her presence the picture would not exist."[32]

Ritchie relies on the assumption that her reading audience is familiar with the main outline of her father's life, for by 1895 at least three biographies of Thackery had already been published. Thus what she can contribute to knowledge of his character is a vision of his private self and a description of his roles as son, father, and friend. Even as she effaces herself, she maintains her position as narrating subject by suggesting the way in which her view is contingent, subjective, and partial, and made all the more valuable for those very qualities:

> As I write on it seems to me that my memory is a sort of Witches' Caldron, from which rise one by one these figures of the past, and they go by in turn and vanish one by one into the mist. . . . From my caldron rise many figures crowned and uncrowned, some of whom I have looked upon once perhaps, and then realized them in afterlife from a different point of view. Now, perhaps, looking back, one can tell their worth better than at the time; one knows which were the true companions, which were the teachers and spiritual pastors, which were but shadows after all.[33]

By asserting that these ghostly representations are neither definitive nor objective and that her point of view, far from being stable, has changed over time— what she writes now could not have been written ten years before and would be written differently ten years later—Ritchie preserves a kind of authority by giving up all pretense of being authoritative. Virginia Woolf's metaphor of light precisely captures this quality in representing her "Aunt Annie's" selfless subjectivity:

> She will be the unacknowledged source of much that remains in men's minds about the Victorian age. She will be the transparent medium through which we behold the dead. We shall see them lit up by her tender and radiant glow. . . . It would have pleased her well to claim no separate lot for herself but to be merged in the greater light of [Thackeray's] memory.[34]

The self Ritchie presents is a self in process and in relation who is revealed only in what she reveals about others.

Ritchie's autobiographical strategy, then, posits the subject as knowable only through its interpersonal interactions, as part of a larger familial and historical framework. Although she writes this text for readers who seek the "true" knowledge of character that can be located only in private experience and that can be, as Sherwood and Ellis claim, best understood only by the women who have made character their primary study, she resists representing that knowledge as independent of her personal, subjective perspective on it. What she knows is a function of her familial position, yet she does not portray herself as a centering subject of knowledge. Like Howitt, Ritchie represents herself as the mediatrix who represents familial relationships to a world eager to know; like Ward, she realizes "that not much detachment *is* possible" (Ward, p.3) when what one tells is the story of one's relation to the past and to others. But for women writing themselves into memoir, "detachment" is not a desirable position. The goal of Ritchie's text is to represent the web of relations that inhered between her life and her father's, and among their other relatives' and friends' lives, and not to tell a story in which she stands apart from the context that has produced and shaped her.

Family Histories: Public/Private, Euphoria/Dysphoria

Ritchie takes what is "private"—family life—and makes it "public," yet she does not represent her "inner life"; nor does she give her reader access to that sort of experience that twentieth-century readers have labeled as the "private," that is, the realm of the psychological. Neither does Mary Ward (1851–1920) in *A Writer's Recollections* (1918). Alan W. Bellringer complains that "it contains little of the usual autobiographical material on private stress"; "instead of inner drama . . . public information has priority over private problems."[35] In the differences between what he understands as the relationship between "private" and "public" and how Ward and Margaret Oliphant understand that relationship lie clues to the differences between their historical moment and our own. For what contemporary bourgeois criticism constitutes as the truly private takes place not in the drawing room, or even in the bedroom, but only within the expert analyst's office. The "private" inhabits the interior of the body as consciousness and unconsciousness, an "inner space" where all "inner dramas," including family psychodramas, are performed by and for an audience of one. But for Ward and Oliphant, the last two literary subjects I will consider, private consciousness is not conventional material for a public text. While both senses of "private"—the familial and the psychological—seem to be operative in their texts, only Oliphant, who began recording her experience without intending to publish it, supplies any explicit detail on "private problems." And what Ward represents as private life—a familial history—does not center on the "inner realm," but rather publicizes a certain version of domestic life.

The "public information" to which Bellringer refers is the history of the Arnolds, their friends, and their associates, the famous people they knew and the famous movements in which they took part, which occupy a central place in Ward's history of herself. While one critic dismisses the text as "a series of anecdotal portraits and descriptions" (*PL*, p. 6), Bellringer rightly asserts that one of the functions of this material is "to form a texture of allusion to an eminent, indeed dominant literary tradition to which, unobtrusively, [Ward] claims the right to belong" (p. 44). As a granddaughter of Thomas Arnold and one of "Uncle Matt's" favorite nieces, Ward is sensitive to the way in which their history shapes hers and how their eminence gives her a place in intellectual circles that, as the granddaughter and niece of "ordinary people," she would not have had. But Ward's text, as the "factual" feminine counterpart to *Tom Brown's Schooldays* (1857), also helps to ensure the preeminence of the Arnold family in Victorian cultural history. And her family history achieves the status of "public information" owing in part to the fact that such novels as Thomas Hughes's and such memoirs as her own were written and published for the marketplace; as Bellringer describes it, she establishes a "continuity in the network of intellectual families who sustain the 'history of ideas' " (p. 43). Chronicling the private record as she knows it, personally and intimately, Ward supplies an insider's view which comes partially to constitute the publicly known, historically accessible story.

As in Ritchie's case but with a more historically and culturally conscious bent, Ward shapes her recollections as a documentary account of an age; with a whole chapter on the origins of *Robert Elsmere* (1888), her first major success, and another on the circumstances surrounding its writing, publication, and enthusiastic reception, she places her own work in a context that stretches from her grandfather's era to the time of writing, in the midst of the Great War. Those who people her text—Charlotte Brontë, Harriet Martineau, George Eliot, Mark Pattison—pass through it, as the lesser lights do through Crosland's, making cameo appearances in the familiar roles they have taken on in the shared public imagination. It is thus not her own interior "drama" that Ward stages, but an external, historical, public one in which she plays her own part. From her privileged position, she conveys an intimate view of important personages, while always remaining "in role"—as granddaughter, niece, and wife, and as lady novelist as well. The memoir format, in other words, allows Ward to construct a text in which what we might think of as "private"—her family's story—can be made "public"; conversely, what is "public"—her work in literature—can be shown to have its genesis in her "private" experience.

In the meeting of the realms we see how these categories begin to lose their force once women can legitimately claim a place in the public sphere: while Ward continues to define herself in relation to the domestic, it is precisely that identification with the familial and the roles it assigns her that enables her public self-representation. Producing the private sphere for public consumption, Ward, like Ritchie, participates in the commodification of "ordinary" familial experience for a mass audience. The only "extraordinary" thing that separates middle-class readers from the celebrities they read about is the fact of celebrity itself, that mark of special talent and brilliance which only the fortunate few possess, that personal access to greatness which can bring Charlotte Brontë and Harriet Martineau into the Arnold family parlor for tea. As we will see in the next chapter, the celebrity autobiographer—whether writer or actress—necessarily lays claim to being both an exceptional woman and an ordinary one, albeit for slightly different ends.

Ward's text does not enact an "inner drama," for interiority is not, as a rule, what the middle-class woman writing secular autobiography demonstrates. While the religious autobiographer could and was indeed expected to represent the spiritual progress of the religious subject, for Ward, whose autobiographical authority also rests on the claim that she is bringing the private out into public, engaging in that kind of self-scrutiny in public would be wholly inappropriate and perhaps impossible. Instead she narrates a bourgeois success story: she is a famous novelist, a worthy Arnold, and a Victorian mother, the descendent of a great family who has proven herself capable of carrying on the tradition.

By contrast, the posthumously published *Autobiography* (1899) of Margaret Oliphant (1828–97) demonstrates the devastating consequences for the writing subject who, imagining her narrative in those same middle-class terms, finds that her life has not met them. Brought up by her mother "with the sense of belonging (by her side) to an old, chivalrous, impoverished race," Oliphant "never got rid of the prejudice" in favor of her family's honor, although she recognizes that "our branch of the Oliphants was [not] much to brag of."[36] The history of this family, unlike Ward's, consists of one disaster after another, and Oliphant writes at length, if sometimes obliquely, of the family misfortunes: the slow demise of her two brothers (one an alcoholic, the other a bankrupt), the early loss of her husband and two daughters, as well as of her love and ambition for her surviving sons, both whom died in the course of the ten or more years it took her to write the later sections of the *Autobiography* without fulfilling the destinies she had envisioned for them. Her family narrative ironically counters Ward's euphoric family text with a vision of what the other story looks like.

Oliphant's resignation is linked not only to family trouble, but also to her estimate of how little her extensive literary production will weigh in the balance of literary history. The financial "deficiencies" for which she hopes her autobiography will make up can be compensated, but her disappointments shadow her candid attempts to assess why she never reached the first rank of contemporary novelists in either sales or skill. Oliphant claims, as Sherwood and Martineau do, that she had "written because it gave me pleasure, because it came natural to me, because it was like talking or breathing" (p. 14). She cites as well "the big fact that it was necessary for me to work for my children," although that "was not the first motive" (p. 14), of which "one quite indisposed to be read" (p. 43) is similarly unwilling to write. When people ask her about her novelistic art, "I laugh inquiries off and say that it is my trade . . . by way of eluding the question which I have neither time nor wish to enter into" (p. 14).

The question Oliphant hesitates to answer, and even to ask, is if under more fortuitous circumstances she could have written a first-class novel, a novel worthy of George Eliot's pen.[37] The question cannot be resolved, of course, but in her description of her life Oliphant makes a point of showing that the cards were overwhelmingly stacked against it. Always for her, writing "was . . . subordinate to everything, to be pushed aside for any little necessity," such as attending to the children, or nursing her sick husband, or sewing a shirt, yet it "ran through everything" (p. 30). Like Howitt, another married writer with domestic duties to juggle, Oliphant "had no table even to myself, much less a room to work in" (p. 30), yet on her devolved all the financial responsibilities of a family that grew to include her older brother and his children.

Additional mouths to feed mean more books to turn out, and that extra burden effectively crushes her hope of creating a masterpiece:

> When my poor brother's family fell upon my hands . . . I remember that I said to myself, having then perhaps a little stirring of ambition, that I must make up my mind to think no more of that, and that to bring up the boys for the service of God was better than to write a fine novel, supposing even that it was in me to do so. . . . It seemed rather a fine thing to make that resolution (though in reality I had no choice); but now I think that if I had taken the other way, which seemed the less noble, it might have been better for all of us. I might have done better work. . . . Who can tell? I did with much labour what I thought the best, and there is only a might have been on the other side.   (p. 16)

Thinking out loud, reviewing the past, she tries to imagine another ending to her story; what I find interesting here, however, is how deeply Oliphant believes that the two alternatives—"a fine novel" or fine boys—are mutually exclusive. As she writes further on, unknowingly echoing Tonna, "one can't be two things or serve two masters": her devotion to her family rules out the "fervour and concentration" (p. 132) necessary to create art that would pass the test of time.[38] Accepting the placeless place in the literary world that both her sex and her economic position assign to her, she thus defines herself in its terms. Unlike Aurora Leigh, who "[put] down the woman's" instinct in her "[passion] to exalt / The artist's" (9. 647, 645–46), Oliphant finds herself writing a dysphoric life that has not satisfied either urge. Neither art nor family can provide her with the story she seeks.

Oliphant began writing her text not for an anonymous reading audience or as a public monument to her family, but for the eyes of the sons who predeceased her.[39] Because she began it as a private journal and later redefined it as a personal legacy to her boys, once she decided to publish it, the change in her intended audience demanded she "change the tone of this record" (p. 86) as well: "I used to feel that Cecco [her second son] would use his discretion,— that most likely he would not print any of this at all, for he did not like publicity, and would have thought his mother's story of her life sacred; but now everything is changed, and I am now going to try to remember more trivial things, the incidents that sometimes amuse me when I look back upon them" (p. 87). With a few pages, however, she questions her effort to write a popular memoir about "trivial things":

> How strange it is to me to write all this, with the effort of making light reading of it, and putting in anecdotes that will do to quote in the papers and make the

book sell! It is a sober narrative enough, heaven knows! and when I wrote it
for my Cecco to read it was all very different, but now that I am doing it
consciously for the public, with the aim (no evil aim) of leaving a little more
money, I feel all this to be so vulgar, so common, so unnecessary, as if I were
making pennyworths of myself. . . . I must try to begin again.   (pp. 95)

Conceptualizing the public in much the same way as Linton does, Oliphant is
repelled at the idea of selling her life—"so vulgar, so common"—and her response is mitigated only by the need to make "a little more money," the hack's
aim to which she has been dedicated throughout her literary career. She ear-
marks the proceeds from the *Autobiography* itself as payment for the debts she
will leave at her death, as "something to make up deficiencies when I am gone."[40]
But whatever value the text might come to possess for her publisher and her
estate, it has none for her, for there is no one still living who will be able to
read it rightly. "It is so strange to think that when I go it will be touched and
arranged by strange hands," she wrote; possibly uncertain that her relatives
would take on the duty of editing the text, she imagined that there would be
"no child of mine to read with tenderness, to hide some things, to cast perhaps
an interpretation of love upon others" (p. 99). Implicitly identifying her life
with her text, Oliphant (somewhat morbidly, to be sure) imagines herself going
unmourned, unloved, misread. What has been vitally important to her, her
domestic family life, is lost and what remains, the work of writing, is no longer
of much moment.

The ironies that shape Oliphant's life shape her text as well. With an ear
finely tuned to the voices of unknown readers who would probably have expected a very different text from someone who had sent forth nearly 100 novels
into the marketplace, she speaks her own sentence on the *Autobiography:* "I
need scarcely say that there was not much of what one might call a literary life
in all this" (p. 137). Even for middle-class women of the nineteenth century,
living "a literary life," in the sense that term might hold for Mill or Dickens
or Trollope, was almost impossible—and so, of course, was writing one. But as
middle-class women who worked for money, who spoke out publicly, and who
tried to represent the difficulties of doing so even as they sought a form and an
idiom that would enable them to represent themselves, these women autobiographers made the first rush at the invisible barriers that other workers, their
contemporaries and their descendents, would continue to struggle to break down.

4

"Artificial Natures": Class, Gender, and the Subjectivities of Victorian Actresses *

IN *Daniel Deronda* (1876), George Eliot's Alcharisi portrays her pursuit of a career on the stage as an escape from marriage and maternity into a world where she could be all she had dreamed of being: in the theater and out of it, she has lived "a myriad lives in one." That this way of evading the constraints of domesticity appeals to the "vulgar" Gwendolen as well underscores the cultural meaning of feminine theatricality: for some Victorian women novelists, as for many of their readers, the actress epitomizes the unconventional woman who enacts the roles that every woman, artist or not, desires to play.[1] One need only think of Lucy Snowe's ambivalent response to Vashti—in its mixture of fear and longing, its fascinated desire for this fictive Rachel's power and its anxious repudiation of it—to summon up a quintessentially middle-class feminine fantasy.[2] In the eyes of her audiences, the actress led a forbidden life, a life in which she could embody and represent an infinite range of possible subjectivities without being contained by any one of them.

The next chapter will further illuminate this aspect of the actress's cultural power, but this one seeks first to dislodge it in the interests of telling another story: by and large, the actresses considered here do not represent their own experiences along the lines of the middle-class novelistic model. Unlike Eliot's or Brontë's characters, and rather more like many of the writers whose autobiographies have already been analyzed, the three actresses studied in this chapter—Fanny Kemble, Madge Kendal, and Marie Bancroft—do not challenge the middle-class ideal of womanhood, but seek to perform it, onstage and off; indeed for Kemble, it is theatricality rather than domesticity that threatens the stability of the middle-class subjectivity to which she lays claim.

Kemble is somewhat exceptional in this regard, however, for most actresses of the period, and particularly those who achieved their professional success in the 1860s and 1870s, had no bourgeois homes to shape their desires; experiences formed Bancroft and Kendal, children of the theater and active performers

---

* The title quotation is from Frances Ann Kemble, *Records of Later Life* (New York, 1882), p. 378.

from a very young age, in ways altogether different from the average middle-class girl. For these two, the entry into middle-class values was not a naturalized process of development that began in the cradle, but part of their training as professionals, something they had to learn as young women in order to play the new roles, onstage and off, that they were called on to perform. Rather than reject the domestic, as Eliot's and Brontë's heroines do, they come to embrace it and to adopt its signs in representing themselves, as part of a specifically professional project. In tracing the changing status of the actress as part of the overall embourgeoisement of the Victorian theater, I argue that this very public adoption of middle-class values makes the actress a respectable public woman, and that Bancroft and Kendal internalize and reproduce these norms not only in their theatrical performances, but also in their autobiographical ones.

My argument thus runs counter to those that would highlight the subversive potential of the actress, much as earlier chapters have sought to undermine the notion that feminine authorship is essentially disruptive of fixed gendered realms of experience. As already demonstrated, those who write autobiography do not necessarily disturb the ideological distinction between the public, masculine world and the private, feminine sphere. The middle-class woman writer generally works from within, not against, patriarchal paradigms: the spiritual autobiographer exposes the inner workings of her soul with full confidence that she is divinely sanctioned to do so, while such writers as Ritchie and Ward represent private familial life for public consumption without exposing what they constitute as the truly private, such as the "subjective musings" that Beatrice Webb records at length in her diaries.[3] In neither case, however, does the representation of women's experience fundamentally alter the contours of gender; in both their lives and their texts, women writers usually remain within, and so help to reproduce, the boundaries of middle-class femininity. Although the parameters of what constitutes privacy and publicity undergo cultural redefinition as we move from Sherwood to Oliphant, just as they do in the sequence that will be traced over the course of the next two chapters, I see an intensification rather than a diminution over time of those norms that signal the textual presence of a properly constituted feminine subject.

Like women writers, actresses, too, work within naturalized, gendered conventions for theatrical and textual performance which increasingly conform to middle-class standards for domestic femininity. Although it may seem paradoxical to claim that Kendal and Bancroft come to achieve the middle-class status of the domestic woman through their public performances, I argue in this chapter that a larger cultural and economic hegemony—the professionalization movement of the Victorian theater—helps to produce this paradoxical effect, for the professionalizing theater takes bourgeois values as its standard at every level of theatrical life. How actresses define themselves on stage and in autobiography thus becomes contingent less on the "facts" of their private lives, and more on how well they can publicly imitate and reproduce the signs and attitudes that mark individuals as belonging to a certain class and gender.

While the actresses studied in this chapter represent domestic femininity for their publics, only Fanny Kemble reveals very much about her personal life. Those who achieve middle-class status through their theatrical work concentrate instead on giving factual accounts of their careers with little reference to who they are in private life, as if the public roles they play fully absorb their personal identities. In their autobiographies, the experience of theatrical representation shapes their representations of their experiences.

Fanny Kemble: Public Acting and Private Being

No woman was so clearly destined for the stage as Fanny Kemble (1809–93), and no one could have detested it more. Niece of Sarah Siddons and John Kemble, daughter of two other accomplished players, she made her debut in 1829, just shy of her twentieth birthday; with her formal preparation limited to three weeks of rehearsal, she took to the stage not by choice, but in order to save her family from financial ruin. She achieved, by all accounts, a spectacular success, not through her native talent (which Leigh Hunt, among others, considered negligible), but for the glamorous history and the promising youth she embodied as heir to a great theatrical tradition. She became a star and a celebrity:

> When I saw the shop-windows full of [Sir Thomas] Lawrence's sketch of me, and knew myself the subject of almost daily newspaper notices; when plates and saucers were brought to me with small figures of me as Juliet and Belvidera on them; and finally, when gentlemen showed me lovely buff-colored neck-handkerchiefs which they had bought, and which had, as I thought, pretty lilac-colored flowers all over them, which proved on nearer inspection to be minute copies of Lawrence's head of me, I not unnaturally, in the fullness of my inexperience, believed in my own success.[4]

Her image commodified and mass-produced, Kemble packed them in at Covent Garden, enabling her father to stave off impending disaster on the strength of her success.

What that success meant in larger terms was that Kemble's image was put into circulation, impressed not only on those in her immediate audience, but also on a wide range of goods distributed throughout a growing national consumer public. Commodifying the public woman's image was not a marketing invention of the nineteenth century; the *Pamela* craze of the 1740s had already largely anticipated it. Nor was it a practice considered suitable only to the actress's special status: Lillie Langtry, for example, was a fully commodified celebrity in the 1880s even before she took to the stage to earn a better living. And Langtry's contemporary, the spiritualist-activist Georgina Weldon, whose story has been retold by Judith Walkowitz, also "enjoyed the ephemeral status of the female celebrity, whose 'face' was her fortune but also a vehicle for the selling of other commodities.[5] Just as Langtry's or Weldon's visage invested an ordinary bar of Pears's soap with the aura of the extraordinary, Fanny Kemble's face made an everyday handkerchief a new kind of icon. This conjunction of the power of a singular personality, defined by the culture as unique, with even the pettiest object of everyday life helped to make Victorian actresses objects of widespread cultural significance.

That celebrity status also had an important effect on Kemble's vision of herself and on how she subsequently constituted herself in writing. Fifty years after her debut, Kemble describes the transformative impact of instant celebrity in *Records of a Girlhood* (1879), one of several autobiographical volumes she produced:

> It would be difficult to imagine anything more radical than the change which three weeks had made in the aspect of my whole life. From an insignificant school-girl, I had suddenly become an object of general public interest. I was a little lion in society, and the town talk of the day. Approbation, admiration, adulation, were showered upon me; every condition of my life had been altered, as by the wand of a fairy.   (p. 226)

Lifted out of the obscurity of private life and set down on a public stage, her every move "of general public interest," Kemble suddenly finds her experience radically altered: from being a private individual, she becomes a public figure. Each of her actions, whether publicly or privately taken, arouses the "interest" of her public audience. And as a public figure of fifty years' standing, Kemble takes her autobiography as the literary space in which she can reconfigure the history of her public life.

In her autobiography, Kemble emphasizes the objectively public events of her life; her stage debut, for example, is given the most narrative play of any life-event. She fills in the off-stage dimension of her first night by narrating the events that lead up to it, the small details of rehearsal and costuming, while also recording her emotions on finding herself in front of an audience for the first time. But Kemble excises personal events that properly belong to the private realm, such as the courtship that led up to her marriage and the events of the disastrous marriage itself, even from the contemporary letters that provide the core material of the text. The "private" information she relates is, like the view Mary Ward gives of the Arnold family, defined as such in relation to what she knows to be a matter of public record. She supplements that record by sketching the personality of the actress, the person to whom those things happened, while she does not write of what she understands as the truly private, that which takes place on a stage inaccessible to public view.

We can explain Kemble's reticence in terms of her primary identification with middle-class values and standards as expressed in antitheatrical terms. Her experience of celebrity and success could not alter her complete distaste for "an avocation which I never liked or honored" (p. 220), of which "every detail . . . from the preparations behind the scenes to the representations before the curtain, was more or less repugnant to me" (p. 191), an aversion so pronounced in *Records of a Girlhood* that some aficionados of the stage took offense at her remarks.[6] Although born into a theatrical family, Kemble had been raised a proper English lady: she attended boarding school on the Continent, devoted her free time to religious and philosophical speculation, and harbored literary aspirations that were partially fulfilled in the writing of two plays, one of which was produced with some success. Had she been left to her own devices, and had she found herself "willing to undergo the drudgery of writing for my bread," literature would have been her chosen profession, for as she notes in a contemporary letter, "my head and heart are engrossed with the idea of exercising and developing the literary talent which I think I possess" (p. 135). A ladylike literary life was what she wanted most for herself, but the decision was not hers to make, and she had to subordinate her desire to familial needs: "It is incumbent upon me to banish all selfish regrets about the surrender of my personal tastes and feelings, which must be sacrificed to real and useful results for myself and others" (pp. 289–90). Even in taking up an unladylike career, she found a wholly ladylike rationale for doing so; to follow her own inclinations would have been "selfish."

Kemble's hatred for the stage derives from her internalization of gendered norms for public behavior. Her objections to it center on her feeling that "a *business* which is incessant excitement and factitious emotion [is] unworthy of a man; a business which is public exhibition, unworthy of a woman" (p. 220). A man who publicly displays "factitious emotion" disturbs the decorums that define the English gentleman; a woman who exhibits herself on a public stage commits no less of a crime against propriety. As a theatrical term, "business" signifies the practices through which the actor and the actress produce their effects, and that "business" is what they exchange, in economic terms, for their means of subsistence. So performers do business in public, which makes Kemble's anxiety about putting her body on stage for an audience of strangers particularly acute: it is "the violence done . . . to womanly dignity and decorum in thus becoming the gaze of every eye and the theme of every tongue," and not "the acting itself," that she finds "disagreeable" (p. 432). Professing literature would not have demanded that exhibition, and even picture postcards and personalized souvenir "plates and saucers" only represent the body and are not the thing itself; making her person the text for public discourse is another story. Like Linton or Oliphant, Kemble defines the public world as the realm of inauthenticity and spectacle. She represents the theater as a calling antithetical to her sense of herself as a proper lady.

One successful Victorian woman novelist, Dinah Mulock Craik, articulated the difference between the writer and "the artiste" in terms that Kemble surely would have seconded. While women authors like Craik herself might "write shelvesful of books, and the errant children of our brain may be familiar half over the known world . . . we ourselves sit as quiet by our chimney-corner, live a life as simple and peaceful as any happy 'common woman' of them all." Craik's verbal echo from *Aurora Leigh* actually aligns the woman writer with the domestic woman in a way that the poem itself does not, and she employs that echo here in order to construct an even more radical difference between the domesticated writer and the public performer. For an artiste "needs to be constantly before the public, not only mentally, but physically: the general eye becomes familiar, not merely with her genius, but her corporeality." And this public dimension makes the artiste an unnatural woman who occupies "a position contrary to the instinctive something—call it reticence, modesty, shyness, what you will—which is inherent"—or should be—"in every one of Eve's daughters."[7] To be a public lady is, for Craik, as for Kemble, a contradiction in terms.

It would be too easy, I think, to dismiss Kemble's aversion to performance as just another instance in a long history of antitheatrical prejudice, although her attack clearly draws on that tradition.[8] We might dismiss it as well and as easily as exemplifying early Victorian prudery or, with more critical authority, as representing the cultural consolidation of the public and private spheres as separate and gendered. Taking the latter line, however, would force us to ignore the fact that it is not only women but also men whom Kemble sees as degraded by public performance, albeit for different reasons. What I would like to argue instead is that Kemble's characterization of theatrical "business" as "unworthy" a lady or a gentleman is primarily grounded in a middle-class concept of the self that locates subjectivity not in surface, but in depth; not in publicity, but in privacy; not in performing, but in imagining.

Remember that while the public display "was utterly distasteful" to Kemble's sense of womanly propriety, the *"acting* itself . . . dramatic personation, was not" (p. 191). Kemble's distinction between the theatrical and the dramatic hinges on her differentiation of public modes of representing the self from private ones. To the private and dramatic she assigns the higher value and the greater truth: it is a mode of expression that reveals the innermost thoughts and emotions of the actor as private utterance spoken only for the relief of the speaker. The dramatic, unlike the theatrical, allows the actress to make a role her own or, as it is more typically represented, to be "possessed" by it.

Kemble makes this distinction clear in an account of what she considered her finest moment on stage, practicing in Covent Garden before an audience of two. She reaches a dramatic pitch she could never again attain:

> Set down in the midst of twilight space, as it were, with only my father's voice coming to me from where he stood hardly distinguishable in the gloom, in those poetical utterances of pathetic passion I was seized with the spirit of the thing; my voice resounded through the great vault above and before me, and, completely carried away by the inspiration of the wonderful play, I acted Juliet as I do not believe I ever acted it again, for I had no visible Romeo, and no audience to thwart my imagination.   (p. 188)

In "a sort of frenzy of passion and entire self-forgetfulness" (p. 191), Kemble's sublime dramatic moment culminates in a loss of self which is, at the same time, an affirmation of self. Although the boundaries between who she is and the role she is playing temporarily blur, Kemble partially defines her subjectivity through this experience. By momentarily losing her sense of difference from that role in being "seized" by it, she recognizes her ontological difference from it as well as her capacity for being selves other than her own ordinary one. Significantly, Kemble has this sublime experience only in a relatively private performance in which she feels free to express herself without self-consciousness; under the actual conditions of the stage, actors and audience inevitably impinge on the dramatic reality she creates best in privacy. In short, her model is a Romantic one: Kemble defines the realm of free expression as that which must remain relatively internal and unseen, and she finds that invisible interiority wholly satisfying.

The opposition between public and private performance that Kemble makes is equivalent to the difference between acting and being: "Juliet . . . I act; but I feel as if I *were* Portia—and how I wish I were!" (p. 249). What one can be or could be, in one's own imagination, is "under very severe though imperceptible restraint" (p. 278) on stage, for the pre-written limits of the role, the necessity of public presentation, the boundaries of the body itself all combine to hem in the performer. Although more free than most to express some part of her interior life through the characters she represents in a public setting, even the actress must work under the everyday constraints of theatrical conventions. But for Kemble, who identifies as middle-class, those constraints are far more real than the ones she experiences in the private realm, where she feels privacy not as deprivation, but as freedom, freedom from being looked at.[9]

For Kemble, the dramatic is individual and solitary while she associates the theatrical with public spectacle and the rules of performance. The experience of acting publicly in the theater creates in Kemble precisely the opposite response to the "self-forgetfulness" described earlier; in the theater, her "natural" being must be put aside for the purposes of artifice. Participating in the theatricality of a staged performance makes Kemble acutely self-conscious of the facts of the performance itself, in all its minute physical details and all its distance from her reality, which she perceives as different from the reality that theater purports to recreate:

> The curious part of acting, to me, is the sort of double process which the mind carries on at once, the combined operation of one's faculties, so to speak, in diametrically opposite directions . . . while I was half dead with crying in the midst of the *real* grief, created by an entirely *unreal* cause, I perceived that my tears were falling like rain all over my silk dress and spoiling it. . . . In short, while the whole person appears to be merely following the mind in producing the desired effect and illusion upon the spectator, both the intellect and the senses are constantly engrossed in guarding against the smallest accidents that might militate against it.   (pp. 246–47)

The "double process" Kemble isolates as the peculiar difficulty of acting in public grows out of her struggle to appear natural by unnatural means in an artificial setting. In order to stage reality, the actress must undertake the most conscious and premeditated movements, disciplining the mind and the body to work together toward the end of "producing the desired effect and illusion" without giving away the unnatural means by which theatrical illusion is brought about.

Kemble's apprehension of the "double process" the actress or actor undergoes while on stage is widely shared among Victorians interested in the theater. Writing about the Alcharisi's demeanor during her first interview with Deronda, Eliot uses the phrase "double consciousness" to articulate the studied way in which this actress represents the emotions that neither Deronda nor Eliot's narrator can be sure she "really" feels. Writing a reply in 1888 to Diderot's influential eighteenth-century treatise on acting, the theater critic William Archer likewise found "the real paradox of acting" to be "the paradox of dual consciousness," and he perceives this doubleness not only in women, but also in men, who are similarly subject to the division of self from role that dramatic impersonation requires.[10] Yet Kemble dislikes public performance for reasons specific to her experience of class and gender. As we will see, actresses of a later period and another class experience, such as Madge Kendal and Marie Bancroft, are differently positioned from Kemble in relation to class standards for femininity; they perform publicly without representing the kind of anxiety about theatricality that Kemble demonstrates here, without recording any kind of discomfort over the "double process" that performance demands. Kemble, however, constantly asserts the primacy of the real life that takes place offstage—the life in which she is an ordinary middle-class daughter—over the fictions of the public theater, where her participation in a disreputable display threatens her sense of identity. The "double process" may be disconcerting to any actress or actor, yet even more so for one who construes the private sphere as her proper place.

For the actress, maintaining the realism of theatrical representation must always have priority over her offstage reality. But for Kemble, the difference between enacting an illusion for public consumption and the private consciousness of how that presentation is being produced makes her unreal to herself: she operates on two levels that she finds wholly incompatible. While Kemble's commentary seems to suggest that the dramatic mode proceeds on a far different principle from the theatrical—that without an audience or fellow actors, one's performance could be perfectly aligned with one's inner needs and motives—the social process of theater, and of representation itself, make the dramatic Romantic moment, and the authenticity that it promises, an impossible ideal for the actress.

The self-representation of a public woman in autobiography is no less a performance than anything she undertakes on stage, and no less a product of the "double process" that operates in any rhetorical act. Yet Kemble herself characteristically refuses artificially to shape an autobiographical self for public representation. Relying on contemporary letters rather than fashioning a narrative, she disingenuously attempts to evade the constraints of public performance; by substituting the supposed sincerity and verisimilitude of the epistolary for the artful reconstruction of the self as subject that a developmental autobiographical narrative demands, Kemble presents herself as textually constituted by and in her own private documentary records of the past. Yet the elisions she makes in the name of decorum and for the sake of middle-class respectability strongly suggest the determining force that the dictates of public performance exert even on what one of her friends in old age, Henry James, called "the private history of the public woman," and particularly on the public woman who would prefer to present herself and her life as wholly private.[11]

Professionalizing the Theater, Domesticating the Actress

When summing up her objections to her profession, Kemble found the actor's lowly social position to be the unkindest cut of all: "for the actor alone the livery of labor is a harlequin's jerkin lined with tatters, and the jester's cap and bells tied to the beggar's wallet" (p. 5). In the days of her aunt Siddons, actors and actresses had believed themselves to be and had been treated as ladies and gentlemen, but in her own time, the actor's work, like the fool's, is not valued by his audience; regarded as a servant rather than as an equal, he is neither respected nor respectable. And "the inexorable element of Respectability," as Kemble puts it, is simultaneously "the preeminently unattractive characteristic of British existence" and "a wholesome, purifying, and preserving element in the homes and lives of many, where, without it, the recklessness bred of inse- cure means and obscure position would run miserable riot" (p. 5). As the glue which holds the middle classes together, the standard against which all behavior is measured, respectability has a power and a value not to be underestimated. Kemble clearly shaped her own life and text by its prescriptions and prohibi- tions, yet found her fellow actors and actresses less than scrupulous in meeting its claims.

In making this judgment she was certainly not alone: in the voluminous literature generated by and about the theatrical establishment in the second half of the century, the issue of respectability is perhaps the central concern. Rarely, however, is it so baldly presented as a gender-related issue as by a journalist for the *Saturday Review*. An anonymous essay from 1862, entitled "The Army and the Stage," assesses the relative standing of the two occupations most closely linked by the press, and in the popular imagination, with sexual license and public immorality. The writer's comparison favors the army, for while soldiers may be unsavory, their profession has a certain dignity, and "very few people think the army a profession to be shunned."[12] The writer attributes the differ- ence between the reputations of the two to the military's "public character": "A body publicly recognised and associated in the face of the world . . . im- poses a code of morality and honour that may be imperfect, but which is infi- nitely better than nothing" (p. 321). The problem of immorality in the theater, the essayist claims, is of far more serious proportions: "The objection to the theatre which most good people make is, that actors and actresses are not vir- tuous characters, or rather, although modesty and prudery may forbid them saying so plainly, they do not much care about the men, but they think that the women are bad. . . . The objection to theatres is therefore really, in the main, an objection to the character of the women" (p. 321). Unlike the army, which enforces a certain discipline by means of its internal rules and regula- tions, the stage is largely unaccountable to public standards of decorum; the writer seeks to clarify the means by which it might be made so, the means by which "the character of the women"—the primary signifier of theatrical licen- tiousness—can be made virtuous and respectable.

In one respect, the writer argues, this end is already on its way to being accomplished, since "the players are not now the mere pets and *protégés* of the rich, but are people on a particular level in the scale of society who have taken to this occupation as to one of the other humbler professions" (p. 322). In this view, one borne out by census statistics on the social origin of actors and actresses from the 1850s onward, the Victorian stage is in the process of becoming a middle-class occupation populated by gentlemen, such as the Etonian Charles Kean and the eminent Macready of a slightly earlier generation, if not yet by ladies. And as acting becomes a profession for gentlemen and a gentlemanly profession, the essayist predicts, the theater will attract recruits from a better class of people. In return, a better class of people, and better women in particular, will begin to frequent the theater and to make it a public venue for respectable entertainment: "Every virtuous and refined woman is helping the world who goes to theatres and imposes on the performers the restraints which her presence ought to impose, and which it will impose" (p. 322). The theater, it seems, cannot be counted on to police itself, as the army can. The presence of women on stage requires the surveillance of domestic women, who will make their errant sisters conform to the unstated standards of middle-class Victorian femininity.

In equating theatrical respectability with respectable women, this writer, like others, explicitly accords the domestic woman the responsibility for establishing the rules of public decorum. By herself appearing in public, not on the stage, but as an audience member—itself a public role requiring a certain degree of acting, the self-discipline of the silent observer—the Victorian woman carries the authority of the domesticated lady with her. She extends the boundaries of the private realm, influencing the theater as she does the home, by imposing "restraints" on those who must presumably be restrained, the performers themselves. Policing the public—not only the theater, but also the hospital, the workhouse, and the domiciles of the poor—middle-class women and their "influence" cast radiant beams over public as well as private behavior. For many Victorians, the woman who would be a "citizen" of the public sphere could only be constituted as such according to the norms of middle-class domesticity and by her function as the civilizing colonizer who imposed those norms on others, particularly on those who were her economic and social, and thus moral, inferiors. The Victorian discourse on middle-class women in their relation to the public sphere is, then, as determined by the norms of class as by those of gender.

The Victorian theater proves to be a particularly revealing cultural locale for analyzing the intersection of class and gender norms. As members of an occupation actively attempting to professionalize itself, actors and actresses needed to obtain the sanction of the middle-class public; in order to achieve professional legitimacy in the economic realm, they had to win over consumers to what they had to sell. The professionalizers of the theater ultimately accomplished their goal by segregating audiences and players according to class differentials, by redefining acting as a specialized art form, and, most importantly, by representing the stage as a viable career for the middle classes. But the centrality of women to the stage made the situation of the Victorian theater different from other occupations involved in a similar process of professionalization: making actors gentlemanly was a far less difficult task to accomplish than making actresses, invariably linked with prostitutes in the public mind (and in the police rolls), ladylike.[13]

Internalizing the norms of respectable, gentlemanly behavior, the actor came to be identified, and to identify himself, with other professionals. "By the end of the century actors, at least the most prominent of them," as Nina Auerbach points out, "were doing their best to prove that they were flesh-and-blood professionals of ordinary stature."[14] But the actress professionalized, too, not by identifying with a preexisting public role for women—there was none that could accommodate her—but by adapting the norms of middle-class private-sphere femininity to a new public role. Both onstage and off, in their theatrical roles and their self-representations, actresses learned to play the part of middle-class women, and in doing so, helped to open the theater to middle-class aspirants. So as we will see in the autobiographical texts of Madge Kendal and Marie Bancroft, there was, by the 1870s and 1880s, no longer a need for the domestic woman to police the theater, because in the process of becoming a middle-class professional, the actress had learned how to police herself.

"In other callings the profession confers dignity on the initiated," wrote the eminently respectable Macready, embittered by his choice of an indecent profession; "on the stage the player must contribute respect to the exercise of his art."[15] With some important individual exceptions—John Kemble, Charles Kean, Macready himself—actors at work during the first half of the century did not achieve the kind of social position regularly accorded the physician, barrister, or clergyman; it was not until he had retired from the stage that Macready could feel an "independence of position" and the "most perfect equality" with those before whom he had once felt "embarrassed."[16] Although "the mid-Victorian and late Victorian theatrical establishment repeatedly issued statements which betrayed their anxiety to expunge the 'bohemian' image of the early nineteenth-century actor" (Baker, pp. 55–56), the attitude lingered on that neither acting nor the actor was quite respectable enough to be considered gentlemanly, despite examples to the contrary. Only in 1895, when Henry Irving became *Sir* Henry Irving, could the actor be said to have arrived at the apex of middle-class fortune.[17]

As Macready's disgust with the low repute of his livelihood suggests, making the actor a respectable gentleman was contingent on making the theater a place that would be frequented by respectable gentlemen and ladies. "The development of a socially exclusive membership" (Baker, p. 94) was the key factor in establishing the actor's claim to professional status, but formidable obstacles stood in the way of drawing the middle classes to the theater. While medicine and law, the two professions most often taken as the models for professionalizing Victorian occupations, had gradually consolidated themselves as professions by making themselves over as thoroughly middle-class in composition and orientation, the theater first needed to differentiate its ranks and its audiences according to class.

The development of two distinct theatrical markets, one for the middle-class "legitimate" drama and one for the music hall, created and sustained different class relations to the theater. For the urban working classes, an evening's amusement at the local hall was not the luxury that a night at the theater was for middle-class suburbanites. Other perquisites of the advantaged, such as the personal attention of a physician or a barrister, were reserved for those who could afford such "luxuries," but music-hall entertainment was cheap and accessible, increasingly controlled by large syndicates and developed as the poor man's and woman's equivalent to the middle-class theater. Experienced by working-class people as one of their few respites from bourgeois norms of work discipline and generally deplorable living conditions, the music hall was clearly necessary to the urban poor as one of the only consistently accessible public alternatives to overcrowded tenements.[18] Two entirely different sectors of what was ostensibly the same occupation thus came to perform for two entirely different audiences. For without breaking what the playwright Henry Arthur Jones later called "the Siamese-Twin connection" between the legitimate theater and the music hall—without making precise and definite distinctions between Dramatic Art and merely popular entertainment—the theater could neither establish itself in a position of equality with the other arts nor have its claims to special professional status taken seriously.[19]

The splitting-off of working-class audiences, as geographically reflected in the distinction between East End and West End theater, resolved one difficulty in professionalizing the stage, but restricting the working classes to a separate theatrical space could not by itself vanquish the theater's long-standing associations with immorality. The prejudice against acting itself as a form of deceit and trickery was another bar to making the theater legitimate. As Dewey Ganzel notes, "The legal recognition of the status of the actor as artist did not come until the act of 6 Victoria (1843) which in effect cleared the court dockets of all cases pending against actors and separated them from 'rogues, vagabonds, vagrants, and sturdy beggars.' "[20] Religious strictures also undermined the argument that the stage could be a moralizing force, and both a history of liaisons between actresses and aristocrats and the frequency with which prostitutes plied their trade at London theaters further identified the stage with sexual transgression.[21]

The absence of formal routes of entry into the theater also hindered actresses and actors from achieving professional status. Long considered the last refuge of the disgraced younger son or the "fallen woman," a sort of domestic Foreign Legion, the theater had no official recruitment or training procedures comparable to those which could be undertaken by the aspiring barrister or physician. As was the case with literature, the ease with which one could enter the ranks of the theatrical world was one of its greatest attractions for someone with nowhere else to turn, but that ease of access also gave acting, like writing, the reputation of being not exclusive enough really to count as a profession. As one journalist put it with regard to his own work in the late 1850s, "A character thus easily put on and off is too indefinite and fugitive to be recognised as a profession."[22]

Thus from a middle-class mid-Victorian perspective, acting lacked credibility as respectable work because it lacked some of the signs and signposts that marked an occupation as higher than trade or superior to wage labor. Contemporary statistics, however, show that the vast majority of those who went on the stage in the first half of the nineteenth century were not middle-class at all: like Marie Bancroft and Madge Kendal, they performed in the theater simply because one or both of their parents had done so. Thus these children, raised in a theatrical milieu and socialized into the trade almost from birth, had no need for training schools or formal initiation procedures. Actors produced actors: Kendal, for example, could trace her theatrical lineage well back into the eighteenth century, for not only her parents, but also her paternal grandparents and even her great-grandparents had been players.[23] Not until the 1870s and 1880s, when the theater became more fully populated with aspirants from middle-class backgrounds, did training schools spring up to prepare those without any previous experience of stage life and dramatic technique for a career in the theater.

As middle-class sons and daughters took to the stage, more and more working-class performers and members of theatrical families were channeled into the urban music halls and the provincial troupes. And as the social origins of its entrants changed, the theater necessarily changed, too, although it is difficult to determine whether the entry of middle-class actors and actresses into the theater or the theater's new attention to middle-class standards did more to promote the embourgeoisement of the stage. In any case, some theaters, the single most important one being Marie Bancroft's Prince of Wales', began by 1865 to cater strictly to the middle classes. Performers of middle-class origin and those who aspired to bourgeois status directed their efforts toward raising the social and moral tone of the theater and the profession; the reforming spirit overtook the stage as it had the slum, the factory, and the school.

The desire to improve the position of the player coincided with the effort to attract a better class of playgoer, "the educated and taste-possessing people . . . whose patronage would be the most discriminating, the most valuable, and the most welcome to the manager," "professional men, and artists, and authors, and students of every kind."[24] The patronage of the educated middle classes could only be secured by providing for members of the audience "the comfort and decency to which they are ordinarily accustomed" (p. 102), and the model for "comfort and decency" theater people imitated in reshaping the entire theatrical experience to fit middle-class norms and tastes was the standard provided by the drawing room. By domesticating the theater, those who ran the London stage of the 1860s and 1870s actively solicited and accommodated a bourgeois audience in their attempt to bridge the theater's distance from mainstream middle-class culture.

As my use of the term "domestication" is meant to indicate, women played a central role in bringing about this transformation. The remarks quoted earlier from the *Saturday Review* suggest that women's role in the theater, if it were to be a respectable and virtuous role, was to bring to bear on the public world the high-minded ideals of Victorian femininity; like their private-sphere sisters, actresses were newly invested with the responsibility for creating and upholding the moral tone of the environment they inhabited and for imbuing the stage with the ideals of domesticity. But the experiences of actresses in their capacity as workers, who merely by the fact of engaging in paid labor outside the home behaved in a way that most of their contemporaries would consider unfeminine, bore little relation to bourgeois Victorian attitudes about what constituted women's natural role. The successful actresses of the 1860s and 1870s, born to the stage, had little in common with the carefully cultivated young ladies of the drawing room.

Like every other walk of life, and particularly public life, the stage felt the effects of the middle-class discourse on true womanhood, and the theater's own preoccupation with achieving professional status made it especially urgent that its women conform as closely as possible to a bourgeois model. That model, however, as Kemble's stance exemplifies, was generally perceived to be entirely incompatible with theatrical representation. As Henry James's ironical Miriam Rooth asks in *The Tragic Muse* (1890), perhaps voicing one of Kemble's oft-stated objections to theatricality, " 'doesn't one have to be [a strange girl], to want to go and exhibit one's self to a loathesome crowd, on a platform, with trumpets and a big drum, for money—to parade one's body and one's soul?' "[25] To domesticate the stage was to strip the theater of precisely those associations between feminine public display and impropriety so lamented by Kemble, to naturalize the presence of women in the public sphere by representing the compatibility of both the stage and the actress with the values of private-sphere femininity. And, strikingly, it is actresses of the theatrical working class—women born to the green room, not the drawing room—who would do the cultural work of transforming the actress from "a strange girl" to a respectable middle-class professional.

Madge Kendal: the Respectable Actress

In some respects, Madge Kendal (1849–1935) had much in common with Fanny Kemble, for both were born to established theatrical families, yet the forty years' difference in their ages made all the difference between them and their lives in the theater. Kemble lived in an era in which to be on the stage, no matter how impeccable one's credentials as an actress or a lady, was to be de-classée. Kendal, on the other hand, came from a far less prominent line of actors, but achieved a reputation for being the most ladylike of actresses. Widely recognized as one of the finest performers of her time and made a Dame of the British Empire in 1926, Kendal earned the unofficial title of "the Matron of the British Drama" from her fans and her peers, and the latter distinction seems to be the one of which she was most proud. The very fact that an actress could be publicly labeled in that way indicates that a shift had taken place in the theater form Kemble's heyday in the 1830s to Kendal's reign in the 1870s and 1880s, first at the Haymarket and later on at the St. James's. While Kemble had left the stage at twenty-five years old to marry and only returned to it years later as a divorcée, forced back behind the footlights in order to make her living, Kendal's marriage to a fellow actor consolidated her position as a successful actress, for it enabled her to represent herself as the most respectable of Victorian ladies.

Like the carefully shaped persona of the archtypical Victorian matron, Kendal's queenly preeminence depended on the close fit between her staged public performances and her known "private" character as an exemplary wife and mother who was as devoted to imposing a salutary feminine influence on the theater as to upholding familial values and virtues. Attempting to expose the secret of Kendal's popularity, a contemporary historian of the stage found that it did not lie in her artistry alone: "It is rather that she is the representative of all the proprieties of private life, the wife, the mother, the champion—with a very loud trumpet—of the respectabilities, in fine, it is as the matron of the British drama that the *pater* and *mater familias* of the middle classes especially patronise her, rather than for her talent."[26] As "the ideal incarnation of generous English womanhood," and the best representative of "the pure and domestic English school," Kendal's reputation depended less on her acting than on the national values and virtues she came to represent.[27]

As an actress and as an autobiographer, Kendal champions the cause of feminine respectability at every turn. Onstage and off, she claims, the actress shares the common experience of femininity with all other women. Far from being extraordinary or unconventional, "in their private life actors and actresses are just like other men and women, moved by the same feelings, affected by the same passions, hurt by the same griefs": like Shylock, Kendal claims to be "fed with the same food, hurt with the same weapons, subject to the same diseases" as are ordinary people.[28] All that distinguishes the actress from the woman in the drawing room is a difference in milieu, a stronger sensibility, and "that little *something* which we cannot describe," that certain indefinable quality that separates the talented artiste from the everyday woman.[29]

What is remarkable about Kendal's own story, when we compare it to Fanny Kemble's, is that Kendal wound up being a far more conventional middle-class lady than Kemble herself, even though Kendal came from a far less advantageously situated family. The youngest of twenty-two children, of whom the eldest was the playwright Tom Robertson, Madge Kendal took to the stage at the tender age of three years; unlike Kemble, she never went to boarding school or any school at all, though she did take voice lessons as part of her informal training for the profession. While her father had been a theatrical entrepreneur, having inherited the theaters of the Lincolnshire circuit from his own father, he lost everything he owned in the railway speculations of the 1840s. "And on the very day and hour when he knew everything was lost," Kendal writes, with self-dramatizing flair, "I was born" (*DO*, pp. 22–23). Like Kemble, she was destined to set the family fortunes aright, but she was no overnight success: it took years of hard work playing child's roles, and later the burlesque boy parts, on the provincial circuit at Bradford, Nottingham, Hull, and Manchester before hear earnings became sufficiently high—ten pounds a week—for her to provide for her aging parents' retirement.

Under these circumstances, we might expect that her autobiography would recount a rags-to-riches story of the kind that was so popular in her period.

But she chooses not to emphasize her struggles in the autobiographical sketches published under the title *Dramatic Opinions* (1890), or in her autobiography proper, *Dame Madge Kendal* (1933); nor does she seem at all aware, in the way that Marie Bancroft is, of how her experiences deviate from the middle-class norm for feminine development. She presents instead the practical standards of behavior and discipline that she sets for herself and for others in pursuing their calling, standards for the responsible and respectable middle-class professional subject. And by making but few references either to her early experiences or to how she rose in the world by means of her own efforts, she assimilates the story of her career to the larger narrative of the theater's gradual progress toward respectability.

Although she was herself no stranger to the art of self-promotion, Kendal's antipathy for how some of her colleagues conducted their public lives marks a clearly professional attitude toward how actresses and actors should behave in society. Expressing her distaste for the "many artists upon the stage who go into society for the sake of being seen, and by that means get a sort of *clientele* of the public who follow them on to the stage" (*DO*, pp., 77–78), Kendal demonstrates her adherence to a newly emerging ethos among players eager to put the stage on a footing above that of patronage. Neither an attractive figure nor a charismatic personality alone will ensure success on the stage: it is "the amount of study, of labour, and of devotion to the art—to say nothing of natural aptitude" (*DMK*, p. 189) informing one's work that raises the ordinary player to the ranks of the skilled professional artist. Self-discipline and self-control, not self-promotion, are Kendal's keys to professional success.

Her personal standards for professional behavior are also ones Kendal advocates for her peers. In a paper she read to the National Association for the Promotion of Social Science at Birmingham in 1884, which she includes in full in *Dame Madge Kendal,* she traces an evolutionary model of progressive improvement in all aspects of the theater, noting the gradual but steady rise in quality of the stagecraft, of the accommodations offered the audience, of the plays written and performed, and, most importantly, of the status of the player in late Victorian culture. Her narrative history of the profession begins in the days of Garrick and Siddons, when "members of all the other professions were glad enough to come and amuse themselves with the outcome of the actor's genius; his ability was recognised . . . but the door of 'society' was closed to him. Now all that is altered" for there is "at last a recognised social position for the professional player" (*DMK*, pp. 188, 187). Maintaining that position, however, is up to the players themselves; like Lewes lamenting the invasion of the literary ranks by the unqualified, Kendal presents herself as an advocate for the true values and moral standards of her calling.

While unscrupulous members of the profession stoop to self-advertisement "as a cloak for incapability" (*DMK*, p. 192), and the public "[runs] after notoriety, and notoriety alone" (*DMK*, p. 196), those who possess both talent and integrity have the responsibility to reclaim the profession from those who use it only to advance themselves, and in doing so, true professionals advance the interests of all:

It is more than a necessity that actors and actresses of position, who have the true interest of their noble art in view, should make their lives an example to those with whom they are associated, and to those who are to come after them. By this means, and by this means only, can the Theatrical Profession expect to maintain its dignity and to secure the high position it should hold in the estimation of the public. It behoves actors and actresses of every degree, while cultivating their talents to elevate and amuse, to lead such lives that those who have regarded the Stage with a suspicious eye will at last give it its proper place in the world of Art.   (*DMK*, p. 196)

Kendal obliges "actors and actresses of position" to conduct themselves publicly in ways befitting ladies and gentlemen so as to "make their lives an example" to others inside and outside the profession; to be exemplary is to secure oneself from potential criticism. Maintaining the high tone of the theater while in the theater is not enough, for professional actors, even as public figures, are also subject to the standards that govern private behavior. Recasting the admonition given by the *Saturday Review*, Kendal reminds her peers that the mark of a real profession is that it can and will police itself. The responsibility of actors and actresses to their art and to their colleagues requires them to make their private lives, as well as their public ones, above reproach.

The actress's particular part in professionalizing the stage was well cast by Dinah Mulock Craik, who warned the aspiring performer never to "be moulded by her calling, but mould her calling to herself; being, as every woman ought to be, the woman first, the *artiste* afterwards" (p. 48). Being "the woman first" means proclaiming the fitness of women for theatrical life as well as taking a leading role in shaping the morals of the audience. "I do not think there is a thing in the world that a woman could be better than an actress," Kendal asserts, motherhood apparently notwithstanding; "there is no other calling in which she can earn so much money,—no other calling in which she can set a better example and do more good. . . . she holds a position which is unique if she has the necessary qualifications" (*DO*, p. 79). Virtuous wives and mothers who are also actresses make the theater safe for everyone, for while the uninitiated seem to believe that the green room is saturated with "a number of bad influences," Kendal "entirely [denies] this": "What influences would there have been, for instance, at the St. James's Theatre that I should have had to keep my girl out of?" (*DO*, p. 169). The actress who practices her training in feminine decorum and virtue wherever she is eliminates the difference that is presumed to exist between the home and the stage. As Kendal puts it, reaffirming the continuity between private and public femininity, "there are the same influences behind the scenes of a theatre as there are in a drawing-room" (*DO*, p. 169).

Kendal's insistence on the compatibility of life on the stage with private-sphere feminine experience made her an influential advocate for the professionalizing Victorian theater. By both her words and her example, she offered a skeptical public a model for what a respectable, public, professional woman could be and shaped her public image by drawing on the authority of the domestic. That she could do so without having been formed in a middle-class milieu suggests the relative ease with which the norms of bourgeois private life could be reproduced and represented even by those whose acquaintance with them was secondhand at best. And as Kendal's example also suggests, the tensions between the bourgeois narrative of private femininity and the actress's experience of public work demand that one be subordinated to the other, insofar as the experience of work departs from the norms of femininity. Whereas Kendal succeeds in creating an apparently seamless public persona that remains consistent with those norms, and indeed pays homage to them, the problems of being a public woman emerge clearly in Marie Bancroft's narrative of her early years in the theater, which illustrates her experiential distance from middle-class life even as it charts the course by which she, too, became a respectable professional.

Marie Bancroft: Class, Gender, Professionalization

It should come as little surprise to find that Marie Bancroft (1839–1921), the driving force behind the Prince of Wales' Theatre in the first two years of its existence, was the daughter of parents who had lost middle-class status by taking to the stage. In the first pages of the autobiography she co-authored with her husband upon their retirement, *On and Off the Stage* (1886), Bancroft narrates the story of her parents' fall into the social abyss of the theater, a fall that took on substantial implications for her own professional experience. Carefully recording a genealogy that includes respectable professionals on both sides of her family, she briefly relates the circumstances that led her father, "infatuated" by the stage, to give up his intended vocation for the clergy in favor of the theater, thus incurring the everlasting wrath of his relatives. "To be an actor," she writes ruefully of the 1830s, "meant exile from home, family, friends, and general respectability."[30] Her regaining of the status her parents had lost by working on the stage through her own theatrical work exactly parallels the transformation of the theater from outcast to professional standing: her story takes the shape of a return from exile, a homecoming she achieves by conforming to middle-class standards, and particularly those that define femininity.

Bancroft's effort to write her story from "the beginning," as bourgeois autobiographers often do, is comparable in this regard to the working-class autobiographies that Regenia Gagnier analyzes: for those who begin work at an early age, "the period of 'childhood' is problematic," since they may understand their own particular experience solely in terms of lack.[31] As a member of a culture that romanticized youth as a period of innocence and freedom, Bancroft compares her early experiences to this fictive standard, which she has, by adulthood, fully internalized as one her own childhood did not meet:

> I wish I could recall a happy childhood; but, alas! I can remember only work and responsibility from a very tender age. No games, no romps, no toys . . . nothing which makes a child's life joyous. I can recollect a doll, but not the

time to play with it, for we only met at night, when it shared my pillow; and as I looked into its face, before I fell asleep after my work, I wished that I could play with it sometimes.

When other children were cosily tucked up in bed, dreaming of their sunny lives, their limbs tired only by the romps and pleasures of the day, I was trudging by my father's side in all weathers to the theatre, where I had to play somebody else's child. . . . I was, of course, much petted by the public; but oh, the work! My poor little body was often sadly tired; I was roused many a time from sleep to go upon the stage . . .   (p. 7)

Not being able to "recall a happy childhood," or anything approximating an ordinary middle-class childhood at all, Bancroft's retrospective narrative can only be constituted in relation to what she imagines a happy childhood might be. Idealizing the youth of others, she presents her own early years in terms of a series of disjunctions between what should have been and what was. As "somebody else's child," she represents onstage what she was not in real life, learning what childhood is supposed to be not by living it, but by mimicking it.

Her relationship to another norm of Victorian childhood experience, a stable home life, is similarly mediated by her idea of the norm. For young Marie Bancroft, "there seemed . . . to be constant travelling in my childhood days; I cannot remember a settled home, and recall only a very restless life" (p. 12): the family needed to move around in search of work, with her father sometimes taking her to one city while her mother remained elsewhere with their other children. Like Kendal, Bancroft shouldered the burden of family finances, which her father could not carry alone, as "the main support of [her] family" (p. 60) until her sisters married. The experience of uncertain living conditions and itineracy, and her unconventional and unfeminine part as family breadwinner, fed Bancroft's desire for the stability that middle-class life seemed to provide, a desire repeatedly foiled until she took over at the Prince of Wales'.

Marie Bancroft differed from most middle-class girls because she engaged in public, paid labor outside the home; she differed from some of her colleagues as well in that the roles she played during her first twenty years in the theater were not "feminine" ones. On the stage as on the street, gender was invariably marked for Victorians by costume and bearing. While cross-dressing on stage had been common in the Victorian theater—Kendal, too, had played burlesque boy parts in her youth, and even Mrs. Patrick Campbell, the original Second Mrs. Tanqueray, wore breeches on stage before her London success—it was increasingly relegated, by the 1880s and 1890s, to such music-hall performers as Vesta Tilley. As Auerbach notes in *Private Theatricals*, "The respectable theatre that began to take shape after mid-century suppressed much of [the] metamorphic play" associated with cross-dressing, pantomime, and other theatrics; "it simulated instead the more rigid identities endorsed by the society" (p. 15). Physically typecast from an early age until well into adolescence because of her slenderness, Bancroft's playing of "burlesque boys" marks her as an actress who, albeit against her will, transgressed the fixed gender boundaries of Victorian culture.[32]

In a letter to John Forster of December 1858, Charles Dickens records the mind-boggling experience of seeing Marie Bancroft act one of the many boys' parts she played at the Strand Theatre:

> I really wish you would go, between this and next Thursday, to see the Maid and the Magpie burlesque there. There is the strangest thing in it that ever I have seen on the stage. The boy, Pippo, by Miss Wilton [Bancroft]. While it is astonishingly impudent (must be, or it couldn't be done at all), it is so stupendously like a boy, and unlike a woman, that it is perfectly free from offence. I never have seen such a thing. . . . A thing that you *can not* imagine a woman's doing at all; and yet the manner, the appearance, the levity, impulse, and spirits of it, are so exactly like a boy that you cannot think of anything like her sex in association with it.[33]

Dickens's wonder at Bancroft's ability to represent a boy so convincingly is equally matched by his amazement at her really being a woman; indeed, he seems to ask if she can really be a woman at all, given that no ordinary woman could do such a thing. It is not, however, the fact of the impersonation itself that Dickens finds startling: what shocks him is that it appears to be no impersonation at all. Onstage, for all intents and purposes, Marie Bancroft is a boy, and her ability to appear so threatens to unfix the stable gender boundaries on which the gendered subjectivities of her patrons, including Dickens's own, depend.

But the momentary disequilibrium Dickens experiences as an observer is as nothing to Bancroft's own discomfort at being its cause: her ability to play a male role to perfection did not prevent her from ardently wishing she could play her own and be a woman onstage as well as off. Her "circumstances," however, "would not permit [her] to pick and choose" (p. 77): a great success as a boy meant that no profit-conscious manager would allow her to play more than a part or two in a skirt. "Season after season I found myself still a boy," she writes, expressing her dismay. " 'Oh, dear me! Why can't I be allowed to be a girl? It's all very well to be a great favourite with the public, and to be told that I am so natural and real in a boy's dress. Well, if so, why was I not born a boy?' " (pp. 82–83). Unlike some of her middle-class contemporaries, who longed for the freedom that the hoydenish heroine Maggie Tulliver envies her brother Tom, Bancroft wanted to conform to the gendered categories of middle-class culture. And like Lucy Snowe, who will dress as a man only from the waist up when forced to take a man's role onstage, Bancroft shies away from the transgressive implications of her own performance.

Bancroft's desire to wear women's clothes is, moreover, inseparable from her wish to advance in the theatrical world: "I did not object to burlesque itself . . . but my training and ambition had pointed to a different class of acting. . . . If I could have been sometimes cast for girls I should have grown more patient; but [playing] those Cupids had made authors think, and, perhaps, the public believe, I could not play anything but boys" (p. 83). For the ambitious and socially sensitive Bancroft, to play a boy is to be identified with a lower "class of acting," in which burlesque is synonymous with the disreputable underside of the theater world; to play a girl is to move up the ladder.

Marie Bancroft's opportunity to get out of breeches arrived when, with the help of a well-to-do brother-in-law and the artistic support of the melodramatist H. J. Byron, she opened the Prince of Wales' in 1865. This professional move eventually gave her the autonomy to choose her own roles; through them, she ultimately became the lady she wanted so desperately to be. In order to create a celebrated theater of which she would be the star, she had to make her new East End theater, previously patronized primarily by working- and lower-middle-class audiences, a magnet for fashionable West Enders. The autobiography explicitly connects her personal ambition with the creation of a middle-class theater as she relates a revealing vignette:

> One night, while the old Queen's was still in existence, Mr. and Mrs. Byron and myself occupied a private box, and saw the performance. It was a well-conducted, clean little house, but oh, the audience! My heart sank! Some of the occupants of the stalls (the price of admission was, I think a shilling) were engaged between the acts in devouring oranges (their faces being buried in them), and drinking ginger-beer. Babies were being rocked to sleep, or smacked to be quiet. . . . "Oh, Byron!" I exclaimed, "do you think people from the West End will ever come into those seats?" "No," he replied, "not *those* seats." (pp. 178–79)

They did, however, because Bancroft's reputation drew them there, and her canny remodeling of the theater and her own persona kept them coming back. She appeared in the first night's fare at the Prince of Wales' not as a lady, but as the principal boy of Byron's burlesque, *La! Sonnambula! or, the Supper, the Sleeper, and the Merry Swiss Boy*, taking the latter title part; six months later, as William Kleb notes, she was still playing the principal boy in the closing pantomime every night even as she was starring in Tom Robertson's *Society*.[34] Only when the success of the theater was assured could she triumphantly shed her boys' clothes for the final time:

> At Christmas, we produced Byron's *Little Don Giovanni*, the hero being the last burlesque character he ever wrote for me, as the success of our management made me firmly insist on my original intention to give up acting that kind of part. . . . The burlesque was removed from the bill in the early spring, when I said farewell to that branch of the drama for ever. *Society* played for a hundred and fifty nights. (pp. 203–204)

Professional success, for Marie Bancroft, meant being permitted to represent middle-class womanhood onstage and off; if it is true, as one contemporary observed, that the comedic roles she played from that time onward were still "*gamin's* parts and burlesque scenes," it is nonetheless more significant that "the *gamin* was pettitcoated [sic] and the burlesque scenes set in a comedy."[35]

Bancroft achieved her success by conforming to standards for femininity that were largely in conflict with the facts of her own experience; she internalized and sought to uphold those standards in her joint management with her husband at the Prince of Wales' and the Haymarket, just as Madge and W. H. Kendal did at the Haymarket and the St. James'. As part of a husband and wife team, Bancroft became one of the most celebrated of Victorian actresses, beloved for her portrayal of a succession of Robertsonian heroines, of whom her favorite was Naomi Tighe in *School* (1869), a character she described as an "artless . . . sunny . . . open . . . romantic . . . lovable thing" who, significantly, "had no drunken father" (p. 413). Identified with ladylike comic roles, she became a real Lady upon Squire Bancroft's elevation to the peerage in 1897, having, in the playwright-critic Clement Scott's words, "made art earnest" and "kept it pure." No more accurate estimate of the confluence of the professional ethos and the feminine ideal on the Victorian stage could be imagined.

The success story narrated in *On and Off the Stage* resembles the story of the Prince of Wales' itself in that the Bancrofts transformed both their lives and their theater to create a new middle-class ideal. Among London theaters, the Prince of Wales' took the lead in producing an experience that would be more attractive to middle-class playgoers than anything that had preceded it. By remodeling the theater stage and auditorium to reproduce the style and atmosphere of a domestic interior, for example, the Bancrofts drew middle-class men and women away from the secure comforts of home entertainments to their new fashionably cozy theater.[36] Suburban trappings—upholstery, antimacassars, and the like—were imported from the family parlor to the theater hall. And while the actors were more completely divided from the audience in physical terms, with the stage proper visually and spatially set off from the pit, smaller houses afforded a sense of greater intimacy: as a *Times* review of Tom Robertson's *M.P.* (1870) reported, the actors of the Prince of Wales' troupe were "almost at an arm's length of an audience who sit, as in a drawing-room, to hear drawing-room pleasantries, interchanged by drawing-room personages."[37]

Writing many years later, Squire Bancroft attributed the change in theater decor to a change in the attitude of management toward patron, a change based on a newly articulated "respect for the audience": creating a homely, comfortable environment for its guests, the Bancrofts treated them as "visitors whose good-will it was sought to conciliate."[38] In representing itself as a home away from home, as a house belonging to known equals rather than strangers or social inferiors, the Prince of Wales' blurred the boundaries between the public and private spheres in bringing the comforts of home into a public place.

As the *Times* review points out, the new drama also contained a new emphasis on the experience of domesticity, as plays promoted and reproduced the middle-class experience of strict familial and social divisions along the lines of class and gender. Robertson's "cup-and-saucer" drama, the so-called realist plays that formed the mainstay of the Bancrofts' repertory for almost twenty years, replaced melodrama (even as it retained melodramatic elements) as the favored form of entertainment for those who began to look to the theater, as they had to the novel, for standards of decorum and lessons in how to conduct themselves as ladies and gentlemen.

The first of Robertson's plays to be produced at the Prince of Wales', *Society* (1865) offers a particularly vivid example of how the new class lines drawn in the audience are symbolically represented on stage as well. By an improbable turn of events, *Society* concludes with an impecunious gentleman marrying a high-born lady; beating out the ungentlemanly nouveau bourgeois (aptly named Chodd, Junior) for both the hand of Maud Hetherington and a seat in Parliament, Sidney Daryl emerges as the hero who wins his dual reward by virtue of his gentlemanliness alone. In its relation to its audience, *Society* thus instructs members of the new bourgeoisie on the kind of behavior they should avoid, while it also confirms the prejudices of the established upper middle class: as Henry Arthur Jones analyzed its class dynamics, a character such as Chodd, Junior makes "blunders . . . so dwelt upon and exaggerated that any pit or gallery spectator can instantly detect them and pride himself upon his superior breeding to the person who makes them."[39] Michael R. Booth asserts that "what [the audience] got from Robertson was reassurance, the comic exploitation but not the discrediting of an unshakeable class position, and the fulfillment of class dreams"; with more bite in his critique, Jones condemned the Robertsonian repertory as consisting of "plays that confirm and flatter [the middle classes] in their own self-content and genial, ignorant self-worship."[40] And far from remaining a Bohemian himself, Robertson "now defended the social rank which he had attained against both the enemies above"—the aristocrats he lampooned—"and the enemies below" (Filon, p. 131)—*nouveaux riches* like the Chodds.

From the Robertson plays, with their focus on love relationships within and across classes, to the later work of Pinero, we can trace an almost direct lineage, particularly in view of the focus on the domestic that nearly all successful middle-class drama of the period comes to adopt. The subject matter that appeared startling and unconventional to contemporary reviewers of Robertson's drawing-room comedies was increasingly taken for granted as the legitimate focus for all bourgeois theater. While Henry James might sneer that *Caste* (1867) could well "have been written by a clever under-teacher for representation at a boarding-school," even he could not deny that Robertson and the Bancrofts had gained the public eye and ear whereas *Guy Domville* never would.[41]

In sum, the Bancrofts and their playwright domesticated the public space of the Victorian playhouse in every particular, making it shape and reflect middle-class norms as it disseminated the signs of private domesticity in a new public forum. And with the new emphasis on the drawing room came a new role for the actress in the theater, or rather, an old role recast for a new home: with the transposition of the domestic sphere into the public arena of the theater, actresses became respectable public professional women, asserting their ties to the privacy of the middle-class drawing room.

5

Bourgeois Subjectivity and Theatrical Personality in the Late Victorian Theatre

AS A PROFESSIONAL ideal, achieving respectability meant more than merely conducting one's life in accordance with middle-class standards. Those who worked in and invested in theatrical productions sought to meet real economic goals, and the commercial theater became a financially lucrative enterprise by attracting those who had both leisure time and money to spend in the style befitting a bourgeois way of life. By the 1870s and 1880s, going to the theater was not only an acceptable thing to do, but also a fashionable pastime. And making the theater respectable also made it one of the few public sites where middle-class people of both sexes could gather without threatening their own particular sense of either gender or class identity, for in the middle-class theater, on stage and in the audience, those categories were stabilized. In the newly domesticated theater, bourgeois spectators watched newly respectable performers act out the drama of middle-class life: the world of the theater was no longer completely "other" to their own existence, but literally encouraged them to make themselves at home, to see the performers not as alien creatures but as people who were, in some important respects, "just like us." The new respectable theater thus became one venue for staging the creation of public personality, in which not only actors and actresses, but also spectators themselves played critical roles.

The public player and the private middle-class theatergoer became more equal in social status, I have suggested, because the theater publicly reproduced the ideals of private domesticity. Yet Victorian audiences simultaneously confronted the differences and distances that separated performers from spectators: worshipping the stars of the stage—the Kendals, the Bancrofts, Ellen Terry and Henry Irving, to mention just the most prominent—Victorian playgoers invested actors and actresses with the aura of the extraordinary and the power of the professional. Analyzing the relationship between artist and spectator in Victorian culture, Richard Sennett notes that "the relation between the audience and this art form began to be one of dependence. The theatre was doing for them that which they could not easily do for themselves." Like other professionals, actors came to fulfill an ostensibly necessary public function, for they possessed the unique capacity to represent the unspoken or repressed emotions and feelings of quotidian existence: "People who were gradually losing a belief in their own expressive powers . . . elevated the artist as someone who was special because he could do what ordinary people could not do in everyday life; he expressed believable feelings clearly and freely in public."[1] Once the ability to express emotion and feeling within the public realm had been centered in a certain figure and commodified, the actor achieved a negotiable power—the power of his own personality—in the marketplace.

But the nature and extent of that power varies according to a number of factors, gender chief among them, for gendered economic differences played a significant if often unacknowledged part in the life of the Victorian theater and in theatrical lives. Institutionalized economic structures deeply affected the lot of Victorian actresses, as they did women in other occupations; in the theater, men held the power to determine what plays would be performed, who would act in them, and, to some extent, how actresses would represent themselves to their audiences. Even the most successful women who worked in the commercial theater were largely debarred from asserting control over their own work, for they had little or no economic pull. "Not even actresses who by some fluke had proved their powers," writes the erstwhile actress Elizabeth Robins, "had any choice as to what they should act. Not Ellen Terry herself, adorable and invaluable as she was, had any choice of parts, nor choice of how the parts chosen for her should be played."[2]

At the same time, the actresses whose lives and texts will be examined here—Ellen Terry, Stella Campbell, and Irene Vanbrugh—all achieved tremendous popular acclaim in the late Victorian and Edwardian theater, in part because all three were believed to possess the power over their audiences that effaced their relative economic powerlessness, the power of the magnetic public personality. The life of Ellen Terry is perhaps the best example of this phenomenon, for in the estimation of many, she "played but one part—herself; and when not herself, she couldn't play it": Terry's acting-that-was-not-acting depended for its compelling effects not on the roles she played, but on the impression she gave that the roles did not matter, that the reality of acting lay not in outwardly reproducing the character written for her, but in allowing her audience to see past and through the character and play to the women within.[3] In looking less at Terry's representations of herself and more at how others represent her, I argue that the power of Terry's personality, as it was and still is culturally constructed, consists in its being constituted as something both known and unknowable. She comes to represent the modern self whose depths cannot be plumbed, yet whose very unfathomability allows each of those who come under that power—whether from witnessing her theatrical performances, or otherwise "reading" her—to claim really to know her.

The emphasis on personality in the late Victorian theater corresponds to a relocation of the theatrical real. The movement from what one critic called the "trivial surface matters" of Robertsonian realism to the interiorized psychological drama of Jones and Pinero is made possible, as I have implied, by larger currents at work in the Victorian theater, and in particular, by the domestication of the theater, the drama, and the actress.[4] Although the English theater of the 1890s did not forego social mimesis, its apparent innovation lay in its attention to character, and what comes to be considered most "real" for the late Victorians is that which is most private and interior. As I will demonstrate later, the representation of the "inner drama" of bourgeois femininity becomes the actress's task on the late Victorian stage; it becomes as well the task of the middle-class actress who writes autobiography.

The two middle-class actresses who will be my other subjects in this chapter—Stella Campbell and Irene Vanbrugh—had vital roles to play in promoting this new psychological drama: Campbell starred in Pinero's two biggest successes, *The Second Mrs. Tanqueray* (1893) and *The Notorious Mrs. Ebbsmith* (1895), while Vanbrugh's less Ibsenesque Pinero roles included the leads in *Trelawny of the 'Wells'* (1898) and *The Gay Lord Quex* (1899). Rather than examine those theatrical roles in detail, however, I look at how these actresses represent themselves in relation to them, how the actress's subjectivity is shaped, in Campbell's case, by her experience of playing antidomestic New Women, and in Vanbrugh's, by the experience of public work itself. In both of their texts we find subjectivities constituted very differently from either the middle-class writer's or the upwardly mobile actress's: in Campbell and Vanbrugh, we see, for the first time, the kind of interiority James asked for—the "inner drama," "the private history of the public woman." Yet we see as well that inner drama is itself produced; these texts demonstrate how thoroughly the conventions of the dramatic and the conditions of theatrical work shape the subject's consciousness of herself.

Commodifying Theatrical Personality

In "Mummer-Worship" (1889), the essay that touched off a prolonged debate between the actor-managers of the commercial theater and the advocates of experimental repertory theater, George Moore indicts stage and society alike for reducing acting to a matter of celebrity. "The actor is applauded not for what he does, but for what he is," Moore claims; he achieves social and economic power not by his skill, but by the personal mystique he builds up through performance and self-promotion.[5] Perhaps unintentionally echoing Wordsworth's words from the 1815 "Essay," Henry Arthur Jones had anticipated Moore's attack some years earlier: "Every manager, every actor, every author, who has made himself secure in an honourable position, has done so by creating and educating his own audience, by imposing his own will, his own tastes, and his own personality on them."[6] In Jones's pragmatic formulation, the success of the actor-manager depends on his ability to capitalize his own personality in much the same way that Wordsworth, Carlyle, or legal and medical professionals do, and to shape his public image in ways that will appeal to his audience.

The Bancrofts were among the first to capitalize their own personalities in the manner to which Moore objects, and they did so less in the interests of art than in their own economic self-interest. The "tastes" to which Jones refers were not "naturally" the Bancrofts' own, but rather their approximation of what middle-class tastes and values were; creating their theater and their own public personae after middle-class models, the Bancrofts both responded to and shaped audience expectations about what the theatrical experience ought to be. Profiting from what Moore calls "the alliance between the stage and society" (p. 128), an alliance that the Bancrofts and the Kendals had been instrumental in forging, the commercial theater of the 1880s and 1890s similarly made its success not by appealing to those who had formed their taste for fine acting on the fare of the Comédie Française, as Moore, Arnold, and James had, but by forming its audience's taste for particular commodified personalities, such as Henry Irving's and Ellen Terry's.

Moore's critique of theatrical embourgeoisement is aimed precisely at the kind of personality the new English theater chooses to commodify. In *A Mummer's Wife* (1885) and, more polemically, in *Confessions of a Young Man* (1888), he attacks the respectable artist for murdering art:

> Respectability!—a suburban villa, a piano in the drawing-room, and going home to dinner. Such things are no doubt very excellent, but they do not promote intensity of feeling, fervour of mind; and as art is in itself an outcry against the animality of human existence, it would be well that the life of the artist should be a practical protest against the so-called decencies of life. . . . In the past the artist has always been an outcast; it is only latterly he has become domesticated, and judging by results, it is clear that if Bohemianism is not a necessity it is at least an adjuvant.[7]

Moore objects to the anaesthetizing influence of middle-class life on the artist's temperament: "a suburban villa" with "a piano in the drawing-room" may be all very nice for the average Philistine, but such bourgeois amenities discourage "intensity of feeling, fervour of mind," those qualities which Moore sees as necessary to aesthetic achievement. The artist ought not to be just like everyone else, Moore asserts, for art should be "a practical protest" against the banality of ordinary life, a protest the artist should embody in her or his own person and personality.

In revolt against his own respectable middle-class upbringing, Moore can see in theatrical embourgeoisement only a loss to art and the apotheosis of everything he despises. But to such actresses as Bancroft and Kendal, for whom middle-class status is not a birthright but an acquisition made through their own work in public representation, embracing the cultural fiction of individualism means access to the success and status achieved only by those who willingly adopt and reproduce the values of the dominant class. Thus Bancroft and Kendal assume middle-class identities through their work in the theater; as Raymond Williams has written of Jones and Pinero, star playwrights of the late Victorian theater, Kendal and Bancroft "were not of ['fashionable Society'] but, like other theatre people, serving it and, as agents of the image, making their way into it."[8] Becoming what they represent, they identify their accession to bourgeois values and bourgeois femininity, the very targets of Moore's attack, as a positive gain.

While the critique Moore makes is ostensibly antibourgeois, it rests on one crucial, unexplored, and characteristically middle-class assumption: like Clement Scott, the early enthusiast for the Bancrofts who was to become the most fierce antagonist to Ibsen and the new theater of the 1890s, Moore believes that "acting is mainly a matter of temperament and personality."[9] In seeing personality as the mainspring of acting, Moore unwittingly accepts a bourgeois model of what acting is about: to act is to express one's personality, one's individual being, in public. While he objects to the particular kind of "temperament and personality" middle-class life and theater create, represent, and commodify, Moore nonetheless bases his critique of Madge Kendal on his perception that she is not "right" for or "suited" to certain parts: "Mrs. Kendal nurses children all day and strives to play Rosalind at night. What infatuation, what ridiculous endeavour! To realise the beautiful woodland passion and the idea of the transformation, a woman must have sinned, for only through sin may we learn the charm of innocence" (*Confessions of a Young Man*, p. 142). Kendal thus fails as Rosalind because nothing in her "experience" or in her straitlaced "personality"—as those "private" qualities have been publicly represented—has prepared her to play the transvestite part of the woodland nymph. Only a woman who has sinned and felt passion could act Rosalind properly—that is to say, improperly. To say this, however, is to consent to the fundamental tenet of the ideology of public performance in late Victorian theatre: actors act best when there is no distance between the parts they play on stage and who they are in "real life."

Moore believes that Kendal cannot *act* Rosalind because Kendal's roles and her vigorous vigilance over her own public image have made him believe she cannot *be* Rosalind. Her self-representations have so successfully fixed her image in the eyes of her audience that any deviation from it makes her appear false to who she "really is." As Percy Fitzgerald remarks in *The Art of Acting*, "The real attraction for the audience is the exhibition of *character*; and the accurate presentation of character . . . is what constitutes *acting*" (p. 69): Scott and Moore would add that one's acuity in the "presentation of character" depends on the congeniality of the part played to one's own personal style and temperament. Yet, as we have seen in the Kendal and Bancroft autobiographies, the actress who is born into the theater has her "character" shaped in great part by the roles she plays and the roles she wants to play, roles both theatrical and social; who she becomes to the public is neither naturally ordained nor completely determined by external forces, but requires her active participation in making that public character, and in gaining her audience's assent to it.

Always to be, onstage and off, the personality she has created in public and in whom the public believes is the measure of the successful actress in Victorian culture; paradoxically, however, the most successful actress is one who appears as if she were not acting at all. Maintaining a consistent public identity throughout the course of her career enables the actress to play any number of different parts so long as those parts accord with the character that has been created in public and for the public. George Bernard Shaw's words about Ellen Terry are highly instructive in this regard. "She never needed to perform any remarkable feat of impersonation: the spectators would have resented it" had she been anyone other than who they expected her to be. "They did not want Ellen Terry to be Olivia Primrose: they wanted Olivia Primrose to be Ellen Terry."[10] The illusion successful actresses of the late Victorian theater created, to recall Kemble's distinction, is that they were not acting, but being; the stage was merely the medium through which they represented who they really were. And whereas Fanny Kemble could never feel enough "at home" in a public theater to be the person she was to herself, late Victorian actresses had to "be themselves" in order to succeed, for what the theater required of them was precisely that.

To be always the same, to represent consistently a known, acceptable, often conventional feminine role is both to establish the unassailability of one's own position and to ensure one's continuing marketability; like Mary Ward, Victorian actresses publicly reproduced private values in domestic dramas, and they also got paid for doing it. As a strategy for authorizing their public work, a strategy not available to Kemble, representing the private in a public medium enabled Victorian actresses to advance the status of the profession as a whole and to achieve personal success, for professional ideology presented their work as both a corporate endeavor and an individual pursuit. And unlike Kemble, who perceived her subjectivity as prior to both acting and writing, Kendal and Bancroft constructed their subjectivities in public and for the public, both on-stage and in autobiography; these texts help to illustrate the distance between middle-class notions of "temperament and personality" as something natural and the experience of many actresses, who were not born into but theatrically and professionally educated into being able to adopt those categories in describing and presenting themselves.

The most successful actor-managers in the commercial theater of the 1890s—Henry Irving, George Alexander, Beerbohm Tree, John Hare, Johnston Forbes-Robertson, Charles Wyndham, all eventually knighted for their services to the Empire—were the consummate professionals of their day. Nearly all of them were middle-class by birth, and they all subscribed to "the star system": what guaranteed the success of a play was not the play itself, but the popularity of the actors and actresses who performed it. Defending the actor-manager against such critics as Moore, Bram Stoker, familiar to us as the author of *Dracula* (1899) but better known in his own time as Henry Irving's righthand man, countered attacks on the commercial theater with a strong dose of capitalist common sense: "A manager must have some attractive personality in his theatre. No matter how good the play or how complete and pleasing its environment, there cannot be success without good players. The successful actor, therefore, who goes into management, starts with one great attraction—his own reputation with the great public."[11] That popular reputation "becomes a valuable stock-in-trade or capital, which only requires to be properly used to become realisable" (p. 1044), for an "attractive personality" and an attractive performer will sell far more tickets than any performance of Ibsen.

Like the professional barrister or physician, the professional actor-manager wins his place by parleying the power of his personality "into wealth, influence, position" (p. 1044), and as Charles Wyndham states in the same series of articles, that power is his inalienable capital:

> There are some kinds of goodwill which are transferable, there are others which
> are not; and among the latter class are the talent and popularity of an actor.
> All assets which are not negotiable or communicable must be used if their
> value is not to be lost altogether; and exactly the same considerations which
> induce a particularly gifted and popular member of a medical or legal or other
> professional firm to dedicate his own personal time and attention and skill to
> the practice of his firm, knowing that the public expects it and would otherwise
> keep away, induces the actor-manager to utilise for the benefit of his business
> the talents and experience which have commended themselves to the public
> voice.[12]

Assimilating the actor's situation to the professional model, both Stoker and Wyndham point to personality as the means by which the actor achieves his reputation and as the particular guarantee of his continued success. From this angle, the actor looks like the perfect type of the Victorian professional. His body is the very medium of his profession; his charisma and popularity are not "transferable," for his own "talents and experience" are what he trades on. Yet the validity of this reading holds only if we restrict its application to the successful actor-managers at the top who controlled the marketplace among themselves. Both of these interested commentators neglect to point out that the actor-manager attains and maintains that position by appropriating the ostensibly inalienable capital of his fellow actors (not to mention stagehands, dressers, and ticket-sellers) as part of his "stock-in-trade." Thus the actor can be his own commodity only if he appropriates the labor of others as his own capital.

What presumably justifies such a move is that the actor-manager who succeeds is "a particularly gifted and popular member" of the profession, but achieving that status depends in great part on his being able to make good use of other people's talents, and particularly his leading lady's. In his late-century book on Ellen Terry, Charles Hiatt noted that "the most precious of all Irving's qualifications as an actor is beyond question the possession of a 'magnetic personality' "; as a manager, however, his supreme stroke of genius was in choosing the right partner, a partner "whose personality should harmonize with his own" and be its "complement."[13] Hiatt's language here almost too readily lends itself to a gendered analysis, but even Terry herself considered her greatest asset as Irving's helpmate at the Lyceum to be her "usefulness" as an actress. And representing herself in this conventional womanly mode ties her text to Kendal's and Bancroft's as well as to Howitt's and Oliphant's:

> If it is the mark of the artist to love art before everything, to renounce every-
> thing for its sake, to think all the sweet human things of life well lost if only
> he may attain something, do some good, great work—then I was never an
> artist. I have been happiest in my work when I was working for some one else.
> I admire those impersonal people who care for nothing outside their own am-
> bition, yet I detest them at the same time, and I have the simplest faith that
> absolute devotion to another human being means the greatest happiness.[14]

Refusing to put art "before everything," ahead of "the sweet human things of life" and the pleasure of "working for some one else," Terry places herself in the line of women who subordinate self to others. The distribution of chapters in *The Story of My Life* (1908) also reflects this tendency to put others ahead of herself: Henry Irving appears more strongly and clearly in Terry's text than she does, while Jessie Millward's *Myself and Others* (1924) records as much of her leading man, William Terriss, and of Irving as of Millward herself. Their feminine modesty, a recurring trope of middle-class women's autobiographies, conditions their texts perhaps even more than it did their lives.

Although these Victorian stage wives were widely acknowledged to be more popular and more skilled performers than their husbands, Bancroft and Kendal publicly ceded managerial authority to their spouses. After launching the Prince of Wales' on her own initiative, Marie Wilton, in becoming Marie Bancroft, gave up the reins of management to her husband, while Madge Kendal, who retained the role of stage manager in all Kendal productions, makes an even more dramatic and emphatic statement in this regard: "Man and wife are one; when I write *I*, I mean *we*, and when I write *we*, I mean *he*."[15] Like other Victorian wives, who could not legally possess property in their own right until 1880, Bancroft, Kendal, and (to a lesser extent) Terry merge their own identities, and their own capital, in the men who come to represent them and their interests.

In Kendal's remarks we see yet another facet of domestication taking place in the theater: as in the larger economy, middle-class women's economic identities and capacities are subordinated to dominant masculine breadwinners and heads of household. This was not always readily acknowledged by the profession (as it referred to itself), for the theater had long prided itself on giving men and women equal status and equal remuneration for their work: the American feminist Olive Logan claimed that in the theater, as in literature, "men and women stand on an absolutely equal plane in the matter of cash reward" because "women have worked as long as men work—with the same purpose in lifelong occupation that men have."[16] The British actress, writer, and feminist Cicely Hamilton contests this assertion: "players who are box-office attractions," be they men or women, may be paid according to "their power of drawing the public," but with those "whose names have no drawing power, the rule obtains that the average woman is paid less than the average man."[17] While equal pay, if indeed equal, is a reward we should not underestimate, another long-standing tradition—managing the theater on the model of the patriarchal family, with the actor-husband at the head and the actress-wife playing the role of his supporter—was clearly given new force in both the Bancroft régime and at Irving's Lyceum. Squire Bancroft explicitly compares the "*ensemble*" of the Prince of Wales's to the familial paradigm: "The factors of the company changed from time to time, but the principle regulating the whole seemed immutable. The secret of this was declared to be good management, by which the spirit was transmitted by a sort of hereditary descent from actor to actor, so that, though the men and women went, the family remained intact."[18]

Though the players change, the "immutable" structure remains, watched over and enforced by the head of the theatrical household.

In the same vein, Edward Gordon Craig—an antifeminist with strong leanings toward authoritarianism in art and politics, and a fervent admirer of Henry Irving, to whom he always referred as his "Master"—described what he saw as the real state of affairs at the theater where his mother spent twenty years of her career: "We hear of the *partnership* of Irving and Ellen Terry, as meaning that both had the same power—it was no such thing. There was only one head of the house, and it was Irving. This house was the Lyceum Theatre, which was at the head of the English Theatrical world" (Craig, p. 152). In domesticating the stage, then, influential members of the profession did more than import the imagery of the patriarchal household into the theater; in Craig's account, the most powerful Victorian actor-manager acted as "head of the house," reproducing the structure of domestic authority by annexing the personality and capital of his stage "wife" as part of his "stock-in-trade."

Other readings of Ellen Terry's life inevitably contest Craig's view of her as subject to Irving's economic and managerial authority. His characterization of his mother as Irving's devoted helpmate is itself a response to the very different portraits of Ellen Terry painted by his sister, Edy Craig, and her partner, Christopher St. John, as well as by George Bernard Shaw, who all tend to underplay the gendered economic control Irving exercised over Terry. They rather locate her power in a personality that transcended the roles she was called on to perform. But these conflicting visions of Terry serve to demonstrate precisely how the late Victorian actress comes to be the figure through whom the commodification of personality takes place in public representation. For on the contested ground of who Ellen Terry is—Irving's subordinate, or a powerful being in her own right?—we see how a bourgeois conception of personality as something to be "revealed" to individuals in an interpersonal transaction takes hold of all the participants in this struggle; each wants to define her as someone to whom each alone holds the key.

Ellen Terry: Actress, Audience, Interpersonal Exchange

Craig's version of his mother did not and does not sit well with other readers and interpreters of Ellen Terry (1847–1928), of whom Virginia Woolf is the most famous and Nina Auerbach the most recent. Both Woolf and Auerbach locate in Terry's life a resistance to authority and convention that belies her characterization of herself as merely "useful," and identify that resistance in her ability to play many different roles without being contained by any one of them. In Woolf's words, "Each part seems the right part until she throws it aside and plays another. Something of Ellen Terry it seems overflowed every part and remained unacted."[19] Still more imbued with a late twentieth-century model of personality as consisting in and of depth, Auerbach's reading clearly takes up where Woolf's leaves off: "Ellen Terry's intimations of mystery within, of a mobile and opaque self beneath her roles, were the charm that lured audiences; she shot tantalizing glimpses of suppressed identities."[20] Those "identities" had to be "suppressed," Auerbach argues, because of the special place Terry occupied in the public imagination—she "reflected collective dreams"—and because of women's subordinate status in social and theatrical life; like many another charismatic woman of her age, Terry "mirrored the passing needs of successive phases of culture" (p. 17).

Auerbach's mirroring Terry thus looks much like Eliot's Alcharisi: "This woman's nature was one in which all feeling—and all the more when it was tragic as well as real—immediately became matter of conscious representation: experience immediately passed into drama, and she acted her own emotions."[21] Or like James's Miriam Rooth: "She was always acting . . . her existence was a series of parts assumed for the moment; each changed for the next, before the perpetual mirror of . . . some spectatorship that she perceived or imagined in the people about her." For Peter Sherringham, the recognition "that [Miriam's] identity resided in the continuity of her personations" is a horror: "such a woman was a kind of monster."[22] For Auerbach, however, such fluidity of identity makes Ellen Terry a heroine, in that Auerbach locates the only possible resistance a Victorian actress could make to the conventional roles—theatrical, social, and personal—Terry had to play in her ability to shift among different personae.

All discussions of Ellen Terry seem to agree that her personality onstage and off transcended her public and private identities, and I do not mean to discount such power, for it helps to explain the existence of the Terry cult. Those who have written about Terry all attest to her extraordinary force, exercised even more directly over those who knew her best. In this light, Gordon Craig's insistence on his mother's subordination to Irving and his relentless infantilizing of her can be explained, as Shaw was first to realize, as manifesting his need to contain textually the one woman, powerful in her own right, whom he could never really control. But in every discussion, even in Auerbach's portrait of Ellen Terry as an ultimately indeterminate being, the writer claims a special and privileged position for determining who Ellen Terry is and is not.

For Gordon Craig, who textually split his mother in two along the lines of the public celebrity and the private woman, "The elder of the two was the great and famous actress—the important figure—known to everyone, admired by all and by me: the young one was the little girl Nelly—known to hardly anyone—my mother—and adored by me" (Craig, p. 15). In a different vein, Edy Craig and Christopher St. John asserted their right to shape Terry's image when they prepared her memoirs for a new edition in 1931. They shut down what had been an open-ended text by supplying copious footnotes on information Terry had excluded; rewriting the last chapters to make them more linear and coherent, they appended long chapters on the last twenty years of Terry's life to bring her story—which had also become theirs—to the moment of her death.[23] Marshaling a vast historical and biographical apparatus, and armed with the insights of feminist theory and criticism, Auerbach does battle for Terry by recreating the context in which she lived, acted, and wrote. The disparate, sometimes irreconcilable conclusions about her we may draw from these texts serve only to demonstrate, however, that a certain model for interpersonal relations determines our notions of what constitutes "personality." All three accounts presume that the observer—or, in theatrical parlance, the spectator—has a particular, unique access to the identity of the performing subject which provides the authoritative view.

Herself an actress and an autobiographer, Irene Vanbrugh describes the distinct quality of what she and many others called Ellen Terry's "charm" as being the means by which she established a privileged bond with every member of her audience:

> It is a bloom, but the bloom has to have a rare foundation to hold it; a foundation of generosity, of giving out to your audience, a quality of crystal clarity which lets your audience see into your soul and understand your feelings without ever yourself parading those feelings. It means teaching your audience to ask and to want to know, and then letting that feeling reveal itself to them so simply that each individual might think it was to them [sic] alone you had shown it.[24]

Whereas James and Auerbach present the actress as a mirror, Vanbrugh figures her first as a flower, which achieves its radiance through being nourished by its "foundation" in "generosity"; then, changing her metaphor, she portrays Terry's power as residing in her ability to open a window onto her own soul into which everyone who wishes can look and can see not the actress playing a part, but the woman revealing her deepest self. Vanbrugh's final assessment of the relation between performer and spectator emphasizes the collaborative process at work in this almost mystical interchange: "You don't belong to yourself; you have encouraged others to see into your innermost thoughts, into your very soul, and you have thus accepted a responsibility which is sacred" (p. 142).

Harold Simpson, who wrote the foreword to Margaret Cooper's *Myself and My Piano* (1909), described the full arc of this interpersonal transaction in strikingly similar terms:

> You feel, when you are listening to her, that she is singing to you and you alone; the rest of the huge audience fades away to nothingness. You watch her inimitable gestures, you see her fingers caressing the notes with that indescribable something appertaining to genius . . . and all the time you are conscious of one feeling, that these things are part of a personality which exists simply to give you pleasure. Then the fabrication of your fancy is vividly dispelled by the thunder of applause that echoes all around you. You realize that there are others who have been feeling what you felt. Your sense of splendid isolation is shattered in a hundred pieces.[25]

Like Vanbrugh, Simpson singles out the distinctive quality of the gifted performer as the ability to make the observer feel as if he or she alone were the intended receiver of the performance, as if all the strength of that personality were directed at that one observer. That a spectator could indulge this illusion of private, interpersonal communion as taking place in a public theater may seem incongruous with what we think of as the determining conditions of public performance, but this experience, which Richard Sennett calls "public privacy" (p. 217), is the culminating effect of the whole tendency toward publicizing the private that I have traced. As the actress's personality is made publicly accessible through (and perhaps even in spite of) her performances, the public itself is also simultaneously privatized: like the Victorian home, the theater is made a space in which one can come to participate on terms of nominal equality in an exchange that appears to transcend the economic, but which necessarily depends on the economic and social subordination of one sex and one class to another.

Ellen Terry's power is thus shown to reside in the personal and interpersonal skills conventionally associated with women, rather than in some combination of those skills with the self-determining individualism of the male actor-manager. That feminized position, moreover, has an impact on the form and tone of her textual self-representation. She asserts, in the preface to *The Story of My Life* (1908), that "I was not leaving a human document for the benefit of future psychologists and historians, but telling as much of my story as I could remember to the good, living public which has been considerate and faithful to me for so many years." Like Stella Campbell's dedication of *My Life and Some Letters* (1927) to an anonymous fan who once stood waiting for hours outside the stage door just to catch a glimpse of her idol, Terry's prefatory remarks represent her reading audience as strangers who are not strangers, for the mutual intimacy between performer and spectators has been carried on throughout her entire stage career.

This public mode of interaction makes the writing subject less introspective than she might otherwise be, for the text leaves open a space for the reader's investment in the identity of the writer; like her stage performances, Terry's text invites the reader's participation in making her particular identity. That identity necessarily varies from reader to reader, according to the dynamics of the public interpersonal exchange, because each individual's experience of it is presumed to be uniquely different, "something that [takes spectators] beyond the immediate and into wider, deeper areas of themselves."[26] So if, as she stated and her interpreters have seconded, Terry had a self she did not know, everyone else knew it, or thought they did, for her performances, dramatic and textual, made them believe they did. Quite possibly, Terry may have derived her sense of her own unknowableness from representations similar to Eliot's or James's; in this light, she would be once more a mirror for and of bourgeois spectators. That Kantian quality—of being simultaneously known and unknowable, consumable yet inexhaustible—is the one on which her allure as a commodity depends, yet it is also what occludes her status as commodity: the interpersonal structure of the relationship between performer and spectator obscures the fact that this illusory experience of direct contact can be endlessly reproduced.[27] In being someone whom everyone could potentially "know" as well as they knew members of their own family, in being a familiar object of everyday discourse, Ellen Terry was still a mystery even to herself. And in that combination of familiarity and mystery, as she and her culture constituted it, lies the never-to-be-depleted value of the extraordinary public personality.

Stella Campbell and the Melodramatic Life

Bernard Shaw's review of Pinero's *The Notorious Mrs. Ebbsmith* says little or nothing about the play, which he sees as no more than a medium through which Stella Campbell (1865–1940) creates "a projection which sweeps the play aside and imperiously becomes the play itself":

> She creates all sorts of illusions, and gives one all sorts of searching sensations. It is impossible not to feel that those haunting eyes are brooding on a momentous past, the parted lips anticipating a thrilling imminent future, whilst some enigmatic present must no less surely be working underneath all that subtle play of limb and stealthy intensity of tone. . . . Mr. Pinero has hardly anything to do with it. When the curtain comes down, you are compelled to admit that, after all, nothing has come of it except your conviction that Mrs. Patrick Campbell is a wonderful woman.[28]

Like Ellen Terry, Stella Campbell exceeds not only her role, but the play and the playwright; her personality overwhelms all else. Shaw figures her as a modern-day Wateresque Mona Lisa: with a "momentous past," "a thrilling imminent future," and an "enigmatic present" all written on her face and body, she is clearly no ordinary actress, but "a wonderful woman," a woman with whom Shaw could—and did—fall in love.[29] And as such, Campbell was the ideal actress for Pinero's new dramas; her position in relation to her roles closely parallels the plight of Paula Tanqueray, who commits suicide rather than live like a "sleek, well-kept, well-fed" pet, and Agnes Ebbsmith, the freethinker who converts to Anglican piety. Confined within dramatic and social conventions which seal off the fierce energy of the heroines she played by the final curtain, Stella Campbell found herself out of sympathy with the conventional representation of "the woman with a past" on which Pinero's society dramas were based.[30]

The continuing presence of that past haunts Paula and Agnes and divides them against themselves. Her youthful innocence corrupted by her first false steps, Paula has been the mistress of many men, and this experience has coarsened her and obscured her "better self": as she states, and as her husband's and her saintly stepdaughter's attitudes to her also affirm, "I've two sides to my nature, and I've let the one almost smother the other" (2:96). For Agnes, marriage, not promiscuity, has done the damage to her psyche. For a year, her husband "treated me like a woman in a harem, for the rest of the time like a beast of burden."[31] This disastrous union converts her to atheism and political activism, but the man she chooses to be her partner in political work turns out to be, on further acquaintance, no better or worse than a conventional British gentleman. An emotional appeal from her lover's wife reminds Agnes of how attached she really is to all she had abjured and returns her to the fold of the domestic pieties, and along with his critical advocates, Pinero represents this return as wholly consistent with her character. Revealed to have been harboring a streak of bourgeois femininity all along, Agnes, unlike Paula, is able to overcome the contradictory pulls on her soul and to choose, instead of suicide or the mistress's role her lover offers her, rustic retirement to a country parson-age.

Although Pinero's supporters often favorably compared his work with Ib-sen's, the modern critical consensus makes the difference between the two play-wrights quite clear: "Whereas Ibsen's aim was to reexamine the conventions and where necessary undermine them, Pinero's was insidiously to bolster them up while only appearing to put them daringly in question."[32] And while the Ibsenite William Archer saw in *The Notorious Mrs. Ebbsmith* "character work-ing itself out entirely from within," the more Shavian Stella Campbell saw only Pinero's failure to live up to the original promise of the iconoclastic character he had created:

> The *rôle* of Agnes Ebbsmith and the first three acts of the play filled me with ecstasy. There was a touch of nobility that fired and inspired me, but the last act broke my heart. I knew that such an Agnes in life could not have drifted into the Bible-reading inertia of the woman she became in the last act: for her earlier vitality, with its mental and emotional activity, gave the lie to it. . . . To me Agnes was a finer woman, and the part a greater one, than Mrs. Tan-queray. In those days, not so long ago, she was a new and daring type, the woman agitator, the pessimist, with original, independent ideas—in revolt against sham morals.[33]

Campbell's critique reflects her dissatisfaction with the prescripted dramatic plot, "that rounding off of plays to make the audience feel comfortable" (p. 99); while the "advanced" playwright of the 1890s could "sympathetically" repre-sent a woman who transgresses the norms of bourgeois femininity, Pinero pun-ishes Agnes for her sins at the end, perhaps in order to appease his audience.

Herself "in revolt against sham morals," Campbell was no political "woman agitator." While she participated in some of the activities of the Actresses' Franchise League, founded in 1908 to work for women's suffrage, she never became a member; however, her assault on the last act of Pinero's play suggests that whatever her reluctance about taking a public stand for women, her dra-matic and political sympathies lay with the progressive forces of Ibsen and the New Woman, and not with Pinero's watered-down Noras. For in formal terms, Pinero's plays retain the moral framework of melodrama, in which the conven-tionally "good" are rewarded and the stereotypically evil vanquished, even as he draws on new theatrical norms which, as Michael R. Booth notes, demand that "characters have interior interest; their motivation and psychology are significant."[34]

Yet however much Campbell kicked against the constraints of Pinero's dra-maturgy, she nonetheless mixes melodrama and psychological realism in rep-resenting the "dramatic" moments in her own life, the best example being her account of the long night of reflection during which she decides, despite familial disapproval, to go on the stage. Her husband's poor health and fiscal insolvency make it necessary for Campbell to get a job to support her growing family, and she represents the process of making her decision with almost novelistic flair:

> I walked up and down that little garden, now and then looking up at the win-dow of the rooms where my husband and little son were asleep, until daylight,

thinking and wondering what was to be done. I knew that Pat was not strong enough to continue working in the city, and that I must help. I could not imagine what work I could do. . . . My lovely baby, and another coming in a few weeks, must be provided for. I was bewildered—lost.

With the daylight coming something entered my soul, and has never since left me—it seemed to cover me like a fine veil of steel, giving me a strange sense of security. Slowly I became conscious that within *myself* lay the strength I needed, and that I must never be afraid.   (p. 25)

Like Eliot's Dorothea Brooke or James's Isabel Archer, secular heroines who also undergo a type of conversion experience, Campbell arrives at her critical turning point after a prolonged temporal process of solitary introspection. The symbolic sunrise signals the conclusion of this process, at which point she comes to an important resolution which spurs her to action. Campbell's decision-making process thus converges with a literary/theatrical pattern for representing it when "the melodrama of consciousness," as Peter Brooks calls this structure with reference to James, is textually enacted in Campbell's scene.[35] All the elements necessary for portraying the feminine heroine at an experiential crossroads are present here: the ailing husband, the helpless babies, the woman with nowhere to turn for aid who must take on herself a burden almost too heavy to bear. But her salvation comes not from without, as it would in classical melodrama, but from within, as in the bourgeois realist novel; no fortuitous accident solves her problem, but her own inner strength guides her steps, and she recognizes this strength through introspection. The language of a psychologized subjectivity—which locates strength or weakness "within *myself"*—makes the experience of everyday life an ongoing drama, acted out on a stage so familiar to us as to seem almost banal.

"A fragile, unsophisticated young woman, still almost a girl, whose heart and nerves had been torn by poverty, illness, and the cruel strain of a long separation from the husband she loved . . . passionately living in a dream world of her own" (p. 81). Campbell's sketch of herself at the time of her debut similarly presents her experience in literary terms, in that she makes herself seem much like Hardy's unhappy Tess. But discovering strength within the self—"a fine veil of steel" capable of protecting her against all external circumstances, a strength which Pinero denied his heroines—makes Campbell both a strong woman and a gifted actress, and she claims that this power is innate, an integral part of her personality from childhood onward.

Even as a young child, "the desire was always with me to tell a secret. . . . I did not know what the secret was, but if only people would stand quite still and listen, then I would know right enough" (pp. 14–15). Later she hypothesizes that it was "the call of my 'secret' " (p. 26) from within that made her resolve to go on the stage, and that the "secret" is also what enabled her to " 'hold an audience' ": it is "a gift from God" (p. 15). It also inspired her first performance as Paula at a dress rehearsal, with Pinero as sole spectator: "I implored him not to speak to me, and I would play the part for him. I kept my word, and to that dark, silent house and that solitary man I poured out my 'secret' with the fire and feeling of my temperament and imagination" (p. 70).

The "secret" revealed, interestingly enough, is still constituted as a secret, although it can be communicated through the medium of the stage; unlike the fictional secret of Lady Audley, which that novel resolves by rational means, or the secret of Paula Tanqueray's past, which must be exposed to the audience and for which Paula must atone, the exact nature of the extraordinary performer's "secret" must remain sealed even as it is put into discourse.[36]

Like Fanny Kemble playing to her father, Campbell performs well in semi-privacy, but she can also reenact "the fire and feeling" of this performance for a larger audience as well; moreover, Campbell's secret is not something she keeps to herself, but something she can and must share, if only allusively, for she constitutes it as an interior voice which requires an audience, "people [who] would stand quite still and listen," a "solitary man" or a gallery full of auditors. By referring throughout her text to the secret as something inside her which is not precisely under her own control, something which has its own laws yet is very much a part of who she is, Campbell represents the private self as that which determines her public self, even as I have tried to show how textual and dramatic conventions shape Campbell's private self. But in making her self-representation in those terms, Campbell still retains, as Terry does, the quality of the enigmatic.

Irene Vanbrugh: the Middle-Class Subject at Work

Irene Vanbrugh's autobiography, *To Tell My Story* (1948), has as dramatic a flavor to it as Campbell's, but balanced by a more explicit discussion of how the experience of public work shapes her sense of self. Granddaughter of a barrister, her father a country parson, and herself one of Ellen Terry's numerous middle-class protégées, Vanbrugh (1872–1949) entered the theater in 1888 in order to earn a living after a short apprenticeship in a provincial theater at Margate, which was "more of a 'finishing school' for the stagestruck members of middle-class families than a systematic training school" (Baker, p. 153). Unlike Campbell, who claimed a mysterious and romantic Italian background on one side of her family and spent some of her youth abroad, Vanbrugh was brought up in ways conventionally English and middle-class. Each year was "naturally divided into the school terms" rather than theatrical seasons; summers were spent at the shore, not in provincial stock companies, as Terry's had been.[37] She passed her mornings at the local high school and the afternoons in study, as well as in taking "music, calisthenics, and dancing lessons" (p. 7), and this genteel discipline regulated the life of her whole family, "a discipline to which," Vanbrugh writes, identifying the seeds of her own personality just as Campbell does, "I attribute a natural, rather silent characteristic in later years" (p. 6). In every respect, then, her experience of life matches a middle-class norm; even when she goes on the stage, she does so by her own choice, believing the life of an actress better suits her "temperament and personality" than nursing, teaching, or writing, the other options open to women of her class in the 1880s.

Constituted as a middle-class subject by her experience of family and education, her gender and class identity clearly formed along the lines of the idealized model for the bourgeois woman, Vanbrugh unexpectedly problematizes the whole issue of personal identity in writing about her experience as an actress. Her text emphasizes the division she perceived between her public, professional, celebrity self, which she describes as her "second self," and her private, feminine, ordinary self, referred to throughout as the "nobody." This division is not based on her fear of losing caste in gendered or economic terms by going on the stage, as in Kemble's case; rather, Vanbrugh confronts a radical doubt about identity itself, a doubt that derives from her public role-playing. And her experience of division precisely reverses the value Kemble assigns to these terms: Vanbrugh, too, feels the doubleness of being both public performer and private woman, but while she assigns the private self ontological priority, she gives her strongest allegiance to the professional, public self.

"Most people are many persons, but who and what is that person who spends more than half his or her life impersonating other people, impersonating them strongly enough not only to convince themselves, but to convince thousands of others. . . . What, then, is the reality; how far has this constant recreation of yourself obliterated the original?" (p. 101). Even in expressing her epistemological doubt about the grounds of personal identity, a doubt familiar to us postmoderns, Vanbrugh relies on the assumption that there is an "original" self prior to public performance. While Campbell, too, holds this belief, neither Bancroft nor Kendal seems to share it, for like Moore's concept of temperament, it is an assumption based on a certain experience of class. Yet what follows this assertion of a primary self behind the public roles is a dramatization of a crisis in middle-class subjectivity. A radical disjunction underlies her doubt, a disjunction Vanbrugh perceives in being a woman who both participates in public work in the marketplace and experiences herself as a private, ordinary person.

For Vanbrugh, the plethora of possible subjectivities that acting different roles offers, "this constant recreation" of herself in public, resolves itself into two distinct identities, herself when working and when not. The way she describes this split is itself instructive, for we see her taking herself as the object of her discourse, analyzing her own experience of a radical discontinuity within the self in a way that other autobiographers I have examined, such as Martineau and Howitt, similarly experience but do not problematize. In a remarkable passage, in which she switches back and forth between second- and third-person pronouns without any internal consistency of reference, Vanbrugh describes the differences between her two identities.[38]

To be an actress, she writes, "a sort of double life must be led. You are nobody, yet inside you there is a second self who has a way of suddenly appearing and obliterates you completely, a second self that you can look at and criticize with a detachment that is almost physical." This "second self" "obliterates" the "nobody" self, the person she is when she is out of work (and not merely when she is not acting). The "second self" is "vividly brought alive by a letter from a manager to go and see him"; only within the context of her professional work does she experience the sense of fullness and energy with which this extraordinary second self invests her.

Later Vanbrugh redefines the second self as an "inward demon" who "refuses to be silenced or listen to any argument"—put forth, presumably, by the "nobody"—which would suggest that the manager's summons "may be nothing after all—probably a bad part, perhaps an understudy." The second self "comes even more alive" when she gets "a good part, salary more than she had before." She goes to work with zeal, and transforms her ordinary existence: "The days are ruled by her performances at the theatre; time for other duties has to be fitted in somewhere. This insistent second self dictates all her movements and reorganizes her life." But the ordinary "nobody" makes her reappearance when the production ends and no other part comes along. In the interim between roles, "she sinks into insignificance . . . the sparkle has gone out. . . . Then, again a door opens and the inward demon reasserts itself, and disappearing behind number two you theoretically stand again on the top of the world" (pp. 102–3). The interplay between the two selves shows how the middle-class woman, trained to believe she is "nobody" special, responds with fervor, as Florence Nightingale and other advocates for middle-class women's work had once prophesied she would, to the possibilities that a working life seems to offer.

Yet in embracing the working life and the professional self, Vanbrugh must reject the "nobody," and that rejection makes her as divided in her own way as any of Pinero's heroines. In her account, the "second self," the "inward demon," is everything that the other self, the "nobody," cannot be: she is competitive, aggressive, dedicated, hard-working, and ambitious. The experience of work makes everything else seem unimportant and trivial, but that ordinary self "who is so different yet so allied to her" is presented as the "original" self, the one who is always present although often subordinated to the rule of the professional self and its alien, demonic energy. Fueling this narrative of the divided self is a dilemma that makes the professional ideal an inadequate prescription for women's ills. Given the opportunity to pursue her own work and to actualize her ideal, an opportunity denied to many and stigmatized for most middle-class women, Vanbrugh can still only experience that pursuit as predicated on a division. To put it another way, when Vanbrugh embarks on her autobiographical project of self-creation, she takes as her model for identity the very metaphor that necessarily predicates a division of self from others as the human condition. Thus she reproduces an individualist paradigm by constructing herself as alienated from others—and even from herself—rather than locate her personal experience within a context that would or could make what determines individual destiny not the psychological, but the social, material, historical, or cultural.

For some of what Vanbrugh experiences in not being able to bring her two selves into harmony is caused by the instability of work itself: periodic disruptions of labor occur in the capitalist marketplace because the demand for workers is uncontrollable and unpredictable. For a fledgling actress without credentials to find work had always been difficult, and never more so than in the 1890s, when one's standing with the public largely determined one's worth to a manager. Vanbrugh's contemporary, Cicely Hamilton, writes in her autobiography that choosing a theatrical career meant entering into "a life where long periods of unemployment were taken as a matter of course" (p. 33), an unsurprising statement when we consider census figures of the time, which show that from 1881 to 1911 the number of actresses looking for work nearly quadrupled.[39] Only the very few achieved the kind of success that this high-profile profession seemed to promise; the many experienced the poverty and deprivation that had been the lot of Kendal and Bancroft in their early years.[40] Vanbrugh's text, however, is remarkably silent about her own material struggles. She presents her crisis as a problem internal to the self, unaffected by anything outside it.

Her use of an individualist paradigm to describe her own situation dictates that she adopt it when describing the profession as a whole. The keen competitiveness for the few available jobs makes life in the theater seem like a Darwinian struggle for existence, and Vanbrugh employs that idiom to characterize the situation of her professional colleagues:

> An actress's life is one long fight, a fight that never ceases while she continues her professional career. She can never rest on her laurels unless she wishes to be passed in the race by others who are quicker and cleverer than herself. However great her name, however popular she may be today, she must always remember that she does not stand alone. There are others, many others, in the field and if she stops fighting for a single moment she will be trampled underfoot. . . . On the stage people are only too ready to run down other "fighters." So each one must fight a lone battle, using the tools in his or her own basket for all they are worth. Reliance on others is fatal; stick up for yourself, believe in yourself, and you will get others to believe in you.   (p. 91)

By basing her professional self on aggressive economic individualism, the "pursuit of self-interest" model that had previously been available only to men, Vanbrugh creates a dichotomy within the self which she cannot satisfactorily resolve. Her advice to aspiring actresses metaphorically sets up the marketplace as a sphere ruled by the natural laws of competition, a world in which there can be no possibility of trust or mutuality between workers, a battlefield on which one has no allies, only enemies.

In the essay "Cassandra," Nightingale, too, had used the language of conquest to talk about women's work, but "the fierce and continued struggle necessary to accomplish" the great victory she imagines would be carried out by women working together to bring it into being.[41] For Vanbrugh, faced with pragmatic economic realities she cannot control but also wholly implicated in the fictions of bourgeois individualism, the recognition "that she does not stand alone" is not an assertion of solidarity with her fellow "fighters" but a reminder that achieving middle-class success is a solitary pursuit. While the professional ideals that Nightingale and even Kendal support are based, in different ways, on a notion of communal interests, Vanbrugh's experience of the marketplace suggests that a cooperative model has no place in the world of work.

Some actresses of the 1890s attempted to circumvent just this kind of problem by organizing companies and productions of their own; moreover, that such women as Janet Achurch, Florence Farr, and Elizabeth Robins were more interested in producing and playing Ibsen than Pinero or Jones signals a rebellion against the power of actor-managers and playwrights, as well as an effort to assert control over the conditions of work that helped to produce Vanbrugh's experiential split. Her own "solution" to that division, however, is wholly within the terms of middle-class Victorian femininity and precisely opposite the protofeminist response. Vanbrugh's marriage to the actor-manager Dion Boucicault makes "the interim lapses" in her theatrical life "almost non-existent because Dot was there to stand by me and guide my two selves to merge and help each other" (p. 103); in union with him and under his tutelage, the two identities could blend, in a pattern familiar to us from *Aurora Leigh*. Culturally invested with the capacity to transform lives and reshape identities, the dual experience of love and work bring together what would otherwise remain separate in Vanbrugh's view of herself: the "nobody" and the "inward demon" can unite when love and professional success provide the necessary medium for their reconciliation. What had seemed improbable in fiction becomes exceptional in life.

Vanbrugh's account reveals problems common to many middle-class working women of her time as well as our own. Imagining access to and practice of professional work as a panacea for their problems, women from Martineau to Vanbrugh respond eagerly to new structures of economic and social opportunity only to find that professional work has radically alienating limitations of its own, of which women's continuing economic and social inequality is but the most obvious. The public identities that actresses make are, moreover, shaped by norms of gender and class that impose all sorts of limits on who and what women can be, to themselves and to others. The fierce individualism Vanbrugh's text demonstrates at its worst shows how in entering the professional work force, women may do little or nothing to change the structure itself: while she feels and represents the tension between the two selves, it never occurs to Vanbrugh—as indeed it does not to many women today—that it is not only the self, but also and especially the structure that needs to be transformed.[42] For if professional women's lives, or any working women's lives, are to provide a felicitous interchange between self and world, the model of competitive individualism will not suffice. In looking at autobiographies by suffragettes in the next chapter, some of them fiercely devoted to bourgeois individualism, others reliant on a cooperative model that structures not only their politics, but also their subjectivities, I will show how these two paradigms emerge on the contested ground of the political arena, when "the fierce and continued struggle" for equality took to the streets.

6

Representation and Subjectivity in the Edwardian Suffrage Movement

THE ACTRESSES OF the Victorian and Edwardian theater were the most prominent but not the sole group of women to claim and achieve professional status at the turn of the century.[1] With the rise of educational and occupational opportunities for middle-class women came the reiteration of the demand for political enfranchisement, a demand which had been made periodically throughout the nineteenth century, most forcefully by John Stuart Mill and his associates in 1867. The suffrage campaign of 1905–14 marked another concerted effort by women from all classes, those who worked inside as well as outside the home, to gain the vote.

The focus here will be less on the politics and history of "the Cause" and more on the subjectivities of those who participated in it, as constituted by and through their numerous autobiographical accounts. Like the writers and actresses already discussed, suffrage autobiographers also adopt self-representational strategies that both uphold and undercut the precepts of bourgeois femininity, yet there is a difference among these texts in that their authors actively reshape feminine norms in an explicitly feminist context. The selflessness of Mary Howitt, who understood her family's needs as prior to her own, or of Ellen Terry, who mirrored the projections of spectating consumers, has an important place in the suffragettes' self-conceptions: members of the Women's Social and Political Union (WSPU) redefined selflessness as a positive political value and as a counter to the culture of individualism, as an important element of a politicized subjectivity. I argue that the militant suffragettes forged a collective identity and established an intersubjective model for selfhood through the material practices of hunger-striking and forcible feeding, prominent features of suffragette experience as represented in the writings of Sylvia Pankhurst, Mary Richardson, and Constance Lytton.

Some Edwardian feminists who left the movement, however, criticized the ethic of feminine self-sacrifice as a patriarchal imposition and the intersubjective model as too idealist in its premises. Those who dissented from the ideological

150

orthodoxy that Christabel and Emmeline Pankhurst sought to impose on their followers repudiated the sacrifice of women's lives and bodies on the grounds that the price of self-sacrifice was excessively high. Like the Pankhursts themselves, apostates from "the Cause" made most of their arguments for the vote by claiming women's historical and social differences from men and men's institutions. But such women as Teresa Billington-Greig, Hannah Mitchell, and Cicely Hamilton also objected to the autocratic structure of the suffragette movement, asserting that it just replaced the old prison of family life with a new and no less oppressive servitude. I suggest, then, that women fought not only for the vote, but also for their own visions of what constituted women's political "good," and that their conceptions of the "good" imply particular modes of subjectivity. As Sandra Stanley Holton remarks of the militant suffragettes, commitment to this struggle "must be understood primarily in terms of a cast of mind, a moral philosophy, a way of looking at the world"; so, too, I would add, must rejection of the militant movement be examined for its subjective underpinnings.[2] My tactic here will be to juxtapose a reading of suffragette intersubjectivity with its critique in order to give voice to the disparate philosophical and political positions articulated by women within the movement.

This chapter differs from those that have preceded it in two important ways. First, I pay much less attention here to individual autobiographies, with the exception of Constance Lytton's *Prisons and Prisoners* (1914). I look instead at the kinds of claims about themselves that suffragettes make in their autobiographical writings so as to establish the subjective consequences of political action for those who engage in it. Second, I draw quite explicitly on both a communitarian critique of the autonomous individual and a critique of the communitarian ideal itself in order to situate the struggle over aims and ends within the suffragette movement in terms of the contemporary discourse on difference. In terms of my analysis here, the most relevant difference among suffrage workers concerns class, whereas for U.S. feminism today, race and heterosexism are the more salient issues. While I do not assume that the particular struggles within the suffrage movement and the contemporary feminist one are at all identical, I do see an analogy between the two in that then as now, feminists and others working for social and political change must deal with questions of differences among and within us.

That this chapter, like some of the earlier ones, highlights questions of differences is very much a function of my own position as a white, heterosexual, working-class-identified feminist academic; I, too, continue to grapple with issues that surfaced within the suffragette movement as part of my coming to terms with feminist politics in a multicultural U.S. context. What I offer here, then, is an interested and partial history, written more to work through certain intellectual and political questions of my own, and of my generation perhaps, than to provide a "true" narrative of a particular historical network of relations.[3] My belief is that many contemporary feminist and feminist-identified readers will recognize themselves in the account I produce; my hope is that this reading may inspire us to do some things differently.

The Question of Representation

In *Ancilla's Share* (1924), a text highly critical of both gendered inequality and the organized suffrage movement, the American-born actress, writer, and feminist Elizabeth Robins spoke for many when she enounced her perception of the disparity between men's ostensibly enlightened views and their benighted practices: "It is clear that intelligent representation of women cannot be left to men who, however modern they think themselves, have as regards women the medieval mind."[4] Robins's point—that antiquated male attitudes toward the other sex made it impossible for men to understand or represent modern women—had its basis in middle-class women's experience.[5] Most feminists, however, believed that the new and visibly different position of women in English culture at the turn of the century, as demonstrated on many fronts and best symbolized by the suffrage movement, demanded a transformation of law and legislation as well as male views. "A change of the customary habits and usages of the nation is what is required," argued the socialist-feminist Teresa Billington-Greig, "and this must be preceded by a change of opinion, a change of outlook."[6] While Billington-Greig assigns temporal priority to changing attitudes and opinions rather than to getting the vote, in practice suffrage workers sought both ends at once.

That twofold task was difficult to accomplish on either front. As a founding member of the Actresses' Franchise League (AFL) and one of the only actresses in management during the first decade of the new century, Lena Ashwell points out the differences between her actual practice as a theatrical lessee and the legal anomaly which made her something less than a proper individual in the eyes of the law:

> I was the sole proprietor and licensee of the Kingsway Theatre; I engaged the company, the staff, the manager, the solicitor, and the chartered accountants. When the income tax returns were filled in by my accountants . . . I disappeared utterly from view because the paper had to be signed as correct in every detail by my husband who knew nothing about the theatre or the work of the stage.[7]

Ashwell's complaint highlights the paradox: while she is, in fact, the sole agent of her enterprise, and legally responsible for the paying of taxes, she is not, in law, an autonomous individual because she is a married woman. Her husband's signature makes her "[disappear] utterly from view," and thus she is not misrepresented, but represented indirectly, only through him. Despite her financial contribution to the maintenance of the state, the state did not recognize her existence, and the contradiction contained therein became a prime target for suffrage activists. As Christabel Pankhurst argued in her own defense at her trial in October 1908, "The law of the land is that taxation and representation must go together. The law of the land is that who obeys laws must have a share in making them. Therefore . . . we are asking the Government to abandon the illegal practice of denying representation to those who have a perfect right to enjoy it."[8]

From this quintessentially liberal point of view, what the suffrage activists asked was a remedy for a legalized inequality that no longer represented an actual state of affairs: for women to affix their signatures to tax returns and to fill out their own ballots at polling places would be visible signs of the changes that had taken place in English culture. Women had progressively achieved equality of access to economic opportunity and political power, and to give women the vote would mark yet another step toward full democracy, similar to those nineteenth-century extensions of the franchise to middle-class and working-class men. Drawing on the political rhetoric that represented English history as a continuous and progressive movement toward a just goal, Emmeline Pethick-Lawrence, one of the leaders of the suffragette movement up until 1912, called the agitation for the ballot "the final stage of the greatest bloodless revolution that has taken place since history began."[9] And J. Keir Hardie, Welsh Labour MP and true friend to the women's movement, thought the enfranchisement of all women—and particularly those who worked as wage labor—only logical: "Since, then, women are more and more taking part in the world's work, it surely follows that they ought also to enjoy the chief right of citizenship. Otherwise they will suffer from sex legislation quite as much as men have hitherto suffered from class legislation."[10] Giving women the vote would signal the long-protracted but inevitable triumph of progressive ideals.

Another story from Ashwell's autobiography reveals a second facet of the feminist struggle, the battle to change male attitudes about women's place. Immediately after she cites the problem of the tax return, Ashwell records an instance in which women would not have been represented or allowed to represent themselves had they not objected to their own exclusion. In the gala performance planned to celebrate King George's coronation in 1910, all the leading actor-managers gave themselves leading roles, while only two or three women were cast in supporting parts; Ashwell fired off a letter of protest to Sir Charles Wyndham, head of the Managers' Association, and got a Jonson masque with a wholly female cast onto the program (pp. 167–68). That women could be eliminated, overlooked, erased from the stage as from the tax return as if they did not exist was, for Ashwell, a critical fact of her everyday experience. The political difficulty for this actress-manager, and for many women, was thus not only to gain access to political representation, but also to make men realize that women counted. In altering the legal and economic structures that made women's interests and experience invisible, feminist activists also simultaneously sought to alter the everyday practices of individuals and institutions.

Founded in 1908, the AFL was but one of a host of professional women's organizations formed in support of "the Cause."[11] Writers, artists, physicians, university graduates, and others all established groups of their own, with each participant usually holding a concurrent membership in one of the three major suffrage alliances, the National Union of Women's Suffrage Societies (NUWSS), the Women's Freedom League (WFL), and the WSPU.[12] Aside from the various contributions members made through the use of the skills that had brought them together, each organization had an important role to play in the mass marches held to promote the extension of the franchise. These demonstrations were carefully orchestrated by a team of volunteers and staged to produce the strongest possible impact on both the House of Commons, skeptical of the extent of electoral support for "the Cause," and a heterogeneous public whose fervor for "Votes for Women" could not otherwise be reliably measured.

Relying on pageantry to get their points across, the leaders of the movement, and especially those of the WSPU, accurately gauged the tenor of the times in adapting "theatrical methods" to a political cause.[13] As George Bernard Shaw wrote sardonically and somewhat proleptically in his preface to *Plays Pleasant*, "Public and private life become daily more theatrical: the modern Kaiser, Dictator, President or PM is nothing if not an effective actor; all newspapers are now edited histrionically; and the records of our law courts show that the stage is affecting personal conduct to an unprecedented extent."[14] But in all those institutions—politics, journalism, law—those who determined what would be represented were men, whereas the organizers of suffrage street theater, and the majority of the participants (with the important exception of the police), were women.

Always at issue for suffrage workers in any public event were questions of representation and self-representation. Most activists criticized the newspapers for suppressing and misrepresenting their activities. "It was impossible to obtain fair publicity in the Press," complained Dora B. Montefiore, an adult suffragist not affiliated with the WSPU, because those in control of the mass media were "so ignorant, prejudiced and malicious, that the general public thought we were a band of ill-behaved viragoes with raucous voices and abominable manners."[15] To counteract these images, suffragists and suffragettes alike always made sure to dress for the public in thoroughly respectable, even modishly feminine attire; as Martha Vicinus puts it, they "emphasized the importance of femininity and feminine values even as [they] were performing unfeminine acts" (p. 264). In staging mass protests and confrontations with the police, women "were indeed part of the spectacle," Lisa Tickner argues, "but they also produced and controlled it; as active agents they need not passively endure the gaze of onlookers who were curious or perhaps indifferent." With "full self-consciousness and with great skill and ingenuity," the militant women attempted, with varying degrees of success, to effect political change by influencing the ways in which they were publicly represented.[16]

Emmeline and Christabel Pankhurst, leaders of the WSPU, committed themselves to tactics that saturated public consciousness with the story of the struggle. In response to misrepresentation in the newspapers—which invariably printed photographs of middle-class women being mauled by police in the streets of London, but failed to move beyond this level of sensationalism in their editorials—Emmeline Pethick-Lawrence and her husband, Frederick, founded and edited *Votes for Women!*, a weekly newspaper that gathered suffrage news and disseminated propaganda across the country, sold by subscription and by volunteers on streetcorners. "Publicists of the first order," the Pankhursts "embodied the very spirit of successful advertisement," and they drew crowds, sometimes hostile but often admiring, wherever they went.[17] As the campaign escalated and began to receive widespread media coverage, new tactics were invented and old ones temporarily abandoned. Even the truce of 1910–11 could be turned to suffragette advantage, for as Christabel Pankhurst notes of that period in her autobiography, *Unshackled* (1959), "Mild militancy was more or less played out. . . . Strategically, then, a pause in military would be valuable, for it would give time for familiarity to fade, so that the same methods could be used again with freshness and effect." Consciously representing the movement not only as a set of tactical maneuvers but also as a theatrical production, she adds that "much depended in militancy, as it depends in other things, upon timing and placing, upon the dramatic arrangement and sequence of acts and events."[18]

As a result of their methods, the leaders of the suffrage movement became celebrities of the day, compared to and represented as "indistinguishable from the typical actress," and Christabel Pankhurst was particularly singled out as the ingenue of the suffragettes.[19] "She has all the qualities which an actress needs, and of which so few actresses have any," wrote an unusually appreciative Max Beerbohm, who found "her whole body . . . alive with her every meaning."[20] When by fleeing to Paris she eluded the police who sought to arrest her, "by her daring and successful escape she . . . once again made herself as popular with the masses as any reigning cinema Star" (p. 267), according to Emmeline Pethick-Lawrence. Her sister Sylvia saw that Christabel's appealing beauty paved the way to her audience's hearts and minds: "That she was slender, young, with the flawless colouring of a briar rose, and an easy grace . . . were delicious embellishments to the sterner features of her discourse."[21]

In *The Convert* (1907), the novel based on her play, *Votes for Women!* (1907), Elizabeth Robins compares the leader of the suffragettes, a character clearly modeled on Christabel Pankhurst, to "an overblown Adelphi heroine"; more seriously, she analyzes the source of Christabel's success as her seeming artlessness.

> [It] was impossible not to feel that when she herself smiled it was because she couldn't help it, and not, singularly enough, because of any dependence she placed upon the value of dimples as an asset of persuasion. What she seemed to be after was to stir these people up. It could not be denied that she knew how to do it, any more than it could be doubted that she was ignorant of how large a part of her success was played by a peculiarly amusing and provocative personality.[22]

To represent the suffragette as actress—part innocent charmer, part conscious performer, gifted with an "amusing and provocative personality"—and to see that personality as the key to political (as to professional) power was not new to the discourse on femininity for, as I have already argued, personality was seen to make all the difference between success and failure for the actress. Nor was it new to the discourse of politics; one of the most striking and problematic things about the suffragette movement, as Martha Vicinus has shown, is that it wrenched familiar tropes from old contexts and remixed them in a new one, in the service of feminist politics. For if Ellen Terry had been the Victorians' paradigmatic Portia, then Christabel Pankhurst—granddaughter of an amateur actor, daughter of political radicals, a woman who had studied law without even the possibility of being admitted to the bar—became "the Portia of the Law Courts" for an adoring Edwardian public.

The Pankhursts wrote the script, and their followers played their parts to the letter; even during her Parisian exile, Christabel was always at center stage, producer, director, and star. Describing her trial in 1908, she makes the dramatic metaphor explicit and concrete, collapsing its allegorical and literal levels as she puts patriarchy on the witness stand, remaking that metaphor to serve her own ends:

> The day came: the two Ministers [Lloyd George and Herbert Gladstone] were there. The Court was packed: the atmosphere was tense. . . . There was the relief of knowing women at that moment of political combat humanly even and equal with men. True, they still held back our vote, but they had to reckon with us as representing womanhood. We were in the dock, but they that day were also there. For the witness box of the Police Court was really the dock in that larger and higher Court of public opinion, and indeed of history, before which we Suffragettes, the advocates for womanhood, were arraigning these two Ministers and political leaders on the charge of illiberality and injustice.   (*Unshackled*, p. 108)

The symbolic reversal enacted here brilliantly captures the rhetorical and representational charge of militancy, which made every masculine venue a site at which those who accused women themselves became the accused. While the Pankhursts were the guilty lawbreakers in the eyes of the law and its representatives, these "advocates for womanhood" refused to be bound by laws which they had no part in making; they arraigned Cabinet ministers, MPs, and magistrates for violating the ostensibly universal principles these officials were pledged to uphold. Taking the law court as her stage, Christabel Pankhurst represents the suffrage struggle in feminist terms.

The power Christabel Pankhurst's visionary militancy held over her followers rested in large part on the absolute distinctions she drew between male persecutors and their female victims and, over time, she became even more separatist in her rhetoric: by 1913, she was claiming that men's sexual depravity was the root cause of all inequality and counseling her followers to have nothing to do with men.[23] As I will subsequently explore in further detail, women who became disaffected from the movement left because they could no longer accept what the Pankhursts imposed. The strongest critic of the Pankhursts, Teresa Billington-Greig, argued that casting the struggle in terms of male violence and female innocence completely obscured the "true cases of victimisation caused by the conditions of which we complained"; in provoking repeated confrontations between militant women and the police, in inciting Liberal leaders to use force against women whose main purpose was to pose for the daily photographers, the Pankhursts "set out to create an arbitrary supply of artificial victims" who were, in Billington-Greig's view, themselves victimized by the Pankhursts' indifference to them.[24] "For women who were concerned to build a firm foundation for radical social change," Vicinus states, "the leaders of the WSPU were maddening in their utter reliance upon personal appeal, demagoguery, and drama" (p. 258). Yet however we assess the tactics of the suffragette leaders, the experience of being a part of the movement clearly transformed the self-conceptions of those who joined it, whether they played leading roles or remained relative unknowns. Participation in radical politics, and particularly in the brand of action the Pankhursts promulgated, was a powerful force in shaping subjectivity for the women who gave their time, their energies, and even their bodies to "the Cause."

Self and Community: Suffragette Intersubjectivity

One of the apparent contradictions of the militant movement is that its leaders criticized the Asquith government for being tyrannical and antidemocratic, but themselves employed autocracy in the WSPU's internal organization. All those who disagreed with Emmeline and Christabel Pankhurst's policy—from Billington-Greig and Charlotte Despard, two of the Pankhursts' first supporters, and the Pethick-Lawrences, the Union's financiers and associate tacticians, to Christabel's socialist sisters, Adela and Sylvia—were exiled from the center of WSPU power. Those who remained were subject to the will and orders of Christabel, as was Annie Kenney, converted to suffrage by the force of Christabel's personality and subsequently her most loyal lieutenant. Kenney's faith in Christabel, which amounts to utter, even abject personal devotion, made her more than willing to implement to the letter her leader's plans, but that devotion is not, as some Pankhurst critics claim, wholly without a pragmatic basis, which Kenney establishes in her own account, *Memories of a Militant* (1924). While she writes of her position on the WSPU executive that "to put me on a committee was like putting a doll or a dummy there" and of her repeated arrests that "I never had the least objection to being moved about on the political chess-board," her compliance is rooted in a deep trust of Christabel's character and in her sense that being trusting made her trustworthy.[25] Kenney defends the autocracy as creating the conditions under which the personal freedom of individual members became possible: "Paradoxical as it may seem, though we were an acknowledged autocracy, never did members have greater liberty of action, provided they kept strictly to the main policy laid down. The discipline the new members had to undergo was good for character building, but once they were proved to be 'true blue' they had militant materials given to them to utilize as they thought best" (p. 80). Constance Lytton echoes this point of view when she claims that "far from tending to produce uniformity of type," autocratic leadership "enhanced individuality."[26] Only by initially giving up her claim to self-determination could the militant suffragette become self-determining; renouncing the power to forge her own ends and purposes, the suffragette came to possess a new self, dedicated to a common ideal.

Heroine-worship of the Pankhursts' has been said by some to verge on fascism, and I will discuss later a few of the dissidents who leveled just this charge at the WSPU. But within the context of this movement, and of feminist consciousness during the prewar period, renouncing the self was for many a necessary and even glorious step: as Olive Schreiner argues in *Woman and Labor* (1911), for each and every woman in the movement, "the abiding consciousness of an end to be attained, reaching beyond her personal life and individual interests . . . binds with the common bond of an impersonal enthusiasm into one solid body."[27] While such antisuffragists as Ethel Colquhoun accused the suffragettes of preaching "the gospel of individualism," the suffragettes themselves represented the ends of the mere individual as altogether subsidiary to the common cause, in which the impersonal pursuit of political justice was the highest goal.[28] "To lose the personal in a great impersonal is to live!" (p. 78) wrote Christabel Pankhurst, coining what might have served as an unofficial motto for the whole movement; for women who had so long been consigned to the personal, the private, and the familial, the opportunity to live for something other than that must have been a heady experience.

While put to a new political use, this ethic of personal renunciation is continuous with some aspects of the Victorian ideology of femininity. As we have already seen, Victorian women's claims to autonomy had always been rejected on the basis of their prescribed part as the servants of others' needs and aims, and even independent women were used to defining themselves in terms of self-sacrifice and self-abnegation. As political theorist Jean Bethke Elshtain notes, "When any previously excluded group enters the public sphere . . . the terms of that entry will reflect [its] prior privatization": suffragette ideology in this way reveals its own indebtedness to the very system against which it was rebelling.[29] And suffragette ideologists often adopted the essentializing rhetoric that portrayed all men as oppressors while eliding historical differences among women, as in Robins's sweeping claim that "the Woman Suffrage Movement has tapped those deep reservoirs of spiritual devotion and consecrated selflessness from which the world has, from the beginning, drawn its moral and religious strength."[30]

Other claims about women's subjectivity by suffragettes further underline the problematic status of this emphasis on selflessness in that they present an uncritical view of the relation between political action and personal change. Those who joined the militant movement and later wrote about it constantly recur to its revolutionary impact on their outlook, enumerating the practical differences militancy made in their lives. The wealthy daughter of a mine-owning MP and one of the founders of the feminist periodical *Time and Tide*, Margaret Haig sums up a prevalent opinion about the influence of the movement on her generation: "It required an almost unbelievable effort of will before a woman brought up with all the inhibitions of the decent Victorian 'lady' could bring herself to throw stones through a street window. The women who did it broke more than windows with the stones; they broke the crust and conventions of a whole era."[31] Yet in representing bourgeois femininity as a matter of social "conventions" rather than a deeply internalized, complex structure of beliefs and attitudes, suffragettes underestimated the power of the multiple structures that had shaped the ideologies of middle-class femininity; moreover, they subscribed to a belief in the deep self beneath the "crust" which would emerge under new conditions. Militancy "meant to women the discovery of their own identity," wrote Emmeline Pethick-Lawrence, "the *real* person that often remains throughout a life-time hidden under the mask of appearances" (p. 215).

Part of the movement's emancipatory promise, then, was that it would enable women to be who they really were, a premise of which today's poststructuralist feminists are duly suspicious. As Rita Felski argues in the context of 1970s American feminism, "The 'authentic self' is very much a social product, and the attempt to assert its privileged autonomy can merely underline its profound dependence upon the cultural and ideological systems through which it is constituted."[32] Promising access to "the true self" beneath the masks or roles, suffragette ideology perpetuated the norms of bourgeois subjectivity, yet at the same time, it appropriated a discourse of liberation that made possible a certain mode of thinking through questions of subjectivity. Only by historicizing ideologies that link subjectivity with politics, as Julia Kristeva does in "Women's Time," or as Felski does in relation to 1970s feminist consciousness-raising, can we see both their scope and their limits, their importance to the movement in its moment and their necessary contingency on a whole complex of factors.[33]

While the suffragette ethic of renunciation represented a revision of Victorian ideology rather than a radical break with it, the opening of a specifically political space for women's altruism and activism enabled women to experience themselves as political and public agents of social transformation. To be sure, many suffragettes had already taken advantage of the new political and economic opportunities afforded to Victorian women of the 1870s and 1880s: Emmeline Pankhurst had been very active in Independent Labour Party politics and had served as a Poor Law Guardian in Manchester; Emmeline Pethick-Lawrence had worked in London settlements among the poor; countless anonymous others had cut their political teeth in trades union activity or in the women's auxiliaries to the major political parties.[34] Just as those middle-class girls who had chosen to go on the stage had fought their families, women who decided to take up public work on behalf of the working class or women's issues often met with vehement parental disapproval. "The very idea that women should leave their homes and live in the comparative freedom of a community, in order to carry out rather subversive principles of social sharing," wrote Pethick-Lawrence, "was a bombshell" to the conventional (p. 72). Women freed from home duties were likely to do all sorts of unthinkable things, and to do them not as individuals, but in concert with other women (and sometimes men); in collectives, women began to build a sense of themselves not as isolated atoms, but as a united force for change. "Out in the open women begin to combine, and what is more, they begin to look abroad over the great world of industrial life, and to perceive that its progress consists of ever-growing powers of combination"; in doing so, they threatened not only the economic foundations of contemporary life, but also the old domestic order. "Those who take part in [public] life," the socialist-feminist Margaret McMillan concludes, "cannot long be home-workers in the old sense."[35]

The political impact of the movement aside, the collective gathering of women around a shared project altered the material circumstances of their lives. As Kenny remarks, "The changed life into which most of us entered was a revolution in itself. No home-life, no one to say what we should do or what we should not do, no family ties[;] we were free and alone in a great brilliant city, scores of young women scarcely out of their teens met together in a revolutionary movement, outlaws or breakers of laws, independent of everything and everybody, fearless and self-confident" (p. 110). The novelty of this experience for women throws Rachel Ferguson back onto male models for collective identity when she attempts to describe it in the 1930s: "The suffrage campaign . . . was our Eton and Oxford, our regiment, our ship, our cricket-match."[36] "In that living identification of the self with the corporate whole" (p. 215), Pethick-Lawrence writes approvingly, women learned discipline, loyalty, and courage in the service of "the Cause."

While the movement might have been as hierarchically structured as any public school, and even militarist in its tone, its overall tenor was emancipatory and liberationist. And Ferguson's analogy captures the sense of collegiality and camaraderie that the movement fostered among its members, a sense of common purpose that, for many of the participants, overrode all other differences. The composer Ethel Smyth writes of her experience in prison "that during those two months in Holloway, for the first and last time in my life I was in good society. Think of it! More than a hundred women . . . one and all divorced from any thought of self, forgetful of everything save the cause for which they had faced imprisonment."[37] Pethick-Lawrence speaks of "women of the upper, middle and working classes [realizing] a new comradeship with each other. Neither class, nor wealth, nor education counted any more, only devotion to the common ideal. No longer did women feel loneliness or isolation or inhibition" (p. 188). A collective movement, she claims, breeds unity across class difference.

While other suffrage autobiographers and many historians contest Pethick-Lawrence's assessment, some participants held that class background made no apparent difference at all; belonging to a community that had professed to transcend all difference inspired individuals to do things of which they had not supposed themselves capable. The daughter of millworkers who herself began working in the mills at ten years, Kenney found that working for the movement freed her from the factory for good, and gave her a new identity: "I knew *the* change had come into my life. The old life had gone, a new life had come . . . I felt absolutely changed. The past seemed blotted out" (p. 42). Invested with a sense of mission, the suffragette Mary Richardson, who later slashed the Rokeby Venus, converted the Bishop of London to "the Cause," but took no personal responsibility for it: "It was as if I were compelled by something outside me to speak as I did. . . . The idea that I could feel satisfied with myself had not entered my mind. At such moments I was no longer my small personal self. The cause had triumphed: that was what mattered."[38]

These features of suffragette subjectivity—the ethic of renunciation and the consequent premium placed on selflessness and impersonality, the tendency to attribute agency to the movement rather than to the individual, and the transcendence of difference—were criticized from within the movement from various points of view, as I will establish later; they are neither unproblematic in and of themselves nor necessarily constitutive of all women's political identities. Indeed, the historicity of this subjectivity is all the more apparent because it only emerges in autobiography when middle-class women begin to participate in groups other than the family and to develop a sense of women as a group. But I do want to suggest that this subjectivity has radical potential which only becomes visible if we take seriously that last statement of Richardson's: "I was no longer my small personal self. The cause had triumphed: that was what mattered." If we think of "the Cause" not as an abstract political goal, but as a living movement composed of women (and some men) working together, suffering, struggling, marching, speaking, and acting, then we will see that Richardson's claim refers us beyond an individualist paradigm for identity and toward a collectivist model.

The relationship of the individual to the collective within suffrage texts corresponds to what Michael Sandel calls an "intersubjective conception" of personal identity. As he puts it, "The relevant description of the self may embrace more than a single, individual human being, as when we attribute responsibility or affirm an obligation to a family or community or class or nation." Under certain "moral circumstances," one's sex, one's race, or a political movement may be considered just such a suprapersonal entity.[39] By contrast, orthodox liberal theory locates agency within the individual, and considers groups merely as aggregates of individuals; from that point of view, Richardson's claim is nonsensical, antirational, almost mystical. As the agent of conversion, the one who reasoned, argued, and persuaded another to accept her position, she surely embodies the principles that define the Cartesian subject of cognition. But as Ruth L. Smith and Deborah M. Valenze note in their study of Victorian working-class women's moral frameworks, the "character of moral behavior among those who do not privilege the autonomous individual" as rational, independent agent "presents a challenge—and an alternative"—to liberal individualism.[40]

In a recent critique of "the ideal of community," Iris Marion Young takes issue with Sandel, among other communitarian theorists, for "[invoking] a conception of community to project an alternative to the individualism and abstract formalism they attribute to liberalism," a critique to which my own theorizing here is also potentially subject. As she rightly points out, "the neat distinction between individualism and community thus generates a dialectic in which each is a condition for the other," and thus, according to her logic, no truly revolutionary subversion can take place by the mere reversal of valorized terms.[41] Yet she also acknowledges that "asserting the value of community over individualism . . . does have some critical force with respect to the dominant ideology and social relations" (p. 306): while she finds that value negligible to contemporary U.S. conditions, for the suffrage movement—with its own historical differences from our contemporary U.S. feminist, antiracist, and anticapitalist struggles—that "critical force" was highly significant. And Young's conception of "the ideal of community"—which, she claims, "presumes subjects can understand one another as they understand themselves" (p. 302)—fails to register the possibility that it is through a particular community, such as the one the suffragettes created, that individual subjects not only form bonds around shared commitments, but also work through, collectively and subjectively, differences of various and particular kinds. By opposing a "politics of difference" to "the ideal of community," Young implies that the two are mutually exclusive, whereas my reading of the suffragette movement suggests that the notion of intersubjectivity—which attends to individuals as sites of community-building, and to communities as shaping forces of individuals—can potentially allow for both identification and conflict, both connection and difference.[42]

The intersubjective character of "the Cause," I suggest, enabled its participants to identify as and with women, and not just as individuals bound to particulars of family or class, so that when "the Cause" triumphs, meeting that collective goal satisfies—even as it constitutes—the subject's needs and desires, and reaffirms the worth of her participatory identity. If "this sense of participation in the achievements and endeavors of (certain) others engages the reflective self-understandings of the participants," Sandel continues, "we may come to regard ourselves, over the range of our various activities, less as individuated subjects with certain things in common, and more as members of a wider (but still determinate) subjectivity . . . as participants in a common identity" (p. 143): it is this "common identity" as suffragettes that the movement forged and from which it drew its strength. Yet that "common identity" did not wholly blot out the significant political and experiential gaps among subjects; it provided a ground for intersubjective connections rather than a solution to or an escape from material and ideological differences.

Later on, I will sketch some of the implications for both autobiography and suffrage history of understanding "the Cause" as an intersubjective movement. But first I would like to look closely at Constance Lytton's account of her experience in the movement, for it provides the most dramatic extant autobiographical example of suffragette intersubjectivity.

Hunger-Striking, Forcible Feeding and the Case of Constance Lytton

On 24 June 1909, the suffragette painter Marion Wallace Dunlop was arrested; days later, she was sentenced to a month's imprisonment in Royal Holloway Prison after refusing to be bound over to keep the peace. The authorities would not place her in the First Division, and thus denied her the political prisoner status that she had requested; in response she began a hunger strike which lasted for almost four days, until she was released on account of her physical condition. Wallace Dunlop's action was voluntary and apparently unpremeditated; as others began to adopt it, the WSPU instituted it as policy. Over time, it became one of the suffragettes' best weapons against the government: as an act of noncompliance, a protest against unfair imprisonment and unjust treatment, the hunger strike was an individual act that made, when undertaken by many, a powerful collective statement of solidarity.

It is possible to argue, as Jane Marcus does, that the hunger strike represents the suffragettes' "symbolic refusal of motherhood": when those socially cast as nourishers and nurturers deny themselves material sustenance, they sever the link between women's reproductive power and their prescribed cultural destiny.[43] And if we add to Marcus's analysis the political theorist Carole Pateman's provocative discussion of women's reproductive ability as that which makes women simultaneously "deficient in a specifically *political* capacity" and "naturally subversive of men's political order," we can see this protest operating in two registers: by denying their prescribed reproductive function, suffragette hunger-strikers were contesting patriarchal definitions of woman-as-mother while also appropriating what had been the political tool of other, mostly male, dissidents to make their own argument.[44] Of course, as Helena Michie suggests, the decision not to eat can be viewed as wholly in line with Victorian norms for women's conduct: what she calls an "aesthetics of deprivation" among middle-class women "forced eating to become a private activity and abstemiousness a public avowal of femininity."[45] The very title of Susie Ohrbach's book on modern anorexia—*Hunger Strike*—suggests that women who refuse to eat take social norms for women's bodies to an extreme that threatens the viability of their existence, and so personally and politically expose the painful contradictions to which female forms are socially subjected.[46] But whether or not we agree with Elaine Showalter's claim that suffragette hunger-strikers "put the symptomatology of anorexia nervosa to work in the service of a feminist cause," the imprisoned suffragette's refusal to eat announced her willingness to use her body as a political stake and so to contest the cultural construction of the middle-class feminine body as marginal to the realm of politics.[47]

There is, however, altogether less emphasis on the practice and meaning of the hunger strike in suffragette texts and rather more on forcible feeding: instead of analyzing the implications of an act voluntarily undertaken as a sign of resistance to institutional male power, suffrage writers painstakingly document the force used to overcome that resistance. As Lisa Tickner represents it, "the women who suffered" forcible feeding "felt [it] as a kind of rape" (p. 107): a male doctor or doctors, assisted by female wardresses who held down the struggling prisoner, would insert a long tube through the patient's mouth or nose and pour liquid into her stomach. While there is no real need to reach for sexual metaphors to describe the experience, it makes sense to speak of forcible feeding as a violation of the boundaries between the self and the world, or between those invested with power and those subject to it. Elaine Scarry's analysis of torture in *The Body in Pain*, which resonates on a number of levels with suffragette accounts of forcible feeding, suggests that "in the most literal way possible, the created world of thought and feeling, all the psychological and mental content that constitutes both one's self and one's world . . . ceases to exist" for one whose body is violated as a means of violating the sanctity and integrity of her spirit.[48] "One feels sometimes," wrote one survivor of forcible feeding in declining to describe her sufferings, "as if it were a violation of oneself to write of them."[49]

By mid-September 1909, the Home Secretary, Herbert Gladstone, had devised a plan for foiling the hunger-strikers: those who refused food were to be forcibly fed. A year later, after a period of grace in which Winston Churchill granted "special privileges to prisoners of good character but without admitting the political nature of the women's protest" (Vicinus, p. 269), suffragettes renewed the hunger strike in defiance of the government's intransigence about the ballot. And forcible feeding was once again used, ostensibly to save women's lives, in practice to weaken their physical powers of resistance, perhaps even to break their minds and spirits. For as Scarry writes of torture, the explicit purposes of the powerful in inflicting bodily punishment—to elicit information, for example—often mask what is really at stake: it is "precisely because the reality of that power is so highly contestable, the régime so unstable" (p. 27), that the display of force manifested in the act of forcible feeding becomes necessary. In challenging male domination, the suffragettes provoked the wrath of their adversaries. And by claiming that feeding the hunger-strikers was "for their own good," the Asquith government attempted to legitimate actions which were, to many, inconceivably brutal, actions which created, in Brian Harrison's words, "suffering so great as almost to pass the limits of what can humanly be endured" (p. 68).

Mary Richardson, who on one occasion underwent the painful, violent process twice a day for nearly ten weeks, wrote that "forcible feeding, in some strange way, disintegrated me, soul and body" (p. 84): to continue a fast while resisting the temptation to eat the meals brought to one's cell would have been difficult enough, but to fight against the doctors, to have the tube forced through one's body, to vomit as much as one could, as Sylvia Pankhurst did, and always to know that the whole process would be repeated again and again was to be forced to submit, to give what Pankhurst called "a shameful consent, an encouragement to the maintainers of outrage" (p. 446). Her own account of the aftermath of an episode, however, shows that "consent" and submission were not appropriate categories to invoke in terms of this experience, for the practice of forcible feeding highlights the fact that women, as disenfranchised, legal nonsubjects, could not truly be said to consent to anything.

The physical and psychological disintegration Richardson notes is the very ground of Pankhurst's experience; the assault on her body is also an attack on the integrity of her identity.

> Sometimes when the struggle was over, or even in the heat of it, in a swift flash I felt as though my entity had been broken up into many selves, of which one, aloof and calm, surveyed all this misery, and one, ruthless and unswerving, forced the weak, shrinking body to its ordeal. Sometimes, breaking forth, it seemed, from the inner depths of my being, came outraged, violated, tortured selves; waves of emotion, fear, indignation, wildly up-surging.
>
> Whilst all these selves were struggling, resisting, shrinking from the tortures, would rise in them a fierce desire to scream. . . . Then a small fear would creep up, lest all those voices, of those maddened, agonized sensations, those huge, untamable emotions, should overwhelm alike the ruthless and the calm self, and, with great effort, I would silence them—lie still and, when I could, clean off all the filth left from the outrage.   (pp. 444–45)

One self is distant, detached, while another "forced the shrinking body"—the object under siege—"to its ordeal." Madness lies within: in suppressing "a fierce desire to scream," Pankhurst preserves some hedge against total break-down. Cut off from the suffragette community which was operative even in prison, her struggle becomes wholly isolated and wholly internal.

Sylvia Pankhurst survived the disintegrating process by asserting what will she had left, and by painting and writing in her cell. Mary Richardson made contact again with the world by communicating covertly with other prisoners, but she would also feel "an influence, almost of a presence, beside me which gave me consolation and sympathy" (p. 84) as she lay recovering. Once the Prisoners' Temporary Discharge for Ill-health Act—popularly known as the Cat and Mouse Act—passed the Commons with Home Secretary McKenna's full approval in April 1913, forcible feeding became even more of an ordeal: hunger-strikers were forcibly fed until they became dangerously ill, were re-leased for a week or so, and then taken back to prison to complete their sen-tences. Only those with the highest public profiles, such as Emmeline Pank-hurst and Annie Kenney, were spared forcible feeding. Other women left prison and the movement broken in health and in spirit. "For the women constrained under the misery of forcible feeding," Sylvia Pankhurst writes, "the joy and the splendour of the struggle was attenuated to so fine a point, that it might well become imperceptible" (p. 588).

Forcible feeding tested the limits of the ethic of selflessness by making bod-ily sacrifice a real choice. Women who underwent it, some repeatedly, experi-enced in and through their bodies the concrete realization of suffragette ideol-ogy; they renounced the claims of the self in giving themselves completely to "the Cause." Yet paradoxically, it was embodiment that both formed the ground for building that ideology and marked each woman's separation from other women: women formed a "sex-class" on the basis of a common culturally con-structed biology, but the intensely personal experience of forcible feeding was directed at the individual and designed to break down all connections between self and world. Suffragettes attempted to transcend separation by participating in a set of common experiences—interrupting Liberal meetings, selling papers in the streets, marching in processions, going on deputations—all of which made individual women subject to physical violence; by their collective action they asserted solidarity across and despite difference. Under forcible feeding, how-ever, each prisoner was disciplined as an embodied individual, and doctors dis-ciplined differentially: relatively unknown women, like Mary Richardson, and working-class women were far more likely to be forcibly fed than women whose surnames or reputations conveyed social or economic standing. It is in this context that Constance Lytton's radical gesture—entering prison in disguise so that she, too, could be forcibly fed—represents in miniature the problem of difference within the suffragette movement as a whole.

Lytton's background made the disguise a practical necessity: member of a prominent aristocratic family, sister of a peer, and "a chronic invalid" (p. 1), she was wary of special treatment from the authorities, as she records in *Pris-*

ons and Prisoners: Some Personal Experiences. On her first deputation, she disguised herself slightly "so that the police . . . should not recognise me and so be tempted not to arrest me; for people whose relatives might make a fuss effectively are considered awkward customers" (p. 35). Sentenced to four weeks in Royal Holloway Prison, she spent most of her term in the infirmary, trying to win her way into an ordinary prisoner's cell. Other suffragette prisoners in far greater physical need were treated far worse than was she, and the inequity "exasperated" her: "The action of the authorities made no pretence at inflexible, even-handed justice, and the partiality shown was all on behalf of the prisoner who needed it least" (p. 152). In January 1910, to avoid the effects of that "partiality," she chose secretly to be arrested as "Jane Warton," an unattractive, unmarried, friendless working woman, and was imprisoned in Liverpool's Walton Gaol. The disguise proved the need for it: after extensive medical examination, Lady Constance Lytton had been pronounced unfit for prison routine because of a cardiac problem; Jane Warton—whose cursory exam by the junior medical officer at Walton found her to have, in his words, a " 'ripping, splendid heart' " (p. 275)—was forcibly fed eight times before being released.

Disguising herself as a working woman enabled Lytton to meet the aims she set herself when she joined the movement and decided to go to prison: "to have personal experience of the inflictions which a Liberal Government thought suitable to women Suffragists, to share every incident of the treatment which my leaders and friends had suffered in our cause and to gain some experience of prison life from within for the sake of one day being equipped to work for prison reforms" (p. 96). These aims all share a common basis in that each rests on the principle that it is only through "personal experience" of injustice and oppression that one comes to understand it; only being in prison can prepare Lytton to address issues of reform.

This "hands on" approach to social questions is widespread among Lytton's contemporaries, and suggests the backlash against the "lady bountiful" mode of Victorian philanthropy.[50] When, in the last stages of making her decision to become a social investigator, Beatrice Webb went to live among workers—also disguising her identity—she did so in order to acquire what she thought would be a truer point of view.[51] Pethick-Lawrence "came to London with vague ideas of brotherhood and equality," but soon realized "that all attempts to help people from a platform of superiority were futile from the point of view of the helper, and of those who wanted help" (p. 95). Dora B. Montefiore likewise felt that she "must study at close quarters working-class conditions," hoping to "train my imagination and intelligence to see eye to eye with the workers in their class struggle" (p. 63). But as Virginia Woolf points out in her "Introductory Letter" to *Life as We Have Known It,* a collection of autobiographical writings by members of the Women's Cooperative Guild, material differences between the experiences of women from different classes prevent full identification, differences Woolf locates in bodily experience. "Because one's body had never stood at the wash-tub; one's hands had never wrung and scrubbed and chopped up whatever the meat may be that makes a miner's supper," the middle-class observer, however interested, could not claim to represent or understand working-class experience and subjectivity: "our sympathy was largely ficti-tious. It was aesthetic sympathy, the sympathy of the eye and of the imagina-tion, not of the heart and the nerves."[52] While middle-class women could assert solidarity with working-class women on the grounds that they shared a com-mon identity as women, women with different class positions and experiences differently experienced their embodiment as women. Training the "imagination and intelligence" to see and feel what working-class women saw and felt would not suffice, for Woolf or for Lytton—but Lytton set out to try to know, through "the heart and the nerves," what it would be to be not herself, but another, a nonprivileged, unknown other.

Early on in her account, Lytton engages the question of how she can pre-sume to represent another's position by situating herself concretely and mate-rially as a woman of the aristocracy:

> My own point of view was definite enough, but I did not feel equipped to speak
> for others. When deciding to go on the Deputation I had, however, taken stock
> of my representative character and asked myself for which group of women I
> should stand, what was my atom's share in this movement if I did not strain
> after any vicarious office but merely added my own personal weight to the
> scale? Without doubt I myself was one of that numerous gang of upper class
> leisured class spinsters, unemployed, unpropertied, unendowed, uneducated,
> without equipment or training for public service, economically dependent en-
> tirely upon others, not masters of their own leisure, however oppressively
> abundant that might seem to the onlooker.   (p. 39)

Her "representative character" as a dependent creature enables her, in the pages that follow, to critique the condition of women in her class, to protest the circumstances that make the spinster "a distortion, an abnormality, an untidi-ness of creation" (p. 41).

Lytton speaks from her own experience here: her family having assumed that "being past the age when marriage was likely, I should always remain at home," her "yearning" for a career in music or journalism "finding no favour" with her mother or siblings, "these wishes . . . had in each case eventually to be repressed" (p. 1). Generalizing from her particular experience to affirm her membership in a particular social group, she then identifies her lack of an in-dependent career as characteristic of other women in her situation: "The notion of a vocation apart from my family and home remained as foreign to my ideas as it was then to the average British spinster of my class" (p. 3). Lytton's recognition of the circumstances she shares with other women of her class is as important as the analysis she delivers because it establishes the standpoint from which she writes as grounded in her experience of her class and gender, and because she takes up her position as a "representative character" with a high degree of consciousness as to how that standpoint unites her with some women and separates her from most others.[53]

Lytton's subsequent reflections further underscore the importance of her identifying her position, for in doing so she realizes the limits Woolf delineates, yet also finds a provisional means of negotiating them. Asserting that it is on the case of "the working women, the bread-winning woman" (p. 41) that the best appeal for women's suffrage rests, she acknowledges her own inability to represent those whose experiences are not hers:

> Though at all times at one with [working women] in point of sympathy from theoretic understanding of their troubles and needs, I was not in direct touch and had no first-hand experience that I could share with them. I read the petitions of factory workers, of the sweated home workers, of the professions— teachers, nurses, medical women—with respect and whole-hearted sympathy, but how could I stand for them when I was not equipped to represent them?   (p. 42)

When she marches in a suffrage procession, however, she "[hears] for the first time with my own ears the well worn taunt 'Go home and do your washing' " (p. 42): she is identified by her street audience as a woman worker, although herself only "an amateur scrubber and laundry-woman in the same spirit as other unemployed females dabble in water-colour drawings or hand embroidery" (p. 43). Her "magic response" (p. 42) to the taunt awakens reverence in her for those who "under unsuitable conditions, without the necessary equipment, in a small house or single room, surrounded by children, with a stinted water supply, inadequate firing utensils, a weary body and a mind distraught as to how to exist from day to day" carry out the material work of everyday life, unrewarded, unpaid, unenfranchised (p. 43). The points of similarity that she identifies—her gender, and her affinity for "the washers, the renewers week by week, the makers clean" (p. 43)—later enable Lytton, on a deputation to the Prime Minister, to prepare to assert her authority despite her difference, not by claiming to represent others, but by affirming the value of their labor: "I determined, if I should find myself the solitary representative of the Deputation and its untrained spokeswoman, I should point to the collars and shirt fronts of the gentlemen who received me and claim the freedom of citizenship for the washers" (p. 43). In this way, she avoids the pitfall of an idealized solidarity, but also maintains a position from which she can make her stand as a suffragette; her response is imaginatively and genuinely intersubjective, because it respects the integrity of others' labor rather than merely appropriating it for purely personal ends.

What ensues in Lytton's text is a minutely detailed account of her prison experiences which records every aspect of prison life from the cramped trip to jail in "Black Maria," the archaic holding van, to the wardrobe of the prisoners and the furnishings of their cells. "Now I myself was one of the criminals. I should know the sensations from actual experience, literally from within" (p. 61), and the materiality of her account conveys to her readers what those experiential "sensations" were and are; yet it was not until she was incarcerated as Jane Warton that Lytton could make the appeal to experience with fuller authority.

Having already recognized that justice operates differentially and unequally, Lytton represents her first experience of forcible feeding from a bifurcated perspective, as both Constance Lytton and Jane Warton. Through the violation of her body, she comes to understand "from within" how class inequality *is* difference because treated *as* difference:

The horror of it was more than I can describe. I was sick over the doctor and wardresses, and it seemed a long time before they took the tube out. As the doctor left he gave me a slap on the cheek, not violently, but, as it were, to express his contemptuous disapproval, and he seemed to take for granted that my distress was assumed. Then suddenly I saw Jane Warton lying before me, and it seemed as if I were outside of her. She was the most despised, ignorant and helpless prisoner that I had seen. When she had served her time and was out of the prison, no one would believe anything she said, and the doctor when he had fed her by force and tortured her body, struck her on the cheek to show how he despised her! That was Jane Warton, and I had come to help her. (pp. 269–70)

Through the doctor's gesture—which exemplifies power's posture toward the powerless—Lytton sees Jane Warton as others see her: "despised, ignorant, and helpless," and also voiceless. Unlike Lytton's own words about her experience, which went widely reported after her release, Jane Warton's independent account of her treatment would have had no authority against the testimony of officialdom; as an unknown working-class woman, "no one would believe anything she said," except perhaps those working-class women who knew from their own experiences the accuracy of her account. By approximating for the Jane Wartons a voice to which those outside the movement would listen, a voice which they could not easily ignore because of the class privilege of the speaking subject, Constance Lytton made her own point of view more authentically if not wholly representative.

"Heretical Individualists"

Lytton's action dramatized the plight of the anonymous suffragette for an audience of thousands; it proved as well, in Mary Richardson's words, that the British Government was "no respecter of persons" (p. 26) even as it illustrated "the glaring gap between legal and human values" (pp. 68–69). But the class bias on the part of the authorities that Lytton's experience proved was also widely felt to exist among the suffragette leaders themselves. Although Christabel Pankhurst had begun her political career organizing women textile workers in Manchester, and had based her original arguments for the vote on the grounds that the ballot would "advance the industrial conditions of women," her incipient Toryism and her courting of wealthy supporters led many to conclude, as Sylvia Pankhurst did, that "what interest she had ever possessed in the Socialist movement . . . she had shed as readily as a garment" (pp. 247–48).[54] As the WSPU gained national attention, it left its socialist roots behind and downplayed the role of working-class women in the movement. Without recapitulating the historians' argument as to whether or not the WSPU was as middle-class in membership and orientation as it often accused the NUWSS of being, I think it is important to note that both groups drew most of their support from middle-class women and made their public case for the vote on the familiar liberal ground of equality of opportunity and access for women to traditional male prerogatives. Even within a liberal ideological framework, however, problems of class difference can be attended to, if not wholly resolved, and Lytton's actions represent a material effort to give differences that attention.

To this point, I have tried to suggest that suffragette ideology and suffragette experience mutually constitute each other: Lytton's desire to believe in the power of "the Cause" to unite individuals across difference leads her to test it, and in testing it she comes to reinforce her own, and her readers', belief in that power. But while the intersubjective point of view she arrives at, intellectually and experientially, supports suffragette claims, other suffrage activists had quite a different response to the self-denying actions carried out in the name of "the Cause." Arguing against the autocracy, dissidents criticized the WSPU for exploiting its members, ignoring the material costs of militancy, and depriving its followers of the very autonomy for which they were fighting.

The WSPU's most vocal critics tended to be either working-class in background, socialist in politics, or both, and as such they were suspicious of the Pankhursts' increasingly single-minded emphasis on women's right to the ballot. The WFL, to which both Hannah Mitchell and Billington-Greig belonged, advocated "a political analysis which argued," in Les Garner's words, "that women's emancipation went beyond the mere gaining of the vote": the League retained its connections "with the Labour movement and the problems of working class women."[55] Many socialist women saw in the WSPU's tactics an utter betrayal of the commitment to changing the material conditions of women's lives. These critics attacked the suffragette leaders for having, in Billington-Greig's words, "sacrificed [the woman] to the getting of the vote" (p. 221); the Pankhursts "had cut themselves off completely from vital things, from the lives women lived, from the injuries they suffered."[56] While suffragette ideology preached transcendence, "heretical individualists," as Billington-Greig labeled them, totaled the material costs of mass martyrdom and found them too heavy to bear; the middle-class suffragette martyrs who chose to make themselves victims could not be considered in the same light as those working-class women whose oppression derived from socioeconomic determinants which they were, as individuals, powerless to change.

Critics charged that WSPU leaders exploited willing women by subjecting them to violence at the hands of the government, and then capitalized on their victimization for publicity's sake. The pages of *Votes for Women!* and, later, *The Suffragette* contained many members' accounts of their imprisonments, hunger strikes, and incidents of forcible feeding; like Lytton's "personal experiences," these testimonials were designed to convert readers to the justice of the WSPU's claims and to inspire members to imitate the actions recorded. "By reprieve petitions, by propaganda speeches and articles, the names and the stories of these unfortunates were torn from their obscurity" (p. 226), noted Sylvia Pankhurst; Billington-Greig, too, condemned "the exploitation of revolutionary forces and enthusiastic women for the purposes of advertisement."[57]

As the Pankhursts adopted new and more dangerous forms of militancy— stone-throwing, mailbox-burning, and finally arson—their followers incurred proportionally higher risks of imprisonment; moreover, these attacks on private property alienated many of those who had, somewhat perversely, been sympathetic when women themselves were the only real victims of militant action. Most who were opposed to the use of such violence had already left the WSPU by 1912, when militancy became even more pronounced as strategy; among the last to go were the Pethick-Lawrences, who rightly predicted that the arson campaign would prove unacceptable and unpopular with the public. "For these unknown girls there would be no international telegrams," Sylvia Pankhurst said of the arsonists; "the mead of public sympathy would be attenuated" (p. 401). By August 1913, four months after the passage of the Cat and Mouse Act, "a kind of grim and fanatical bitterness had crept into the struggle," according to Evelyn Sharp, a writer and WSPU official; maintaining the spirit of the movement was difficult in the face of so much personal suffering.[58]

Although the WSPU did not intend to kill anyone through violence—occupied buildings were never burned—some former suffragettes objected to this extreme form of militancy on the grounds that it might injure the interests of innocent people. "Personally, I did not like the destruction of an ancient church," wrote Mitchell, a working-class socialist who had joined the WFL at the time of the first split, "or the burning of letters which may have contained poor people's money."[59] But most dissident opposition to the WSPU tried to establish a link between the material costs of militancy and the effects of autocracy, for they saw the Pankhursts' insistence on complete loyalty as the direct cause of the hardships their followers suffered. Having herself lived through it, Sylvia Pankhurst recognized the suffragettes' submission to the hunger strike and forcible feeding as a form of mass suicide undertaken at the behest of her mother and sister: "The women under forcible feeding were slowly being done to death; those faithful zealots who did the will of their leaders" (p. 587) forfeited the very rights for which they were fighting.

Well in advance of the events of 1912–14, Teresa Billington-Greig published her critique of the WSPU in *The Militant Suffrage Movement* (1911).[60] Making autocracy the target of her attack, she claims that "the will of the leaders rapidly came to be substituted for the will of the members; free choice and personal liberty dwindled into insignificance" (p. 167) under the influence of the Pankhursts' rhetoric. Giving themselves up to "the Cause" meant that women relinquished personal autonomy, and so autocracy "imposed upon women the very evils of subjection from which it sets itself to deliver them" (p. 180). In doing so, autocratic leadership, even with women as leaders, reproduces a patriarchal strategy for keeping women in their place: "the women who succumb to it exhibit a type of self-subjection, not less objectionable than the more ordinary self-subjection of women to men, to which it bears a close relation" (p. 181). Breaking with what she identifies as an inherently oppressive paradigm, Billington-Greig exposes the ethic of selflessness as a historical construct that denies women the opportunity to shape their own lives:

> Ages of self-suppression and the yielding up of self have developed this capacity in women to such an extent as to make a vice out of a virtue. Woman has not only failed to assert her own right to consideration, her right to be herself,

she has given herself away, and given herself away for nothing. The militant movement, while asserting the woman's right to political liberty, has only continued the cultivation of this spirit of self-sacrifice. It has not only exploited the divine thing. It has continued its degradation.   (p. 205)

While self-sacrifice is not a bad thing, but "the divine thing," Billington-Greig objects to what women are sacrificing themselves for: to the Pankhursts, the vote had become an end in itself, rather than a means to any number of better ends, such as the material improvement of the lives of working women and their children, or of middle-class girls with limited economic opportunities other than marriage. "The only consoling reflection" about the Pankhursts' policy, she adds, "is that self-forgetfulness has been provided with an avenue of courage in place of the old-time avenue of suppression" (p. 205), but under autocracy, even this makes little material difference. The woman who follows the will of others without independently evaluating the impact of what she is doing makes herself a "creature of the leaders": "her sufferings redound to their credit and add to their glory while she herself passes through the fiery furnace—and into oblivion," for she "can be chosen and cast off, can be made and unmade, and is always under direction."[61]

Billington-Greig was not alone in identifying "subjection" to autocracy as a practice that contradicted the explicit principles of "the Cause" and that exacted a great personal cost from many. As Sylvia Pankhurst writes, "Movements for liberation bring with them, to some, opportunities of personal advancement and release from uncongenial drudgery; to others, loss of livelihood, lowering of status, a double load of toil" (p. 200). As a student pursuing a degree at the London School of Economics, Rachel Barrett had volunteered for the WSPU during her vacations, but she was soon called to do more: "Christabel Pankhurst asked me to give my whole time to the movement and to become an organiser. I was sorry to give up my work at the School and all that it meant, but it was a definite call and I obeyed."[62] Hannah Mitchell had traveled extensively in the early years of the campaign, but finally broke down from fatigue; as a working-class wife and mother, she "knew that arrears of work, including the weekly wash, awaited my return" (p. 162) from lecture tours. Her socialist husband was sympathetic only to a point, and while "public disapproval could be faced and borne . . . domestic unhappiness, the price many of us paid for our opinions and activities, was a very bitter thing" (p. 130).

Even so zealous a suffragette as Mary Richardson found herself questioning the costs of militancy. Coming to Bloomsbury as an aspiring writer, she "[gave] up my pleasant life to sit in a dismal attic all day" (p. 4) at a local WSPU office; after repeated arrests, she "was unable any longer to read poetry: it seemed but the vapourings of a world that had grown unreal" (p. 129). Convalescing from a particularly harsh jail term, she received a call from an anonymous organizer who ordered her to burn a country mansion, and she recoiled at the thought: "There was fierce rebellion in my heart. I felt this was the last straw. It was just too much. I felt no enthusiasm for what I was undertaking and was convinced we would fail" (p. 178). She went through with it, but only as an "automaton" (p. 179) would, without thought or feeling. These sacrifices, made in the name of "the Cause," represent only a handful among many; those that went unrecorded obviously cannot be traced. The important point is that some women gave up as much as or more than they gained by their participation. No matter how powerful selflessness was as a moral and political ideology, it could not repair the material losses women experienced.

The dissident critique of the suffragette movement thus argued that the WSPU required its members to pay too high a price—their own independence, the rights they were struggling for—in return for the franchise. It is not surprising that this critique comes from socialist and working-class women, who were oppressed, and fought oppression, on the basis of class as well as gender, for these women had worked long and hard for some measure of personal freedom. Politics had given Mitchell "the opportunity for a wider life" (p. 88) that she had craved, but she would not give to the movement that which she denied her own family, "being no more inclined to sink my individuality in my child than I had been to do so for my mother or my husband" (p. 183). Billington-Greig's response to her position within her large working-class family parallels her refusal to abdicate the claims of self for "the Cause": "I knew from the life around me and from my reading what sort of life loomed ahead for the family drudge, the spinster sacrificed to family needs. . . . My dream of achieving an education . . . was to be utterly broken. . . . The capacities *I* knew I had— the capacities *they* knew I had—to be wasted. It was utterly impossible for me to submit."[63] Their hard-won battles to gain some of the privileges that many middle-class Edwardian women already possessed by birthright instilled in many socialist women the desire to extend these opportunities to other women of their class, and not to promote a political ethic that would reinscribe women's cultural disposition to self-sacrifice.

Socialist-feminist criticism of Pankhurst autocracy links up with another critical perspective on the suffragette movement, one which also saw in collectivism a threat to individual autonomy. Some creative artists who were active suffrage workers claimed that the collective basis of the movement threatened to destroy the individuality of those who participated in it; in their responses to this mass movement, and especially in Sylvia Pankhurst's case, we see familiar but still crucial problems in mediating the mutual claims of individuals and communities.

Art, Politics, Subjectivity

For Cicely Hamilton, actress, writer, and feminist, the dangers of autocracy came into focus only in hindsight; what she had disliked as policy during the suffrage campaign she later came to identify as the first signs of totalitarianism. Writing in the mid-1930s, as fascism and Stalinism started to sweep across Europe, she portrayed the militant suffrage movement as "the beginning—the first indication" of what was to come: "Not the Fascists but the militants of the Women's Social and Political Union first used the word 'Leader' as a reverential title. . . . Emmeline Pankhurst, in this respect, and on a smaller scale, was the forerunner of Lenin, Hitler, Mussolini—the Leader whose fiat must not be questioned, the Leader who could do no wrong!"[64] Since she states early on in *Life Errant* (1935) that "community life does not suit me" (p. 14), Hamilton is perhaps not well-qualified to appraise the positive value of the movement; nevertheless, in calling Emmeline Pankhurst a dictator, she, like other "heretical individualists," casts the Pankhursts' followers as having given up their own wills to serve their leaders.

Describing a meeting of the Women's Liberal Federation that was interrupted repeatedly by suffragettes protesting against Lloyd George, Hamilton identifies her fellow activists in terms usually reserved by suffragettes to characterize the mostly male crowds who attacked them in the streets:

> Gathered together in the Albert Hall, they were violent, they were brutal, they were crazed. . . . And the reason for their violence, for their lack of control, was crowd-life, overpowering sense of membership; for the time being, they had resigned their responsible individuality, and were conscious only of their herd-, their community-life.   (p. 73)

Where others might see women fighting for their right to self-determination, Hamilton sees an unruly mob in which all members had "resigned their responsible individuality." She rejects the collective as requiring her to give up what she will not, her own personhood; with Billington-Greig, Hamilton claimed she could "do better work for the emancipation of women from the outside" (p. 178).

Like Hamilton, May Sinclair was an active member of the Women Writers' Suffrage League, but she, too, opposed the autocracy of the Pankhursts on the grounds that it elevated the claims of the group while robbing the individual of her rights.[65] In her novel, *The Tree of Heaven* (1917), one of Sinclair's characters takes a stand, similar to Hamilton's, against the collective, identifying "the Feminist Vortex" with a brother's experience of public school life:

> Dorothy was afraid of the Feminist Vortex, as her brother Michael had been afraid of the little vortex of school. She was afraid of the herded women. She disliked the excited faces, and the high voices skirling their battle-cries, and the silly business of committees, and the platform slang. She was sick and shy before the tremor and the surge of collective feeling; she loathed the gestures and the movements of the collective soul, the swaying and heaving and rushing forward of the many as one.[66]

In this description, the activists are deprived of whatever individuality they might be presumed to possess: they are "excited faces" and "high voices," but not particularized. This resistance to recognizing particularity among the crowd precisely inverts Dorothy's insistence on her own integrity as an individual: "she would keep the clearness and hardness of her soul. It was her soul they wanted, these women of the Union . . . and she was not going to throw it to them." In her "direct attack on militant feminism," as Laura Stempel Mumford rightly argues, Sinclair uses the image of a "vortex"—which "describes any group activity that involves mass emotion and threatens individuality, personal integrity, and self-control"—as an emblem of "false and dangerous attempts at community."[67] Yet the resistance to the community does not entail an escape for Dorothy into another realm, such as the private sphere or the art world, but an affirmation of another way, another avenue for her to take: "She would fight for freedom, but not in their way and not at their bidding" (p. 124). Sinclair's position, like Hamilton's, suggests that political engagement need not take the form of militancy, and, perhaps, that aesthetic practice itself can constitute an active and activist stance in the political realm.

In the event, however, maintaining a dual commitment to art and to politics was no simple matter. As Wendy Mulford notes of Elizabeth Robins's divided impulses in *The Convert*, "The contradictions between private artistic determinations and those wider goals of making a literary intervention in order to educate people about the inequity of women's lack of enfranchisement caused some conflict, some resistance and heartache."[68] By way of expanding Mulford's point, I want to conclude with a look at Sylvia Pankhurst's life of art and activism, for in her story we see the clash of these two commitments.

As the daughter of Emmeline and Richard Pankhurst, Sylvia was raised in an atmosphere in which politics provided the very medium of life: "the lesser affairs of home and school life were always dwarfed for us by the great social and political struggles, in which our parents were active."[69] Her father had argued the case for women's suffrage alongside John Stuart Mill as early as 1867, and had given the same unswerving attention to the cause of Labour. Like her sister Adela, who eventually emigrated to Australia, Sylvia Pankhurst never wavered in her support for socialist feminism: she ultimately broke with her mother and Christabel to form the East London Federation, an organization of working-class women whose active efforts toward social change continued well into the 1920s. For her, there was no contradiction between socialism and feminism; her goal was "to fortify the position of the working woman" by forwarding "the existence of a strong, self-reliant movement" (p. 416). "To rouse these women of the submerged mass to be, not merely the argument of more fortunate people, but to be fighters on their own account" (p. 417) was Pankhurst's purpose, and her group notably paid as much attention to the class constraints of East End life as to the particular position of women in that community.

Pankhurst's other commitment, the one she finally gave up, was to the arts. As a child, she had shown a precocious talent for drawing, and was awarded a number of competitive scholarships as a young student, including a two-year term at the South Kensington School of Art. Her personal ambition was to be "an artist in the cause of progress" (p. 215): influenced by the examples of William Morris and Walter Crane, she put her talents to work in painting scenes "in the cause of the People and the Poor."[70] At the same time, her residence in London gave the fledgling WSPU a London base, and she divided her time and her energy between her two avocations, overworking herself to the point of exhaustion and exhausting as well her scant financial resources. As the movement grew, she came critically to appraise the social value of being an artist. "Facing alone the hard struggle of life as an unknown artist, nervous, diffident, and in poor health, came the frequent question: Why? As a speaker, a pamphlet-seller, a chalker of pavements, a canvasser on doorsteps, you are wanted; as an artist the world has no real use for you; in that capacity you must fight a purely egotistical struggle" (p. 218).

An external obstacle further complicates this "inner struggle," as Pankhurst notes in another memoir. She comes to see that participating in the capitalist art marketplace could bring her no closer to her dream of producing a revolutionary aesthetic practice: "With my eager desire to work for the Golden Age, I could not be satisfied to win an existence by commercial art, and the deterrent thought at times stirred mockingly in my brain that those who would live by the fine arts must do so at the pleasure of the rich" (MWY, pp. 284–85). Unwilling to paint to the specifications of the elite, unable to paint what she wanted for lack of a market to support her work, she resigned herself to what she imagined as "a prospect too tragically grey and barren to endure"—"giving up the artist's life, surrendering the study of colour and form, laying aside the beloved pigments and brushes, to wear out one's life on the platform and the chair at the street corner" (MWY, p. 285).

Pankhurst sets the terms of her conflict by opposing the artist's lonely and useless life—"a purely egotistical struggle"—to the clear utility of political action, in which every individual contributes something to the common cause; yet the opposition itself is not so clear-cut, for art and politics do not appear as wholly distinct spheres in her own representations. Her ideal art would be political; her ideal politics would include a new aesthetic. "The key to much of her political conduct," as Brian Harrison puts it, "lies in her yearning to harmonize politics with art."[71] Pankhurst's crisis thus replays the scenario earlier noted in the lives of Martineau, Howitt, and Oliphant: she is forced to choose, in Elizabeth Robins's words, "between the ambition that is obliged to concern itself with one's own advantage, and the ambition that is obliged to concern itself with the advantage of other people."[72] For Pankhurst, however, one term of the opposition has, significantly, changed: the "other people" to whom she devotes her energies are not her own family members, but other women and the children who depend on them. And the companion term, the aesthetic, has also been redefined to include the political, as gender itself becomes politicized by being exposed as a discourse of power and powerlessness.

In theory and practice, a sizable number of Victorian and Edwardian women repeatedly interrogated invidious distinctions between the individual and the collective, the aesthetic and the political, the private wish and the public good: in this critique we recognize the revolutionary premise and promise of feminism. That we are all still, women and men alike, under enormous pressure to privilege one side of every dichotomy over the other is perhaps the most devastating fact of contemporary culture. For Pankhurst, the "inner struggle" resolves itself by the force of an external imperative that she could not ignore:

> When the world war came suddenly upon us, and hardship and sorrow descended upon the East End, when husbands and sons were called up and the meagre separation allowances came slowly, if at all, when the factories shut down in panic, prices soared, and little families were rendered destitute, moth-

ers came to me with their wasted little ones. I saw starvation look at me from
patient eyes.

I knew then that I should never return to my art.   (*MWY*, pp. 311–12)

In giving up the life of art that underwrites the culture of individualism at the
very moment when the limits of that ideology were being exposed at home and
abroad, Pankhurst breaks with the founding principles of her society: like her,
many women came to see the rights and privileges for which they had fought
in the suffrage movement as inadequate tools for reconstructing English society. In one of the central ironies of the movement for those who participated
in it, women were legally constituted as autonomous individual subjects just at
the moment when all England learned to its sorrow that, in Vera Brittain's
words, that "no life is really private, or isolated, or self-sufficient."[73]

Autobiography as History

In her recent biography of Sylvia Pankhurst, Patricia W. Romero congratulates
another scholar, Martin Pugh, for being "among the first of the historians writing on the suffrage movement to recognize how invalid most memoirs of the
period are."[74] Widely used by historians as primary sources, suffrage autobiographies are "invalid" because they are not disinterested: "perhaps part of
[Pankhurst's] motivation" for writing *The Suffragette Movement*, Romero suggests, "was to redefine herself in relation to the movement by writing her
version of it" (p. 186). As history, *The Suffragette Movement* is thus hopelessly compromised because the historian-participant's subjective perspective skews
her vision; as autobiography, it takes unpardonable liberties, for Pankhurst "re-
lived her own triumphs . . . while exaggerating her role" (pp. 186–87).

The Romero–Pugh position effectively reproduces the wish Emmeline Pankhurst expresses in her (heavily ghostwritten) autobiography, *My Own Story*
(1914):

> It seemed to me that I had a duty to perform in giving to the world my own
> plain statement of the events which led up to the women's revolution in En-
> gland. Other histories of the militant movement will undoubtedly be written
> . . . when, in a word, all the dreadful and criminal discriminations which exist
> now between the sexes are abolished, as they one day must be abolished, the
> historian will be able to sit down in leisurely fashion and do full justice to the
> strange story of how the women of England took up arms against the blind
> and obstinate Government of England and fought their way to political free-
> dom.[75]

But the moment for Pankhurst's imagined historian to take up her pen has not
arrived, nor will it; moreover, Pankhurst's own description of "the strange story"
unwittingly betrays the impossibility of writing such an account. To some participants and historians, the Asquith administration was "blind and obstinate";
others see it differently. To some, the Pankhursts were tyrants; to others, great

leaders. The point, then, is that the meaning of the suffrage movement is still—as it was in its own time—under contestation. Nowhere is that struggle over its meaning more fiercely staged than in suffrage texts, as I have tried to suggest by juxtaposing two of the most powerful interpretations of its import.

Yet Romero's distinction between history and autobiography belies another ongoing contest. In conventional terms, history is objective, autobiography subjective; at best, autobiography is but a subset of history proper. When using subjective accounts, historian must read enough of them to provide a balanced picture, to contrast and compare them and so to arrive at a fuller version of historical truth. But using autobiographical texts in this fashion inevitably leads the reader to overlook what I have tried to stress throughout this book, the grounded position of the writer in her own experience as constructed in autobiographical texts. If we are to value women's autobiographical writings, we must do as Sylvia Pankhurst does in her preface to *The Suffragette Movement*, and collapse the boundary between history and autobiography:

> I have essayed to describe events and experience as one felt them. . . . In this effort I have often been thrown back upon my own experience. . . . No history, whether of movements or of persons, can be truly expressed apart from the social and economic conditions and thought currents of its time. I have endeavoured to convey these not through the medium of statistics or argument, but by incidents in the moving course of life.   (p. vii)

Subtitling her text "An Intimate Account of Persons and Ideals," Pankhurst uses the autobiographical and the historical as compatible categories; "personal experiences" give her a standpoint, as they gave Lytton hers, but she also attempts to integrate the "subjective" story of her life with the "objective" history of social and political life, and in doing so, she challenges our readerly sense of the distinction.

While generations of academics have tended to repeat the objective history/ subjective autobiography dichotomy, feminist critiques of objectivity, like the autobiographies analyzed here, reveal that it can be collapsed.[76] Since all histories are interested, subjective, laden with value, what distinguishes the autobiographer from the historian is that the historian's experience of the subject is doubly or trebly mediated by text, by time, by distance, while the writing subject's account—the "direct" and "immediate" experience that is also mediated by and through culture and ideology—is more local, grounded, and specific with respect to the events recorded. That we have consistently valued the observer over the participant—the voyaging voyeur over the stationary native, to use Gillian Beer's terms—says much about how we have constructed knowledge and power in the image of the deity we profess to have abjured.[77]

The limits of that knowledge, if we recognize them, need not be perceived as constraint, but as respect for particularity. Annie Kenney's text, for instance, definitely subordinates her story to history: to provide "a clear description . . . of certain but important parts of the Militant Movement for Woman's Suffrage," "the best way will be to write my life" (p. v). Kenney's "certain" is a critical word here, for it delineates her own perspective; the particularity of her experience, I suggest, is what we should prize. More powerfully, Teresa Billington-Greig—"the ideal participant-observer," as the historian Brian Harrison describes her—prefaced *The Militant Suffrage Movement* with a precise reckoning of the motives that drove her to write it and an appeal to her experience as self-authorizing.[78]

> I mush show clearly what were the forces of reason and feeling which drew me into the militant suffrage movement, kept me a willing and earnest worker within its ranks, and made me accept official position and responsibility for five years; I must also show from what events came the growth of that slow disillusionment which gave me my personal freedom again. . . . Unless I make these things clear, the purpose and value of what I write will be seriously endangered. My personal experience and effort alone entitle me to speak with any authority, and I can only say all that is necessary to be said by dealing frankly and personally with the things that I know.   (p. 140)

Again, the standpoint is all: it is not the bias to be wished away or smoothed over, but the very thing that allows us to read these texts in context.

Emmeline Pankhurst considered it "a duty" to give "her own plain statement of facts"; Dora Montefiore sought to tell "the truth, not only about myself, but about many of my fellow-workers" (p. 5); Evelyn Sharp would not "shirk the telling of a tale that otherwise I, having lived through it, would gladly leave untold" (p. 127). Autobiography is history for these autobiographers, yet they do not claim to provide authoritative master narratives; as women who knew that women's history had been erased, they were determined to represent their own. Moreover, the story is not only directed at others, but also for and about others: writing the life means telling it as a legacy for contemporaries and descendants. While suffrage autobiography thus bears a parallel to the nineteenth-century family memoir of Ward or Oliphant, these texts more firmly situate themselves in history, often from their opening pages: Millicent Garrett Fawcett significantly marks the year of her birth as "the year of the Irish Famine and the repeal of the Corn Laws," with the subsequent year "[seeing] the down-fall of half the old autocratic Governments in Europe" (p. 9), while Emmeline Pankhurst's earliest memories are of Fenian riots, the struggle for abolition, and *Uncle Tom's Cabin*. As family provided a generative context for earlier memoirists, so public events, particularly revolutionary ones, are represented as part of the appropriate medium for public women's lives. Thus suffrage autobiographies position themselves in both the particular and the general, as individual account and collective story. It is through this grid, at the intersection of private and public experience, that we should read them.

Afterword

[T]HE UNDERSTANDING OF one's personal condition as a woman in terms social and political, and the constant revision, reevaluation, and reconceptualization of that condition in relation to other women's understanding of their sociosexual positions, generate a mode of apprehension of all social reality that derives from the consciousness of gender.   —Teresa de Lauretis, "The Technology of Gender"*

A feminist confession of faith commits those who make it to the effort to transform life.   —Teresa Billington-Greig, "Feminism and Politics"†

The Great War changed everything. The WSPU devoted its considerable energy and resources to jingoism. Suffragettes who had once sold *Votes for Women!* on street corners instead distributed white feathers to every able-bodied Englishman out of uniform. The NUWSS leadership split across a divide between pacifists and militarists. Women went to work on the land and in the munitions factories. And at the end of the war, some—not all—Englishwomen were rewarded for their patriotism and their labor by being enfranchised.

As the historian Joan W. Scott has recently pointed out, the "war as watershed" argument has been the dominant representation of the war years among feminists and nonfeminists alike, perhaps because it so clearly marks the end of "the Victorian era" and the beginning of "the modern."[1] Within the terms of that argument, there is room for several possible "interested" interpretations of what the war meant to women, and I will repeat only one of them here: we can characterize the Great War as a series of events that freed women from the confines of the private sphere but exacted a devastating social price for that freedom. Virginia Woolf's analysis in *Three Guineas* (1938), most recently taken up by Gilbert and Gubar, asserts that "[women's] unconscious influence was . . . in favour of war":

> How else can we explain that amazing outburst in August 1914, when the daughters of educated men who had been educated thus rushed into hospitals, some still attended by their maids, drove lorries, worked in fields and munition factories, and used all their immense stores of charm, of sympathy, to persuade

*Teresa de Lauretis, "The Technology of Gender," in *Technologies of Gender: Essays on Theory, Film, and Fiction* (Bloomington: Indiana University Press, 1987), p. 20.

†Teresa Billington-Greig, "Feminism and Politics," in *The Non-Violent Militant*, ed. Carol McPhee and Ann FitzGerald (London: Routledge and Kegan Paul, 1987), p. 226.

young men that to fight was heroic, and that the wounded in battle deserved all her care and all her praise? The reason lies in that same education. So profound was her unconscious loathing for the education of the private house with its cruelty, its poverty, its hypocrisy, its immorality, its inanity that she would undertake any task however menial, exercise any fascination however fatal that enabled her to escape. Thus consciously she desired "our splendid Empire"; unconsciously she desired our splendid war.[2]

In blaming the patriarchal division of the world into separate spheres for the loss of a generation of young men, and in suggesting women's unconscious complicity with and "loathing" of that system, Woolf marks the death of an illusion. As Sandra Stanley Holton bluntly remarks, "modern warfare needed the mass mobilisation of women as well as men for its execution. Ironically, the ideology of separate spheres lost much of its former legitimacy as women provided essential support in this way."[3] Through their "influence" and their actions, women supported the war, and in doing so demonstrated that the supposedly innate moral differences between peaceable women and aggressive men, which many suffrage activists had taken as part of the ideological basis for women's right to vote, could no longer be assumed to exist.

For one of the suffrage movement's most compelling arguments for enfranchising women had rested on its claim that voting women would "reconstruct society in accordance with female values and needs . . . suffragists did not seek merely an entry to a male-defined sphere, but the opportunity to redefine that sphere. They rejected the characterisation of political life in terms of masculine qualities, and sought to redefine the state by asserting for it a nurturant role" (Holton, p. 18). Woolf's remarks suggest, however, that the "daughters of educated men" who had been educated in the ways of the private house were not the moral exemplars they seemed: they were not only nurturant, but also angry; not only careful to support their brothers, but also anxious and eager to make lives for themselves outside the private house. The events surrounding the war thus became a kind of proof that women and men were more similar than different (or at least potentially so), that under the pressure and influence of a great national crisis, both sexes would willingly cooperate in national and international destruction.

Even suffrage women who were actively opposed to the war came to feel the fragility of their ideals and to doubt the existence of the gendered differences in morality and outlook between men and women in which they had once believed, as Sylvia Pankhurst's postwar postmortem conveys:

> Gone was the mirage of a society regenerated by enfranchised womanhood as by a magic wand. Men and women had been drawn closer together by the suffering and sacrifice of the War. Awed and humbled by the great catastrophe, and by the huge economic problems it had thrown into naked prominence, the women of the Suffrage movement had learnt that social regeneration is a long and mighty work. The profound divergences of opinion on war and peace had been shown to know no sex.[4]

Like those of many of her contemporaries of other ideological persuasions, Pankhurst's response suggests that differences between women and men, insofar as any existed at all, were culturally and socially produced but not irreversible. Given access to the public sphere, women would not retain their moral superiority, or necessarily be opposed to war, but would simply "be themselves." Their presence and their activities would not inevitably regenerate the public sphere; they, too, would have "profound divergences of opinion on war and peace."

According to this schema, subjectivity depends on the roles one plays: women who have public and economic lives can be more or less ungendered actors in the public sphere, with their opinions, beliefs, and daily practices having little or nothing to do with the experience of gender and everything to do with the particular places—the boardroom, the munitions factory, the nursery—in which they find themselves. Yet while I would never want to claim that being a woman necessarily means that I am innately, naturally, opposed to war, I would also never want to claim that gender is irrelevant to my opinions and beliefs, or that the places I fill in the world are wholly empty of historically accrued content. And even if I were to think of myself as an ungendered actor in the world, my ignorance of how gender operates in everyday life would not protect me from experiencing the cultural effects of being perceived as and oppressed as a woman. In short, while we all might possibly agree that there is no "natural" difference between men and women per se, there is a whole history of difference which I want to hold on to, for reasons that may be difficult to explain.

When John Stuart Mill wrote in *The Subjection of Women* that "what is now called the nature of women is an eminently artificial thing," he was claiming that his contemporaries were mistaking women's cultural role for her natural essence. But today, when many of us no longer believe in the truth of roles or the existence of essences yet still want to insist on some kinds of difference between and among women and men, we must be careful to locate those differences not in biology, but in gender or, more particularly, in the experience of gender and, in de Lauretis's phrase, "the consciousness of gender." Only when we are conscious of ourselves as gendered beings of a certain class and race do we begin to see the way in which the world is still unequally and unjustly arranged. And what "consciousness of gender" entails is not only an apprehension of the present, but also a vision of the past. To study the historical construction of "Woman" over time; to see how that construction changes and how it persists; to correct it with historical evidence and subjective testimony; to believe on the basis of considerable empirical evidence that women's experiences and subjectivities have differed from men's; to hope that we can make these differences a shaping force in institutions and practices: this is the "feminist confession of faith" that commits me and many others to a scholarly and a political project.

It is "consciousness of gender" and class and race that makes possible and necessary the exploration of the social subject. For feminists, this project has particular urgency, based on our growing knowledge and consciousness of our own multiple histories. And it is on the basis of experience and history that women should, as Woolf counsels in *Three Guineas*, "refuse to be separated from the four great teachers of the daughters of educated men—poverty, chastity, derision, and freedom from unreal loyalties" (p. 79). For history lives not only in books, but also in institutions; it makes itself felt, if we allow ourselves to feel it, in the irregular rhythms of our lives. We can hear it and see it all around us. To weave the strands of that history into our "real loyalties" might be the ultimate act of feminist faith.

Notes

Introduction

1. Virginia Woolf to Ethel Smyth, 24 December 1940, *The Letters of Virginia Woolf*, ed. Nigel Nicolson and Joanne Trautman, 6 vols. (New York: Harcourt Brace Jovanovich, 1975), 6:453.

2. Felicity A. Nussbaum, *The Autobiographical Subject: Gender and Ideology in Eighteenth-Century England* (Baltimore: Johns Hopkins University Press, 1989), p. xii.

3. Roy Pascal, *Design and Truth in Autobiography* (Cambridge: Harvard University Press, 1960), p. 148.

4. James Olney, *Metaphors of Self* (Princeton, N.J.: Princeton University Press, 1972), pp. 33–34.

5. See Paul Jay, *Being in the Text: Self-Representation from Wordsworth to Roland Barthes* (Ithaca, N.Y.: Cornell University Press, 1984), pp. 59–72.

6. Paul de Man, "Autobiography as De-facement," *MLN* 94 (December 1979): 919–30.

7. Andreas Huyssen, "Mapping the Postmodern," in *After the Great Divide* (Bloomington: Indiana University Press, 1986), p. 213.

8. Edited anthologies of work devoted to women's autobiographies have only recently begun to appear: Estelle C. Jelinek's volume, *Women's Autobiography: Essays in Criticism* (Bloomington: Indiana University Press, 1980) was the very first, followed in later years by Domna Stanton, ed., *The Female Autograph*, New York Literary Forum 12–13 (1984); Dale Spender, ed., "Personal Chronicles: Women's Autobiographical Writings," a special issue of *Women's Studies International Forum* 10, no. 1 (1987); Shari Benstock, ed., *The Private Self: Theory and Practice of Women's Autobiographical Writings* (Chapel Hill: University of North Carolina Press, 1988); Bella Brodzki and Celeste Schenck, eds., *Life/Lines: Theorizing Women's Autobiography* (Ithaca, N.Y.: Cornell University Press, 1988); and The Personal Narratives Group, eds., *Interpreting Women's Lives: Feminist Theory and Personal Narratives* (Bloomington: Indiana University Press, 1989). See also the essays by Sidonie Smith and Linda Peterson in " 'The Vexingly Unverifiable': Truth in Autobiography," a special issue, edited by Paul H. Schmidt, of *Studies in the Literary Imagination* 23 no. 2 (Fall 1990).

9. See Sidonie Smith, *A Poetics of Women's Autobiography: Marginality and the Fictions of Self-Representation* (Bloomington: Indiana University Press), pp. 3–19; less

detailed critiques of similar texts include Bella Brodzki and Celeste Schenck's introduction to *Life/Lines*, esp. pp. 2–7, and Nussbaum, *The Autobiographical Subject*, esp. pp. 5–10.

10. Surprisingly, even Smith turns to Martineau for her only nineteenth-century example in *Poetics*, just as Linda H. Peterson does in *Victorian Autobiography* (New Haven, Conn.: Yale University Press, 1986). Only Valerie Sanders, in *The Private Lives of Victorian Women: Autobiography in Nineteenth-Century England* (New York: St. Martin's Press, 1989), has displaced the fiction that women have not written autobiography until this century in any quantity or of any interest. Because Sanders's book did not become available to me until my own was substantially finished, I have not been able to incorporate its insights fully; while I find myself disagreeing with her arguments at various points, we have some shared concerns and common texts throughout, as will be evident especially in my Chapter 3.

11. Cora Kaplan, "Pandora's Box: Subjectivity, Class and Sexuality in Socialist Feminist Criticism," in *Sea Changes: Essays on Culture and Feminism* (London: Verso, 1986), pp. 149–50.

12. For a reading of Martineau's life and work with which I find myself in substantial agreement, see Deirdre David, *Intellectual Women and Victorian Patriarchy: Harriet Martineau, Elizabeth Barrett Browning, George Eliot* (Ithaca, N.Y.: Cornell University Press, 1987).

13. For an important contribution to the new feminist revision of genre theory which considers genre as "overdetermined loci of contention and conflict," see Celeste Schenck, "All of a Piece: Women's Poetry and Autobiography," in *Life/Lines*, p. 282ff.

14. Diana Fuss, *Essentially Speaking: Feminism, Nature and Difference* (New York: Routledge, 1989), p. 25.

15. Teresa de Lauretis, *Alice Doesn't: Feminism, Semiotics, Cinema* (Bloomington: Indiana University Press, 1984), p. 31.

16. In *Discerning the Subject* (Minneapolis: University of Minnesota Press, 1988), Paul Smith argues that de Lauretis's theorization of subjectivity lacks a workable concept of agency and offers his own through readings of Althusser, Lacan, and especially Kristeva. While I find myself less than fully convinced by Smith's arguments and formulations, reading his work has been useful to me insofar as it has explicitly problematized agency in ways that my own work does not.

17. Rita Felski, *Beyond Feminist Aesthetics: Feminist Literature and Social Change* (Cambridge: Harvard University Press, 1989), pp. 56–57. Also see Anthony Giddens, *Central Problems in Social Theory: Action, Structure and Contradiction in Social Analysis* (London: Hutchinson, 1976), for his concept of duality of structure; in Chapter 2 of her book, Felski makes very good use of Giddens's work.

18. Nancy K. Miller, "Changing the Subject: Authorship, Writing, and the Reader," in *Subject to Change: Reading Feminist Writing* (New York: Columbia University Press, 1988), p. 106; Elizabeth Fox-Genovese, "My Statue, My Self: Autobiographical Writings of Afro-American Women," in *The Private Self*, p. 67. I want to cite two other theorists who similarly suggest a new direction vis-à-vis the question of female authorship. "What we need, instead of a theory of the death of the author," as Cheryl Walker puts it, "is a new concept of authorship that does not naively assert that the writer is an originating genius, creating aesthetic objects outside of history, but does not diminish the importance of difference and agency in the responses of women writers to historical formations" ("Feminist Literary Criticism and the Author," *Critical Inquiry* 16 [Spring 1990]: 560). And in feminist film studies, Kaja Silverman has recently resuscitated and revised *auteur* theory to investigate a female authorial voice in cinema in "The Female

Authorial Voice," in *The Acoustic Mirror: The Female Voice in Psychoanalysis and Cinema* (Bloomington: Indiana University Press, 1988), pp. 187–233.

19. Walker, "Feminist Literary Criticism," p. 555.

20. Regenia Gagnier, *Subjectivities: A History of Self-Representation in Britain, 1832–1920* (New York: Oxford University Press, 1991). Gagnier's analysis also considers the geographical and occupational locations of the subjects she studies.

21. The best account I know of these debates can be found in Michèle Barrett's *Women's Oppression Today: The Marxist/Feminist Encounter*, rev. ed. (London: Verso, 1988), 8–41.

22. Among these I would include Lillian S. Robinson, *Sex, Class, and Culture* (Bloomington: Indiana University Press, 1978); Mary Poovey, *The Proper Lady and the Woman Writer: Ideology as Style in the Works of Mary Wollstonecraft, Mary Shelley, and Jane Austen* (Chicago: University of Chicago Press, 1984), and *Uneven Developments: The Ideological Work of Gender in Mid-Victorian England* (Chicago: University of Chicago Press, 1988); Judith Lowder Newton, *Women, Power, and Subversion: Social Strategies in British Fiction, 1778–1860* (Athens: University of Georgia Press, 1981); Kaplan, *Sea Changes*; Gagnier, *Subjectivities*; David, *Intellectual Women and Victorian Patriarchy*; and Nancy Armstrong, *Desire and Domestic Fiction: A Political History of the Novel* (New York: Oxford University Press, 1987).

23. Ruth L. Smith and Deborah M. Valenze, "Mutuality and Marginality: Liberal Moral Theory and Working-Class Women in Nineteenth-Century England," *Signs* 13, no. 2 (Winter 1988): 282.

24. M. H. Abrams, *Natural Supernaturalism* (New York: W. W. Norton and Co., 1971).

25. George P. Landow, Introduction to *Approaches to Victorian Autobiography* (Athens: Ohio University Press, 1979), p. xxvii.

26. Quoted in Regenia Gagnier, *Idylls of the Marketplace: Oscar Wilde and the Victorian Public* (Stanford, Calif.: Stanford University Press, 1986), p. 81.

27. In *Discipline and Punish*, trans. Alan Sheridan (New York: Vintage Books, 1979), p. 31.

28. Ray Strachey, *"The Cause": A Short History of the Women's Movement in Great Britain* (1928; reprint ed., Port Washington, N.Y.: Kennikat Press, 1969), p. 6. For "the god trick," see Donna Haraway, "Situated Knowledges: The Science Question in Feminism and the Privilege of Partial Perspective," *Feminist Studies* 14, no. 3 (Fall 1988): 575–99. Haraway's influence on my thinking about questions of history, positionality, and subjectivity has been considerable, and I am indebted here as well to Alex Chasin, Miranda Joseph, and Kelly Mays for the many conversations about Haraway's work that have shaped my understanding of it. I also owe them, as well as Art Casciato and Elizabeth Heckendorn Cook, for especially helpful readings of earlier drafts of this essay.

Chapter 1

1. John Forster, "The Literary Examiner," *The Examiner*, 17 January 1846, p. 35.

2. Thomas Carlyle, "The Hero as Man of Letters," in *On Heroes, Hero-Worship and the Heroic in History*, ed. Carl Niemeyer (Lincoln: University of Nebraska Press, 1966), p. 154.

3. William Wordsworth, "Essay, Supplementary to the Preface" in *Wordsworth's Literary Criticism*, ed. W. J. B. Owen (London: Routledge and Kegan Paul, 1974), p.

210; all subsequent references to Wordsworth's published prose will be to this edition and will be included in the text.

4. Leonore Davidoff and Catherine Hall, *Family Fortunes: Men and Women of the English Middle Classes, 1780–1850* (Chicago: University of Chicago Press, 1987), p. 33.

5. Clifford Siskin, "Wordsworth's Prescriptions: Romanticism and Professional Power," in *The Romantics and Us: Essays on Literature and Culture,* ed. Gene W. Ruoff (New Brunswick, N.J.: Rutgers University Press, 1990), p. 310.

6. Recent work by Marlon B. Ross on Romanticism elaborates the relation of gender identity to the literary vocation in ways that anticipate some aspects of my argument; he sees, for example, Wordsworth's sense of poetry as "defined by a quest for poetic self-identity that is mirrored by the quest for manhood" (p. 35). See *The Contours of Masculine Desire: Romanticism and the Rise of Women's Poetry* (New York: Oxford University Press, 1989), esp. ch. 1.

7. On the position of eighteenth-century writers in relation to the marketplace, see Michael McKeon, "Prefigurations of the Writer's Life in the Early English Novel," (Paper delivered at "The Novel and the Writer's Life" Conference, Stanford University, February 4, 1989). For a discussion of market changes in the Romantic period, see Lee Erickson, "The Poets' Corner: The Impact of Technological Changes in Printing on English Poetry, 1800–1850," *ELH* 52, no. 4 (Winter 1985): 893–911, and more generally, Richard D. Altick, *The English Common Reader* (Chicago: University of Chicago Press, 1957); and for a Marxist analysis of change in the literary marketplace, N. N. Feltes, *Modes of Production of Victorian Novels* (Chicago: University of Chicago Press, 1986). In "The Writer's Ravishment: Women and the Romantic Author—The Example of Byron," in *Romanticism and Feminism,* ed. Anne K. Mellor (Bloomington: Indiana University Press, 1988), pp. 93–114, Sonia Hofkosh provides a wholly engaging account of "the lines of connection between the emergence of women as a force in literary culture and the emergence of a professionalized literary culture" (p. 111).

8. For a recent discussion of many of the issues I am concerned with here, see Mary Poovey, "The Man-of-Letters Hero: *David Copperfield* and the Professional Writer," in *Uneven Developments: The Ideological Work of Gender in Mid-Victorian England* (Chicago: University of Chicago Press, 1988), pp. 89–125. Poovey rightly argues that "because it was conceptualized simultaneously as superior to the capitalist economy and as hopelessly embroiled in it, literary work was the work par excellence that denied *and* exemplified the alienation written into capitalist work" (pp. 105–106), and I take no issue with this characterization. Where I differ from Poovey is in adopting a critical approach to the idea of a "literary profession," for my research suggests that professional discourse attempts to "resolve" the problem of alienation in important ways that literary men pick up on.

9. In *Professional Power* (Chicago: University of Chicago Press, 1986), Eliot Freidson traces the history of the words "profession" and "professional," and finds "a number of overlapping denotations and connotations, few of which are sharply divided from the others" (p. 21). He notes that "even as early as the sixteenth century the word *profession* could be used to mean either a very exclusive set of occupations or the exact opposite—any occupation at all" (p. 22). The ambiguity of the word means that at different historical moments and in different discursive practices, "professional" can convey either "the connotations of the ungentlemanly, the crass, the inappropriately labored or excessive" (p. 22)—as it does when the Romantics deploy it to downgrade the work of their contemporaries—or "good, reliable work of skill and quality"—as it does when literary men use it at mid-century to describe their own activity. I would argue that the word shifts in denotative value for literary men once the transition from an older pa-

tronage model for literary production to a new, fully commodified practice is complete. In any case, "profession" is not "a generic concept," but "a changing historic concept with particularistic roots" (p. 32) in specific cultures and ideologies, "a field of ideological tension" (Feltes, *Modes of Production,* p. 42) continually reworked in nineteenth-century culture.

10. Most of the books in this area that I have consulted use the term "profession" very loosely, without examining the construction of professionalism itself. See A. S. Collins, *The Profession of Letters: A Study of the Relation of Author to Patron, Publisher, and Public, 1780–1832* (London: Routledge and Sons, 1928); Louis Dudek, *Literature and the Press: A History of Printing, Printed Media, and Their Relations to Literature* (Toronto: The Ryerson Press, 1961); John Gross, *The Rise and Fall of the Man of Letters* (New York: Macmillan, 1969); J. W. Saunders, *The Profession of English Letters* (London: Routledge and Kegan Paul, 1969); and Victor Bonham-Carter, *Authors by Profession,* 2 vols. (London: Society of Authors, 1978). In *The Common Writer: Life in Nineteenth-Century Grub Street* (Cambridge: Cambridge University Press, 1985), Nigel Cross takes a slightly more skeptical position toward the idea of a "literary profession." For a critical discussion of Romantic authorship that bypasses the issue of professionalism, see Patrick Parrinder, *Authors and Authority: A Study of English Literary Criticism and Its Relation to Culture, 1750–1900* (London: Routledge and Kegan Paul, 1977). Another good discussion of "the world of the men of letters" can be found in T. W. Heyck, *The Transformation of Intellectual Life in Victorian England* (New York: St. Martin's Press, 1982), esp. ch. 2.

11. Gaye Tuchman, with Nina E. Fortin, *Edging Women Out: Victorian Novelists, Publishers, and Social Change* (New Haven, Conn.: Yale University Press, 1989), p. 36.

12. S. T. Coleridge, *Biographia Literaria,* ed. James Engell and W. J. Bate (Princeton, N.J.: Princeton University Press, 1983), pp. 39, 41.

13. As Noel Parry and José Parry note, "there are two distinctly opposing views about the consequences of the Apothecaries' Act": one side argues that it was "an important reforming measure and a major cause of the rapid improvement in medical education," the other that "the Act and its consequences were retrogressive" (*The Rise of the Medical Profession: A Study in Collective Social Mobility* [London: Croom Helm, 1976], p. 113). From my point of view, the importance of the act is that it demonstrates the growth of self-consciousness among all medical men about the need to organize themselves from within; in the contest over which sector of the profession had the power to make policy for the profession as a whole, we see the struggle for power over the profession itself.

14. My overview of the profession is indebted to the following works: Robert Robson, *The Attorney in Eighteenth-Century England* (Cambridge: Cambridge University Press, 1959); W. J. Reader, *Professional Men: The Rise of the Professional Classes in Nineteenth-Century England* (London: Weidenfeld and Nicolson, 1966); Harold Perkin, *The Origins of Modern English Society, 1780–1880* (London: Routledge and Kegan Paul, 1969); Philip Elliott, *The Sociology of the Professions* (New York: Herder and Herder, 1972); and Parry and Parry, *The Rise of the Medical Profession.*

15. See JoAnne Brown, "Professional Language: Words That Succeed," *Radical History Review* 34 (1986): 33–51, for an imperfect but suggestive analysis of the way in which professionals deploy rhetorical strategies to rationalize their own authority. I am grateful to Frank Donoghue for the reference.

16. The phrase is from William Wordsworth to William Mathews, 23 September 1791, *The Letters of William and Dorothy Wordsworth, Volume I: The Early Years, 1787–1805,* 2d ed., rev., Chester L. Shaver, ed. Ernest de Selincourt (Oxford: Clarendon

Press, 1967), 59; all subsequent references to the Wordsworths' letters will be to this edition and volume and will be included in the text.

17. Quoted in Reader, *Professional Men*, p. 120. For the classic analysis of how ideologies reproduce themselves, see Louis Althusser, "Ideology and Ideological State Apparatuses," in *Lenin and Philosophy and Other Essays*, trans. Ben Brewster (New York: Monthly Review Press, 1971), pp. 127–86.

18. Adam Smith, *An Inquiry into the Nature and Causes of the Wealth of Nations*, 2 vols. (Oxford: Clarendon Press, 1976), 1:122.

19. R. L. Edgeworth, *Essays on Professional Education* (London, 1809), p. 315.

20. Walter Scott to George Crabbe, 1 June 1813, in *The Letters of Sir Walter Scott 1811–1814*, 12 vols., ed. H. J. C. Grierson (London: Constable and Co., Ltd., 1932), 3:281–82.

21. His high-handed assessment and implicit dismissal of literature did not, ironically enough, stop Scott from becoming the professional writer *par excellence* among Romantic writers: financial necessity forced him to turn out one novel after another, culminating in the release of Waverley Edition in 1827, which both established the shape of his *oeuvre* and enabled his estate to pay off its voluminous debts. To the end, however, Scott publicly represented himself as an amateur, establishing a persona which obscured the operation of the material conditions that made literature his profession by default.

22. For accounts of how gender impacts on issues of professional authority in medicine, see Jean Donnison, *Midwives and Medical Men* (New York: Schocken, 1977); and Mary Poovey, "Scenes of an Indelicate Character: The Medical Treatment of Victorian Women," in *Uneven Developments*, esp. pp. 38–50.

23. Maureen Cain, "The General Practice Lawyer and Client: Towards a Radical Conception," in *The Sociology of the Professions: Lawyers, Doctors, and Others*, ed. Robert Dingwall and Philip Lewis (London: Macmillan, 1983), p. 108.

24. Kurt Heinzelman, *The Economics of the Imagination* (Amherst: University of Massachusetts Press, 1980), p. 201.

25. Stephen Gill, *William Wordsworth: A Life* (Oxford: Clarendon Press, 1989), p. 164.

26. M. S. Larson, *The Rise of Professionalism: A Sociological Analysis* (Berkeley: University of California Press, 1977), p. 14.

27. John Locke, *Second Treatise of Government*, ed. C. B. Macpherson (Indianapolis: Hackett Publishing Company, Inc., 1980), p. 19.

28. William Hazlitt, "The Catalogue Raisonné of the British Institution," in *The Complete Works of William Hazlitt*, 21 vols., ed. P. P. Howe (London: J. M. Dent and Sons, Ltd., 1933), 18:109. Also quoted in David Bromwich, *Hazlitt: The Mind of a Critic* (New York: Oxford University Press, 1983), p. 119.

29. D'Israeli's *Essay* was subsequently expanded and revised many times in later editions; although I have consulted the first, all quotations are taken from a late Victorian American edition, entitled *The Literary Character; or the History of Men of Genius* (New York, 1885). All subsequent references to D'Israeli's book will be included in the text. For a discussion of the historical grounding of the concept in eighteenth-century law and society, see Martha Woodmansee, "The Genius and the Copyright: Economic and Legal Conditions of the Emergence of the 'Author,' " *Eighteenth-Century Studies* 17, no. 4 (1984):425–48.

30. *The Protestant Ethic and the Spirit of Capitalism*, trans. Talcott Parsons (1904–5; reprint ed., London: Unwin Paperbacks, 1985) p. 110.

31. For an analysis of the change in early nineteenth-century periodical production,

see Jon P. Klancher, *The Making of English Reading Audiences, 1790–1832* (Madison: University of Wisconsin Press, 1987), esp. chs. 1 and 2.

32. D'Israeli's distinction between authorial production of knowledge and its dissemination by secondary agents reworks a principle of political economy enunciated by Adam Smith, the difference between productive and unproductive labor. In *The Wealth of Nations* (1776), Smith classes writers with professionals as those whose labor is unproductive; the writer's work "perishes in the very instant of its production" because that work cannot "put into motion a quantity of labor equal to that which had originally produced it" (2:330, 331). Despite "the extraordinary inadequacy of this distinction to advanced capitalism," Raymond Williams points out that it was reinscribed by Marx in "a footnote in the *Grundrisse* in which it is argued that a piano-maker is a productive worker, engaged in productive labour, but that a pianist is not, since his labour is not labour which reproduces capital" (*Marxism and Literature* [Oxford: Oxford University Press, 1977], pp. 90–94).

33. The question Franco Moretti asks in analyzing the classical *bildungsroman* is highly relevant here: "How can the tendency toward *individuality*, which is the necessary fruit of a culture of self-determination, be made to coexist with the opposing tendency to *normality*, the offspring, equally inevitable, of the mechanism of socialization?" (*The Way of the World: The "Bildungsroman" in European Culture* [London: Verso, 1987], p. 16). My effort in what follows is precisely to situate Wordsworth's self-representation as an exploration and elaboration of this tension between the unique individual and his cultural medium.

34. Clifford Siskin reads "development" as "an all-encompassing formal strategy underpinning middle-class culture" in *The Historicity of Romantic Discourse* (New York: Oxford University Press, 1988), p. 12; see chapters 4 to 6 for the elaboration of this argument, which is compatible in some respects with my own.

35. William Wordsworth, "Autobiographical Memoranda," in Christopher Wordsworth, *Memoirs of William Wordsworth*, 2 vols., ed. Henry Reed (Boston, 1851), 1:14; a brief account of his years at Hawkshead is given in Gill, *William Wordsworth: A Life*, pp. 26–29. For sympathetic readings of Wordsworth's years at St. John's, see Mary Moorman, *William Wordsworth: A Biography: The Early Years, 1770–1803* (Oxford: Oxford University Press, 1957), ch. 4, and Ben Ross Schneider, Jr., *Wordsworth's Cambridge Education* (Cambridge: Cambridge University Press, 1957); for a more critical reading, see Gill, *William Wordsworth: A Life*, pp. 37–50.

36. William Wordsworth, *The Prelude: 1799, 1805, 1850*, ed. Jonathan Wordsworth, M. H. Abrams, and Stephen Gill (New York: W. W. Norton & Co., 1979), 3:89–90; all subsequent references to Wordsworth's *The Prelude* are to the 1805 edition and will be included in the text.

37. "Present System of Education," *Westminster Review* 4 (July 1825): 152–53.

38. For details of the legacy—which amounted to 900 pounds—see Moorman, *William Wordsworth: A Biography*, pp. 251–53; Shaver, *Letters of William and Dorothy Wordsworth*, 1: 129–34; and Mark L. Reed, *Wordsworth: The Chronology of the Early Years, 1770–1797* (Cambridge: Harvard University Press, 1967), pp. 158–61. For a reading of the legacy as Calvert's "investment" in Wordsworth's future, see Heinzelman, *Economics*, pp. 197–202. I am grateful to Barbara Gelpi for pointing out the importance of the Calvert bequest to Wordsworthian self-fashioning.

39. James K. Chandler, *Wordsworth's Second Nature: A Study of the Poetry and Politics* (Chicago: The University of Chicago Press, 1984), p. 214. Although Chandler considers Wordsworthian discipline as a public mode, he does so in a context altogether

different from mine, as "a psychological manifestation of a national character and a native tradition" (p. 187), and focuses on the relevance of the "spots of time."

40. As we know from Michel Foucault's work, discipline is not only a process to which the individual is subjected, but also a set of procedures and techniques that shapes the conscious and unconscious practices of large bodies of individuals; "the code [the disciplines] come to define is not that of law but that of normalisation" ("Two Lectures," in *Power/Knowledge: Selected Interviews and Other Writings*, ed. and trans. Colin Gordon [Brighton, Sussex: Harvester Press, 1980], p. 106). Thus by acquiring (a) discipline, Wordsworth comes also to wield disciplinary power over others, readers and writers alike. My use of Foucault here and elsewhere is derived mainly from my reading of *Power/Knowledge* and *Discipline and Punish*, trans. Alan Sheridan (New York: Vintage Books, 1979).

41. The persistence of this standard can be seen, from very different points of view, in M. H. Abrams, *Natural Supernaturalism* (New York: W. W. Norton and Co., 1971) and Margaret Homans, *Women Writers and Poetic Identity* (Princeton, N.J.: Princeton University Press, 1980).

42. David Simpson, *Wordsworth's Historical Imagination* (New York: Methuen, 1987), p. 114. The line of thought Simpson pursues in this book, especially in chapter 4 (pp. 113–33), anticipates some aspects of my own argument, but Simpson places somewhat more emphasis than I do on the social and intersubjective elements of Wordsworth's constitution of a poetic self.

43. While commentators on the "glad preamble" long assumed that it was composed during the mid-1790s, John Alban Finch conclusively established its date as November 1799; see "Wordsworth's Two-Handed Engine," in *Bicentenary Wordsworth Studies*, ed. Jonathan Wordsworth (Ithaca, N.Y.: Cornell University Press, 1970), pp. 1–15.

44. While Chandler argues that Rousseau is the primary target of Wordsworth's critique in book five, and Gill (*William Wordsworth: A Life*, pp. 130–31) nominates Tom Wedgwood's educational scheme for the same honor, my research suggests that the English Edgeworth is just as likely a candidate. Having tried to raise his eldest son on the model of *Emile*, and failing miserably (the boy turned out an idler), Edgeworth turned to a more Lockean model of education: to make the mind "obedient to Discipline and pliant to Reason" in its earliest years is, for Edgeworth as for Locke, the aim and end of infant pedagogy (John Locke, *Some Thoughts Concerning Education* [Cambridge: Cambridge University Press, 1898], p. 21). See Marilyn Butler, *Maria Edgeworth* (Oxford: Oxford University Press, 1972), ch. 1, for an account of Edgeworth's experiment. Regardless of whom he is critiquing, Wordsworth's whole point in book five, I think, is to expose the false, mechanical tenor of such artificial discipline.

45. Gayatri Spivak, "Sex and History in *The Prelude*: Books Nine to Thirteen," in *In Other Worlds* (New York: Methuen, 1987), p. 72. Simpson puts it more precisely: "the history of a self must also be the history of a society, or at least of the tension between inner and outer forms of determination" (*Wordsworth's Historical Imagination*, p. 117).

46. Kenneth R. Johnston, *Wordsworth and "The Recluse"* (New Haven, Conn.: Yale University Press, 1984), p. 62.

47. Eli Zaretsky traces the origin of the split Wordsworth is trying to deny to "the development of large-scale industrial production" and "the conflict between the individual and society" that it created: "On the one side appeared society—the capitalist economy, the state, the fixed social core that has no space in it for the individual; on the other, the personal identity, no longer defined by its place in the social division of labor"

(*Capitalism, The Family, and Personal Life,* 2d ed. [New York: Harper and Row, 1986], p. 41). *The Prelude,* I am arguing, attempts to repress this split even as it enacts its effects.

48. Neil Hertz's essay, "The Notion of Blockage in the Literature of the Sublime," now reprinted in *The End of the Line: Essays on Psychoanalysis and the Sublime* (New York: Columbia University Press, 1985), pp. 40–60, first drew my attention to the importance of this book for understanding the relation between personal identity and the threat of the other in *The Prelude;* though I have pursued a historical materialist track in considering this episode in the context of a specifically *literary* crisis, I think my reading is still fundamentally compatible with Hertz's analysis.

David Simpson cites the "clear connections between this improper society of alienated figures and the famous polemic [in the Preface to *Lyrical Ballads*] against what [Wordsworth] called poetic diction," and implicitly recognizes that Wordsworth's encounter with the city constitutes a threat to the entire *Recluse* project—to write the universally applicable poem on "Man, Nature, and Human Life" (*Wordsworth and the Figurings of the Real* [London: Macmillan, 1982], p. 51); however, Simpson does not read the book as a whole in terms of Wordsworth's vocational crisis.

In *The Politics and Poetics of Transgression* (Ithaca, N.Y.: Cornell University Press, 1986), Peter Stallybrass and Allon White conclude their discussion of authorship in the seventeenth and eighteenth centuries with a brief reading of book seven which clearly overlaps at points with my own analysis, as when they note for instance that "the ambivalence of the poetic 'I' is thus inscribed in its ineluctable return *in writing* to that very scene from which it persistently declared its absence" (p. 124). However, they locate Wordsworth's recuperation of a transcendental position in strictly literary terms, in reading his invocation of the "classical aesthetic" as that which enables him to meet "the fair's threat to authorship and identity" (p. 123). What I find particularly helpful in their work is its discussion of issues similar to the ones I address in their reading of Ben Johnson's *Bartholomew Fair* (1614), pp. 66–79.

49. Michael H. Friedman, *The Making of a Tory Humanist: William Wordsworth and the Idea of Community* (New York: Columbia University Press, 1979), p. 52. See also chapter 2 of William Chapman Sharpe, *Unreal Cities: Urban Figuration in Wordsworth, Baudelaire, Whitman, Eliot, and Williams* (Baltimore: Johns Hopkins University Press, 1990), for a more extended treatment of the encounter with the blind beggar.

50. As Hertz puts it, "the self cannot simply think but must read the confirmation of its own integrity, which is only legible in a specular structure, a structure in which the self can perform that 'supererogatory identification with the blocking agent' " ("The Notion of Blockage," p. 56); reading the face and emblem of the blind beggar at first suggests the likeness, and then the difference between the object viewed and the viewing subject.

51. Following Edward Said's *The World, the Text, and the Critic,* Klancher uses this concept in his discussion of the new public discourse being created in the periodical text in the 1790s to describe the way in which "all ranks [of readers] are [presented as] intricately connected, yet also distinct" (*The Making of English Reading Audiences,* p. 26). Such a model allows Wordsworth to believe in the possibility of writing poetry that all classes can read and in which they can read themselves, even as the poetry enacts and encodes the differences that separate one class of readers from another. Interestingly, Wordsworth's universalizing sweep is analogously reproduced in periodicals such as the *Edinburgh Review,* edited by Wordsworth's arch-adversary, Francis Jeffrey; as Klancher puts it, "the quarterly review at every point situates its reader atop a simula-

crum of social order, turning nearly any subject into an intellectual surveyor's social map" (p. 69).

52. Raymond Williams, *The Country and the City* (New York: Oxford University Press, 1973).

53. For a slightly different reading of a similar phenomenon, see Philippe Lejeune, "The Autobiographical Contract," in *French Literary Theory Today: A Reader*, ed. Tzvetan Todorov, trans. R. Carter (Cambridge: Cambridge University Press, 1982), esp. pp. 196–204.

54. See Herbert Lindenberger, "The Reception of *The Prelude*," *Bulletin of the New York Public Library* 64 (1960): 196–208, for a sample of the lukewarm reviews the poem garnered when posthumously published and for an analysis of why the poem had so little impact on the Victorian reading public.

55. Siskin, "Wordsworth's Prescriptions," p. 305.

56. See Carl Woodring, "Wordsworth and the Victorians," in *The Age of William Wordsworth: Critical Essays on the Romantic Tradition*, ed. Kenneth R. Johnston and Gene W. Ruoff (New Brunswick: Rutgers University Press, 1987), pp. 261–75.

57. David Riede, "Transgression, Authority, and the Church of Literature in Carlyle," in *Victorian Connections*, ed. Jerome J. McGann (Charlottesville: University Press of Virginia, 1989), p. 101; this fine article anticipates in some respects my way of thinking about Carlyle.

58. Thomas Carlyle, *Sartor Resartus*, ed. Charles Frederick Harrold (New York: The Odyssey Press, 1937), p. 18; all subsequent references will be to this edition and will be included in the text.

59. For an account of these aborted efforts at obtaining university sinecures, see Fred Kaplan, *Thomas Carlyle: A Biography* (Ithaca, N.Y.: Cornell University Press, 1983), pp. 135–39.

60. Thomas Carlyle to Thomas Murray, 24 August 1814, *The Collected Letters of Thomas and Jane Welsh Carlyle*, 15 vols., ed. Charles Richard Sanders (Durham: Duke University Press, 1970), 1:20–21; all subsequent references will be included in the text and cited as *CL*.

61. Also see *Sartor Resartus* for Teufelsdröckh's abdication of a legal career, which leaves him "without landmark of outward guidance; whereby his previous want of decided belief, or inward guidance, is frightfully aggravated" (pp. 121–22).

62. The quotation, which repeatedly figures in Carlyle's letters, is from *A Midsummer Night's Dream*, 5.1.

63. When hack work went well for Carlyle, he most often expressed his satisfaction as a sense of accomplishment at being able to see the tangible fruits of constant, applied labor: "It would do you good to see with what regularity I progress in translating. Clockwork is scarcely steadier. . . . It is not unpleasant work, nor is it pleasant. Original composition is ten times as laborious. . . . But this present business is cool and quiet; one feels over it, as a shoemaker does when he sees the leather gathering into a shoe; as any mortal does when he sees the activity of his mind expressing itself in some external material shape" (To Jane Welsh, *CL*, 3:59).

64. The choice of a career in medicine for a young Scot of the Carlyles' relatively low socioeconomic standing was not as unusual as it might appear today: as Parry and Parry record, for Scots, "a medical career" was "very attractive as an avenue of individual social mobility" because the Scottish medical system offered "good educational facilities . . . a relative ease of access to training and also a lack of distinction between the traditional ranks in medicine" (*The Rise of the Medical Profession*, p. 107).

65. The language Carlyle uses and the train of thought he pursues here, as in so many similar letters, closely matches Max Weber's description of the relation between Protestant piety, capitalist determinants, and professional behavior, for example, "For everyone without exception God's Providence has prepared a calling which he should profess and in which he should labour"; "A man without a calling thus lacks the systematic, methodical character . . . demanded by worldly asceticism" (*Protestant Ethic,* p. 160). Carlyle reserves the religious imperative for his discussions of authorship as a divine calling, but the conjunction of moral duty and work-as-calling that Weber traces clearly pervades Carlyle's thinking on the professions even when he undercuts it.

In addition, the biographical context of Weber's own work proves equally relevant to the point I am making here. *The Protestant Ethic* was the first text Weber produced after a long period of relative idleness induced by a series of mental and physical illnesses, and thus seems motivated by a particularly strong need to establish the boundaries of what constitutes work; as Gianfranco Poggi writes, "when in *The Protestant Ethic* Weber traced to Luther the attachment of that significance to a worldly calling, he was still groping his way out of years of much diminished activity" (*Calvinism and the Capitalist Spirit: Max Weber's "Protestant Ethic"* [London: Macmillan, 1983]) p. 9. I am grateful to Alexandra Chasin for referring me back to Weber as a supporting text.

66. "Jean Paul Friedrich Richter" (1827), in Thomas Carlyle, *Critical and Miscellaneous Essays,* 5 vols. (New York: AMS Press, 1969), 1:20; also quoted in Kaplan, *Thomas Carlyle,* p. 130.

67. Walter L. Reed, "The Pattern of Conversion in *Sartor Resartus,*" *ELH* 38, no. 3 (September 1971): 415.

68. Jerome J. McGann, *The Romantic Ideology: A Critical Investigation* (Chicago: The University of Chicago Press, 1983), p. 1; Kaplan, *Thomas Carlyle,* p. 54. While McGann has definitely given an impetus to my work, I find the research and conclusions of Stallybrass and White offer a more suggestive model for cultural analysis, as when they argue, for example, that "it is only when such related concepts as critical judgement, taste, authorship and writing are reconnected to their 'planes of emergence' as Foucault has called them, the social points at which such ideas surface, that they can be fully understood" (*Politics and Poetics,* pp. 82–83).

69. G. B. Tennyson, *Sartor Called Resartus* (Princeton, N.J.: Princeton University Press, 1965), p. 170. Tennyson puts *Sartor* in the context of *Fraser's* and relates its method and style to the tone of the magazine and its writers, pointing out the parallels, but he does not speculate as to why Carlyle chose to model his text along the general lines of a *Fraser's* article; nor does he examine the implications of Carlyle's strategy in terms of his position in relation to literary production in the 1830s. I have, however, drawn freely on Tennyson's excellent research and find myself in agreement with him on most of his main points.

70. Walter E. Houghton, "Periodical Literature and the Articulate Classes," in *The Victorian Periodical Press: Samplings and Soundings,* ed. Joanne Shattock and Michael Wolff (Toronto: University of Toronto Press, 1983), pp. 19–20.

71. For all its irreverence, *Fraser's,* too, upheld the dogma of artist-as-genius; its first issue contains an essay "On Poetical Genius, Considered as a Creative Power" by John A. Heraud, one of William Maginn's main collaborators, which cites D'Israeli's *Essay* with unequivocal approval and shares its uncertainty over how to discriminate between different kinds of literary production.

72. George Levine, *The Boundaries of Fiction* (Princeton, N.J.: Princeton University Press, 1968), p. 20.

73. Interestingly, this is a point repeated in the very first paragraph of *Fraser's*

review of *The French Revolution:* "Know you nothing of the author—you shall know nothing of the book" (*Fraser's* 16 [1837]: 85).

74. Carlyle, "Jean Paul Friedrich Richter," (1830), 2:100–101.

75. Paul Jay makes a similar point in his discussion of Carlyle in *Being in the Text: Self-Representation from Wordsworth to Roland Barthes* (Ithaca, N.Y.: Cornell University Press, 1984), p. 105.

Chapter 2

1. Gilbert and Gubar first located the woman writer's anxiety in relation to male precursors in *The Madwoman in the Attic* (New Haven, Conn.: Yale University Press, 1979) as "a radical fear that she cannot create, that because she can never become a 'precursor' the act of writing will destroy her" (p. 49); they assert as well "her fear of the antagonism of male readers, her culturally conditioned timidity about self-dramatization, her dread of the patriarchal authority of art" (p. 50) as additional barriers to women's self-expression. I want not only to acknowledge my own indebtedness to these two "precursors," who provided my earliest introduction to feminist criticism, but also to articulate my difference from them. I am far less concerned than they are with how "great" authors "transcend" their anxiety to produce art or with how their monstrous/revolutionary messages erupt from within the submerged unconscious of literary texts; I look at the explicit register of anxiety as it appears in the autobiographical text and at the culturally sanctioned strategies autobiographers develop for coping with their gendered cultural positioning.

2. Quoted in Carl Ray Woodring, *Victorian Samplers: William and Mary Howitt* (Lawrence: University of Kansas Press, 1952), p. 201.

3. I am grateful to the anonymous reader for Oxford University Press for making this observation.

4. Fanny Burney, Preface to *Evelina* (1778; reprint ed., New York: W. W. Norton and Company, 1965).

5. For an interesting although differently centered analysis of the risks involved in self-exposure for both men and women writers, see Catherine Gallagher, "George Eliot and *Daniel Deronda*: The Prostitute and the Jewish Question," in *Sex, Politics, and Science in the Nineteenth-Century Novel,* ed. Ruth Bernard Yeazell (Baltimore: Johns Hopkins University Press, 1986), where Gallagher argues that Victorian writing and Victorian prostitution—another form of self-exposure to which some women were subject—are metaphorically "linked" . . . through their joint inhabitation of the realm of exchange" (p. 41).

6. Mary Poovey, *Uneven Developments: The Ideological Work of Gender in Mid-Victorian England* (Chicago: University of Chicago Press, 1988), p. 101.

7. See Eli Zaretsky, *Capitalism, The Family, and Personal Life,* 2d ed. (New York: Harper and Row, 1986), for the theoretical exposition of men's relation to the private sphere.

8. For a concise historical summary of these claims, see T. W. Heyck, "The World of the Men of Letters, 1830s–1860s," in *The Transformation of Intellectual Life in Victorian England* (New York: St. Martin's Press, 1982).

9. [George Henry Lewes], "The Condition of Authors in England, Germany, and France," *Fraser's* 35 (March 1847): 285. For a reading of this essay compatible with my own, see Julia Swindells, *Victorian Writing and Working Women* (Cambridge: Polity Press, 1985), pp. 38–43.

10. "Vivian," "A Gentle Hint to Writing-Women," *The Leader* 1 (18 May 1850): 189. As Monica Correa Fryckstedt observes, Lewes makes his remarks "half jokingly, half in despair" ("Defining the Domestic Genre: English Women Novelists of the 1850s," *Tulsa Studies in Women's Literature* 6, no. 1 [Spring 1987]: 10): although Lewes's remarks are deliberately and self-consciously ironic, the valence of the essay also seems to me to be on the side of professional, masculine literary prerogative.

11. Robert Southey [to Charlotte Brontë], March 1837, *The Life and Correspondence of Robert Southey*, 6 vols., ed. Charles Cuthbert Southey (London, 1850), 6:329.

12. For a discussion of the implications of gender for George Eliot's professional project, see N. N. Feltes, *Modes of Production of Victorian Novels* (Chicago: University of Chicago Press, 1986), pp. 36–56.

13. "Encouragement of Literature by the State," *The Examiner*, 5 January 1850, p. 2.

14. "Literary Women," *The London Review* 8 (26 March 1864): 328, 329; all subsequent references to this article will be included in the text.

15. Catherine Gallagher, *The Industrial Reformation of English Fiction: Social Discourse and Narrative Form, 1832–1867* (Chicago: University of Chicago Press, 1985), p. 120.

16. For more on the legal doctrine of coverture, see Poovey, "Covered but Not Bound: Caroline Norton and the 1857 Matrimonial Causes Act," in *Uneven Developments*, esp. pp. 70–80.

17. Elizabeth Barrett Browning, *Aurora Leigh* in *Aurora Leigh and Other Poems*, ed. Cora Kaplan (London: The Women's Press, 1978), 1:398, 403, 406; all subsequent line references will be included in the text.

18. For two readings of the poem that make this point in contexts that differ from my own, see Barbara Charlesworth Gelpi, "*Aurora Leigh*: The Vocation of the Woman Poet," *Victorian Poetry* 19, no. 1 (Spring 1981): 35–48; and Kathleen Blake, "Elizabeth Barrett Browning and Wordsworth: The Romantic Poet as a Woman," *Victorian Poetry* 24, no. 4 (Winter 1986): 387–98.

19. See Helen M. Cooper, who argues that "the central issue in Barrett Browning's work is how a woman poet empowers herself to speak" in *Elizabeth Barrett Browning, Woman and Artist* (Chapel Hill: University of North Carolina Press, 1988), p. 3. Other recent readings that address similar issues include Dorothy Mermin, *Elizabeth Barrett Browning: The Origins of a New Poetry* (Chicago: University of Chicago Press, 1989), pp. 183–224, and Deborah Byrd, "Combating an Alien Tyranny: Elizabeth Barrett Browning's Evolution as a Feminist Poet," *Browning Institute Studies* 15 (1987): 23–41.

20. In an argument with which my disagreement should be obvious, Christine Sutphin claims that this division is satisfactorily resolved by the conclusion of the poem in her "Revising Old Scripts: The Fusion of Independence and Intimacy in *Aurora Leigh*," *Browning Institute Studies* 15 (1987): 43–54.

21. See Margaret Homans, *Women Writers and Poetic Identity* (Princeton, N.J.: Princeton University Press, 1980), esp. ch. 1. The absence of Barrett Browning from Homans's discussion is particularly striking to me here, for *Aurora Leigh* seems boldly to contradict Homans's assertion that "the masculine tradition" is wholly closed to women.

22. Deirdre David, *Intellectual Women and Victorian Patriarchy* (Ithaca, N.Y.: Cornell University Press, 1987), pp. 97–98. I find David's reading of *Aurora Leigh* and of Barrett Browning's sexual politics to be closest to my own.

23. Cora Kaplan, "Pandora's Box: Subjectivity, Class and Sexuality in Socialist Fem-

inist Criticism," in *Sea Changes: Essays in Culture and Feminism* (London: Verso, 1986), p. 149; Dorothy Mermin, "The Damsel, the Knight, and the Victorian Woman Poet," *Critical Inquiry* 13 (Autumn 1986): 65. For an early socialist-feminist formulation of what is at stake in Barrett Browning's positioning of Aurora as subject, see The Marxist-Feminist Literature Collective, "Women's Writing: *Jane Eyre, Shirley, Villette, Aurora Leigh,*" *Ideology and Consciousness* 3 (Spring 1978): 27–48.

24. As David remarks, "What is to be made new, and the means of making it new" at the end of *Aurora Leigh* "are figured in highly traditional, even reactionary terms" (*Intellectual Women*, p. 154).

25. Carole Pateman, *The Sexual Contract* (Stanford, Calif.: Stanford University Press, 1988), pp. 130–31.

26. Jane Tompkins's analysis of the ideological import of nineteenth-century American "sentimental" novels by women, which combine Christian morality and feminine virtue, is relevant here. See "The Other American Renaissance," in *Sensational Designs* (New York: Oxford University Press, 1985), pp. 147–85.

27. See F. J. Harvey Darton's Introduction to *The Life and Times of Mrs. Sherwood* (London: Wells Gardner, Darton and Company, Ltd., 1910), and Margaret E. Tabor, *Pioneer Women* (London: The Sheldon Press, 1930) for more biographical information on Sherwood; for some discussion of her fiction, see Vineta Colby, *Yesterday's Woman: Domestic Realism in the English Novel* (Princeton, N.J.: Princeton University Press, 1974), pp. 159–65.

28. See Colby, *Yesterday's Woman*, pp. 174–78, and Monica Correa Fryckstedt, "Charlotte Elizabeth Tonna & *The Christian Lady's Magazine,*" *Victorian Periodicals Review* 14, no. 2 (Summer 1981): 43–51.

29. Charlotte Elizabeth [Tonna], *Personal Recollections* (New York, 1842), pp. 15, 1; all subsequent references to this autobiography will be included in the text.

30. Mary Martha Sherwood, *The Life of Mrs. Sherwood*, ed. Sophia Kelly (London, 1857), p. 1; all subsequent references to this autobiography will be included in the text.

31. Gallagher, *The Industrial Reformation of English Fiction*, p. 118.

32. Mary Bayly, *The Life and Letters of Mrs. Sewell*, 5th ed. (London, 1890), p. 56. Bayly's book contains a seventy-five page autobiography that Sewell left in manuscript at the time of her death.

33. Sewell's disapproval notwithstanding, there was a tradition of women preaching in public dating back at least to the eighteenth century. For late-eighteenth century evidence documenting the historical record on women preachers in the Methodist revival, see D. Colin Dews, "Ann Carr and the Female Revivalists of Leeds," in *Religion in the Lives of English Women, 1760–1930*, ed. Gail Malmgreen (London: Croom Helm, 1986), pp. 68–87; Deborah Valenze, "Cottage Religion and the Politics of Survival," in *Equal or Different*, ed. Jane Rendall (London: Basil Blackwell, 1987), pp. 31–56; and for Sewell's own period, see Olive Anderson, "Women Preachers in Mid-Victorian Britain: Some Reflexions on Feminism, Popular Religion and Social Change," *The Historical Journal* 12, no. 3 (1969): 467–84.

34. For introductions to and readings of Tonna's politicized industrial fiction, see Ivanka Kovacevic and S. Barbara Kanner, "Blue Book Into Novel: The Forgotten Industrial Fiction of Charlotte Elizabeth Tonna," *Nineteenth-Century Fiction* 25, no. 2 (September 1970): 152–73; Joseph Kestner, "Charlotte Elizabeth Tonna's *The Wrongs of Woman*: Female Industrial Protest," *Tulsa Studies in Women's Literature* 2, no. 2 (Fall 1983): 193–214; and Deborah Kaplan, "The Woman Worker in Charlotte Elizabeth Tonna's Fiction," *Mosaic* 18, no. 2 (Spring 1985): 51–63.

35. Mary Anne Schimmelpenninck, *Life of Mary Anne Schimmelpenninck*, 2 vols., ed. Christiana C. Hankin (London, 1858), 1:219; all subsequent references to this autobiography will be included in the text.

36. Gail Malmgreen, Introduction to *Religion in the Lives of English Women, 1760–1930*, ed. Gail Malmgreen (London: Croom Helm, 1986), p. 7.

37. For an important recent reading of Victorian religious fiction for adolescents along these lines, see Judith Rowbotham, "Religion as a Control on Reality," in *Good Girls Make Good Wives: Guidance for Girls in Victorian Fiction* (London: Basil Blackwell, 1989), pp. 53–98.

38. Elisabeth Jay, *The Religion of the Heart: Anglican Evangelicalism and the Nineteenth-Century Novel* (Oxford: Oxford University Press, 1979), p. 51.

39. Nancy Armstrong, *Desire and Domestic Fiction* (New York: Oxford University Press, 1987), p. 81.

40. For an explication of "the concept of Original Sin" as "the linchpin of the Evangelical creed," see Jay, *Religion of the Heart*, pp. 54–59; for a reading of the Puritan spiritual autobiography in relation to fiction, see G. A. Starr, *Defoe and Spiritual Autobiography* (Princeton, N.J.: Princeton University Press, 1965), and esp. pp. 17–22 on the exemplarity of the autobiographical text.

41. Tonna's autobiography does record a conversion, which I will not report in complete detail; what I find most interesting about it is the way in which it is mediated by the Biblical text. Living in rural Ireland, and thus outside an immediate community of Protestant believers, Tonna's seclusion leads her to undertake a thorough course of religious devotions; when she finds herself unable to pray, she turns to the Bible for guidance so as "to reform myself . . . and become obedient to the whole law" (p. 102), which she carries out through reading and writing—making note of Biblical texts that she should take to heart and pasting them around her room, keeping a little book in which she records all her offenses, and finally understanding the true meaning of the Scriptures by divine guidance. Her career as a writer begins almost immediately after this conversion to Evangelical ways. For a reading of the autobiography as a "failed" conversion narrative, see Elizabeth Kowaleski, " 'The Heroine of Some Strange Romance': The *Personal Recollections* of Charlotte Elizabeth Tonna," *Tulsa Studies in Women's Literature* 1, no. 2 (Fall 1982): 141–53. See also Jay, *Religion of the Heart*, pp. 59–65 and 148–49, for an account of the influence of Evangelical motifs on literary texts, particularly in George Eliot's novels, in which conversion is represented as "continuous warfare with sin" (p. 67), part of an ongoing process of self-scrutiny rather than a sudden and dramatic break from sinfulness to salvation. And for a brief but perceptive reading of *Personal Recollections*, see Valerie Sanders, *The Private Lives of Victorian Women: Autobiography in Nineteenth-Century England* (New York: St. Martin's Press, 1989), pp. 79–82.

42. Carol Edkins, "Quest for Community: Spiritual Autobiographies of Eighteenth-Century Quaker and Puritan Women in America," in *Women's Autobiography: Essays in Criticism*, ed. Estelle C. Jelinek (Bloomington: Indiana University Press, 1980), p. 41. Also see Mary Anne Schofield, " 'Womens Speaking Justified': The Feminine Quaker Voice, 1662–1797," *Tulsa Studies in Women's Literature* 6, no. 1 (Spring 1987): 61–77.

43. "Vivian" [Lewes], "A Gentle Hint to Writing-Women," p. 189.

44. Mary Russell Mitford, *Recollections of a Literary Life*, 3 vols. (London, 1852), 1:249.

45. Sarah Ellis, *The Wives of England* (London, 1843), pp. 344–45. Also see Gallagher's reading of Ellis in *The Industrial Reformation of English Fiction*, pp. 118–20.

46. Margaret Homans makes a similar point—"women's obligation to enact the word of God is thus a compensation for the first woman's conceiving the word of Satan"—in *Bearing the Word: Language and Female Experience in Nineteenth-Century Women's Writing* (Chicago: University of Chicago Press, 1986), p. 159.

47. The middle-class woman's "natural" role as civilizer and moral agent was earlier argued for on the same grounds Schimmelpenninck puts forward. As Hannah More writes in "Strictures on the Modern System of Female Education" (1799), "The general state of civilized society depends, more than those are aware who are not accustomed to scrutinize into the springs of human action, on the prevailing sentiments and habits of women, and on the nature and degree of the estimation in which they are held. . . . I would call [women] to the best and most appropriate exertion of their power, to raise the depressed tone of public morals, and to awaken the drowsy spirit of religious principles" (In *The Complete Works of Hannah More* [New York, 1843], p. 313). Literature, as More's own career demonstrates, provided an obvious means for carrying out the feminine moral mission she recommends.

Chapter 3

1. Mary Howitt, *An Autobiography*, 2 vols., ed. Margaret Howitt (Boston, 1889), 1:70–71; all subsequent references to this autobiography will be included in the text.

2. Harriet Martineau, *Autobiography*, 3 vols. (1877; reprint ed., London: Virago Press, 1983), 1:117–20; all subsequent references to this autobiography will be included in the text.

3. A. Amy Bulley and Margaret Whitley, *Women's Work* (London, 1894), p. 3.

4. After embracing a number of different creeds, Howitt converted to Roman Catholicism shortly before her death as an expatriate in Italy, while Martineau substituted Auguste Comte's "religion of humanity" for traditional orthodoxy and adopted the practices of mesmerism and spiritualism.

5. Carl Ray Woodring, Preface to *Victorian Samplers: William and Mary Howitt* (Lawrence: University of Kansas Press, 1952).

6. Ruth L. Smith and Deborah M. Valenze argue something similar to what I am suggesting here about Howitt in their essay, "Mutuality and Marginality: Liberal Moral Theory and Working-Class Women in Nineteenth-Century England," *Signs* 13, no. 2 (Winter 1988): 277–98): "For [working-class] women, participation in the public realm of work was not a matter of their relationship to capitalism and the state; rather, it was an extension of their roles as sisters, mothers, and wives" (p. 288). While I do not wish to elide the class differences between the woman seamstress and the woman writer, I do believe that Howitt's representation of herself as a worker has a close affinity to what Smith and Valenze report.

7. Mary Howitt, "Margaret von Ehrenberg, The Artist-Wife," in *Stories of Domestic and Foreign Life* (London, 1853), pp. 11–12.

8. Howitt's tableau also fits Elaine Showalter's description of the way in which the "feminine novelists" represented themselves: in order "to present their writing as an extension of their feminine role . . . it was essential that the writing be carried out in the home, and that it be only one among the numerous and interruptible household tasks of the true woman" (*A Literature of Their Own* [Princeton, N.J.: Princeton University Press, 1977], p. 85). Thanks to Barbara Gelpi for reminding me of Showalter's point.

9. Sidonie Smith, *A Poetics of Women's Autobiography: Marginality and the Fic-*

tions of Self-Representation (Bloomington: Indiana University Press, 1987), p. 126. Smith locates "the muted drama of repression" in the psychosexual realm, particularly in terms of Martineau's relation to her mother; she claims that Martineau "suppresses the story of emotional turmoil . . . [giving] her allegiance to the ideology of male selfhood" (p. 144), and thus reproduces the public–private split. This reading tends, in my opinion, to underplay Martineau's conscious manipulation of these categories of experience. For another important critical account of the *Autobiography*, see Linda Peterson, *Victorian Autobiography* (New Haven, Conn.: Yale University Press, 1986), pp. 120–55. Valerie Sanders, *The Private Lives of Victorian Women: Autobiography in Nineteenth-Century England* (New York: St. Martin's Press, 1989), pp. 130–34, contains a far briefer but suggestive account; cited in text as *PL*.

10. I am of course coining the phrase after Adrienne Rich, "Compulsory Heterosexuality and Lesbian Existence," reprinted in *Blood, Bread, and Poetry: Selected Prose 1979–1985* (New York: W. W. Norton and Co., 1986), pp. 23–75.

11. [William Maginn,] "Gallery of Literary Characters: Miss Harriet Martineau," *Fraser's* 8 (November 1833): 576–77.

12. W. R. Greg, "Why Are Women Redundant?" *National Review* 14 (April 1862): 434–60.

13. [G. Poulett Scrope,] "Miss Martineau's *Monthly Novels*," *The Quarterly Review* 49 (April 1833): 151. But see also the more temperate, generally positive review in *The Edinburgh Review* 47 (April 1833): 1–39.

I have argued elsewhere that Martineau's apparently radical stance on (and in) political economy needs to be historicized as part of a hegemonic bourgeois discourse that perpetuates patriarchal structures as much or more than it undercuts them; see my "Feminine Authorship and Spiritual Authority in Victorian Women Writers' Autobiographies," *Women's Studies* 18, no. 1 (1990): 13–29, esp. pp. 13–15. For an extended elaboration of competing ideologies in Martineau's life and work, see Deirdre David, *Intellectual Women and Victorian Patriarchy* (Ithaca, N.Y.: Cornell University Press, 1987), chs. 1–4.

14. The phrase is taken from Richard Polwhele's late eighteenth-century poem, *The Unsex'd Females* (reprint ed., New York: Garland Publishing, 1974).

15. Margaret Walters, "The Rights and Wrongs of Women: Mary Wollstonecraft, Harriet Martineau, Simone de Beauvoir," in *The Rights and Wrongs of Women*, ed. Juliet Mitchell and Ann Oakley (Harmondsworth: Penguin, 1976), p. 336; Valerie Sanders, *Reason Over Passion: Harriet Martineau and the Victorian Novel* (New York: St. Martin's Press, 1986), p. 180.

16. Nancy K. Miller, "Writing Fictions: Women's Autobiography in France," in *Subject to Change: Reading Feminist Writing* (New York: Columbia University Press, 1988), p. 51.

17. [Margaret Oliphant,] "Harriet Martineau," *Blackwood's* 121 (April 1877): 479, 496; all subsequent references to this essay will be included in the text. For an alternative view by a far less critical male reviewer, see Henry S. Richardson, "Harriet Martineau's Account of Herself," *Contemporary Review* 29 (May 1877): 1112–23.

18. In another roughly contemporary article, Oliphant makes a similar criticism of DeQuincey, whom she sees as providing "too much minuteness and distinctness" in his portrait of the Wordsworth circle at home, and so demonstrates that she disapproves of excessive disclosure by either men or women: "such an invasion of the privacy of domestic life, by whomsoever done, is always more or less of a sin against human nature" ("The Opium-Eater," *Blackwood's* 122 [December 1877]: 726).

19. It is worth noting here that Oliphant herself was criticized after the posthumous publication of her *Autobiography* by Meredith Townsend ("Mrs. Oliphant," *The Cornhill Magazine* 79 [1899]: 773–79) for being too harsh on her contemporaries: "we doubt if she ever hated or much disliked anybody, yet some of the kit-cat sketches of acquaintance in the *Autobiography* are drawn in vitriol" (p. 774). Elisabeth Jay has identified passages in the recently discovered manuscript of the *Autobiography* which are highly critical, in personal terms, of George Eliot, G. H. Lewes, Leslie Stephen and others in which Oliphant is also very severe on her hapless sons and brothers (see note 36).

20. For an account of the controversy, see Valerie Kossew Pichanick, *Harriet Martineau: The Woman and Her Work, 1802–76* (Ann Arbor: University of Michigan Press, 1980), esp. pp. 188–92. For a recent reading of Martineau's life and work that analyzes her relationship with her mother in psychological terms, see Diana Postlethwaite, "Mothering and Mesmerism in the Life of Harriet Martineau," *Signs* 14, no. 3 (Spring 1989): 583–609.

21. George Eliot to Mrs. Charles Bray, 20 March 1877, *The George Eliot Letters*, 7 vols., ed. Gordon S. Haight (New Haven, Conn.: Yale University Press, 1955), 6:353–54.

22. In short, this defense is a pure product of liberal political philosophy, which, as Alison M. Jaggar reminds us, "[defines] the legitimate power of the state" by "[distinguishing] between the 'public' realm, where the state may intervene legitimately, and the 'private' realm" (p. 61), which the state empowers to carry out its reproductive functions without interfering in the family's inner workings. See her *Feminist Politics and Human Nature* (Totowa, N.J.: Rowman and Allanheld, 1983).

23. Mary Poovey, *The Proper Lady and the Woman Writer: Ideology as Style in the Works of Mary Wollstonecraft, Mary Shelley, and Jane Austen* (Chicago: University of Chicago Press, 1984), p. 41.

24. [George Henry Lewes,] "The Lady Novelists," *Westminster Review* o.s. 58 (July 1852): 139.

25. Eliza Lynn Linton, *My Literary Life* (London, 1899), p. 72.

26. Mrs. Newton [Camilla Toulmin] Crosland, *Landmarks of a Literary Life 1820–1892* (New York, 1893), p. 1.

27. Sanders, *Private Lives*, p. 6.

28. Mrs. Humphry [Mary] Ward, *A Writer's Recollections* (London: W. Collins Sons & Co. Ltd., 1918), p. 2.

29. Avrom Fleishman describes the memoir as a "breed of writings designed to obscure their own artificiality" (p. 37), by which he means that the absence of "the double focus" (p. 192) of autobiography—in which "the interplay of I-past and I-present" (p. 192) creates a complex psychological narrative structure—from the typical memoir keeps "the focus of attention . . . on the I-past" (p. 192); this accounts for the lower generic status of this form (*Figures of Autobiography: The Language of Self-Writing in Victorian and Modern England* [Berkeley: University of California Press, 1983]). This purely formal definition prizes the continuity of identity over time and the centrality of the writing subject; it also fails to take gender into account.

I use the term "memoir" to denote an autobiographical text that does not tell a story about a centered self, but one in which the writing subject recounts stories of others and events or movements in which she and/or her other subjects have taken part. Valerie Sanders describes Victorian women's memoirs as often telling "the story of a generation" and offering "a slice of representative life in a specific period" (*Private Lives*, pp. 10–11), and I consider this a good way to think about these texts. While I do not care to make hard and fast distinctions any more than Fleishman does, I do want to suggest that the memoir form provides a fitting medium for Victorian women's self-representations.

30. Quoted in Herbert von Thal, *Eliza Lynn Linton: The Girl of the Period* (London: George Allen and Unwin, 1979), p. 154; it is not clear to me from the context what it is that she thinks she "knows" that she will not reveal. For a reading of two Linton novels that argues that she displaced her autobiographical impulse into fiction, see Nancy F. Anderson, "Autobiographical Fantasies of a Female Anti-Feminist: Eliza Lynn Linton as Christopher Kirkland and Theodora Desanges," *Dickens Studies Annual* 14 (1985): 287–301. And also see Sanders, *Private Lives*, pp. 91–95, for another discussion of the autobiographical fiction and a brief analysis of the contradictions between Linton's publicly declared antifeminism and her own personal heterodoxies.

31. For Mitford's response to Bentley's decision, see her letter of July 1851 to James T. Fields, quoted in his *Yesterdays With Authors* (1871; reprint ed., Boston, 1881), pp. 291–93.

32. Winifred Gerin, *Anne Thackeray Ritchie: A Biography* (Oxford: Oxford University Press, 1981), p. 219. For a reading of Ritchie's biographical and autobiographical writings that deals in depth with the way in which she defined her position as narrating subject, see Carol Hanbery MacKay, "Biography as Reflected Autobiography: The Self-Creation of Anne Thackeray Ritchie," in *Revealing Lives: Gender in Autobiography and Biography*, ed. Marilyn Yalom and Susan Groag Bell (Albany: State University of New York Press, 1991).

33. Anne Thackeray Ritchie, *Chapters from Some Unwritten Memoirs* (New York, 1895), p. 58.

34. Virginia Woolf, "Lady Ritchie," in *The Essays of Virginia Woolf: 1919–24*, ed. Andrew McNeillie (New York: Harcourt Brace Jovanovich, 1988), p. 18.

35. Alan W. Bellringer, "Mrs Humphry Ward's Autobiographical Tactics: A Writer's Recollections," *Prose Studies* 8, no. 3 (December 1985): 41; all subsequent references to this article will be included in the text. In suggesting that what is expected of the woman autobiographer is a private story rather than a public account, Bellringer's critique indirectly repeats the psychological model for female identity to which the work of Erik Erikson once gave currency: as Judith Kegan Gardiner states of the Eriksonian account of female development, a woman's "unique 'inner space,' " her particular biological destiny as childbearer, is what "she seeks to fill and to protect . . . rather than forge into outward accomplishments" (p. 350). Ward's focus on the public, then, appears particularly inappropriate to the psychoanalytically inclined male critic. See Erik Erikson, "Womanhood and the Inner Space," in *Identity, Youth and Crisis* (New York: W. W. Norton & Co., 1968), pp. 261–94, and Judith Kegan Gardiner, "On Female Identity and Writing by Women," *Critical Inquiry* 8, no. 2 (Winter 1981): 347–91.

36. *The Autobiography of Margaret Oliphant: The Complete Text*, ed. Elisabeth Jay (Oxford: Oxford University Press, 1990), pp. 21–22; all subsequent references to this autobiography will be included in the text. Jay's new edition, which is based on the manuscript of *The Autobiography*, supercedes the recent University of Chicago Press reprint of the heavily edited 1899 edition. For an essay which covers much of the same ground as I do here but from a very different perspective, see Linda H. Peterson, "Audience and the Autobiographer's Art: An Approach to the *Autobiography* of Mrs. M. O. W. Oliphant," in *Approaches to Victorian Autobiography*, ed. George P. Landow (Athens: Ohio University Press, 1979), pp. 158–74. Sanders includes a brief but perceptive reading of the text in *Private Lives*, pp. 86–91. The most provocative recent reading is Gail Twersky Reimer, "Revisions of Labor in Margaret Oliphant's *Autobiography*,"

in *Life/Lines: Theorizing Women's Autobiography*, ed. Bella Brodzki and Celeste Schenck (Ithaca, N.Y.: Cornell University Press, 1988), pp. 203–20. Reimer expertly addresses the complicated issue of how Oliphant attempts to inscribe both maternal procreativity and literary creativity within the gendered generic boundaries of the form.

37. Oliphant's anxiety about Eliot was, as Elaine Showalter demonstrates, widespread among late Victorian novelists of both sexes; see "Queen George," in *Sexual Anarchy: Gender and Culture at the Fin de Siècle* (New York: Viking, 1990), pp. 59–75.

38. One contemporary critical response to the *Autobiography* makes the family/art split explicit and uses it to denigrate Oliphant's work in terms that match her own. See the discussion of Stephen Gwynn's review in Gaye Tuchman, with Nina E. Fortin, in *Edging Women Out: Victorian Novelists, Publishers, and Social Change* (New Haven, Conn.: Yale University Press, 1989), pp. 190–93.

39. Peterson's essay speculates on how this shift in audience affects the text, and Jay's Introduction provides more information on this point. That the *Autobiography* began as a private journal without any "audience" other than Oliphant—and God— links her writing with the Protestant tradition of spiritual accounting discussed in Chapter 2. See Treva Broughton, who also seems to have examined the unedited manuscript, for more commentary on the audience problem in "Margaret Oliphant: The Unbroken Self," *Women's Studies International Forum* 10, no. 1 (1987): 41–52.

40. Quoted in Vineta and Robert A. Colby, *The Equivocal Virtue: Mrs. Oliphant and the Victorian Literary Market Place* ([Hamden, Conn.:] Archon Books, 1966), p. 233.

Chapter 4

1. For Daniel's mother's history, see chapters 51 and 53; for Gwendolen's turn to the idea of the stage, see chapter 23. My edition of the novel is *Daniel Deronda*, ed. Graham Handley (Oxford: Clarendon Press, 1984). The most suggestive recent reading of the novel is Catherine Gallagher's "George Eliot and *Daniel Deronda*: The Prostitute and the Jewish Question," in *Sex, Politics, and Science in the Nineteenth-Century Novel*, ed. Ruth Bernard Yeazell (Baltimore: Johns Hopkins University Press, 1986), pp. 39–62, in which Gallagher expertly connects the Alcharisi, Gwendolen, and Eliot's authorship with notions of sexuality and writing as exchange.

2. "It was a marvelous sight: a mighty revelation. It was a spectacle low, horrible, immoral" (Charlotte Brontë, *Villette* [London: Dent, 1974], p. 234). For readings of Brontë's attitude toward the stage and to the particular real-life model for Vashti, see Rachel M. Brownstein, "Representing the Self: Arnold and Brontë on Rachel," *Browning Institute Studies* 13 (1985): 1–24, and John Stokes, "Rachel's Terrible Beauty: An Actress Among the Novelists," *ELH* 51 (1984): 771–93. For a briefer discussion set in the context of nineteenth-century fiction, see Gillian Beer, " 'Coming Wonders': Uses of Theatre in the Victorian Novel," in *English Drama: Forms and Developments*, ed. Marie Axton and Raymond Williams (Cambridge: Cambridge University Press, 1977), pp. 164–85.

3. Beatrice Webb, *My Apprenticeship* (1926; reprint ed., Cambridge: Cambridge University Press, 1979), p. 93.

4. Frances Ann Kemble, *Records of a Girlhood* (New York, 1879), pp. 224–25; all subsequent references to this autobiography will be included in the text.

5. Judith R. Walkowitz, "Science and the Seance: Transgressions of Gender and Genre in Late Victorian London," *Representations* 22 (Spring 1988): 20.

6. See, for example, "Mrs. Fanny Kemble and the Stage," *The Theatre* 2 (1 May 1879): 224–27.

7. [Dinah Mulock Craik,] *A Woman's Thoughts About Women* (Leipzig, 1860), pp. 45–46.

8. See Jonas Barish, *The Antitheatrical Prejudice* (Berkeley: University of California Press, 1981) for a comprehensive history of antagonistic attitudes to theatrical representation.

9. For a concise but illuminating history of the word "private" and how it has changed over time—from connoting "deprivation" to "privilege"—see Raymond Williams, *Keywords*, rev. ed. (New York: Oxford University Press, 1983), pp. 242–43.

10. Denis Diderot, *The Paradox of Acting* and William Archer, *Masks or Faces?* (New York: Hill and Wang, 1957), p. 184. For a sociological analysis that also picks up on this idea of a split between self and role, see Erving Goffman, *The Presentation of Self in Everyday Life* (Garden City, N.Y.: Doubleday Anchor, 1959). What Archer and Goffman share is a metaphysical conception of the self as some essence that lies beneath or behind the roles that the theatrical or social actor performs.

11. Henry James to Mrs. Humphry Ward, 9 December 1884, *Letters*, 4 vols., ed. Leon Edel (Cambridge: Harvard University Press, 1980), 3:59.

12. "The Army and the Stage," *Saturday Review* 13 (22 March 1862): 321.

13. The theater is unique in this period as an occupation employing both men and women; the only other major occupations with pretensions to professional and middle-class status that were open to women in the 1860s and 1870s, teaching and nursing, differ from the theater in that women teachers generally taught only girls and had few male colleagues, while nursing was an all-female calling. See Martha Vicinus, *Independent Women: Work and Community for Single Women, 1850–1920* (Chicago: University of Chicago Press, 1985), for discussion of these other dimensions of women's work. For a brief but informative overview of actresses in the Victorian and Edwardian theater, see Christopher Kent, "Image and Reality: The Actress and Society," in *A Widening Sphere*, ed. Martha Vicinus (Bloomington: Indiana University Press, 1977), pp. 94–116.

14. Nina Auerbach, *Private Theatricals: The Lives of the Victorians* (Cambridge: Harvard University Press, 1990), p. 114.

15. Quoted in Michael Baker, *The Rise of the Victorian Actor* (Totowa, N.J.: Rowman and Littlefield, 1978), p. 19.

16. William Charles Macready, 19 March 1851, *The Journal of William Charles Macready, 1832–1851*, ed. J. C. Trewin (London: Longmans, 1967), p. 296.

17. As Nina Auerbach points out, however, while "the theatre had become respectable" with Irving's knighthood, "theatricality would never cease to become an offense": Oscar Wilde was sentenced to prison on the same day that Irving received news of his honor (*Ellen Terry, Player in Her Time* [New York: W. W. Norton & Co., 1987], p. 202).

18. As Gareth Stedman-Jones argues, "In working-class districts, where the multiplicity of occupations, the separation of home from workplace and the overcrowding and impermanence of apartments made any stable community life very difficult [the music hall] fulfilled, if only in an anonymous way, a craving for solidarity in facing the daily problems of poverty and family life" ("Working-Class Culture and Working-Class Politics in London, 1870–1900," in *Languages of Class: Studies in English Working Class History, 1832–1982* [Cambridge: Cambridge University Press, 1983], p. 225). See also Peter Bailey, "Custom, Capital and Culture in the Victorian Music Hall," in *Popular*

Culture and Custom in Nineteenth-Century England, ed. Robert D. Storch (London: Croom Helm, 1982), pp. 180–208.

The music hall provided the working classes with one of the few public spaces available for their use. As M. J. Daunton argues, the middle-class value on domesticity, private space, and self-containment of the family unit meant that working-class urban dwellers were increasingly housed in "rigidly encapsulated" domiciles: "each house was turned in upon itself as its own private world," thus eliminating the semienclosed liminal space between home and street that had once provided urbanites with an alternative to the crowded conditions of the tenement (*House and Home in the Victorian City* [London: Edward Arnold, 1983], p. 12). As the border between public and private space was more sharply drawn, "the sanction for popular use of public space" (Daunton, p. 270) was withdrawn, so that popular street-based recreations increasingly came under the control of the police or were outlawed entirely. In effect, the music hall was one of the few public sites for working-class leisure available on a regular daily basis, and not limited to use only on holidays.

19. Henry Arthur Jones, "The Theatre and the Mob," in *The Renascence of the English Drama* (London, 1895), p. 16.

20. Dewey Ganzel, "Patent Wrongs and Patent Theatres: Drama and the Law in the Early Nineteenth Century," *PMLA* 76 (1961): 386; also see Barish, *The Antitheatrical Prejudice.*

21. See Tracy C. Davis, "Actresses and Prostitutes in Victorian London," *Theatre Research International* 13, no. 3 (Autumn 1988): 239–49, for a good account of the material and symbolic connections that held between these two groups of "public women."

22. "The Profession of Journalism," *Saturday Review* 7 (1 January 1859): 9.

23. According to the tables included in Baker's *The Rise of the Victorian Actor* (pp. 204–10), almost half of the actors cited who made their debuts from 1830–60 were the children of theatrical fathers (actors, managers, and playwrights); in the following thirty years, that proportion dropped to under twenty-five percent. For actresses (pp. 215–19), the figures are even higher: in the first period, more than two-thirds were theater-born, dropping to about fifty percent in 1860–90. Despite the fact that the number of actors and actresses included in these calculations is small relative to the actual numbers who worked in the theater, the statistics still seem significant.

24. "The Cost of Playgoing," *The Theatre* 1 (September 1878): 102.

25. Henry James, *The Tragic Muse* (1890; reprint ed., New York: Harper and Brothers, 1960), p. 130.

26. H. Barton Baker, *History of the London Stage* (London: Routledge and Sons, 1904), p. 468.

27. William Archer, "Mr. and Mrs. Kendal," in *Actors and Actresses of Great Britain and the United States,* ed. Brander Matthews and Laurence Hutton (New York, 1886), p. 184; Clement Scott, *The Drama of Yesterday & To-day,* 2 vols. (London, 1899), 2:129.

28. *Dame Madge Kendal by Herself,* ed. Rudolph de Cordova (London: John Murray, 1933), p. 64; all subsequent references to this autobiography will be included in the text and cited as *DMK; The Merchant of Venice,* act 3, sc. 1, lines 60–62. Shylock, of course, is claiming that likenesses between Jews and Christians override their differences, and Kendal's appropriation of his discourse suggests the extent to which actors identified as outcasts. Thanks to Regenia Gagnier for picking up the echoes in cadence and content.

29. Mrs. [Madge] Kendal, *Dramatic Opinions* (Boston, 1890), p. 52; All subsequent references to this autobiography will be included in the text and cited as *DO.*

30. Mr. and Mrs. Bancroft, *On and Off the Stage,* 3d ed. (London, 1888), p. 5. A

later edition of this work, to be cited later, contains substantially less of Marie Bancroft's personal reminiscences and substantially more information, composed largely by Squire Bancroft, that attempts to put the Prince of Wales' into its historical context, making a strong case for its centrality to the revival of the late Victorian theater. All subsequent references to this autobiography will be included in the text.

31. Regenia Gagnier, "Social Atoms: Working-Class Autobiography, Subjectivity, and Gender," *Victorian Studies* 30, no. 3 (Spring 1987): 344.

32. See Kathy Fletcher, "Planché, Vestris, and the Transvestite Role: Sexuality and Gender in the Victorian Popular Theatre," *Nineteenth Century Theatre* 15, no. 1 (Summer 1987): 9–33, for valuable information on and analysis of female cross-dressing in the 1830s and 1840s.

33. Charles Dickens, "Marie Wilton as a Boy," in *The Dickens Theatrical Reader*, ed. Edgar and Eleanor Johnson (Boston: Little, Brown and Company, 1964), pp. 309–10.

34. William Kleb, "Marie Wilton (Lady Bancroft) As An Actress," *Theatre Survey* 20, no. 1 (May 1979): 45.

35. Augustin Filon, *The English Stage*, trans. Frederic Whyte (London, 1897), p. 121.

36. The novelty of this strategy accounts in part for its appeal. As Raymond Williams notes, "Even the motive for much naturalistic illusion was spectacular: the impressive reproduction of a 'real' environment" ("Social Environment and Theatrical Environment: The Case of English Naturalism," in *English Drama: Forms and Development*, ed. Marie Axton and Raymond Williams [Cambridge: Cambridge University Press, 1977], p. 208).

37. Cited in Charles E. Pascoe, *The Dramatic List: A Record of the Performances of Living Actors and Actresses of the British Stage*, 2d ed. (1880; reprint ed., New York: Benjamin Blom, Inc., 1969), p. 21.

38. Squire and Marie Bancroft, *The Bancrofts: Recollections of Sixty Years* (London: John Murray, 1909), p. 74.

39. Jones, "Religion and the Stage," in *The Renascence of the English Drama*, pp. 30–31.

40. Michael R. Booth, Introduction to *T. W. Robertson: Six Plays* (Derbyshire: Amber Lane Press, 1980), pp. xv–xvi; Jones, "The Theatre and the Mob," in *The Renascence of the English Drama*, p. 12.

41. Henry James, "The London Theatres (1879)," in *The Scenic Art*, ed. Allan Wade (New Brunswick: Rutgers University Press, 1948), p. 124.

Chapter 5

1. Richard Sennett, *The Fall of Public Man* (New York: Alfred A. Knopf, 1974), pp. 176, 266.

2. Elizabeth Robins, *Both Sides of the Curtain* (London: William Heinemann, Ltd., 1940), p. 250. In his essay on Terry in *Bernhardt, Terry, Duse: The Actress in Her Time*, co-authored with John Stokes and Susan Bassnett (Cambridge: Cambridge University Press, 1988), pp. 65–117, Michael R. Booth suggests, however, that Terry had far more latitude in shaping her roles than Robins allows her. Yet he does at the same time subscribe to Robins's basic point by representing Terry as spending "the significant part of her career in the shadow" of Irving (p. 65).

3. Edward Gordon Craig, *Ellen Terry and Her Secret Self* (New York: E. P. Dutton & Co., 1932), p. 10.

4. Percy Fitzgerald, *The Art of Acting* (London, 1892), p. 78.

5. George Moore, "Mummer-Worship" (1889); reprinted in *Impressions and Opinions* (London: T. Werner Laurie, Ltd., 1913), p. 128.

6. Henry Arthur Jones, "The Theatre and the Mob," in *The Renascence of the English Drama* (London, 1895), p. 13.

7. George Moore, *Confessions of a Young Man* (1888; reprint ed., St. Clair Shores, Mich.: Scholarly Press, Inc., 1971), p. 142.

8. Raymond Williams, "Social Environment and Theatrical Environment: The Case of English Naturalism," in *English Drama: Forms and Development*, ed. Marie Axton and Raymond Williams (Cambridge: Cambridge University Press, 1977), p. 218.

9. Clement Scott, *The Drama of Yesterday & To-day*, 2 vols. (London, 1899), 2:87.

10. Bernard Shaw, Preface to *Ellen Terry and Bernard Shaw: A Correspondence*, ed. Christopher St. John (New York: G. P. Putnam's Sons, 1932), p. xiv.

11. Bram Stoker, "Actor-Managers," *The Nineteenth Century* 27 (June 1890): 1045.

12. Charles Wyndham, "Actor-Managers," *The Nineteenth Century* 27 (June 1890): 1055.

13. Charles Hiatt, *Ellen Terry and Her Impersonations* (London, 1898), p. 103.

14. Ellen Terry, *The Story of My Life* (New York: Doubleday, Page & Co., 1908), p. 85.

15. Mrs. [Madge] Kendal, *Dramatic Opinions* (Boston, 1890), p. 155. But also see Elizabeth Robins's account of working with Madge Kendal in which she cites a dress rehearsal that proceeded briskly and professionally with *"Mrs. Kendal in charge"* (her emphasis) in *Both Sides of the Curtain*, pp. 144–45. Robins's story suggests that Kendal's representation of herself as merged with her husband may be overstated.

16. Quoted in Albert Auster, *Actresses and Suffragettes: Women in the American Theatre, 1890–1920* (New York: Praeger Publishers, 1984), p. 25. Michael Baker also claims, without supplying evidence, that "actresses were already established on an equal footing with actors" even though relatively few women in the last third of the century could sustain prolonged excursions into managerial work on their own (in *The Rise of the Victorian Actor* [Totowa, N.J.: Rowman and Littlefield, 1978], p. 108).

17. Cicely Mary Hamilton, *Life Errant* (London: J. M. Dent & Sons, 1935), p. 43.

18. Squire and Marie Bancroft, *The Bancrofts: Recollections of Sixty Years* (London: John Murray, 1909), p. 74.

19. Virginia Woolf, "Ellen Terry," in *The Moment and Other Essays* (New York: Harcourt, Brace and Co., 1948), p. 212.

20. Nina Auerbach, *Ellen Terry, Player in Her Time* (New York: W. W. Norton & Co., 1987), p. 15.

21. George Eliot, *Daniel Deronda*, ed. Graham Handley (1876; reprint ed., Oxford: Clarendon Press, 1984), ch. 51.

22. Henry James, *The Tragic Muse* (1890; reprint ed., New York: Harper and Brothers, 1960), p. 150.

23. *Ellen Terry's Memoirs*, ed. Edith Craig and Christopher St. John (New York: G. P. Putnam's Sons, 1932).

24. Irene Vanbrugh, *To Tell My Story* (London: Hutchinson & Co., 1948), p. 93. See also Booth's pertinent remarks on charm, pp. 95–96 in *Bernhardt, Terry, Duse*.

25. Harold Simpson, Foreword to *Myself and My Piano* (London: John Ouseby, Ltd., 1909).

26. Booth, Introduction to *Bernhardt, Terry, Duse*, p. 11.

27. Thanks to Regenia Gagnier for pointing out the Kantian underpinnings of my characterization here.

28. Bernard Shaw, review of *The Notorious Mrs. Ebbsmith*, reprinted in *Our Theatres in the Nineties*, 3 vols. (London: Constable and Company, 1932), 1:61.

29. For the history of the Shaw–Campbell romance, see Margot Peters, *Bernard Shaw and the Actresses* (Garden City, N.Y.: Doubleday & Company, Inc., 1980), chs. 20–22, as well as her *Mrs. Pat: The Life of Mrs. Patrick Campbell* (New York: Alfred A. Knopf, 1984).

30. Arthur Wing Pinero, *The Second Mrs. Tanqueray* in *Plays by A. W. Pinero*, ed. George Rowell (Cambridge: Cambridge University Press, 1986), 2:97; all subsequent references to the play will be by act and page number and included in the text.

31. Arthur W. Pinero, *The Notorious Mrs. Ebbsmith* (London: William Heinemann, 1906), p. 33.

32. John Russell Taylor, *The Rise and Fall of the Well-Made Play* (New York: Hill and Wang, 1967), p. 84.

33. Archer quoted in James Agate, *Those Were The Nights* (London: Hutchinson & Co., [1946]), p. 54; Mrs. Patrick Campbell [Beatrice Stella Cornwallis-West], *My Life and Some Letters* (London: Hutchinson & Co., 1927), pp. 98–99; all subsequent references to this autobiography will be included in the text.

34. Michael R. Booth, *English Melodrama* (London: Herbert Jenkins, 1965), p. 181. For other relevant discussions of Pinero, see John Stokes, *Resistible Theatres* (London: Paul Elek, 1972), pp. 22–23; Agate, *Those Were the Nights*, pp. 49–62, 72–74; and Ian Clarke, *Edwardian Drama* (London: Faber and Faber, 1989), pp. 24–50.

35. In his chapter on James in Peter Brooks, *The Melodramatic Imagination* (New Haven, Conn.: Yale University Press, 1976), pp. 153–97.

36. D. A. Miller's disquisition on secrecy and subjectivity nicely elucidates Campbell's representation:

> I have had to intimate my secret, if only *not to tell it;* and conversely, in theatrically continuing to keep my secret, I have already rather *given it away.* . . . I can't quite tell my secret, because then it would be known that there was nothing really special to hide, and no one really special to hide it. But I can't quite keep it either, because then it would not be believed that there *was* something to hide and someone to hide it. It is thus a misleading common sense that finds the necessity of secrecy in the 'special' nature of the contents concealed when all that revelation usually reveals is a widely diffused cultural prescription, a cliché. . . . secrecy would seem to be a mode whose ultimate meaning lies in the subject's formal insistence that he is radically inaccessible to the culture that would otherwise entirely determine him.

See "Secret Subjects, Open Secrets," reprinted in *The Novel and the Police* (Berkeley: University of California Press, 1988), pp. 194–95.

37. Vanbrugh, *To Tell My Story*, p. 6; all subsequent references to this autobiography will be included in the text.

38. For a theoretical discussion of autobiography in the second or third person, see Philippe Lejeune, "The Autobiographical Contract," reprinted in *French Literary Theory Today: A Reader*, ed. Tzvetan Todorov (Cambridge: Cambridge University Press, 1982), esp. pp. 194–95.

39. Census figures cited in Michael Sanderson, *From Irving to Olivier: A Social History of the Acting Profession in England, 1880–1983* (New York: St. Martin's Press, 1984).

40. See Jan McDonald, "Lesser Ladies of the Victorian Stage," *Theatre Research International* 13, no. 3 (Autumn 1988): 234–49, for some discussion of the conditions

and experience of work for those who were not as successful as the actresses considered here.

41. Florence Nightingale, *Cassandra: An Essay* (1928; reprint ed., Old Westbury, N.Y.: Feminist Press, 1979), p. 40.

42. For a discussion of similar issues in an American context, see Penina Migdal Glazer and Miriam Slater, *Unequal Colleagues: The Entrance of Women into the Professions, 1890–1940* (New Brunswick: Rutgers University Press, 1987). Glazer and Slater argue that the first generation of American professional women sought to create women's networks, but by and large had to adopt the standards of the male establishment if they were to succeed. As in England, women who married were assumed to be unable to fulfill the dual demands of motherhood and paid work.

Chapter 6

1. In the growing literature on middle-class women's work, see especially Sandra Berman, ed., *Fit Work for Women* (New York: St. Martin's Press, 1979); Lee Holcombe, *Victorian Ladies at Work: Middle-Class Working Women in England and Wales, 1850–1914* (Hamden, Conn.: Archon Press, 1973); Jane Lewis, *Women in England 1870–1950: Sexual Divisions and Social Change* (Bloomington: Indiana University Press, 1984); Louise A. Tilly and Joan W. Scott, *Women, Work and Family* (New York: Holt, Rinehart and Winston, 1978); Martha Vicinus, *Independent Women: Work and Community for Single Women 1850–1920* (Chicago: University of Chicago Press, 1985); and Martha Vicinus, ed., *A Widening Sphere: Changing Roles of Victorian Women* (Bloomington: Indiana University Press, 1977).

2. Sandra Stanley Holton, " 'In Sorrowful Wrath': Suffrage Militancy and the Romantic Feminism of Emmeline Pankhurst," in *British Feminism in the Twentieth Century*, ed. Harold L. Smith (London: Edward Elgar, 1990), p. 10. Holton's essay in some ways anticipates the focus of my own, but with, I think, some significant differences, especially in her use of "classical" and "romantic" as conceptual categories employed to distinguish the constitutionalists from the militants.

3. In the large body of feminist writing that takes up the question of local and interested narratives, see especially Donna Haraway, "Situated Knowledges: The Science Question in Feminism and the Privilege of Partial Perspective," *Feminist Studies* 14, no. 3 (Fall 1988): 575–99.

4. [Elizabeth Robins,] *Ancilla's Share*, 2d ed. (London: Hutchinson and Co., 1924), p. 132.

5. Dale Spender comments on Robins's "uncompromising and caustic criticisms of male power" and says that "the only man she appears to have praised in any way was Henrik Ibsen—for his portrayal of women" in *Time and Tide Wait for No Man* (London: Pandora Press, 1984), p. 48. Robins is a fascinating figure in the histories of women's literature, the late Victorian theater, and feminist theory and practice, but—unbelievably—the sole sustained analysis of her work remains Jane Marcus's doctoral dissertation, "Elizabeth Robins," Northwestern University, 1973.

6. Teresa Billington-Greig, "Feminism and Politics," in *The Non-Violent Militant: Selected Writings of Teresa Billington-Greig*, ed. Carol McPhee and Ann FitzGerald (London: Routledge and Kegan Paul, 1987), p. 231.

7. Lena Ashwell, *Myself a Player* (London: Michael Joseph Ltd., 1936), p. 166.

8. Christabel Pankhurst, "The Trial of the Suffragette Leaders" (1908), in *Suffrage and the Pankhursts* (London: Routledge and Kegan Paul, 1987), p. 57.

9. Emmeline Pethick-Lawrence, Preface to *My Part in a Changing World* (1938; reprint ed., Westport, Conn.: Hyperion Press, Inc., 1976).

10. J. Keir Hardie, "Women and Politics," in *The Case for Women's Suffrage*, ed. Brougham Villiers (London: T. Fisher Unwin, 1907), p. 81.

11. The history of the AFL, founded in late 1908, has been told in brief by Claire Hirshfield, "The Actresses' Franchise League and the Campaign for Women's Suffrage, 1908–1914," *Theatre Research International* 10, no. 2 (Summer 1985): 129–53, and in fuller detail by Julie Holledge, *Innocent Flowers: Women in the Edwardian Theatre* (London: Virago, 1981). Holledge's work also uncovers the story of the suffrage theater—organized by actresses and playwrights who sympathized with "the Cause"—as well as that of the Pioneer Players, the women's theater group headed by Edy Craig, Ellen Terry's daughter, which continued performing well into the 1920s. See Eleanor Adlard, ed., *Edy* (London: Frederick Muller, Ltd., 1949), and Nina Auerbach, "Edy's Women," in *Ellen Terry: Player in Her Time* (New York: W. W. Norton & Co., 1987), pp. 365–436. For a sampling of suffrage drama, see Bettina Friedl, ed., *On to Victory: Propaganda Plays of the Woman Suffrage Movement* (Boston: Northeastern University Press, 1987) and *How the Vote Was Won, and Other Suffragette Plays* (London: Methuen, 1985).

All the leading actresses of the London stage, as well as many more unknowns, joined the AFL: Ellen Terry and Madge Kendal both attended the first meeting, and Terry played one of the leading roles in Cicely Hamilton's *Pageant of Great Women* (1910), directed by Edy Craig. Hamilton was very active in feminist causes: her *Marriage as a Trade* (1909) is one of the landmark texts in British feminism, and her women-centered work for the theater includes *Diana of Dobson's* and *How the Vote Was Won*. See as well her autobiography, *Life Errant*, cited later. Irene Vanbrugh was an early supporter, but left the AFL when she came to feel that its membership was too much in favor of militant methods; see *To Tell My Story* (London: Hutchinson and Co., 1948), pp. 82–84, for her account of a meeting and her reasons for quitting. Eva Moore, another leading West End actress, served as a vice-president of the AFL, made speeches, and acted in suffrage theater, including a role in a play written by her husband, Harry Esmond; see her *Exits and Entrances* (New York: Frederick A. Stokes Co., 1923), pp. 89–100, for more on her activities. Other notables who participated include Stella Campbell, who often rode in the mass suffrage processions, and Lillie Langtry, who had a starring role in a suffrage play called *Helping the Cause* (1912). Even Lillah McCarthy, the original Ann Whitefield in Shaw's *Man and Superman*—and allegedly one of Asquith's mistresses during the campaign—was an ardent supporter of the movement: "We were all suffragettes in those days. . . . I had walked in processions. I had carried banners for Mrs. Pankhurst and the Cause" (*Myself and My Friends* [New York: E. P. Dutton and Co., 1933], p. 148).

The relationship of the theater and the theatrical to the suffrage movement goes deeper than the widespread participation by actresses. In her Introduction to *Suffrage and the Pankhursts*, pp. 1–17, Jane Marcus self-consciously uses the drama as her "chief metaphor" for the suffrage movement, and examines its uses in other texts; she points out the misogyny in some and the melodrama in others, especially Sylvia Pankhurst's *The Suffragette Movement*, cited later, which Marcus claims is the "source" for the metaphor, a conclusion not borne out by my reading of earlier texts—including Elizabeth Robins's *Votes for Women*—and Christabel Pankhurst's own writings. Despite the ambiguity of her commitment to socialist feminism and her outright distaste for what she calls "the battle of heterosexuality" acted out in *The Suffragette Movement*, Marcus's brief text is yet valuable for calling attention to some of the underrepresented thematics of the movement and for bringing a theoretical perspective to bear on issues of subjectivity and self-representation.

12. In general, I will dwell very little on the differences in policy and history between these organizations; consult the sources cited for extensive accounts.

The NUWSS, founded in 1897 as an umbrella group uniting the independent suffrage societies of Manchester, Bristol, London, and Edinburgh and led by Millicent Garrett Fawcett, sought to gain the ballot by constitutional, nonmilitant means, such as petitions, voter education, and canvassing of MPs. Its members were known as "suffragists," rather than "suffragettes"; the latter term was coined by the *Daily Mail* in 1906 as a label for WSPU activists. The NUWSS's traditional ties to the Liberal Party were ultimately severed in 1912, after the Asquith government repeatedly failed to honor its promises; thereafter, the NUWSS formed an Election Fighting Fund to contest seats held by Liberals at elections and made a flexible alliance with the Labour Party. The best accounts of the NUWSS are in Ray Strachey, *"The Cause": A Short History of the Women's Movement in Great Britain* (1928; reprint ed., Port Washington, N.Y.: Kennikat Press, 1969); Constance Rover, *Women's Suffrage and Party Politics in Britain 1866–1914* (London: Routledge and Kegan Paul, 1967), pp. 53–71; Leslie Parker Hume, *The National Union of Women's Suffrage Societies, 1897–1914* (New York: Garland Publishing, Inc., 1982); Les Garner, *Stepping Stones to Women's Liberty* (London: Heinemann, 1984), pp. 11–27; and especially Sandra Stanley Holton, *Feminism and Democracy* (Cambridge: Cambridge University Press, 1986). See as well Millicent Garrett Fawcett, *What I Remember* (1925; reprint ed., Westport, Conn.: Hyperion Press, Inc., 1976) for a personal history.

Emmeline Pankhurst, with her daughters Christabel and Sylvia, founded the WSPU in Manchester in 1903 as an alternative to the constitutionalist program with a particular focus on the need for the vote among working-class women. The Pankhurst family's traditional ties were to the Labour Party, and especially to Keir Hardie, but the WSPU became increasingly hostile to Labour as well as to the Liberals over the course of the campaign; Christabel Pankhurst, in fact, later stood as a Tory candidate for the Commons. See E. Sylvia Pankhurst, *The Suffragette: The History of the Women's Militant Suffrage Movement, 1905–1910* (1911; reprint ed., New York: Source Book Press, 1970); Rover, *Women's Suffrage*, pp. 72–101; Antonia Raeburn, *The Militant Suffragettes* (London: Michael Joseph, 1973); Andrew Rosen, *Rise Up, Women! The Militant Campaign of the Women's Social and Political Union, 1903–14* (London: Routledge and Kegan Paul, 1974); Brian Harrison's essay, "The Act of Militancy: Violence and the Suffragettes, 1904–1914," in *Peaceable Kingdom: Stability and Change in Modern Britain* (Oxford: Clarendon Press, 1982), pp. 26–81; and Garner, *Stepping Stones*, pp. 44–60. Some of Martha Vicinus's conclusions in "Male Space and Women's Bodies: The Suffragette Movement," in *Independent Women* (Chicago: University of Chicago Press, 1985), pp. 247–80, match my own; her compelling argument has helped shape my thinking.

The smallest of the three, the WFL, was led by Charlotte Despard and Teresa Billington-Greig and formed as a splinter group from the WSPU after the split in the fall of 1907; when the Pankhursts and their financial supporters, Emmeline and Frederick Pethick-Lawrence, made the decision to institute a strict hierarchy and greater autocracy, many socialist women joined together to start this nonmilitant group. See Garner, *Stepping Stones*, pp. 28–43, and Andro Linklater's biography of Charlotte Despard, *An Unhusbanded Life* (London: Hutchinson and Co., 1980) as well as the texts cited on the WSPU for more information.

Three more books should be mentioned here: Jill Liddington and Jill Norris, *One*

Hand Tied Behind Us (London: Virago, 1978), which recounts working-class women's role in the movement and focuses on the grass-roots struggle outside London; Jill Liddington, *The Life and Times of a Respectable Rebel: Selina Cooper (1864–1946)* (London: Virago, 1984), a biography of a working-class suffragist that contextualizes Cooper's life within the political and social movements she took part in; and Susan Kingsley Kent, *Sex and Suffrage in Britain, 1860–1914* (Princeton, N.J.: Princeton University Press, 1987), which explores various activists' differing attitudes toward issues of sexuality, marriage, and chastity.

13. Both Holledge *(Innocent Flowers)* and Rosen *(Rise Up Women!)* use the term "theatrical methods" in referring to the suffragettes' tactics.

14. George Bernard Shaw, Preface to *Plays Pleasant* in *The Bodley Head Bernard Shaw*, 6 vols. (London: Max Reinhardt for the Bodley Head, 1970), 1:378.

15. Dora B. Montefiore, *From a Victorian to a Modern* (London: E. Archer, 1927), pp. 7, 6.

16. Lisa Tickner, *The Spectacle of Women: Imagery of the Suffrage Campaign 1907–14* (London: Chatto and Windus, 1987), p. 81. Tickner relies a little too heavily here, from my point of view, on terms like "agency" and "full self-consciousness" in making her case, but I am sympathetic to her focus on the conscious choices suffragettes made in representing themselves. Martha Vicinus's tack nicely qualifies Tickner's point here when she rightly argues that the militant suffragettes "could not effectively prescribe the desired response" *(Independent Women*, p. 264) to either their femininity or their politics.

17. The characterization of the Pankhursts is by Janet E. Courtney, one of the original "Antis," as members of the National League for Opposing Women's Suffrage were called, in *The Women of My Time* (London: Lovat Dickson Ltd., 1934), p. 171.

18. Dame Christabel Pankhurst, *Unshackled* (London: Hutchinson, 1959), p. 153.

19. Israel Zangwill, quoted in Albert Auster, *Actresses and Suffragists: Women in the American Theatre, 1890–1920* (New York: Praeger Publishers, 1984), p. 86.

20. Max Beerbohm, quoted in Christopher St. John, *Ethel Smyth: A Biography* (London: Longmans, Green & Co., Ltd., 1959), p. 147.

21. E. Sylvia Pankhurst, *The Suffragette Movement: An Intimate Account of Persons and Ideals* (London: Longmans, Green and Co., 1931), p. 221; all subsequent references to this autobiography will be included in the text.

22. Elizabeth Robins, *The Convert* (1907; reprint ed., Old Westbury, N.Y.: The Feminist Press, 1980), pp. 87, 113.

23. See Kent, *Sex and Suffrage*, for discussion of Christabel's radical sexual politics as well as Jane Marcus's Introduction to *Suffrage and the Pankhursts* and Elizabeth Sarah, "Christabel Pankhurst: Reclaiming Her Power," in *Feminist Theorists*, ed. Dale Spender (London: The Women's Press, 1983), pp. 256–84.

24. Billington-Greig, "The Feminist Revolt: An Alternate Policy," in *The Non-Violent Militant*, p. 242.

25. Annie Kenney, *Memories of a Militant* (London: Edward Arnold & Co., 1924), pp. 72, 101. For an alternative view of Kenney's life and text that argues for her textual resistance to what the Pankhursts imposed upon her, see Jill Eichhorn, "Autobiography as Dissent: A Working-Class Suffragette Speaks Out," unpublished seminar paper, Miami University, 1990.

26. Constance Lytton, *Prisons and Prisoners: Some Personal Experiences* (London: William Heinemann, 1914), p. 50; all subsequent references to this book will be included in the text.

27. Olive Schreiner, *Woman and Labor*, 7th ed. (New York: Frederick A. Stokes Co., Publishers, 1911), p. 128.

28. Mrs. Archibald [Ethel] Colquhoun, *The Vocation of Woman* (London: Macmillan, 1913), p. 20.

29. Jean Bethke Elshtain, *Public Man, Private Woman* (Princeton, N.J.: Princeton University Press, 1981), p. 176.

30. Robins, "Shall Women Work?" in *Way Stations* (London: Hodder and Stoughton, 1913), p. 272.

31. Margaret Haig [Viscountess Rhondda], *This Was My World* (London: Macmillan and Co., 1933), p. 162.

32. Rita Felski, *Beyond Feminist Aesthetics: Feminist Literature and Social Change* (Cambridge: Harvard University Press, 1990), p. 104.

33. See Felski, *Beyond Feminist Aesthetics*, esp. chs. 2 and 3, and Julia Kristeva, "Women's Time," reprinted in *The Kristeva Reader*, ed. Toril Moi (New York: Columbia University Press, 1986), pp. 188–213.

34. For two accounts of women's political organizations, see Dorothy Thompson, "Women, Work and Politics in Nineteenth-Century England: The Problem of Authority," pp. 57–81, and Linda Walker, "Party Political Women: A Comparative Study of Liberal Women and the Primrose League, 1890–1914," pp. 165–91, both in *Equal or Different: Women's Politics 1800–1914*, ed. Jane Rendall (London: Basil Blackwell, 1987).

35. Margaret McMillan, "Woman in the Past and Future," in *The Case for Women's Suffrage*, p. 117.

36. *Victorian Bouquet: Lady X Looks On*, ed. Rachel Ferguson (London: Ernest Benn Ltd., n.d.), p. 21. See Vicinus, *Independent Women*, for further discussion of women's communities antecedent to the suffrage movement.

37. Quoted in Christopher St. John, *Ethel Smyth: A Biography*, p. 155.

38. Mary R. Richardson, *Laugh A Defiance* (London: George Weidenfeld and Nicolson, 1953), pp. 46–47, 48; all subsequent references to this autobiography will be included in the text.

39. Michael J. Sandel, *Liberalism and the Limits of Justice* (Cambridge: Cambridge University Press, 1982), pp. 62–63.

40. Ruth L. Smith and Deborah M. Valenze, "Mutuality and Marginality: Liberal Moral Theory and Working-Class Women in Nineteenth-Century England," *Signs* 13, no. 2 (Winter 1988): 280.

41. Iris Marion Young, "The Ideal of Community and the Politics of Difference," in *Feminism/Postmodernism*, ed. Linda J. Nicholson (New York: Routledge, 1990), pp. 305, 307. See also the elaboration of this argument in chapter 8 of her *Justice and the Politics of Difference* (Princeton, N.J.: Princeton University Press, 1990).

42. See Donna Haraway, "A Manifesto for Cyborgs," *Socialist Review* 80 (March/April 1985): 65–107, for more discussion of related issues.

43. Marcus, Introduction to *Suffrage and the Pankhursts*, p. 2.

44. Carole Pateman, *The Sexual Contract* (Stanford, Calif.: Stanford University Press, 1988), p. 96.

45. Helena Michie, *The Flesh Made Word: Female Figures and Women's Bodies* (New York: Oxford University Press, 1987), p. 20.

46. Susie Orbach, *Hunger Strike: The Anorectic's Struggle as a Metaphor for Our Age* (New York: W. W. Norton, 1986). For more on anorexia and its potential political implications, see Joan Jacobs Brumberg, *Fasting Girls: The Emergence of Anorexia Ner-*

vosa as a Modern Disease (Cambridge: Harvard University Press, 1988), and Susan R. Bordo, "The Body and the Reproduction of Femininity: A Feminist Appropriation of Foucault," in *Gender/Body/Knowledge: Feminist Reconstructions of Being and Knowing*, ed. Alison M. Jaggar and Susan R. Bordo (New Brunswick: Rutgers University Press, 1989), pp. 13–33.

47. Elaine Showalter, *The Female Malady: Women, Madness, and English Culture, 1830–1980* (New York: Pantheon, 1985), p. 162.

48. Elaine Scarry, *The Body in Pain* (New York: Oxford University Press, 1985), p. 30.

49. Ada Cecile Wright, manuscript autobiography, Suffragette Fellowship Collection (on microfilm), p. 5.

50. See F. K. Prochaska, *Women and Philanthropy in Nineteenth-Century England* (New York: Oxford University Press, 1980), and Vicinus, *Independent Women*, ch. 6.

51. See Beatrice Webb, *My Apprenticeship* (1926; reprint ed., Cambridge: Cambridge University Press, 1979), pp. 151–72, for an account of how what begins as "a sentimental journey" (p. 152) ends in solidifying Webb's commitment to sociology.

52. Virginia Woolf, "Introductory Letter" to *Life as We Have Known It*, ed. Margaret Llewellyn Davies (1931; reprint ed., New York: W. W. Norton and Co., Inc., 1975), pp. xxi, xxvi.

53. Feminist standpoint theory, on which I am drawing here, originates with Nancy C. M. Hartsock, *Money, Sex, and Power: Toward a Feminist Historical Materialism* (New York: Longman, 1983), esp. ch. 10, and finds its best exposition in Alison M. Jaggar, *Feminist Politics and Human Nature* (Totowa, N.J.: Rowman & Allanheld, 1983), pp. 369–89. Taking off from Hegel's master–slave dialectic, standpoint theorists argue that women, as members of an oppressed group, have particular views of the world that provide necessary and corrective insights that are left out of universalist masculine theory and practice. Because standpoint theory insists on the particularity of perspectives, Lytton's interrogation of her own position in *Prisons and Prisoners* seems to me exemplary, since she takes both class and gender into account in articulating her own starting point. But see Haraway, "Situated Knowledges," for the necessary critique of standpoint theory, which acknowledges that no viewpoints, even those of the oppressed, can be innocent.

54. Sylvia Pankhurst, quoted in Rosen, *Rise Up, Women!*, p. 36.

55. Les Garner, *Stepping Stones*, p. 42.

56. Billington-Greig, "Feminism and Politics," in *The Non-Violent Militant*, p. 229.

57. Billington-Greig, *The Militant Suffrage Movement* in *The Non-Violent Militant*, p. 138; all subsequent references to Billington-Greig's writing included in the text will be to this long essay unless otherwise indicated by note.

58. Evelyn Sharp, *Unfinished Adventure* (London: John Lane, 1933), p. 145.

59. Hannah Mitchell, *The Hard Way Up*, ed. Geoffrey Mitchell (London: Faber and Faber, 1968), p. 176; all subsequent references to this autobiography will be included in the text. Not coincidentally, most of those who left the WSPU later became dedicated opponents of the war: while Christabel and Emmeline Pankhurst threw themselves into pro-government propaganda work in August 1914, Billington-Greig, Sylvia Pankhurst, Mitchell, and Pethick-Lawrence all put their efforts into local and internationalist alliances against conscription and militarism.

60. For more biographical information and a trenchant discussion of Billington-Greig's political thinking, see chapter 2 of Brian Harrison, *Prudent Revolutionaries: Portraits of British Feminists between the Wars* (Oxford: Clarendon Press, 1987), pp. 45–72.

61. Billington-Greig, "The Feminist Revolt: An Alternate Policy," p. 242.

62. Rachel Barrett, manuscript autobiography, Suffragette Fellowship Collection (on microfilm), p. 2.

63. Billington-Greig, "Autobiographical Fragments," p. 57.

64. Cicely Mary Hamilton, *Life Errant* (London: J. M. Dent and Sons, 1936), p. 68. For a discussion of fascist psychology that bears a number of parallels to Hamilton's and May Sinclair's perspectives, see Theodor W. Adorno, "Freudian Theory and the Pattern of Fascist Propaganda," in *The Essential Frankfurt School Reader*, ed. Andrew Arato and Eike Gerhardt (New York: Urizen Books, 1978), pp. 118–37.

Both Hamilton and Sinclair, along with Amber Blanco White, have recently come under attack from Jane Marcus for their criticism of the suffragettes. Citing White's description of the WSPU as "towards the end, an organization run on Fascist lines and characterized by an authentically Fascist violence and emotionalism and exaggeration," Marcus takes her to task for her repudiation of her mother's activism; with reference to Hamilton and Sinclair, she remarks on "how quickly the intellectuals come to the aid of their country, rejecting the feminist, pacifist, and socialist reforms needed at home to agree to internationalist slaughter of a whole generation in the name of democracy" ("Corpus/Corps/Corpse: Writing the Body in/at War," in *Arms and the Woman: War, Gender, and Literary Representation*, ed. Helen M. Cooper, Adrienne Auslander Munich, and Susan Merrill Squier [Chapel Hill: University of North Carolina Press, 1989], pp. 133–34). While I see the grounds for and to some extent share Marcus's desire to abjure such representations, I am more concerned than she with taking the Hamilton–Sinclair critique seriously, since for me it echoes some of the working-class women's discontent with the aims and methods of the militants.

65. For one study of Sinclair's attitudes to suffrage and her fictional representations of the campaign, see Diane F. Gillespie, " 'The Muddle of the Middle': May Sinclair on Women," *Tulsa Studies in Women's Literature* 4, no. 2 (Fall 1985): 235–51.

66. May Sinclair, *The Tree of Heaven* (New York: Macmillan, 1917), p. 124. See Regenia Gagnier, " 'From Fag to Monitor; Or, Fighting to the Front': Art and Power in Public School Memoirs," in *Victorian Learning*, ed. Robert Viscusi (*Browning Institute Studies*, 16, 1990), pp. 15–38, and "The Construction of Middle-Class Identities: School and Family," chapter 5 of her *Subjectivities: A History of Self-Representation in Britain, 1832–1920* (New York: Oxford University Press, 1991), for a reading of the public school experience to which Sinclair here refers; Gagnier reports that "the analogy school/totalitarianism is explicit in countless twentieth-century memoirs" ("From Fag to Monitor," p. 32).

67. Laura Stempel Mumford, "May Sinclair's *The Tree of Heaven*: The Vortex of Feminism, The Community of War," in *Arms and the Woman*, pp. 169, 170.

68. Wendy Mulford, "Socialist-Feminist Criticism: A Case Study, Women's Suffrage and Literature, 1906–14," in *Re-Reading English*, ed. Peter Widdowson (London: Methuen, 1982), p. 188.

69. Sylvia Pankhurst, *The Suffragette Movement*, p. 124.

70. Sylvia Pankhurst, in *Myself When Young: By Famous Women of To-Day*, ed. Margot Asquith (London: Frederick Muller Ltd., 1938), p. 285; all subsequent references to this brief memoir will be included in the text and cited as *MWY*.

71. Harrison, *Prudent Revolutionaries*, p. 211.

72. Robins, "The Feminist Movement in England," in *Way Stations*, pp. 39–40.

73. Vera Brittain, *Testament of Youth* (1933; reprint ed., London: Wideview Books, 1980), p. 472.

74. Patricia W. Romero, *E. Sylvia Pankhurst: Portrait of a Radical* (New Haven, Conn.: Yale University Press, 1987), p. 293.

75. Emmeline Pankhurst [with Rheta Childe-Dorr], *My Own Story* (1914; reprint ed., New York: Source Book Press, 1970), p. 323.

76. For feminist critiques of objectivity, see (among others) Susan Bordo, *The Flight to Objectivity: Essays on Cartesianism and Culture* (Albany: State University of New York Press, 1987); Jane Flax, "Political Philosophy and the Patriarchal Unconscious: A Psychoanalytic Perspective on Epistemology and Metaphysics," in *Discovering Reality: Feminist Perspectives on Epistemology, Metaphysics, Methodology and Philosophy of Science*, ed. Sandra Harding and Merrill Hintikka (Dordrecht: Reidel, 1983); Evelyn Fox Keller, *Reflections on Gender and Science* (New Haven, Conn.: Yale University Press, 1985); Haraway, "Situated Knowledges"; and Sandra Harding, *The Science Question in Feminism* (Ithaca, N.Y.: Cornell University Press, 1986).

77. Gillian Beer, "Can the Native Return?," (Paper delivered at the Stanford Humanities Center, March 8, 1989).

78. Harrison, *Prudent Revolutionaries*, p. 54.

Afterword

1. See Joan W. Scott's analysis of gender and historiography in "Rewriting History," in *Behind the Lines: Gender and the Two World Wars*, ed. Margaret Randolph Higonnet et. al. (New Haven, Conn.: Yale University Press, 1987), pp. 21–30. And see as well Jo Vellacott, "Feminist Consciousness and the First World War," *History Workshop Journal* 23 (Spring 1987): 81–101.

2. Virginia Woolf, *Three Guineas* (1938; reprint ed., New York: Harcourt, Brace and Jovanovich, 1966), p. 39. See Sandra M. Gilbert, "Soldier's Heart: Literary Men, Literary Women, and the Great War," in *Sexchanges*, volume 2 of Gilbert and Gubar's *No Man's Land: The Place of the Woman Writer in the Twentieth Century* (New Haven, Conn.: Yale University Press, 1989), pp. 258–323.

3. Sandra Stanley Holton, *Feminism and Democracy* (Cambridge: Cambridge University Press, 1986), p. 146.

4. E. Sylvia Pankhurst, *The Suffragette Movement* (London: Longmans, Green and Co., 1931), p. 608.

Bibliography

Abrams, M. H. *Natural Supernaturalism*. New York: W. W. Norton and Company, 1971.

Adlard, Eleanor, ed. *Edy*. London: Frederick Muller, Ltd., 1949.

Adorno, Theodor W. "Freudian Theory and the Pattern of Fascist Propaganda." In *The Essential Frankfurt School Reader*, edited by Andrew Arato and Eike Gebhardt, pp. 118–37. New York: Urizen Books, 1978.

Agate, James. *Those Were the Nights*. London: Hutchinson & Co., [1946].

Althusser, Louis. "Ideology and Ideological State Apparatuses." In *Lenin and Philosophy and Other Essays*, translated by Ben Brewster, pp. 127–86. New York: Monthly Review Press, 1971.

Altick, Richard D. *The English Common Reader*. Chicago: University of Chicago Press, 1957.

Anderson, Nancy F. "Autobiographical Fantasies of a Female Anti-Feminist: Eliza Lynn Linton as Christopher Kirkland and Theodora Desanges." *Dickens Studies Annual* 14 (1985): 287–301.

Anderson, Olive. "Women Preachers in Mid-Victorian Britain: Some Reflexions on Feminism, Popular Religion and Social Change." *The Historical Journal* 12, no. 3 (1969): 467–84.

Archer, William. *Masks or Faces?* 1888. Reprint. New York: Hill and Wang, 1957.

Armstrong, Nancy. *Desire and Domestic Fiction: A Political History of the Novel*. New York: Oxford University Press, 1987.

"The Army and the Stage." *Saturday Review* 13 (22 March 1862): 321–22.

Ashwell, Lena. *Myself a Player*. London: Michael Joseph Ltd., 1936.

Asquith, Margot, ed. *Myself When Young: By Famous Women of To-Day*. London: Frederick Muller Ltd., 1938.

Auerbach, Nina. *Ellen Terry: Player in Her Time*. New York: W. W. Norton & Co., 1987.

———. *Private Theatricals: The Lives of the Victorians*. Cambridge: Harvard University Press, 1990.

Auster, Albert. *Actresses and Suffragists: Women in the American Theatre, 1890–1920*. New York: Praeger Publishers, 1984.

Bailey, Peter. "Custom, Capital and Culture in the Victorian Music Hall." In *Popular*

217

Culture and Custom in Nineteenth-Century England, edited by Robert D. Storch, pp. 180–208. London: Croom Helm, 1982.

Baker, H. Barton. *History of the London Stage.* London: Routledge and Sons, 1904.

Baker, Michael. *The Rise of the Victorian Actor.* Totowa, N.J.: Rowman and Littlefield, 1978.

Bancroft, Squire, and Bancroft, Marie. *The Bancrofts: Recollections of Sixty Years.* London: John Murray, 1909.

———. *On and Off the Stage.* 3d ed. London, 1888.

Barish, Jonas. *The Antitheatrical Prejudice.* Berkeley: University of California Press, 1981.

Barrett, Michèle. *Women's Oppression Today: The Marxist-Feminist Encounter.* Rev. ed. London: Verso, 1988.

Barrett Browning, Elizabeth. *Aurora Leigh and Other Poems.* Edited by Cora Kaplan. London: The Women's Press, 1978.

Bayly, Mary. *The Life and Letters of Mrs. Sewell.* 5th ed. London, 1890.

Beer, Gillian. "Can the Native Return?" Paper delivered at the Stanford Humanities Center, 8 March 1989.

———. " 'Coming Wonders': Uses of Theatre in the Victorian Novel." In *English Drama: Forms and Development,* edited by Marie Axton and Raymond Williams, pp. 164–85. Cambridge: Cambridge University Press, 1977.

Bellringer, Alan W. "Mrs Humphry Ward's Autobiographical Tactics: A Writer's Recollections." *Prose Studies* 8, no. 3 (December 1985): 40–50.

Benstock, Shari, ed. *The Private Self: Theory and Practice of Women's Autobiographical Writings.* Chapel Hill: University of North Carolina Press, 1988.

Berman, Sandra, ed. *Fit Work for Women.* New York: St. Martin's Press, 1979.

Billington-Greig, Teresa. *The Non-Violent Militant: Selected Writings of Teresa Billington-Greig.* Edited by Carol McPhee and Ann FitzGerald. London: Routledge and Kegan Paul, 1987.

Blake, Kathleen. "Elizabeth Barrett Browning and Wordsworth: The Romantic Poet as a Woman." *Victorian Poetry* 24, no. 4 (Winter 1986): 387–98.

Bonham-Carter, Victor. *Authors by Profession.* 2 vols. London: Society of Authors, 1978.

Booth, Michael R. *English Melodrama.* London: Herbert Jenkins, 1965.

Bordo, Susan R. "The Body and the Reproduction of Femininity: A Feminist Appropriation of Foucault." In *Gender/Body/Knowledge: Feminist Reconstructions of Being and Knowing,* edited by Alison M. Jaggar and Susan R. Bordo, pp. 13–33. New Brunswick: Rutgers University Press, 1989.

———. *The Flight to Objectivity: Essays on Cartesianism and Culture.* Albany: State University of New York Press, 1987.

Brittain, Vera. *Testament of Youth.* 1933. Reprint. London: Wideview Books, 1980.

Brodzki, Bella, and Schenck, Celeste, eds. *Life/Lines: Theorizing Women's Autobiography.* Ithaca, N.Y.: Cornell University Press, 1988.

Bromwich, David. *Hazlitt: The Mind of a Critic.* New York: Oxford University Press, 1983.

Brontë, Charlotte. *Villette.* London: Dent, 1974.

Brooks, Peter. *The Melodramatic Imagination.* New Haven, Conn.: Yale University Press, 1976.

Broughton, Treva. "Margaret Oliphant: The Unbroken Self." *Women's Studies International Forum* 10, no. 1 (1987): 42–52.

Brown, JoAnne. "Professional Language: Words that Succeed." *Radical History Review* 34 (1986): 33–51.

Brownstein, Rachel M. "Representing the Self: Arnold and Brontë on Rachel." *Browning Institute Studies* 13 (1985): 1–24.

Brumberg, Joan Jacobs. *Fasting Girls: The Emergence of Anorexia Nervosa as a Modern Disease.* Cambridge: Harvard University Press, 1988.

Bulley, A. Amy, and Whitley, Margaret. *Women's Work.* London, 1894.

Burney, Frances. *Evelina.* 1778. Reprint. New York: W. W. Norton & Co., 1965.

Butler, Marilyn. *Maria Edgeworth.* Oxford: Oxford University Press, 1972.

Cain, Maureen. "The General Practice Lawyer and Client: Towards a Radical Conception." In *The Sociology of the Professions: Lawyers, Doctors, and Others,* edited by Robert Dingwall and Philip Lewis, pp. 106–30. London: Macmillan, 1983.

Campbell, Mrs. Patrick [Beatrice Stella Cornwallis-West]. *My Life and Some Letters.* London: Hutchinson & Co., 1927.

Carlyle, Thomas. *Critical and Miscellaneous Essays.* 5 vols. New York: AMS Press, 1969.

———. *On Heroes, Hero-Worship and the Heroic in History.* Edited by Carl Niemeyer. Lincoln: University of Nebraska Press, 1966.

———. *Sartor Resartus.* Edited by Charles Frederick Harrold. New York: Odyssey Press, 1937.

Chandler, James K. *Wordsworth's Second Nature: A Study of the Poetry and Politics.* Chicago: University of Chicago Press, 1984.

Clarke, Ian. *Edwardian Drama.* London: Faber and Faber, 1989.

Colby, Vineta. *Yesterday's Woman: Domestic Realism in the English Novel.* Princeton, N.J.: Princeton University Press, 1974.

———, and Colby, Robert A. *The Equivocal Virtue: Mrs. Oliphant and the Victorian Literary Market Place.* Hamden, Conn.: Archon Books, 1966.

Coleridge, Samuel Taylor. *Biographia Literaria.* Edited by James Engell and W. J. Bate. Princeton, N.J.: Princeton University Press, 1983.

Collected Letters of Thomas and Jane Welsh Carlyle. 15 vols. Edited by Charles Richard Sanders. Durham: Duke University Press, 1970.

Collins, A. S. *The Profession of Letters: A Study of the Relation of Author to Patron, Publisher, and Public, 1780–1832.* London: Routledge and Sons, 1928.

Colquhoun, Mrs. Archibald [Ethel]. *The Vocation of Woman.* London: Macmillan, 1913.

Cooper, Helen. *Elizabeth Barrett Browning, Woman and Artist.* Chapel Hill: University of North Carolina Press, 1988.

Corbett, Mary Jean. "Feminine Authorship and Spiritual Authority in Victorian Women Writers' Autobiographies." *Women's Studies* 18, no. 1 (1990): 13–29.

"The Cost of Playgoing." *The Theatre* 1 (September 1878): 99–103.

Courtney, Janet. *The Women of My Time.* London: Lovat Dickson Ltd., 1934.

Craig, Edith, and St. John, Christopher, eds. *Ellen Terry's Memoirs.* New York: G. P. Putnam's Sons, 1932.

Craig, Edward Gordon. *Ellen Terry and Her Secret Self.* New York: E. P. Dutton & Co., 1932.

[Craik, Dinah Mulock.] *A Woman's Thoughts About Women.* Leipzig, 1860.

Crosland, Mrs. Newton [Camilla Toulmin]. *Landmarks of a Literary Life, 1820–1892.* New York, 1893.

Cross, Nigel. *The Common Writer: Life in Nineteenth-Century Grub Street.* Cambridge: Cambridge University Press, 1985.

Darton, F. J. Harvey. *The Life and Times of Mrs. Sherwood.* London: Wells Gardner, Darton and Company, Ltd., 1910.

Daunton, M. J. *House and Home in the Victorian City.* London: Edward Arnold, 1983.

David, Deirdre. *Intellectual Women and Victorian Patriarchy: Harriet Martineau, Elizabeth Barrett Browning, George Eliot.* Ithaca, N.Y.: Cornell University Press, 1987.

Davidoff, Leonore, and Hall, Catherine. *Family Fortunes: Men and Women of the English Middle Classes, 1780–1850.* Chicago: University of Chicago Press, 1987.

Davis, Tracy C. "Actresses and Prostitutes in Victorian London." *Theatre Research International* 13, no. 3 (Autumn 1988): 221–34.

de Lauretis, Teresa. *Alice Doesn't: Feminism, Semiotics, Cinema.* Bloomington: Indiana University Press, 1984.

———. "The Technology of Gender." In *Technologies of Gender: Essays on Theory, Film, and Fiction*, pp. 1–30. Bloomington: Indiana University Press, 1987.

de Man, Paul. "Autobiography as De-facement." *MLN* 94 (December 1979): 919–30.

Dews, D. Colin. "Ann Carr and the Female Revivalists of Leeds." In *Religion in the Lives of English Women, 1760–1930*, edited by Gail Malmgreen, pp. 68–87. London: Croom Helm, 1986.

D'Israeli, Isaac. *The Literary Character; or the History of Men of Genius.* New York, 1885.

Donnison, Jean. *Midwives and Medical Men.* New York: Schocken, 1977.

Dudek, Louis. *Literature and the Press: A History of Printing, Printed Media, and Their Relations to Literature.* Toronto: The Ryerson Press, 1961.

Edgeworth, R. L. *Essays on Professional Education.* London, 1809.

Edkins, Carol. "Quest for Community: Spiritual Autobiographies of Eighteenth-Century Quaker and Puritan Women in America." In *Women's Autobiography: Essays in Criticism*, edited by Estelle C. Jelinek, pp. 39–52. Bloomington: Indiana University Press, 1980.

Eichhorn, Jill. "Autobiography as Dissent: A Working-Class Suffragette Speaks Out." Unpublished manuscript, Miami University, 1990.

Eliot, George. *Daniel Deronda.* Edited by Graham Handley. Oxford: Clarendon Press, 1984.

Ellen Terry and Bernard Shaw: A Correspondence. Edited by Christopher St. John. New York: G. P. Putnam's Sons, 1932.

Elliott, Philip. *The Sociology of the Professions.* New York: Herder and Herder, 1972.

Ellis, Sarah Stickney. *The Wives of England.* London, 1843.

Elshtain, Jean Bethke. *Public Man, Private Woman.* Princeton, N.J.: Princeton University Press, 1981.

"Encouragement of Literature by the State." *The Examiner*, 5 January 1850, p. 2.

Erickson, Lee. "The Poets' Corner: The Impact of Technological Changes in Printing on English Poetry, 1800–1850." *ELH* 52, no. 4 (Winter 1985): 893–911.

Erikson, Erik. *Identity, Youth and Crisis.* New York: W. W. Norton & Co., 1968.

Fawcett, Millicent Garrett. *What I Remember.* 1925. Reprint. Westport, Conn.: Hyperion Press, Inc., 1976.

Feltes, N. N. *Modes of Production of Victorian Novels.* Chicago: University of Chicago Press, 1986.

Felski, Rita. *Beyond Feminist Aesthetics: Feminist Literature and Social Change.* Cambridge: Harvard University Press, 1989.

Fields, James T. *Yesterdays with Authors.* Boston, 1881.

Filon, Augustin. *The English Stage.* Translated by Frederic Whyte. London, 1897.

Finch, John Alban. "Wordsworth's Two-Handed Engine." In *Bicentenary Wordsworth Studies*, edited by Jonathan Wordsworth, pp. 1–15. Ithaca, N.Y.: Cornell University Press, 1970.

Fitzgerald, Percy. *The Art of Acting*. London, 1892.

Flax, Jane. "Political Philosophy and the Patriarchal Unconscious: A Psychoanalytic Perspective on Epistemology and Metaphysics." In *Discovering Reality: Feminist Perspectives on Epistemology, Metaphysics, Methodology and Philosophy of Science*. Edited by Sandra Harding and Merrill Hintikka. Dordrecht: Reidel, 1983.

Fleishman, Avrom. *Figures of Autobiography: The Language of Self-Writing in Victorian and Modern England*. Berkeley: University of California Press, 1983.

Fletcher, Kathy. "Planché, Vestris, and the Transvestite Role: Sexuality and Gender in the Victorian Popular Theatre." *Nineteenth Century Theatre* 15, no. 1 (Summer 1987): 9–33.

Forster, John. "The Literary Examiner." *The Examiner*, 17 January 1846, pp. 35–36.

Foucault, Michel. *Discipline and Punish*. Translated by Alan Sheridan. New York: Vintage Books, 1979.

————. *Power/Knowledge: Selected Interviews and Other Writings*. Edited and translated by Colin Gordon. Brighton, Sussex: Harvester Press, 1980.

Fox-Genovese, Elizabeth. "My Statue, My Self: Autobiographical Writings of Afro-American Women." In *The Private Self: Theory and Practice of Women's Autobiographical Writings*, edited by Shari Benstock, pp. 63–89. Chapel Hill: University of North Carolina Press, 1988.

Freidson, Eliot. *Professional Power*. Chicago: University of Chicago Press, 1986.

Friedl, Bettina, ed. *On to Victory: Propaganda Plays of the Woman Suffrage Movement*. Boston: Northeastern University Press, 1987.

Friedman, Michael H. *The Making of a Tory Humanist: William Wordsworth and the Idea of Community*. New York: Columbia University Press, 1979.

Fryckstadt, Monica Correa. "Charlotte Elizabeth Tonna & *The Christian Lady's Magazine*." *Victorian Periodicals Review* 14, no. 2 (Summer 1981): 43–51.

————. "Defining the Domestic Genre: English Women Novelists of the 1850s." *Tulsa Studies in Women's Literature* 6, no. 1 (Spring 1987): 9–26.

Gagnier, Regenia. " 'From Fag to Monitor; Or, Fighting to the Front': Art and Power in Public School Memoirs." *Victorian Learning*. Edited by Robert Viscusi. *Browning Institute Studies* 16 (1988).

————. *Idylls of the Marketplace: Oscar Wilde and the Victorian Public*. Stanford, Calif.: Stanford University Press, 1986.

————. "Social Atoms: Working-Class Autobiography, Subjectivity, and Gender." *Victorian Studies* 30, no. 3 (Spring 1988): 335–63.

————. *Subjectivities: A History of Self-Representation in Britain, 1832–1920*. New York: Oxford University Press, 1991.

Gallagher, Catherine. "George Eliot and *Daniel Deronda*: The Prostitute and the Jewish Question." In *Sex, Politics, and Science in the Nineteenth-Century Novel*, edited by Ruth Bernard Yeazell, pp. 39–62. Baltimore: Johns Hopkins University Press, 1986.

————. *The Industrial Reformation of English Fiction: Social Discourse and Narrative Form, 1832–1867*. Chicago: University of Chicago Press, 1985.

Ganzel, Dewey. "Patent Wrongs and Patent Theatres: Drama and the Law in the Early Nineteenth Century." *PMLA* 76 (1961): 384–96.

Gardiner, Judith Kegan. "On Female Identity and Writing by Women." *Critical Inquiry* 8, no. 2 (Winter 1981): 347–61.

Garner, Les. *Stepping Stones to Women's Liberty.* London: Heinemann, 1984.

Gelpi, Barbara Charlesworth. "*Aurora Leigh:* The Vocation of the Woman Poet." *Victorian Poetry* 19, no. 1 (Spring 1981): 35–48.

The George Eliot Letters. Edited by Gordon S. Haight. 7 vols. New Haven, Conn.: Yale University Press, 1955.

Gerin, Winifred. *Anne Thackeray Ritchie: A Biography.* Oxford: Oxford University Press, 1981.

Giddens, Anthony. *Central Problems in Social Theory: Action, Structure and Contradiction in Social Analysis.* London: Hutchinson, 1976.

Gilbert, Sandra M., and Gubar, Susan. *The Madwoman in the Attic.* New Haven, Conn.: Yale University Press, 1979.

——. *Sexchanges. No Man's Land: The Place of the Woman Writer in the Twentieth Century,* Volume 2. New Haven, Conn.: Yale University Press, 1989.

Gill, Stephen. *William Wordsworth: A Life.* Oxford: Clarendon Press, 1989.

Gillespie, Diane F. " 'The Muddle of the Middle': May Sinclair on Women." *Tulsa Studies in Women's Literature* 4, no. 2 (Fall 1985): 235–51.

Glazer, Penina Migdal, and Slater, Miriam. *Unequal Colleagues: The Entrance of Women into the Professions, 1890–1940.* New Brunswick: Rutgers University Press, 1987.

Goffman, Erving. *The Presentation of Self in Everyday Life.* Garden City, N.Y.: Doubleday Anchor, 1959.

Greg, W. R. "Why Are Women Redundant?" *National Review* 14 (April 1862): 434–60.

Gross, John. *The Rise and Fall of the Man of Letters.* New York: Macmillan, 1969.

Haig, Margaret [Viscountess Rhondda]. *This Was My World.* London: Macmillan and Co., 1933.

Hamilton, Cicely Mary. *Life Errant.* London: J. M. Dent & Sons, 1935.

Haraway, Donna. "A Manifesto for Cyborgs: Science, Technology, and Socialist Feminism in the 1980s." *Socialist Review* 50 (March–April 1985): 65–107.

——. "Situated Knowledges: The Science Question in Feminism and the Privilege of Partial Perspective." *Feminist Studies* 14, no. 3 (Fall 1988): 575–99.

Hardie, J. Keir. "Women and Politics." In *The Case for Women's Suffrage,* edited by Brougham Villiers, pp. 78–83. London: T. Fisher Unwin, 1907.

Harding, Sandra. *The Science Question in Feminism.* Ithaca, N.Y.; Cornell University Press, 1986.

Harrison, Brian. *Peaceable Kingdom: Stability and Change in Modern Britain.* Oxford: Clarendon Press, 1982.

——. *Prudent Revolutionaries: Portraits of British Feminists between the Wars.* Oxford: Clarendon Press, 1987.

Heinzelman, Kurt. *The Economics of the Imagination.* Amherst: University of Massachusetts Press, 1980.

Hertz, Neil. "The Notion of Blockage in the Literature of the Sublime." In *The End of the Line,* pp. 40–60. New York: Columbia University Press, 1985.

Heyck, T. W. *The Transformation of Intellectual Life in Victorian England.* New York: St. Martin's Press, 1982.

Hiatt, Charles. *Ellen Terry and Her Impersonations.* London, 1898.

Hirshfield, Claire. "The Actresses' Franchise League and the Campaign for Women's Suffrage, 1908–1914." *Theatre Research International* 10, no. 2 (Summer 1985): 129–53.

Hofkosh, Sonia. "The Writer's Ravishment: Women and the Romantic Author—the

Example of Byron." In *Romanticism and Feminism*, edited by Anne K. Mellor, pp. 93–114. Bloomington: Indiana University Press, 1988.

Holcombe, Lee. *Victorian Ladies at Work: Middle-Class Working Women in England and Wales, 1850–1914*. Hamden, Conn.: Archon Press, 1973.

Holledge, Julie. *Innocent Flowers: Women in the Edwardian Theatre*. London: Virago, 1981.

Holton, Sandra Stanley. *Feminism and Democracy*. Cambridge: Cambridge University Press, 1986.

———. " 'In Sorrowful Wrath': Suffrage Militancy and the Romantic Feminism of Emmeline Pankhurst." In *British Feminism in the Twentieth Century*, edited by Harold L. Smith, pp. 7–24. London: Edward Elgar, 1990.

Homans, Margaret. *Bearing the Word: Language and Female Experience in Nineteenth-Century Women's Writing*. Chicago: University of Chicago Press, 1986.

———. *Women Writers and Poetic Identity*. Princeton, N.J.: Princeton University Press, 1980.

Houghton, Walter E. "Periodical Literature and the Articulate Classes." In *The Victorian Periodical Press: Samplings and Soundings*, edited by Joanne Shattock and Michael Wolff, pp. 3–27. Toronto: University of Toronto Press, 1983.

How the Vote Was Won, and Other Suffragette Plays. London: Methuen, 1985.

Howitt, Mary. *An Autobiography*. Edited by Margaret Howitt. 2 vols. Boston, 1889.

———. *Stories of Domestic and Foreign Life*. London, 1853.

Hudson, Lynton. *The English Stage 1850–1950*. London: George G. Harrap and Co., Ltd., 1951.

Hume, Leslie Parker. *The National Union of Women's Suffrage Societies, 1897–1914*. New York: Garland Publishing, 1982.

Huyssen, Andreas. *After the Great Divide: Modernism, Mass Culture, Postmodernism*. Bloomington: Indiana University Press, 1986.

Jaggar, Alison M. *Feminist Politics and Human Nature*. Totowa, N.J.: Rowman and Allanheld, 1983.

James, Henry. *Letters*. 4 vols. Edited by Leon Edel. Cambridge: Harvard University Press, 1974–84.

———. "The London Theatres (1879)." In *The Scenic Art*, edited by Allan Wade, pp. 119–24. New Brunswick: Rutgers University Press, 1948.

———. *The Tragic Muse*. 1890. Reprinted. New York: Harper and Brothers, 1960.

Jay, Elisabeth. *The Religion of the Heart: Anglican Evangelicalism and the Nineteenth-Century Novel*. Oxford: Oxford University Press, 1979.

Jay, Paul. *Being in the Text: Self-Representation from Wordsworth to Roland Barthes*. Ithaca, N.Y.: Cornell University Press, 1984.

Jelinek, Estelle C., ed. *Women's Autobiography: Essays in Criticism*. Bloomington: Indiana University Press, 1980.

Johnson, Edgar, and Johnson, Eleanor, eds. *The Dickens Theatrical Reader*. Boston: Little, Brown and Co., 1964.

Johnston, Kenneth R. *Wordsworth and "The Recluse"*. New Haven, Conn.: Yale University Press, 1984.

Jones, Henry Arthur. *The Renascence of the English Drama*. London, 1895.

The Journal of William Charles Macready, 1832–1851. Edited by J. C. Trewin. London: Longmans, 1967.

Kaplan, Cora. "Pandora's Box: Subjectivity, Class and Sexuality in Socialist Feminist Criticism." In *Sea Changes: Essays on Culture and Feminism*, pp. 147–76. London: Verso, 1986.

Kaplan, Deborah. "The Woman Worker in Charlotte Elizabeth Tonna's Fiction." *Mosaic* 18, no. 2 (Spring 1985): 51–63.

Kaplan, Fred. *Thomas Carlyle: A Biography*. Ithaca, N.Y.: Cornell University Press, 1983.

Keller, Evelyn Fox. *Reflections on Gender and Science*. New Haven, Conn.: Yale University Press, 1985.

Kemble, Frances Ann. *Records of a Girlhood*. New York, 1879.

————, *Records of Later Life*. New York, 1882.

Kendal, Dame Madge. *Dame Madge Kendal by Herself*. Edited by Rudolph de Cordova. London: John Murray, 1933.

————. *Dramatic Opinions*. Boston, 1890.

Kenney, Annie. *Memories of a Militant*. London: Edward Arnold & Co., 1924.

Kent, Christopher. "Image and Reality: The Actress and Society." In *A Widening Sphere*, edited by Martha Vicinus, pp. 94–116. Bloomington: Indiana University Press, 1977.

Kent, Susan Kingsley. *Sex and Suffrage in Britain, 1860–1914*. Princeton, N.J.: Princeton University Press, 1987.

Kestner, Joseph. "Charlotte Elizabeth Tonna's *The Wrongs of Woman:* Female Industrial Protest." *Tulsa Studies in Women's Literature* 2, no. 2 (Fall 1983): 193–214.

Klancher, Jon P. *The Making of English Reading Audiences, 1790–1832*. Madison: University of Wisconsin Press, 1987.

Kleb, William. "Marie Wilton (Lady Bancroft) As An Actress." *Theatre Survey* 20, no. 1 (May 1979): 43–74.

Kovacevic, Ivanka, and Kanner, S. Barbara. "Blue Book Into Novel: The Forgotten Industrial Fiction of Charlotte Elizabeth Tonna." *Nineteenth-Century Fiction* 25, no. 2 (September 1970): 152–73.

Kowaleski, Elizabeth. " 'The Heroine of Some Strange Romance': The *Personal Recollections* of Charlotte Elizabeth Tonna." *Tulsa Studies in Women's Literature* 1, no. 2 (Fall 1982): 141–53.

Kristeva, Julia. "Women's Time." Reprinted in *The Kristeva Reader*, edited by Toril Moi, pp. 188–213. New York: Columbia University Press, 1986.

Landow, George P., ed. *Approaches to Victorian Autobiography*. Athens: Ohio University Press, 1979.

Larson, M. S. *The Rise of Professionalism: A Sociological Analysis*. Berkeley: University of California Press, 1977.

Lejeune, Philippe. "The Autobiographical Contract." In *French Literary Theory Today*, edited by Tzvetan Todorov, pp. 192–222. Cambridge: Cambridge University Press, 1982.

The Letters of Sir Walter Scott. 12 vols. Edited by H. J. C. Grierson. London: Constable & Co., Ltd., 1932.

The Letters of William and Dorothy Wordsworth. The Early Years, 1787–1805, vol. 1. 2d ed. rev. Chester L. Shaver. Edited by Ernest de Selincourt. Oxford: Clarendon Press, 1967.

Levine, George. *The Boundaries of Fiction*. Princeton, N.J.: Princeton University Press, 1968.

[Lewes, George Henry.] "The Condition of Authors in England, Germany, and France." *Fraser's* 35 (March 1847): 285–95.

[Lewes, George Henry] "Vivian." "A Gentle Hint to Writing-Women." *The Leader* 1 (18 May 1850): 189.

[————.] "The Lady Novelists." *Westminster Review* o.s. 58 (July 1852): 129–41.

Lewis, Jane. *Women in England 1870–1950: Sexual Divisions and Social Change.* Bloomington: Indiana University Press, 1984.

Liddington, Jill. *The Life and Times of a Respectable Rebel: Selina Cooper (1864–1946).* London: Virago, 1984.

————, and Norris, Jill. *One Hand Tied Behind Us.* London: Virago, 1978.

Lindenberger, Herbert. "The Reception of *The Prelude.*" *Bulletin of the New York Public Library* 64 (1960): 196–208.

Linklater, Andro. *An Unhusbanded Life.* London: Hutchinson and Co., 1980.

Linton, Eliza Lynn. *My Literary Life.* London, 1899.

"Literary Women." *The London Review* 8 (26 March 1864): 328–29.

Locke, John. *Second Treatise on Government.* Edited by C. B. Macpherson. 1690. Reprint. Indianapolis: Hackett Publishing Company, Inc., 1980.

————. *Some Thoughts Concerning Education.* Cambridge: Cambridge University Press, 1898.

Lytton, Lady Constance. *Prisons and Prisoners: Some Personal Experiences.* London: William Heinemann, 1914.

MacKay, Carol Hanbery. "Biography as Reflected Autobiography: The Self-Creation of Anne Thackeray Ritchie." In *Revealing Lives: Gender in Autobiography and Biography.* Edited by Marilyn Yalom and Susan Groag Bell. Albany: State University of New York Press, 1991.

[Maginn, William.] "Gallery of Literary Characters: Miss Harriet Martineau." *Fraser's* 8 (November 1833): 576–77.

Malmgreen, Gail, ed. *Religion in the Lives of English Women, 1760–1930.* London: Croom Helm, 1986.

Marcus, Jane Connor. "Corpus/Corps/Corpse: Writing the Body in/at War." In *Arms and the Woman: War, Gender, and Literary Representation,* edited by Helen M. Cooper, Adrienne Auslander Munich, and Susan Merrill Squier, pp. 124–67. Chapel Hill: University of North Carolina Press, 1989.

————. "Elizabeth Robins." Ph.D. dissertation, Northwestern University, 1973.

Martineau, Harriet. *Autobiography.* 3 vols. 1877. Reprint. London: Virago Press, 1983.

The Marxist-Feminist Literature Collective. "Women's Writing: *Jane Eyre, Shirley, Villette, Aurora Leigh.*" *Ideology and Consciousness* 3 (Spring 1978): 27–48.

Matthews, Brander, and Hutton, Laurence, eds. *Actors and Actresses of Great Britain and the United States.* New York, 1886.

McCarthy, Lillah. *Myself and My Friends.* New York: E. P. Dutton and Co., 1933.

McDonald, Jan. "Lesser Ladies of the Victorian Stage." *Theatre Research International* 13, no. 3 (Autumn 1988): 234–49.

McGann, Jerome J. *The Romantic Ideology: A Critical Investigation.* Chicago: University of Chicago Press, 1983.

McKeon, Michael. "Prefigurations of the Writer's Life in the Early English Novel." Paper delivered at conference on "The Novel and the Writer's Life," 4 February 1989, at Stanford University.

McMillan, Margaret. "Women in the Past and Future." In *The Case for Women's Suffrage,* edited by Brougham Villiers, pp. 106–21. London: T. Fisher Unwin, 1907.

Mellor, Anne K., ed. *Romanticism and Feminism.* Bloomington: Indiana University Press, 1988.

Melville, Joy. *Ellen and Edy.* London: Pandora Press, 1987.

Mermin, Dorothy. "The Damsel, the Knight, and the Victorian Woman Poet." *Critical Inquiry* 13 (Autumn 1986): 64–80.

Mermin, Dorothy. *Elizabeth Barrett Browning: The Origins of a New Poetry*. Chicago: University of Chicago Press, 1989.

Michie, Helena. *The Flesh Made Word: Female Figures and Women's Bodies*. New York: Oxford University Press, 1987.

Miller, D. A. *The Novel and the Police*. Berkeley: University of California Press, 1988.

Miller, Nancy K. *Subject to Change*. New York: Columbia University Press, 1988.

Mitchell, Hannah. *The Hard Way Up*. Edited by Geoffrey Mitchell. London: Faber and Faber, 1968.

Mitford, Mary Russell. *Recollections of a Literary Life*. 3 vols. London, 1852.

Montefiore, Dora B. *From a Victorian to a Modern*. London: E. Archer, 1927.

Moore, Eva. *Exits and Entrances*. New York: Frederick A. Stokes Co., 1923.

Moore, George. *Confessions of a Young Man*. 1888. Reprint. St. Clair Shores, Mich.: Scholarly Press, Inc., 1971.

————. "Mummer-Worship." In *Impressions and Opinions*, pp. 120–38. London: T. Werner Laurie, Ltd., 1913.

Moorman, Mary. *William Wordsworth: A Biography. The Early Years, 1770–1803*. Oxford: Oxford University Press, 1957.

More, Hannah. *The Complete Works of Hannah More*. New York, 1843.

Moretti, Franco. *The Way of the World: The "Bildungsroman" in European Culture*. London: Verso, 1987.

"Mrs. Fanny Kemble and the Stage." *The Theatre* 2 (1 May 1879): 224–27.

Mulford, Wendy. "Socialist-Feminist Criticism: A Case Study, Women's Suffrage and Literature, 1906–14." In *Re-Reading English*, edited by Peter Widdowson, pp. 179–92. London: Methuen, 1982.

Mumford, Laura Stempel. "May Sinclair's *The Tree of Heaven*: The Vortex of Feminism, the Community of War." In *Arms and the Woman: War, Gender, and Literary Representation*, edited by Helen M. Cooper, Adrienne Auslander Munich, and Susan Merrill Squier, pp. 163–83. Chapel Hill: University of North Carolina Press, 1989.

Nightingale, Florence. *Cassandra: An Essay*. 1928. Reprint. Old Westbury, N.Y.: Feminist Press, 1979.

Nussbaum, Felicity A. *The Autobiographical Subject: Gender and Ideology in Eighteenth-Century England*. Baltimore: Johns Hopkins University Press, 1989.

Oliphant, Margaret. *The Autobiography of Margaret Oliphant: The Complete Text*. Edited by Elisabeth Jay. Oxford: Oxford University Press, 1990.

————. "Harriet Martineau." *Blackwood's* 121 (April 1877): 472–96.

————. "The Opium-Eater." *Blackwood's* 122 (December 1877): 717–41.

Olney, James. *Metaphors of Self*. Princeton, N.J.: Princeton University Press, 1972.

Orbach, Susie. *Hunger Strike: The Anorectic's Struggle as Metaphor for Our Age*. New York: W. W. Norton, 1986.

Owen, W. J. B., ed. *Wordsworth's Literary Criticism*. London: Routledge and Kegan Paul, 1974.

Pankhurst, Dame Christabel. *Unshackled*. London: Hutchinson, 1959.

Pankhurst, Emmeline. *My Own Story*. 1914. Reprint. New York: Source Book Press, 1970.

Pankhurst, E. Sylvia. *The Suffragette: The History of the Women's Militant Suffrage Movement, 1905–1910*. 1911. Reprint. New York: Source Book Press, 1970.

————. *The Suffragette Movement: An Intimate Account of Persons and Ideals*. London: Longmans, Green, and Co., 1931.

————. "Sylvia Pankhurst." In *Myself When Young: By Famous Women of To-Day*, edited by Margot Asquith, pp. 259–312. London: Frederick Muller Ltd., 1938.

Parrinder, Patrick. *Authors and Authority: A Study of English Literary Criticism and Its Relation to Culture, 1750–1900*. London: Routledge and Kegan Paul, 1977.

Parry, Noel, and Parry, José. *The Rise of the Medical Profession: A Study in Collective Social Mobility*. London: Croom Helm, 1976.

Pascal, Roy. *Design and Truth in Autobiography*. Cambridge: Harvard University Press, 1960.

Pascoe, Charles E., ed. *The Dramatic List: A Record of the Performances of Living Actors and Actresses of the British Stage*. 2d ed. 1880. New York: Benjamin Blom, Inc., 1969.

Pateman, Carole. *The Sexual Contract*. Stanford, Calif.: Stanford University Press, 1988.

Perkin, Harold. *The Origins of Modern English Society, 1780–1880*. London: Routledge and Kegan Paul, 1969.

The Personal Narratives Group, ed. *Interpreting Women's Lives: Feminist Theory and Personal Narratives*. Bloomington: Indiana University Press, 1989.

Peters, Margot. *Bernard Shaw and the Actresses*. Garden City, N.Y.: Doubleday & Company, Inc., 1980.

————. *Mrs. Pat: The Life of Mrs. Patrick Campbell*. New York: Alfred A. Knopf, 1984.

Peterson, Linda H. "Audience and the Autobiographer's Art: An Approach to the *Autobiography* of Mrs. M. O. W. Oliphant." In *Approaches to Victorian Autobiography*, edited by George P. Landow, pp. 158–74. Athens: Ohio University Press, 1979.

————. *Victorian Autobiography*. New Haven, Conn.: Yale University Press, 1986.

Pethick-Lawrence, Emmeline. *My Part in a Changing World*. 1938. Reprint. Westport, Conn.: Hyperion Press, Inc., 1976.

Pichanick, Valerie Kossew. *Harriet Martineau: The Woman and Her Work, 1802–76*. Ann Arbor: University of Michigan Press, 1980.

Pinero, Arthur W. *The Notorious Mrs. Ebbsmith*. London: William Heinemann, 1906.

————. *The Second Mrs. Tanqueray*. In *Plays by A. W. Pinero*. Edited by George Rowell. Cambridge: Cambridge University Press, 1986.

Poggi, Gianfranco. *Calvinism and the Capitalist Spirit: Max Weber's "Protestant Ethic."* London: Macmillan, 1983.

Polwhele, Richard. *The Unsex'd Females*. Reprint. New York: Garland Publishing, 1974.

Poovey, Mary. *The Proper Lady and the Woman Writer: Ideology as Style in the Works of Mary Wollstonecraft, Mary Shelley, and Jane Austen*. Chicago: University of Chicago Press, 1984.

————. *Uneven Developments: The Ideological Work of Gender in Mid-Victorian England*. Chicago: University of Chicago Press, 1988.

Postlethwaite, Diana. "Mothering and Mesmerism in the Life of Harriet Martineau." *Signs* 14, no. 3 (Spring 1989): 583–609.

"Present System of Education." *Westminster Review* 4 (July 1825): 147–76.

Prochaska, F. K. *Women and Philanthropy in Nineteenth-Century England*. New York: Oxford University Press, 1980.

"The Profession of Journalism." *Saturday Review* 7 (1 January 1859): 9–10.

"The Profession of Literature." *Westminster Review* o.s. 58 (October 1852): 507–31.

Raeburn, Antonia. *The Militant Suffragettes*. London: Michael Joseph, 1973.

Reader, W. J. *Professional Men: The Rise of the Professional Classes in Nineteenth-Century England*. London: Weidenfeld and Nicolson, 1966.

Reed, Mark L. *Wordsworth: The Chronology of the Early Years, 1770–1797*. Cambridge: Harvard University Press, 1967.

Reed, Walter L. "The Pattern of Conversion in *Sartor Resartus*." *ELH* 38, no. 3 (September 1971): 411–31.

Reimer, Gail Twersky. "Revisions of Labor in Margaret Oliphant's Autobiography." In *Life/Lines: Theorizing Women's Autobiography*, edited by Bella Brodzki and Celeste Schenck, pp. 203–20. Ithaca, N.Y.: Cornell University Press, 1988.

Rendall, Jane, ed. *Equal or Different: Women's Politics, 1800–1914*. London: Basil Blackwell, 1987.

Rich, Adrienne. "Compulsory Heterosexuality and Lesbian Existence." In *Blood, Bread, and Poetry: Selected Prose 1979–1985*. New York: W. W. Norton, 1986.

Richardson, Henry S. "Harriet Martineau's Account of Herself." *Contemporary Review* 29 (May 1877): 1112–23.

Richardson, Mary R. *Laugh A Defiance*. London: George Weidenfeld and Nicolson, 1953.

Riede, David. "Transgression, Authority, and the Church of Literature in Carlyle." In *Victorian Connections*, edited by Jerome J. McGann, pp. 88–120. Charlottesville: University Press of Virginia, 1989.

Ritchie, Anne Thackeray. *Chapters from Some Unwritten Memoirs*. New York, 1895.

[Robins, Elizabeth.] *Ancilla's Share*. 2d ed. London: Hutchinson and Co., 1924.

Robins, Elizabeth. *Both Sides of the Curtain*. London: William Heinemann, Ltd., 1940.

———. *The Convert*. 1907. Reprint. Old Westbury, N.Y.: The Feminist Press, 1980.

———. *Way Stations*. London: Hodder and Stoughton, 1913.

Robinson, Lillian S. *Sex, Class, and Culture*. Bloomington: Indiana University Press, 1978.

Robson, Richard. *The Attorney in Eighteenth-Century England*. Cambridge: Cambridge University Press, 1959.

Romero, Patricia W. *E. Sylvia Pankhurst: Portrait of a Radical*. New Haven, Conn.: Yale University Press, 1987.

Rosen, Andrew. *Rise Up, Women! The Militant Campaign of the Women's Social and Political Union, 1903–14*. London: Routledge and Kegan Paul, 1974.

Ross, Marlon B. *The Contours of Masculine Desire: Romanticism and the Rise of Women's Poetry*. New York: Oxford University Press, 1989.

Rover, Constance. *Women's Suffrage and Party Politics in Britain 1866–1914*. London: Routledge and Kegan Paul, 1967.

Rowbotham, Judith. *Good Girls Make Good Wives: Guidance for Girls in Victorian Fiction*. London: Routledge and Kegan Paul, 1967.

Sandel, Michael. *Liberalism and the Limits of Justice*. Cambridge: Cambridge University Press, 1982.

Sanders, Valerie. *The Private Lives of Victorian Women: Autobiography in Nineteenth-Century England*. New York: St. Martin's Press, 1989.

———. *Reason over Passion: Harriet Martineau and the Victorian Novel*. New York: St. Martin's Press, 1986.

Sanderson, Michael. *From Irving to Olivier: A Social History of the Acting Profession in England, 1880–1983*. New York: St. Martin's Press, 1984.

Sarah, Elizabeth. "Christabel Pankhurst: Reclaiming Her Power." In *Feminist Theorists*, edited by Dale Spender, pp. 256–84. London: The Women's Press, 1983.

Saunders, J. W. *The Profession of English Letters*. London: Routledge and Kegan Paul, 1969.

Scarry, Elaine. *The Body in Pain*. New York: Oxford University Press, 1985.

Schenck, Celeste. "All of a Piece: Women's Poetry and Autobiography." In *Life/Lines: Theorizing Women's Autobiography*, edited by Bella Brodzki and Celeste Schenck, pp. 281–305. Ithaca, N.Y.: Cornell University Press, 1988.

Schimmelpenninck, Mary Anne. *Life of Mary Anne Schimmelpenninck*. 2 vols. Edited by Christiana C. Hankin. London, 1858.

Schmidt, Paul H., ed. " 'The Vexingly Unverifiable': Truth in Autobiography." *Studies in the Literary Imagination* 23, no. 2 (Fall 1990).

Schneider, Ben Ross, Jr. *Wordsworth's Cambridge Education*. Cambridge: Cambridge University Press, 1957.

Schofield, Mary Anne. " 'Womens Speaking Justified': The Feminine Quaker Voice, 1662–1797." *Tulsa Studies in Women's Literature* 6, no. 1 (Spring 1987): 61–77.

Schreiner, Olive. *Women and Labor*. 7th ed. New York: Frederick A. Stokes Co., Publishers, 1911.

Scott, Clement. *The Drama of Yesterday and To-day*. 2 vols. London, 1899.

Scott, Joan W. "Rewriting History." *Behind the Lines: Gender and the Two World Wars*, edited by Margaret Randolph Higonnet et al., pp. 21–30. New Haven, Conn.: Yale University Press, 1987.

[Scrope, G. Poulett.] "Miss Martineau's *Monthly Novels*." *Quarterly Review* 49 (April 1833): 136–52.

Sennett, Richard. *The Fall of Public Man*. New York: Alfred A. Knopf, 1974.

Sharp, Evelyn. *Unfinished Adventure*. London: John Lane, 1933.

Sharpe, William Chapman. *Unreal Cities: Urban Figuration in Wordsworth, Baudelaire, Whitman, Eliot, and Williams*. Baltimore: Johns Hopkins University Press, 1990.

Shaw, George Bernard. *The Bodley Head Bernard Shaw*. 6 vols. London: Max Reinhardt for the Bodley Head, 1970.

———. *Our Theatres in the Nineties*. 3 vols. London: Constable and Company, 1932.

Sherwood, Mary Martha. *The Life of Mrs. Sherwood*. Edited by Sophia Kelly. London, 1857.

Showalter, Elaine. *The Female Malady: Women, Madness and English Culture, 1830–1980*. New York: Pantheon, 1985.

———. *A Literature of Their Own*. Princeton, N.J.: Princeton University Press, 1977.

———. *Sexual Anarchy: Gender and Culture at the Fin de Siècle*. New York: Viking, 1990.

Silverman, Kaja. *The Acoustic Mirror: The Female Voice in Psychoanalysis and Cinema*. Bloomington: Indiana University Press, 1988.

Simpson, David. *Wordsworth and the Figurings of the Real*. London: Macmillan, 1982.

———. *Wordsworth's Historical Imagination*. New York: Methuen, 1987.

Simpson, Harold. Foreword to *Myself and My Piano*. London: John Ouseby, Ltd., 1909.

Sinclair, May. *The Tree of Heaven*. New York: Macmillan, 1917.

Siskin, Clifford. *The Historicity of Romantic Discourse*. New York: Oxford University Press, 1988.

———. "Wordsworth's Prescriptions: Romanticism and Professional Power." In *The Romantics and Us: Essays on Literature and Culture*, edited by Gene W. Ruoff, pp. 303–21. New Brunswick: Rutgers University Press, 1990.

Smith, Adam. *An Inquiry into the Nature and Causes of the Wealth of Nations*. 2 vols. 1776. Reprint. Oxford: Clarendon Press, 1976.

Smith, Paul. *Discerning the Subject*. Minneapolis: University of Minnesota Press, 1988.

Smith, Ruth L., and Valenze, Deborah M. "Mutuality and Marginality: Liberal Moral Theory and Working-Class Women in Nineteenth-Century England." *Signs* 13, no. 2 (Winter 1988): 277–98.

Smith, Sidonie. *A Poetics of Women's Autobiography: Marginality and the Fictions of Self-Representation.* Bloomington: Indiana University Press, 1987.

Southey, Charles Cuthbert, ed. *The Life and Correspondence of Robert Southey.* 6 vols. London, 1850.

Spender, Dale, ed. "Personal Chronicles: Women's Autobiographical Writings." *Women's Studies International Forum* 10, no. 1 (1987).

———. *Time and Tide Wait for No Man.* London: Pandora Press, 1984.

Spivak, Gayatri. "Sex and History in *The Prelude.*" In *In Other Worlds*, pp. 45–76. New York: Methuen, 1987.

Stallybrass, Peter, and White, Allon. *The Politics and Poetics of Transgression.* Ithaca, N.Y.: Cornell University Press, 1986.

Stanton, Domna, ed. *The Female Autograph.* New York: New York Literary Forum, 1984.

Starr, G. A. *Defoe and Spiritual Autobiography.* Princeton, N.J.: Princeton University Press, 1965.

Stedman-Jones, Gareth. "Working-Class Culture and Working-Class Politics in London, 1870–1900." In *Languages of Class: Studies in English Working Class History, 1832–1982*, pp. 179–238. Cambridge: Cambridge University Press, 1983.

St. John, Christopher. *Ethel Smyth: A Biography.* London: Longmans, Green and Co., 1959.

Stoker, Bram. "Actor-Managers." *The Nineteenth Century* 27 (June 1890): 1040–51.

Stokes, John. "Rachel's 'Terrible Beauty': An Actress Among the Novelists." *ELH* 51 (1984): 771–93.

———. *Resistible Theatres.* London: Paul Elek, 1972.

———; Booth, Michael R.; Bassnett, Susan. *Bernhardt, Terry, Duse: The Actress in Her Time.* Cambridge: Cambridge University Press, 1988.

Strachey, Ray. *"The Cause": A Short History of the Women's Movement in Great Britain.* 1928. Reprint. Port Washington, N.Y.: Kennikat Press, 1969.

Suffrage and the Pankhursts. Introduction by Jane Marcus. London: Routledge and Kegan Paul, 1987.

The Suffragette Fellowship Collection. Brighton, Sussex: Harvester Microform, 1985.

Sutphin, Christine. "Revising Old Scripts: The Fusion of Independence and Intimacy in *Aurora Leigh.*" *Browning Institute Studies* 15 (1987): 43–54.

Swindells, Julia. *Victorian Writing and Working Women.* Cambridge, England: Polity Press, 1985.

Tabor, Margaret. *Pioneer Women.* London: The Sheldon Press, 1930.

Taylor, John Russell. *The Rise and Fall of the Well-Made Play.* New York: Hill and Wang, 1967.

Tennyson, G. B. *Sartor Called Resartus.* Princeton, N.J.: Princeton University Press, 1965.

Terry, Ellen. *The Story of My Life.* New York: Doubleday, Page & Co., 1908.

Thompson, Dorothy. "Women, Work and Politics in Nineteenth-Century England: The Problem of Authority." In *Equal or Different: Women's Politics 1800–1914*, edited by Jane Rendall, pp. 57–81. London: Basil Blackwell, 1987.

Tickner, Lisa. *The Spectacle of Women: Imagery of the Suffrage Campaign 1907–14.* London: Chatto and Windus, 1987.

Tilly, Louise A., and Scott, Joan W. *Women, Work and Family*. New York: Holt, Rinehart and Winston, 1978.

Tompkins, Jane. *Sensational Designs*. New York: Oxford University Press, 1985.

[Tonna,] Charlotte Elizabeth. *Personal Recollections*. New York, 1842.

Townsend, Meredith. "Mrs. Oliphant." *The Cornhill Magazine* 79 (1899): 773–79.

Tuchman, Gaye, with Nina E. Fortin. *Edging Women Out: Victorian Novelists, Publishers, and Social Change*. New Haven, Conn.: Yale University Press, 1989.

T. W. Robertson: Six Plays. Introduction by Michael R. Booth. Derbyshire: Amber Lane Press, 1980.

Valenze, Deborah. "Cottage Religion and the Politics of Survival." In *Equal or Different*, edited by Jane Rendall, pp. 31–56. London: Basil Blackwell, 1987.

Vanbrugh, Irene. *To Tell My Story*. London: Hutchinson & Co., 1948.

Vellacott, Jo. "Feminist Consciousness and the First World War." *History Workshop Journal* 23 (Spring 1987): 81–101.

Vicinus, Martha. *Independent Women: Work and Community for Single Women, 1850–1920*. Chicago: University of Chicago Press, 1985.

———, ed. *A Widening Sphere*. Bloomington: Indiana University Press, 1977.

Victorian Bouquet: Lady X Looks On. Edited by Rachel Ferguson. London: Ernest Benn Ltd., n.d.

Villiers, Brougham, ed. *The Case for Women's Suffrage*. London: T. Fisher Unwin, 1907.

Von Thal, Herbert. *Eliza Lynn Linton: The Girl of the Period*. London: George Allen and Unwin, 1979.

Walker, Cheryl. "Feminist Literary Criticism and the Author." *Critical Inquiry* 16 (Spring 1990): 551–71.

Walker, Linda. "Party Political Women: A Comparative Study of Liberal Women and the Primrose League, 1890–1914." In *Equal or Different: Women's Politics 1800–1914*, edited by Jane Rendall, pp. 165–91. London: Basil Blackwell, 1987.

Walkowitz, Judith R. "Science and the Seance: Transgressions of Gender and Genre in Late Victorian London." *Representations* 22 (Spring 1988): 3–28.

Walters, Margaret. "The Rights and Wrongs of Women: Mary Wollstonecraft, Harriet Martineau, Simone de Beauvoir." In *The Rights and Wrongs of Women*, edited by Juliet Mitchell and Ann Oakley, pp. 304–78. Harmondsworth: Penguin, 1976.

Ward, Mrs. Humphry [Mary]. *A Writer's Recollections*. London: W. Collins Sons & Co. Ltd., 1918.

Webb, Beatrice. *My Apprenticeship*. 1926. Reprint. Cambridge: Cambridge University Press, 1979.

Weber, Max. *The Protestant Ethic and the Spirit of Capitalism*. Translated by Talcott Parsons. London: Unwin Paperbacks, 1985.

Williams, Raymond. *Keywords*. Rev. ed. New York: Oxford University Press, 1983.

———. *Marxism and Literature*. Oxford: Oxford University Press, 1977.

———. "Social Environment and Theatrical Environment: the Case of English Naturalism." In *English Drama: Forms and Development*, edited by Marie Axton and Raymond Williams, pp. 203–39. Cambridge: Cambridge University Press, 1977.

Woodmansee, Martha. "The Genius and the Copyright: Economic and Legal Conditions of the Emergence of the 'Author.'" *Eighteenth-Century Studies* 17, no. 4 (1984): 425–48.

Woodring, Carl Ray. *Victorian Samplers: William and Mary Howitt*. Lawrence: University of Kansas Press, 1952.

———. "Wordsworth and the Victorians." In *The Age of William Wordsworth: Critical Essays on the Romantic Tradition,* edited by Kenneth R. Johnston and Gene W. Ruoff, pp. 261–75. New Brunswick: Rutgers University Press, 1987.

Woolf, Virginia. "Ellen Terry." In *The Moment and Other Essays,* pp. 205–12. New York: Harcourt, Brace and Co., 1948.

———. "Introductory Letter." In *Life As We Have Known It.* Edited by Margaret Llewellyn Davies. 1931. Reprint. New York: W. W. Norton and Co., Inc., 1975.

———. "Lady Ritchie." In *The Essays of Virginia Woolf: 1919–24,* edited by Andrew McNeillie, pp. 16–20. New York: Harcourt Brace Jovanovich, 1988.

———. *The Letters of Virginia Woolf.* Edited by Nigel Nicolson and Joanne Trautman. 6 vols. New York: Harcourt Brace Jovanovich, 1975.

———. *Three Guineas.* 1938. Reprint. New York: Harcourt Brace Jovanovich, 1966.

Wordsworth, Christopher. *Memoirs of William Wordsworth.* 2 vols. Edited by Henry Reed. Boston, 1851.

Wordsworth, William. *The Prelude: 1799, 1805, 1850.* Edited by Jonathan Wordsworth, M. H. Abrams, and Stephen Gill. New York: W. W. Norton & Co., 1979.

Wyndham, Charles. "Actor-Managers." *The Nineteenth Century* 27 (June 1890): 1054–58.

Young, Iris Marion. "The Ideal of Community and the Politics of Difference." In *Feminism/Postmodernism,* edited by Linda J. Nicholson, pp. 300–23. New York: Routledge, 1990.

———. *Justice and the Politics of Difference.* Princeton, N.J.: Princeton University Press, 1990.

Zaretsky, Eli. *Capitalism, The Family, and Personal Life.* 2d ed. New York: Harper and Row, 1986.

Index